Civil-Military Relations

Civil-Military Relations

Changing Concepts in the Seventies

Charles L. Cochran

Fp
THE FREE PRESS
A Division of Macmillan Publishing Co., Inc.
New York
Collier Macmillan Publishers
London

The Free Press
A Division of Macmillan Publishing Co., Inc.
866 Third Avenue, New York, N.Y. 10022

Collier-Macmillan Canada Ltd.

Library of Congress Catalog Card Number: 73–17646

Printed in the United States of America

printing number
1 2 3 4 5 6 7 8 9 10

Library of Congress Cataloging in Publication Data

Cochran, Charles L
Civil-military relations.

Includes bibliographical references.
1. Civil supremacy over the military--United States--Addresses, essays, lectures. 2. Civil supremacy over the military--Addresses, essays, lectures. I. Title.
JK558.C6 350'.895 73-17646
ISBN 0-02-905670-5

Contents

Preface

The last decade has been a particularly trying time in the nation's history, in large measure because of its involvement in Southeast Asia. Vietnam was traumatic in that the purpose of American involvement, both ends and means, was still uncertain even after the last prisoner was returned. The lack of consensus on what our politico-military objectives were, or even should be, spilled over into other areas of public policy from health care to poverty and the role of the military in American society.

The conflict, which began and ended in ambiguity, has proven to be very difficult for society to accept with equanimity. There is an awareness that it may signal the era of a new type of warfare with a potential for vast expenditures in human and material resources for an inconclusive result. Consequently, a greater understanding of the military and its influence in society is more important than ever before.

It is the purpose of this book to provide selected original readings pertaining to the military that relate to the areas generally covered in courses on civil-military relations and national security policy. The selections will examine the role of the military in a world order in which war as an institution unfortunately still exists and nations prepare for the contingency of a future confrontation.

There are some basic assumptions in this theme. One is that military establishments are, at present and for the foreseeable future, both necessary and unavoidable. This is as true for the technically advanced nations as for the less developed countries of the world. A second assumption is that national experiences will differ in accordance with the political and social contexts in which they develop.

This work is an attempt to contribute to the understanding of the role of the military not only in our society but also in other societies as well, for only through understanding can there be a hope of shaping military power and policy wisely.

The present study is the result of the cooperative efforts of some twelve people, present or former members of the political science faculty of the U.S. Naval Academy. The book grew out of a feeling that much that has been written about the military suffers from being too highly specialized or has proceeded only within strict disciplinary lines and that it usually has neglected any comparative analysis in terms of the development and role of the military in other cultures and politico-military settings. The attempt here is to bring together a collection of studies of the military and national security from different perspectives and provide a basis for comparative analysis in relation to other states.

While all authors of chapters worked diligently in the preparation of the entire manuscript, a special debt is acknowledged to those who made especially important contributions to the final product, particularly to John R. Probert, Chairman of the Department of Political Science, for his constant encouragement and advice and to my colleagues Professors G. Pope Atkins and Rocco M. Paone for their assistance in many decisions along the way. Appreciation is expressed also to Lt. John A. Williams for his thoughtful critiques and comments, and particular appreciation goes to Joseph Smaldone for his editorial assistance and to Frances Nasso for typing the manuscript.

This work reflects the views of the individual authors and is not necessarily the official position of the U.S. Naval Academy, the U.S. Navy, or the Department of State.

About the Contributors

G. Pope Atkins, Associate Professor of Political Science at the U.S. Naval Academy, is a graduate of the University of Texas and holds the M.A. and Ph.D. degrees from American University. He has lived in Argentina and Ecuador, and has taught at the University of Guayaquil (Ecuador), American University, and the University of Texas. He is the co-author of *The United States and the Trujillo Regime* (1972) and has published several articles on Latin American politics, including "La Junta Militar Ecuatoriana, 1963–1966," *Aportes* (1972) and, as co-author, "German Military Influences in Argentina," *Journal of Latin American Studies* (1973). He has been a guest scholar at the Institute of Latin American Studies (University of London) and the Brookings Institution. He is an associate editor of the *Journal of Political and Military Sociology*.

Robert A. Bender is an Associate Professor in the Political Science Department, Princeton University, A.B. 1942, M.A. 1949. Professor Bender has taught in the economics and political science departments since joining the faculty in 1951.

Charles L. Cochran, Associate Professor of Political Science at the U.S. Naval Academy, is a graduate of Mt. St. Mary's College. He received an M.A. from Niagara University and a Ph.D. from Tufts University. Professor Cochran has been a contributor to several different journals. Related research includes "Midshipman and Cadet Profiles and the National Norms: A Comparison," which appeared in the *Naval War College Review* (May 1972). He is also an associate editor of the *Journal of Political and Military Sociology*.

Charles R. D'Amato was a member of the Department of Political Science at the U.S. Naval Academy from 1969 to 1972. A graduate of Cornell University, Lt. D'Amato received an M.A. from the Fletcher School of Law and Diplomacy in 1965 and an M.A.L.D. the following year. He is currently a doctoral candidate at Fletcher. He is also presently assigned to the *U.S.S. King, DLG*.

Harry Gilmore is a Foreign Service Officer of the U.S.A. At the time he wrote the chapter entitled "Civil-Military Relations in the USSR" he was on assignment to the U.S. Naval Academy as an exchange officer. Mr. Gilmore received a B.A. degree at the University of Pittsburgh in 1960. After engaging in two years of graduate study of the USSR and Eastern Europe at Indiana University, he entered the Foreign Service in September, 1962. His overseas assignments in the Foreign Service have included Ankara, Budapest, and, from 1969 to 71, Moscow. During his tour of duty at the Naval Academy, Mr. Gilmore taught courses on Soviet politics and civil-military relations in the USSR as well as comparative communist theory and practice. He is currently serving as Officer-in-Charge of Yugoslav Affairs.

John P. Lovell is Professor and Director of Graduate Studies in the Political Science Department at Indiana University. He is a graduate of West Point, with a Ph.D. from the University of Wisconsin. The essay for this book was begun during the 1971–72 academic year when he served as a Visiting Professor at the Naval Academy. Lovell is author of *Foreign Policy in Perspective,* editor of and contributor to the *Military and Politics in Five Developing Nations,* and co-editor and contributor to *New Civil-Military Relations: The Agonies of Adjustment to Post Vietnam Realities.* He has served as Chairman of the Section on Military Studies of the International Studies Association from 1970–74. Currently he is working on a book-length study of *Organizational Change at the U.S. Service Academies.*

Luis R. Luis was an Assistant Professor in the Department of Economics at the U.S. Naval Academy. He received a bachelor's degree from St. Edward's University and a Ph.D. from the University of Notre Dame. He has been a Fulbright Lecturer at the University of Trujillo in Peru. After temporary leave from the Naval Academy to serve as a Project Director for "Problems of Unemployment in Selected West Indian Countries," to the Organization of American States, he became the Senior Economic Adviser to the OAS.

Elmer J. Mahoney is Professor of Law and former Chairman of the Political Science Department of the U.S. Naval Academy. He has also served as Professorial Lecturer at the George Washington University. As a Lieutenant Commander in the Naval Reserve, he was on active duty from 1942 to 1946. Professor Mahoney received his A.B. from Western Maryland College and his J.D. degree from the University of Maryland's School of Law. He is a member of the bar and has been admitted to the practice of law in the state of Maryland. He has been a contributor and consultant to the *U.S. Naval Institute Proceedings* for several years.

Phillip A. Mangano is an Associate Professor of Political Science and International Relations at the U.S. Naval Academy. A graduate of Yale University, he has an M.A. from the University of Rochester and a J.D. from the National Law Center of George Washington University. He saw service as a Naval officer assigned to the Office of Strategic Services in Italy and the Mediterranean area during World War II. His State Department career (1942–63) included nine years as a specialist on international security affairs in the State Department's Bureau of UN Affairs and periodically, as a member of U.S. delegations to UN General Assembly sessions or UN field commissions. His foreign service tours included assignments as political officer and as Charge d'Affaires in Tunisia, in the Middle East, and on home assignment in Washington with work on North and East African affairs. He has lectured in courses at American, Catholic, and Maryland Universities.

Rocco M. Paone, Professor, Political Science Department, U.S. Naval Academy, received his Ph.D. from Georgetown University. He has served as Advisor to the General Staff, U.S. Army, on Foreign Military Aid; Consultant to the U.S. Army Command and General Staff College; is co-author of *Geography and National Power;* contributing author to *Guide to American Military History;* and editor and co-author of *Political-Military Relations and United States Foreign Policy Formulation: An Anthology*. He has also published several articles in various journals.

John R. Probert, Professor and Chairman of the Political Science Department, United States Naval Academy, served in the U.S. Army in World War II and the U.S. Army Reserve until his retirement with the rank of colonel in February 1972. A specialist in national security administration, his Reserve assignment was in Civil Affairs. He has been a consultant in national security policy and administration. Professor Probert did his undergraduate work at Lafayette College and received his Ph.D. from the University of Pennsylvania. His publications include: *Military Assistance Management: A Proposal for Change* (co-author); "Streamlining the Foreign Policy Machine," *Public Administration Review*; and "Pentagon Reorganization: Phase Three," *U.S. Naval Institute Proceedings*.

Joseph P. Smaldone, a Captain in the U.S. Marine Corps, received his Ph.D. from Northwestern University in 1970. His special research interest is African military history and modern African military affairs, about which he has written several articles which have appeared in *The Journal of African History* and *A Current Bibliography on African Affairs*.

1

At Home

Introduction

Vast energies were expended by the United States in the costly experience of Vietnam. Although there has been opposition to previous wars in the nation's history, none, except for the Civil War, can compare to the deep divisions in society that accompanied this most recent affair.

Ordinarily in wartime there is the expectation, of questionable validity, that politics stops at the water's edge, that when the military is engaged in external combat Americans will unite to achieve the prescribed goal of victory. Vietnam produced not unity but the reverse; it exacerbated the divisions largely because it was perceived by many as an extension of conflicts within the United States over domestic priorities. The expenditure in terms of resources and lives, when no threat to national security was perceived by the public at large, was great, while at the same time governmental programs to deal with a whole host of problems including poverty, disease, education, and environmental protection were significantly reduced in size and scope, postponed, and in some instances cancelled.[1]

Civilian and military personnel who planned and executed policy claimed to have the support of most Americans and hoped that successive increases in military power would bring the collapse of the North Vietnamese and a victory that would vindicate both their position and the earlier investment. The failure to achieve success frustrated policy-makers who apparently believed that the North Vietnamese would come to terms very quickly once the seriousness of the American commitment was demonstrated. When the North Vietnamese did not abandon their objectives or activities after military pressure was escalated on a major scale, it was easier for the decision-makers to conclude that domestic opposition to those military policies had convinced the "enemy" at each step that no greater escalation would be tolerated than to conclude that the North Vietnamese could not be defeated by the application of American military force.

The military failure resulted also in ever-increasing disillusionment and alienation among the public. Some reached the conclusion that the divisions at home were fomented by domestic enemies. If the domestic enemies could be completely discredited, unity would follow. Statements by officials attacking "welfare cheats," "hippies," "radiclibs," "elitists," and the like only

[1] See Bruce M. Russett, "Who Pays for Defense?" *The American Political Science Review*, Vol. LXIII, No. 2, June 1969, pp. 412–426, for an empirical study dealing with the negative impact increased defense spending has on these sectors of the economy.

served to polarize the society rather than deal with the fundamental issue of the wisdom of military involvement in Southeast Asia.

Indeed the effect of the Vietnam experience has been, at the very least, to swing popular support away from the military. That there would be a decline in the prestige of the military in the aftermath of conflict containing such broad and deep cleavages was inevitable. The military is identified in the public mind as the arm of the government to be used in the defense of critical national security requirements. When national security policy enjoys a consensus of national support, the prestige of the military is assured to the extent that it is tied to these "high" national goals. But the opposite is also true. Whatever the extent of civilian control, when United States foreign and national security policies are not supported by a clear majority of the population, the military is as tied to the major military decisions as if they had been made by the Joint Chiefs of Staff, with a resulting decline in prestige.

Probably more than any other profession in American society the military is concerned with its "image" and constantly strives to live up to its ideal. The spectre of the decline in the level of its esteem haunts the military at the present time. The opposition of many American men toward military service reflected in the opposition to ROTC programs on some college campuses is indicative of the trend. Alexis de Tocqueville expressed the problem in the following way:

> . . . When the military spirit foresakes a people, the profession of arms immediately ceases to be held in honor, and military men fall to the lowest rank of the public servants; they are little esteemed and no longer understood. The reverse of what takes place in aristocratic ages then occurs; the men who enter the army are no longer those of the highest, but of the lowest class. Military ambition is indulged only when no other is possible. Hence, arises a circle of cause and consequence . . . the best part of the nation shuns the military profession because that profession is not honored, and the profession is not honored because the best part of the nation has ceased to follow it.
>
> . . . The soldier feels that he occupies an inferior position, and his wounded pride either stimulates his desire for hostilities that would render his services necessary or gives him a desire for revolution, during which he may hope to win by force of arms the political influence and personal importance now denied him.[2]

Recent American experience in Southeast Asia, then, has heightened concern over civil-military relations. A thoroughgoing reappraisal of traditional roles and values is underway. The military is trying to reshape its image to fit the new mood throughout the country, as well as on college

[2] Alexis de Tocqueville, *Democracy in America* (1835), Henry Reeve, translator (New York: Langley, 1840), Vol. II, Book III, pp. 266–267.

campuses. Admiral Zumwalt's famed "Z-grams" permitting longer hair and beards are an example of military adaptation, although these policies are not without their critics within the military. Providing more responsibility and command positions to younger officers in the Navy is yet another example. The expanded role of women in the military and greater recruitment efforts among ethnic minority groups illustrate a new orientation that will have profound consequences for the military as an institution.

Professor Lovell suggests, in Chapter 1, that the traditional dichotomy of "civil" and "military" relations is an inadequate perspective from which to view the problem. The model assumes that if the problem is conceived in terms of providing for civilian control of the military, then one may categorize elements within the state as being essentially "civilian" or "military." Problems could then be analyzed in terms of a proper relationship between civilian and military sectors of the society. Professor Lovell cites Alfred Vagts' view that civilians within a society may be as militaristic or more so than military professionals.

Lovell suggests that civil-military relations should be viewed in a political context. The term *politics* may be used to describe the value-allocation process in subsystems of a national political system or in international politics. Politics and political views are rooted in differing priorities that each of us tends to establish as the result of individual value systems, although to governments national security is almost always of prime concern. Civil-military relations should be viewed more broadly, then, as an issue within a context of politics and policy-making in which it is impossible to make sharp distinctions between military and civilian sectors of the society.

Professor Mahoney agrees in Chapter Two that it is impossible to delineate clearly separate military and civilian sectors. In "The Constitutional framework of Military-Civilian Relations," he explores the role of the armed forces in the constitutional system. While the modern conceptualization gives a better vantage point, it does not come to grips with the problem of how a democratic society can insure that arbitrary military power is held in check. Mahoney's investigation reflects the Founding Fathers' distrust of military power and how they attempt to restrain it by making the users of such power subservient to civilian authority. He examines the roles which the President, Congress, and the Judiciary have played in spelling out the meaning of the "war powers" in our constitutional history and evaluates the performance of each in its constitutionally assigned function.

Contrary to the conventional wisdom, it is suggested that the abuse of military force in American history has resulted more frequently from military decisions made by civilians than from those made by the military. Nonetheless, while Professor Mahoney argues for the necessity of maintaining civilian control over the military in a democratic society, his analysis indicates that this is no simple task.

In his essay in Chapter Three, Professor Mahoney analyzes from a historical perspective the eternal balancing task that a free society has in harmonizing liberty and national security. Preserving this balance is complicated by the fact that the one institution indispensable to the nation's security, the military, exercises a power not necessarily in harmony with an open democratic society. While acknowledging that each of the coordinated branches of the national government has a role to play, he focuses mainly on the Supreme Court as the weight-master in balancing military necessity against guaranteed individual rights. He does not find the Court to be a jealous guardian of civil rights when faced with war's felt necessities. Mahoney demonstrates that the historical development of the trade-offs between military necessity and individual rights is a study in the realities of constitutional law.

Rocco Paone's discussion in Chapter Four of the role of the military as an institutional mechanism in the foreign-policy formulation process examines the structure and function of various organizations within the Defense Department. This study represents a more traditional view applied to the present-day civil-military relationships. He treats them in relation to such modern institutions as the National Security Council, the International Security Affairs Office of the Department of Defense, and the Bureau of Politico-Military Affairs of the Department of State. He reaffirms the need for cohesion and coordination between the military and civilian policymakers at the highest levels of government.

By necessity, the military must advise civil authorities on the nature of possible military threats. In proposing strategies to cope with these threats the military must include in their analysis not only military power but foreign policies of other nations as well. Through the formulation of national security policy, then, the military "has acquired a political role in the formulation of foreign policy." Department of Defense policy recommendations in regard to foreign affairs are submitted formally to the President via the National Security Council Staff. The Secretary of Defense, who has a separate avenue, has on many occasions been influential in determining United States policy positions. One need only recall Secretary Laird's persistent warnings of caution in the Strategic Arms Limitation Talks with the Soviet Union.

The role of the military in the process of foreign-policy formulation is interesting to consider in relation to the formulation of the defense budget. Robert A. Bender's study in Chapter Five argues that the military operates much as any other interest group in the society. He presents a picture of the making of the military budget and its allocation among the services as essentially a political phenomenon. Normally this process is thought of as a fairly objective and realistic compromise between military need and economic limitations. In actuality it is the same accommodation to the strengths and demands of interest groups as in other areas of government budget-making, albeit with its own particular set of twists and turns.

Bender shows that rather than developing a defense budget to support a particular strategy, the military authorities may develop a defense strategy to fit felt budgetary requirements. The imponderables of the defense question, "How much is enough?" indicate that there is no clearly rational way to determine how much should be spent on defense. The conflict over priorities between the military and the other sectors of the society, together with the imponderables of the defense question, requires that the size of the defense allocation be decided in the political arena. Bender cites Professor Huntington's observation that strategies, like other policies, are the end result of conflict, bargaining, and compromise involving interest groups. Failure to recognize this fact has led many to criticize these policy-makers for acting as participants characteristically act in a political process.[3]

To illustrate the strength of the popular belief that the military is apolitical, that military budgets and strategies are unrelated to politics, Professor Bender notes the outraged reactions to the award-winning television documentary *The Selling of the Pentagon.* Liberals were furious that the Pentagon was propagandizing as any interest group does, although in this instance with taxpayers' money; while conservatives and the military denied that the Pentagon was either propagandizing or behaving as interest groups typically act.

As the military is very much involved in the political process, the political and social orientation of the officer corps will have an effect ultimately on the policies and programs endorsed by the military. The clash of values over priorities in foreign and domestic policy may be more deep-seated than differences over the role played by the military in defense of national security vis-à-vis the civilian society. In Chapter Six Luis R. Luis and I explore the suggestion that the political, economic, and social convictions of an individual often form a board and coherent pattern that expresses deep-seated personality characteristics. If these convictions are jointly held by a group of people, then there exists an identifiable "spirit" or "ethic." Samuel Huntington and Morris Janowitz, among others, have written extensively about the military ethic.[4] Huntington referred to the military spirit as one of "conservative realism":

[3] Samuel P. Huntington, *The Common Defense: Strategic Programs in National Politics* (New York: Columbia University Press, 1961), pp. 145–155.

[4] Samuel P. Huntington, *The Soldier and the State* (Cambridge, Mass.: Harvard University Press, 1957), p. 79. Morris Janowitz's model of the ideal military man differs from Huntington's. He combines the heroic leader model with managerial skills and the capability of organizing the newer technical skills of the military. This would require a slightly different orientation than Huntington's.

> The military ethic emphasizes the permanence, irrationality, weakness, and evil in human nature. It stresses the supremacy of society over the individual . . . [and] the importance of order. . . . It recognizes the continuing likelihood of wars among nation states. It emphasizes the importance of power (and national interest) in international relations. . . . It exalts obedience as the highest virtue of military men. . . .

He concludes that the military ethic is pessimistic, power-oriented, and nationalistic. Huntington by no means intends his assessment to be pejorative, as these qualities are needed for the military.

This chapter would tend to bear out at least a part of Huntington's model. It is one of the findings of our study that individuals who attend the Naval Academy have a great deal in common. They exhibit, among other things, great potential in academic and leadership endeavors. They also tend to be conservative generally in terms of their social and economic views. It is very possible that a considerable amount of anticipatory socialization is occurring at the service academies. Nonetheless, their attitudes are an important indicator of the attitudes of the military in relation to political priorities.

John Probert deals with the outlook and views of the military in the post-Vietnam period in Chapter Seven. Vietnam brought about a thoroughgoing introspection by the U.S. military, occasioned by its decline in prestige, cuts in the armed forces, and pronounced antimilitarism in American society. In view of the traumatic impact of the war on the professional military, a critical examination of what they are thinking, particularly about their role in politico-military affairs, is of importance. The problem of how the military should present its views to an administration, particularly in its advisory, representative, and advocatory roles, is explored. The issue of how these views are to be presented to the public is also raised; this is especially delicate if the views held are at variance with an administration's policy.

Although a substantive role for the military in which the military would attempt to overturn established military or other policy of the administration by engaging in overt political activity is generally prohibited, one must be aware that there may be differing subjective opinions as to when the military moves from an advocatory role to a substantive role. Critics have often pointed to the public relations efforts of the military as an attempt to "sell" policies to the public and the administration. If administrations place more emphasis on domestic programs in the post-Vietnam era partly because of a disenchantment with the military, one might expect the military to be more inclined to engage in this publicity activity in the years ahead to restore its prestige and position.

On the whole, however, the American military is engaged in a continuing self-critical examination of their role in government. Above all, they continue, according to Probert, to see their role in terms of the traditional professional military ethic of civilian primacy within the system.

The press may be put to limited use by the military through public relations programming. But an inquiry only into military influence on the press would be far from complete because it would miss the reciprocal influence of the press on national security policy. Charles R. D'Amato discusses the interaction between the press and the policy-makers in Chapter Eight. The influence of the press is emphasized in the personal relationships established among policy-makers and the major correspondents. Public officials, both military and civilian, may use the press to condition public attitudes or float a trial balloon concerning a new policy.

D'Amato's implications are clear. If the relationship between the press and the policy-makers is closer to collusion than to antagonism, the result might well be a failure to see major problems. The Bay of Pigs is a case in point. In the name of national security, many reporters were persuaded by various governmental officials during the buildup to write nothing. The easiest course for a reporter was to go along for fear of offending officials and having a news source run dry in the future. President Kennedy's criticism of the press was that it had not printed more information prior to the ill-fated invasion. D'Amato quotes JFK's statement to Turner Catledge, "If you had printed more about the operation you would have saved us from a colossal mistake."

Kennedy's conclusion was that other government agencies, in acting like interest groups in the formulation of national security policy, had been misleading in their advice. The suggestion is that the press may be better at analyzing some public policy than the government.

The lessons learned from that collusion have made the press more reluctant to be used by subsequent administrations as another interest group. As Jefferson said, "Were it left to me to decide whether we should have a government without newspapers or newspapers without a government, I should not hesitate a moment to prefer the latter."

The interrelationship and interdependence of military and civilian societies is nowhere more in evidence than in the Reserves and the National Guard. Members of these organizations transcend the traditional dividing-lines of both societies. Professor Probert deals with the problems and potentials of these organizations in Chapter Nine.

In 1970, then Secretary of Defense Melvin R. Laird, speaking for the Nixon Administration, redesignated the military Reserves as the "initial and primary source for augmentation of the active forces in any future emergency requiring a rapid and substantial expansion of the active forces." This had been the traditional role of the Reserves in the national defense structure, but reliance on the draft to build up the active forces for the war in Vietnam was a significant departure from that traditional role.

The military Reserves, half civilian and half military, are in a key position in our society to enlist popular support for national defense while acting as a check on military adventurism. However, unless they are actually relied upon as the primary source of military manpower to supplement the active forces, these salutary effects are not likely to accrue. The case study of Vietnam, with the incremental and gradual buildup of the armed forces via the draft rather than an extensive Reserve call up, is examined as a crucial case in point. Regardless of the eventual outcome of reliance on a Reserve call-up rather than the draft for Vietnam manpower requirements, the results for the United States could scarcely have been worse. A Reserve call-up might have provoked widespread public discussion, the posing of alternatives, and a basic reevaluation of our involvement in Vietnam. In short, the salutary processes of democracy could have been brought to bear on the making of American foreign policy for Vietnam.

1

Civil-Military Relations: Traditional and Modern Concepts Reappraised

JOHN P. LOVELL

In the formal-legalistic approach that characterized most writing on politics in the United States until after World War II, political phenomena were usually described and evaluated in terms of formal institutions, lawful authority, and the relationship of actions and decisions to legal guidelines. The traditional approach (a term that we shall use interchangeably with "formal-legalistic approach") was typical also of discussions of civil-military relations and indeed continues to be reflected in much current popular writing and some scholarly analysis.

From a formal-legalistic perspective, the problem in civil-military relations lies primarily in the threat posed by a military establishment (especially a large standing army) to popular control of government and to individual liberty. The solution to the problem is perceived to lie in the maintenance of "civil control" of the military, established through a series of constitutional "checks and balances."

The limitations of a formal-legalistic approach to the study of politics generally have become increasingly evident with the onslaught of behavioral critiques.[1] The traditional approach tends to neglect important informal patterns of interaction and sources of power other than lawful authority and to inadequately explain actions and decisions that are not shaped or inhibited by prevailing legal norms. Similarly, as Robert Dahl has noted, the concept of constitutional checks and balances obscures the subtle ways in which formal constitutional prescriptions may become undermined or ob-

[1] Of course, critiques of formal-legalistic approaches to the study of social phenomena predate the post-World War II "behavioral revolution." Thorstein Veblen, John Dewey, and Charles Beard are among the early twentieth-century forerunners. See Morton White, *Social Thought in America: The Revolt Against Formalism*, 2d ed. (Boston: Beacon Press, 1957).

solete in practice and—perhaps more importantly—ignores informal and internalized restraints that often in politics are more important than formalized constraints.[2]

Inadequacies of the traditional approach to civil-military relations have been demonstrated by a number of critics in recent decades. The writings of Huntington, Millis, Lasswell, Vagts, and Lyons (although not all behavioral in methodology) illustrate important criticisms of formal-legalistic approaches to civil-military relations.

INADEQUACIES OF THE TRADITIONAL APPROACH

In the first place, as Samuel Huntington especially has emphasized (supported by several other social scientists), the vast majority of American military professionals accept civil control virtually as an article of faith.[3] Thus, anxieties about the dangers to American society of a "man on horseback"—that is, supplanting of civilian rule by military takeover—seems unfounded. The *Seven Days in May* scenario makes lively reading, but lacks credibility.[4] If the problem of civil-military relations were merely (as suggested by the traditional view) one of getting the military to accept the legitimacy of constitutional provisions establishing civilian supremacy, then available evidence would suggest that in the American case the problem has been solved. However, phenomena such as the prolonged agony of war in Southeast Asia, massive defense expenditures, and cost overruns indicate that many important problems remain regarding the relationship of the military establishment to American society—problems that do not fit neatly, if at all, into the traditional framework.

The concept of "civil control" was born, as Walter Millis has observed, "in the eighteenth-century fear and loathing of a standing army as a menace to the liberties of the people." But as Millis has pointed out, even by 1945 this "greatest and most enduring of the old principles . . . was not, in fact, of much relevance to the practical issues which confronted the country," in

[2] Robert A. Dahl, *A Preface to Democratic Theory* (Chicago: University of Chicago Press, 1956), esp. Chapter 1.

[3] Samuel P. Huntington, *The Soldier and the State: The Theory and Politics of Civil-Military Relations* (Cambridge, Mass.: Belknap Press of Harvard Univ. Press, 1957). Also see John W. Masland and Laurence I. Radway, *Soldiers and Scholars: Military Education and National Policy* (Princeton, N.J.: Princeton Univ. Press, 1957); and Morris Janowitz, *The Professional Soldier: A Social and Political Portrait* (Glencoe, Ill.: Free Press, 1960).

[4] Fletcher Knebel and Charles W. Bailey, *Seven Days in May* (New York: Harper & Row, 1962).

spite of continued reference to the concept in political rhetoric. The three great civil-military issues of the post-World War II decade, Millis noted, were the administration of the occupied territories, the development and control of atomic energy, and the reorganization of the military establishment. As he has observed of these issues, "none raised a valid question of the locus of power, of civilian control in the old sense [that is, in the sense of concern for military domination] . . . ." Rather, he argued:

> the fundamental problem in each was whether the technical military advice as to force levels, weapon systems, expenditures, could be combined with the political, civilian advice as to diplomacy, budget and tax policy and popular acceptance into a coherent and adequate national strategy on the world stage.[5]

Harold Lasswell, writing on the eve of American entry into World War II, argued that the question of "the locus of power" and of threats to individual liberty would continue to be important issues—far more important than in any earlier period. However, like Millis, Lasswell saw that the problem was not that of "civilian control in the old sense." Rather, Lasswell depicted the problem as one in which the state as a whole, experiencing external threats, would generate demands that "specialists on violence" would be peculiarly equipped to satisfy. The result might be, Lasswell warned, the emergence of a "garrison state" in which individual freedom would be sacrificed on the altar of military preparedness.[6] The salient point here is not support or challenge of the accuracy of the "garrison state hypothesis." Rather, the point lies in Lasswell's recognition that problems of popular control of government and the maintenance of individual liberty are broader than the concept of "civil control" would suggest.

Like Lasswell, Alfred Vagts has recognized that militarism is a problem that extends beyond the institutional confines of the military organizations. Indeed, as Vagts has pointed out, civilians within a society may be as militaristic as military professionals or even more so. Basing his observations on the experience of a number of nation-states throughout history, Vagts made an important distinction between "militarism" and "the military way." He has used the former term to describe institutions and attitudes that glorify war or romanticize or perpetuate military practices, customs, or attributes beyond their purpose of contributing to combat efficiency. "The military way," in contrast, refers to techniques and practices of military organizations designed to enable them to perform their assigned tasks with efficient utiliza-

[5] Walter Millis, "Reorganization," in Millis, with Harvey Mansfield and Harold Stein, *Arms and the State* (New York: Twentieth Century Fund, 1958).

[6] Harold D. Lasswell, "The Garrison State," *The American Journal of Sociology*, 46 (January 1941), pp. 455–468. The article has been reprinted in the Bobbs-Merrill reprint series in the social sciences, No. 161.

tion of resources. Thus, Vagts has emphasized that although any truly professional military establishment will adhere to "the military way," military professionals are not necessarily militaristic in their outlook.[7] Although Vagts did not carry his argument this far, one might further contend that in a democratic society it is perfectly appropriate for military professionals to be anti-militaristic (but not anti-military).[8]

Gene Lyons, in an oft-cited article on "the new civil-military relations" published in 1961, noted that the traditional view of civil-military relations, with its exaltation of "civil control" as the guiding principle for such relations, retains little contemporary significance. Like Millis, Lyons pointed out that the boundaries between "civilian" and "military" in the American political system have become increasingly blurred, with civilians performing tasks essentially "military" in nature and military professionals assigned to roles indistinguishable from those of civilian counterparts. Moreover, Lyons observed, the military are not a monolithic group; they are factionalized, with intra-service differences often being more important than are differences between military and civilian viewpoints. Furthermore, like Huntington, Lyons argued that the vast majority of military professionals in the United States accept the principle of civilian supremacy.[9]

As summarized in Table 1, traditional (18th and 19th century) images of civil-military relations have been altered in the light of 20th century experiences and institutions. Contingencies or abuses of power that are the object of concern have shifted; fear of a military coup or involvement in European wars has to a large extent given way to anxiety about militarism, the "military-industrial complex," cost-overruns, and undue emphasis on military solutions to diplomatic problems. A belief in the efficacy of formal-

[7] Alfred Vagts, *A History of Militarism: Civilian and Military*, revised ed. (New York: Free Press, 1959).

[8] Reformists within the West German Army recently have adopted a position that is quite explicitly anti-militaristic. The current German experience is interesting and controversial (within the German army itself as well as among interested observers). For instance, after several years of official efforts to integrate the German army into society and to grant soldiers political rights comparable to those of civilians, a high-level military staff published a secret paper highly critical of the reforms and arguing that liberalization of the Bundeswehr must be halted. In reply, a group of young lieutenants circulated nine theses, with the general theme, "I want to be an officer of the Bundeswehr who. . . ." Two of the nine assertions read, " . . . refuses to display an allegedly 'officerlike' behavior. On the contrary, I am not prepared to live up to any specific officer role," and " . . . is not satisfied with maintaining peace but also wants to shape it." The heated debate continues. Dietrich Genschel, M.A., Oberstleutnant, "Armed Forces and Society in the Federal Republic of Germany," a paper delivered at the annual conference of the Inter-University Seminar on Armed Forces and Society, Chicago, Nov. 18–20, 1971.

[9] Gene M. Lyons, "The New Civil-Military Relations," *American Political Science Review*, 55 (March 1961), 53–63.

TABLE 1. CHANGING PERCEPTIONS OF U.S. CIVIL-MILITARY RELATIONS

Changing Perceptions of the Problem				
The Problem in General Terms	*18th-19th Centuries*	*Early 20th Century*	*Post-WW II Liberal or Radical*	*Post-WW II Conservative (Huntington)*
Threat to Individual Liberty	"Man on horseback" (Military rule—e.g. Napoleon)	Prussian militarism	Militaristic culture "Garrison state"	
Threat to Popular Control (Accountability, Political Equality)	Military adventurism Involvement in foreign (i.e. European) wars	Warrior caste (e.g. West Point), All-powerful General Staff	Military-industrial complex; "Power elite" unresponsive to popular will and needs	Blurring of civil-military areas of special competence; Mutual meddling; Inter-service rivalry; Waste; Inefficiency

Changing Perceptions of the Cure				
General Terms	*18th-19th Centuries*	*Early 20th Century*	*Post-WW II Liberal or Radical*	*Post-WW II Conservative (Huntington)*
Civil control	Constitutional "checks and balances." Keep standing army small	Same as 19th, into 1930s	Divide and rule; Strengthen civilian Sec. of Defense	Maintain boundaries; Promote military professionalism

legalistic cures attainable through keeping the army small or through congressional control of appropriations to some extent has been supplanted by a recognition of the importance of internalized restraints on behavior and informal political checks. (However, to a greater extent than can be depicted in Table 1, radicals, liberals, and conservatives have disagreed about the nature of the problem and on the specific measures that ought to be taken to cope with the problem.)

It is true that some current writings expressing alarm about alleged dangers of an all-volunteer army have a clearly eighteenth-century ring to them; and books with titles such as "How to Control the Military" attract a wide audience.[10] However, the size of the audience for such writings is attributable more to a pervasive disillusionment with defense-related matters, in the aftermath of Vietnam, Cambodia, and Laos, than to a rejection of behavioral analysis in favor of the formal-legalistic approach.

LIMITATIONS OF MODERN APPROACHES

Among the "attentive public," if not throughout the public as a whole, it seems clear that formal-legalistic views of civil-military relations have been superceded by the views of their critics. However, the concepts and theories thus far developed by those modern writers who depart from traditional approaches have their own limitations, which must be noted. These include (1) the parochialism of many modern treatments of civil-military relations by American writers; (2) the continuing dichotomization of "civil" and "military" sectors in most models that move beyond parochialism to a comparative perspective; and (3) the *a priori* nature of assumptions made about the value systems of military professionals and of salient civilian groups.

Parochialism

First, a number of the critiques that have been made of formal-legalistic approaches to civil-military relations have been parochial in scope (e.g. Millis, Lyons), offering analyses that have considerable validity in the American context but much less validity elsewhere. For instance, it is an

[10] John Kenneth Galbraith, *How to Control the Military* (Garden City, N.Y.: Doubleday, 1969). In suggesting that traditional notions of "civil control of the military" have little usefulness for policy-making or for analysis, I do not mean to suggest that the military should be unrestrained or immune from criticism. Moreover, although I contend that some of the alarm that has been expressed about an all-volunteer army has an anachronistic quality, many other expressions of concern are timely and analytically persuasive. Some examples of the latter may be found in a special edition of the Columbia University *Teachers College Record,* 73 (Sept. 1971); the theme of the special edition was "The Quest for Equity: National Service Options."

accurate criticism of formal-legalistic arguments to observe that the "man on horseback" threat is of little significance to civil-military relations in the United States today. However, clearly the "man on horseback" is an accurate representation of the problem that many political systems in the world do face. In many of the states of Latin America, the Middle East, Africa, and Asia, the military coup d'etat is a common if not a chronic problem. Thus, concern for civil control, in the traditional sense of protection of governmental institutions and individual liberty from domination by the armed forces, is a fundamental reality. Even in political systems not plagued by the threat or reality of military coups d'etat, such as the Canadian, problems in the relationship of the military establishment of society are in many instances distinctively different from those found in the United States. The salient point, therefore, is that a useful framework for discussion and analysis of the relationship of military establishments to societies ought to accommodate the varied problems and experiences of nation-states throughout the world. Even if one's major policy or analytical interest is focused on the United States, a comparative framework has the advantage of better enabling one to recognize aspects of the American experience that are attributable to peculiarities of American culture and traditions and other aspects that may be common to a number of political systems (for example, common to all democracies, common to all advanced industrialized nation-states, and so forth).

Perpetuation of the Civil-Military Dichotomy

Some modern students of civil-military relations have moved beyond a parochial American frame of reference to a comparative one. Characteristically, attempts to develop a comparative framework have taken the form of criteria for classifying political systems in terms of the political role of the armed forces. Typically, role categories such as "total domination," "veto group," "political interest group," and "no influence," are depicted.[11] Although such categories can be useful for comparing and contrasting the experience of political systems in which the uniformed armed forces are sharply differentiated in organizational structure and in function from civilian groups, the classification scheme is much less useful for analysis of systems such as the American one in which the boundaries between "military" and "civil" have become blurred. Indeed, by focusing on a continuum of military

[11] See for example, S. E. Finer, *The Man on Horseback: The Role of the Military in Politics* (New York: Praeger, 1962); and Morris Janowitz, *The Military in the Political Development of New Nations: An Essay in Comparative Analysis* (Chicago: University of Chicago Press, 1964). An interesting attempt to establish categories of military roles while treating as variable the degree of integration of the boundaries of the military is made by A. R. Luckham, "A Comparative Typology of Civil-Military Relations," *Government and Opposition,* 6 (Winter 1971), 5–35.

influence or intervention in politics, such taxonomies tend to neglect problems associated with civilian participants in the national security process (for example, Secretary of Defense McNamara and his "whiz kids"; presidential advisor Henry Kissinger). Moreover, the framework is insensitive to fluctuations that occur within a single category (for instance, changing values and behavior of the military as an interest group). Thus, paradoxically, the comparative frameworks that have been developed in recent years usefully carry analysis beyond a parochial American focus; but many of them are limited, especially in their applicability to complex civil-military interrelationships such as those experienced currently in the United States.

A Priori Conclusions

Another important limitation of modern treatments of civil-military relations has been the foundation on which conclusions rest. There has been a notable dearth of empirical data to support generalizations about important questions such as what value preferences are held by military professionals and civilian political leaders, respectively. The theoretical framework developed by Samuel Huntington in *The Soldier and the State* is a case in point.

Probably no other work since World War II has influenced serious discussions of civil-military relations to the extent that Huntington's has. From a review of writings and discussions by those who have drawn heavily upon this pioneering work, however, it would appear that few of his many readers have been sensitive to the largely deductive process by which Huntington arrived at the portrait of "the professional military ethic" that provides the major part of the foundation for his model of civil-military relations. Instead, the professional military ethic that Huntington describes often is cited as a valid empirical description of values held by military professionals in contrast to the values of civilians. (Indeed, it is a tribute to Huntington's influence that many critics of the military as well as many military professionals have seized upon Huntington's discussion to support their mutually contrasting views.) Because of the central role that *The Soldier and the State* has played in shaping modern discussions of civil-military relations, a rather detailed examination of the approach utilized by Huntington in developing the theoretical framework of the book is required.[12]

It is important to note at the outset that although many readers have

[12] See especially Samuel P. Huntington, *The Common Defense: Strategic Programs in National Politics* (New York: Columbia University Press, 1961). (Chicago: University of Chicago Press, 1964.) An interesting attempt to establish categories of military roles while treating as variable the degree of integration of the boundaries of the military, is made by A. R. Luckham, "A Comparative Typology of Civil-Military Relations," *Government and Opposition*, 6 (Winter 1971), pp. 5–35.

badly misinterpreted what Huntington was attempting to do in Part One (the theoretical portion) of the book, Huntington himself was quite explicit about his approach. In developing a theory of the military profession and its relationship to society, Huntington was following the lead of Max Weber, whose analysis of bureaucracy had depicted its distinguishing characteristics as an "ideal type" rather than as elements inductively identified through empirical study of any particular organization.

Huntington's depiction of the military profession as an "ideal type" begins with a discussion of features that distinguished "professions" from other occupations; the root of the term, to profess, provides the key clue.[13] A career in the law, in medicine, in the clergy, or as an officer in the military has been regarded as "a calling," demanding a special oath or commitment of service to the society. Thus Huntington depicts a strong sense of social responsibility as one of the defining characteristics of professionalism. Second, to a large extent professions tend to be self-regulating, to establish their own standards of admission and advancement and their own norms of acceptable professional conduct. A sense of commitment to the profession and its ideals is thus another characteristic of professionalism, according to Huntington. Third, professionals are identifiable by their highly developed expertise.

The distinctive nature of the expertise that is possessed becomes central to determining the content of the professional ethic. Because (according to Huntington) "the management of violence" is the skill that distinguishes the military from other professions, the nature of such expertise tends to mold the content of the professional military ethic (together with the commitment to professional corporateness and social responsibility). A preference for discipline and order, a desire to avoid military adventurism but a belief in the continuing likelihood of war among nations, and an acceptance of the view that military men are servants of statesmen are among the tenets of value and belief that Huntington views as *functional for military organizations, given their distinctive skill requirements and their organizational relationship to the state*. Therefore, he includes such values in his description of the professional military ethic. As he summarizes it, "the military ethic is thus pessimistic, collectivist, historically inclined, power-oriented, nationalistic, pacifist, and instrumentalist in its view of the military profession. It is, in belief, realistic and conservative."[14]

[13] The distinction between "professions" and other occupations is examined in some detail also by Everett C. Hughes, "Professions," *Daedalus,* 92 (Fall 1963), pp. 655–668. The entire issue of the journal is devoted to articles on the professions. Included is one by Huntington on "Power, Expertise and the Military Profession," pp. 785–807, providing an analysis of post-World War II trends in the American military profession.

[14] Huntington, *The Soldier and the State,* p. 79. All subsequent Huntington citations are to this work.

One might object to Huntington's contention that a military man who fails to display the values that he defines as essential components of the professional ethic is not "truly" professional. Further, one might object to his blanket assertion that "the military ethic is a constant standard by which it is possible to judge the professionalism of any officer corps anywhere anytime." [15] But such objections, in the final analysis, are definitional, not substantive. Huntington's description of "the professional military ethic" is a definition. It is a way of saying, "I am going to use the term, 'professional military ethic,' to mean the following . . . ," much as one might say, "Let *v* equal velocity" in a mathematical analysis. Definitions cannot be proven true or false; they are merely useful or not useful according to their clarity and according to the purpose for which they are developed or applied.

Thus, the salient question to be asked about Huntington's discussion of the values and beliefs that comprise the professional military ethic is not whether his description is true or false—being definitional, it is neither true nor false. Rather, the salient question is *whether,* the discussion is useful *as a basis for making theoretical and policy inferences about civil-military relations.*

In defense of Huntington, one might argue that his concern in *The Soldier and the State* is primarily normative rather than empirical in terms of the applicability of his framework. That is, primarily he seems to be interested in developing a model that will enable civilian policy-makers as well as military professionals to understand what structural arrangements are "best" and how each "ought" to behave in order to attain the "most desirable" civil-military relationship. The prescriptive key lies in maximizing military professionalism (as Huntington defines it), thereby attaining what he terms "objective civilian control." "Objective civilian control" is a more realistic and desirable goal for most modern political systems, according to Huntington, than is "subjective civilian control." The latter could be attained only by "civilianizing" the military, "making them the mirror of the state"; to do so would erode military professionalism and therefore (by definition) greatly diminish the usefulness of the military to the state.[16]

The frequent references to Huntington's model over a period of years are ample testimony to the appeal of the model. However, even when one acknowledges the normative rather than empirical intent and the deductive rather than inductive process of theory-building, one must turn to the "real world" (that is, to empirically observable reality) in order to apply pre-

[15] Huntington, p. 62. A critique of Huntington by two Army officers who were serving on the faculty at West Point raises objections of the sort described. The authors complain that Huntington is stereotyping the "military mind." Lt. Col. Zeb B. Bradford, Jr., and Maj. James R. Murphy, "A New Look at the Military Profession," *Army* (Feb. 1969), pp. 59–64.

[16] Huntington, *The Soldier and the State,* p. 83.

scriptions inferred from the model. Such empirical observation reveals deficiencies that, in my judgment, call into serious question the usefulness of the model for even normative purposes.

Because Huntington's concept of "the professional military ethic" is central to his theorizing, it becomes especially pertinent to consider the implications of the degrees of "professionalism" that would be judged true of actual military officers and organizations if his norms were applied. For instance, empirical observation suggests numerous cases where the trends in the development of military organizations are not historically concurrent along each of the three dimensions that Huntington describes as defining characteristics of professionalism. Technological proficiency and general expertise have increased sharply over the past fifty years in the British, Canadian, and U.S. armies (as they have in many other armies); however, in the cases cited, evidence suggests that the sense of organic unity among military professionals has declined rather than grown, reflecting a somewhat diminished importance attached to the traditions and mystique of corporate membership and a somewhat greater emphasis upon individuality. Moreover, if one considers "social responsibility," another defining characteristic of professionalism which for military professionals includes an acceptance of civilian supremacy, according to Huntington, one finds a number of instances (e.g. Pakistan, South Korea, Ethiopia, Ghana) in which forcible intervention by the military in politics came *after* a moderate level of professional expertise had been acquired, not during the period when expertise was lowest.[17] Likewise, a recent content analysis of U.S. Army professional journals over a fifty year period indicates that American Army officers have become more politicized, rather than more apolitical in orientation, during a half-century characterized by heightened military professionalism in other respects.[18] If a military organization (or individual) is developing along one dimension of "professionalism," but receding along another dimension, how is one to describe the degree of "professionalism" of the organization or its members?

[17] See for example the studies in Henry Bienen (ed.), *The Military Intervenes: Case Studies in Political Development* (New York: Russell Sage, 1968). The flurry of military coups d'etat in Africa further illustrates the point at hand, as Smaldone's analysis in the present volume reveals. Likewise, Stepan's excellent analysis of the role of the military in Brazil reveals that increased intervention by the military in politics, and the abandonment of the "moderating pattern" of civil-military relations, was in part the product of increased professionalism (among sergeants) and in part stimulated by the concern among officers about threats to military professionalism. Alfred Stepan, *The Military in Politics: Changing Patterns in Brazil* (Princeton, N.J.: Princeton University Press, 1971).

[18] Clarence L. Abercrombie, III, and Major Raoul H. Alcalá, USA, "The New Military Professionalism," in *Military Force and American Society,* ed. Bruce M. Russett and Alfred Stepan (New York: Harper & Row, 1973), pp. 34–58.

To be sure, Huntington is not oblivious to cases of this sort; but for the most part they are explained away in *The Soldier and the State* as a failure of military men to live up fully to professional ethics or as failures of civilian statesmen to respect the professionalism of the military and thereby allow it to develop "normally." [19] One might argue instead (and I do so argue) that it is more useful to abandon Huntington's *a priori* definition of "the professional military ethic" in favor of a framework that can accommodate variety and complexity in the structure and skill requirements of modern military organizations, in the tasks such organizations have been assigned, in the circumstances under which tasks are performed, and in the composition and value preferences of those who pursue military careers.

Large military establishments such as the American one are not monolithic structures, describable in terms of a single function and a single set of skill requirements. Rather, like other complex organizations, every large military establishment is a complex of smaller organizations, each of which performs a distinctive function and is likely to have distinctive skill requirements. As current differences among the U.S. Army, Navy, Air Force, and Marines reveal (as do intra-branch differences within each arm of service), each component is likely to define in distinctive terms its recruitment needs, its training requirements, the leadership styles that are appropriate, and the organizational ethos that embodies its distinctive traditions and mission.

Moreover, as a recent critique of the Huntington model by two American field-grade Army officers correctly points out:

> Military expertise is not a constant: it is contingent and relative. Military expertise will vary according to whatever is required of the profession to support the policies of the state. The range of possibilities includes "management of violence," "peacekeeping," "deterrence," "nation-building," "revolutionary development," "civic action" or "pacification." There are many examples of military establishments being required to do all sorts of "non-military" tasks. To name only a few in the American experience, we can point to the construction of the Panama Canal, the building of the railroads to the West, the rehabilitation of domestic social groups, conservation of natural resources, work projects for the unemployed and even polar and space exploration.[20]

Furthermore, there are important differences of viewpoint and value preference among members of most large modern military establishments

[19] Huntington, *The Soldier and the State,* pp. 74–78.

[20] Bradford and Murphy, *Army* (Feb. 1969), p. 60. I agree with this and several other points made by Bradford and Murphy. However, as I have suggested earlier (n. 15 and related discussion), many of their objections to the Huntington model confuse essentially definitional statements with empirical conclusions. Moreover, Bradford and Murphy do not clearly distinguish their own definitional efforts from empirical observations about the modern U.S. military officer.

(as there are among many other professions in modern society). In the American military, attitudes cluster to some extent according to branch of service, to some extent according to occupational specialty within service, to some extent according to common career experiences, race and ethnic origin and according to age and grade.[21] But even within a particular branch, specialization, career path, racial or age cohort some variety exists. The variety of value preferences among military career personnel cannot be explained accurately by attributing differences simply to differing degrees of "professionalism." An analytical framework adequate to cope with such variety, therefore, must go beyond the one developed in *The Soldier and the State*.

The Critique of Modern Approaches Summarized

To summarize the past several pages of discussion, modern treatments of civil-military relations generally represent an analytical step forward from formal-legalistic treatments. However, most of the concepts and theories developed in recent decades in this field of inquiry have had important shortcomings of their own, which include: (1) a parochial focus exclusively upon the American experience by some scholars; (2) a tendency by several of those analysts who have moved beyond a parochial framework to a comparative one to perpetuate the view of "civil" and "military" sectors as sharply differentiated; and (3) an *a priori* approach to generalizing about the value preferences of military professionals and civilians concerned with national security policies, to the neglect of pertinent empirical data. What is needed is a framework for empirical and normative analysis, one that can accommodate the experience of political systems in which structures and values are complex and varied and in which boundaries between "military" and "civilian" are blurred, as well as accommodating the experience of political systems in which the military *qua military* do pose a threat of political domination.

[21] Differences of outlook that have contributed to inter-service rivalry have been a recurring feature of American politics since World War II. Of special interest in the current era are differences of outlook attributable to race, on the one hand, and age, on the other. On racial attitudes and policies in the American military, see Charles C. Moskos, Jr., "The American Dilemma in Uniform: Race in the Armed Forces," in *The Annals* of the American Academy of Political and Social Science (March 1973; entire issue devoted to "The Military and American Society"), pp. 94–106. The "generation gap" in the military, especially as it divides the outlook of senior military professionals from junior ones, and ranking NCO's from younger enlisted men, has been identified in a study conducted by the U.S. Army War College, *Leadership for the 1970's,* 1 July 1971. See also Commander James A. Barber, Jr., "Is There a Generation Gap in the Naval Officer Corps?", *Naval War College Review,* 22 (May 1970), 24–33.

AN ALTERNATIVE FRAMEWORK

Politics, as Easton put it, is the process by which values are authoritatively allocated in a society. The term *politics* also may be used to describe the value-allocation process in subsystems of a national political system (e.g. state politics, urban politics, community politics, corporation politics) or in superordinate systems (e.g. international politics). Politics are ubiquitous because value differences are ubiquitous. Or to state the point somewhat differently, politics are rooted in the differing priorities that each of us tends to establish regarding values that we hold dear. The problem of political analysis is complicated (in part) because differences arise not only over goal-values (what should be done—or done first, with the most resources?), but also over instrumental values (what course of action should be pursued, or what means utilized, in order to attain various goal-values?).

Because national security is of paramount concern to most national governments, the questions of what values are deemed instrumental to achieving the goal of "national security" and of what trade-offs with other values are made in order to try to maintain national security are central to an understanding of the politics of most nation-states. I would suggest further that such questions provide a useful alternative manner of depicting the analytical task that traditionally has been described as "the study of civil-military relations." In Lasswellian terms, the questions that are of interest to us from an alternative conceptual framework are: who gets what, when, and how, in the struggle over national security policies, and with what effect in terms of the allocation of security and competing values?

In the study of a political system in which there is a broad commitment of the populace to "democracy" (however vaguely articulated by the populace), it becomes of special interest analytically to examine the trade-offs made in the political arena between values conventionally associated with national security (for example, military strength, "preparedness," efficiency in military training, in the development of weapons systems, and in the conduct of military operations) and values associated with democratic practices (popular control of government, political equality, individual liberty). Of course, disagreement exists among political theorists as well as among laymen regarding the "essential ingredients" of democracy and the extent to which particular values (such as individual liberty) must be satisfied before it is appropriate to describe a political system or its practices as "democratic." However, we do not insist here upon an arbitrary definition of "democracy." Rather, for purposes of illustrating the kinds of issues that might be of policy or theoretical interest, I suggest merely that "popular control," "political equality," and "individual liberty" are values that often are competitive with national security values in the politics of societies where the aspiration to "democracy" (however defined) is high.

To say that democratic values often are competitive with national security values is not to argue that attainment of the former necessarily involves costs in terms of the latter, or vice versa. It is only to argue that in many historical instances those who have placed a high priority on national security (for example, in wartime) have claimed that some compromise in democratic values (for instance, more secrecy, more restrictions on dissent) was essential to the attainment of effective security. To some extent, the reverse is also evident; those who have demanded more liberty or more equality many times have contended that their goals were important enough to warrant accepting greater risks in terms of national security (for example, risks produced by large reductions in military force levels).

However, the analytical task in identifying the process of bargaining and tradeoffs among competing values in the arena of national security politics is complicated for a variety of reasons, among the most important of which is the fact that the most heated battles in politics frequently are over means (instrumental values) rather than ends (goal values); and rarely is information complete or fully reliable as to which means lead to which ends. As a consequence, in addition to the situation implicit in the preceding discussion, in which a party (that we shall call Able) favoring national security values even at some cost to democratic values is in conflict with another party (whom we shall call Baker) that seeks to advance democratic values even at some risk to national security values, one encounters the following situations.

(1) Able and Baker have value-preferences as described above; but Able *erroneously* believes that action X (for example, more secrecy) will contribute to national security when in fact X is unrelated to, or may even detract from, the goal that Able seeks to advance. Baker, in turn, erroneously believes that action Y (for example, a protest demonstration that disrupts traffic leading to the Pentagon) will reduce militarism and enhance individual liberty, when in fact Y may increase militarism and induce repression.

(2) Able and Baker *agree* on goal-values (that is, they have the same priorities), but *disagree* as to the probable consequences of a particular course of action. For example, both Able and Baker highly value political equality. However, Able favors an all-volunteer army because he believes that it will be more equitable than a system that relies in part on conscription, whereas Baker opposes an all-volunteer army because he believes that the recruitment-base will consist primarily of lower socio-economic class youth, thereby heightening inequities.

(3) Able and Baker agree on the priorities to be established when national security values conflict with other values (e.g. social welfare), but disagree on the "facts" regarding trends in the allocation of resources. For example, using figures for defense expenditures as a percent of the gross

national product (GNP), Able contends that expenditures for U.S. national security have been declining in the 1970s, whereas expenditures for welfare (including state and local as well as federal governmental expenditures) have been rising. Baker, on the contrary, includes in his definition of "defense expenditures" not only DOD expenditures but also those for veterans benefits, military assistance, atomic energy, and a substantial portion of the repayments on the federal debt. Therefore, Baker argues that military spending has been rising in the 1970s, just as it rose in the 1960s; he further claims that in periods when the government invests heavily in defense it tends to cut back on social welfare spending. Choosing between these competing arguments is not a matter of selecting truth and rejecting falsehood. Each argument is "true," if one accepts the terminology and assumptions of the advocate of the position. Consequently, the choice is not between Able's conclusions and those of Baker; rather, it is a choice between the premises and kinds of data that Able relies upon, and the premises and data consulted by Baker.[22]

A framework sensitive to the range of values that are at stake in the resolution of national security issues is outlined in Table 2. In contrast to approaches criticized earlier in the chapter, analysis from the alternative framework begins not with an image of structures in conflict (military versus civilian), but rather with an assessment of issue areas in which national security values are at stake. Such issue areas can be categorized in terms of the various functions that all political systems perform, such as political recruitment, political socialization, interest articulation, and others such as those identified in the landmark studies of developing nations edited by Almond and Coleman.[23] The framework emphasizes that considerations of strategic and tactical effectiveness in national security policy-making represent values that typically compete with (and sometimes complement) other values, such as individual liberty, social welfare, and commitments to the development of international institutions. The individuals, groups and institutions that will be associated with competing value preferences are not identified on an *a priori* basis in the framework; rather such identification is left to empirical inquiry. Empirical analysis no doubt will reveal that in most political systems there are issues that arise which pit the value preferences

[22] Cf. "Highlights of the New Defense Budget," *Military Directions* (Fact Sheet published by the Center for Defense Information, Washington, D.C., Feb. 1973), with testimony of Secretary of Defense Melvin Laird and other DOD officials in U.S. Congress, House of Representatives, Committee on Appropriations, Subcommittee on Department of Defense, *Hearings: Department of Defense Appropriations for 1973*, 92d Cong., 2d sess., 1972, Part 3.

[23] Gabriel A. Almond and James S. Coleman, eds., *The Politics of the Developing Areas* (Princeton, N.J.: Princeton University Press, 1960). See also refinements of the framework in Gabriel A. Almond and G. Bingham Powell, Jr., *Comparative Politics: A Developmental Approach* (Boston: Little, Brown, 1966).

of most military professionals against the values of most of the civilian sector; such analysis will also reveal, however, numerous instances in which the configurations of political views and political alliances are much more complex and diversified (with elements of the military on opposing sides of an issue, for instance).

The framework can be used to generate normative and empirical questions. Focusing upon issues in the American context (although the framework could be applied to other systems as well), normative questions of interest include: How wide a range of authority should the President have to commit troops? How much discretionary authority should be granted to military commanders? How much of the national budget should be allocated for military purposes? How should the defense budget be divided? How much political dissent, and in what forms, should be permitted in time of war?

Normative issues might be approached from an individual rather than a societal perspective. For instance, one might ask: which political candidate's position on defense spending do I find most attractive? Should I petition my congressman to prevent further expansion of the ABM system? What is my obligation to the state—should I refuse to accept military service if I disagree with the military policies of the state? If I have to choose between jail and abstention from acts of civil disobedience that I believe are justified, what choice do I make?

Empirically, one might explore a series of questions not in terms of what ought to be, but rather in terms of what is (or what has been or will be). For instance, what kinds of constraints have been placed on presidential commitment of troops? How much discretionary authority has been allocated to military commanders and under what circumstances? What factors of urgency, personality, organizational routine, or political climate determine the amount of discretionary authority that will be allocated? How much of the national budget has been allocated for military purposes—and how was the level of military spending established? How has the defense budget been divided? Which groups are most successful in gaining funds? What political strategies do they employ, and what factors explain their success? What has been the fate of political dissidents in time of war?

As one reflects upon such questions in the light of American political experience in recent decades, he might attempt to formulate and to test hypotheses such as the following, in an effort to develop empirical generalizations relevant to his normative concerns.[24]

[24] These and additional hypotheses relevant to the problem area under examination are discussed in John P. Lovell, *Foreign Policy in Perspective* (New York: Holt, Rinehart and Winston, 1970), Chaps. 9 and 11.

TABLE 2. CIVIL-MILITARY RELATIONS VIEWED WITHIN THE CONTEXT OF THE POLICIES OF NATIONAL SECURITY

Political Functions Performed in the Political System	National Security Issues Relevant to Each Function	Values to be Allocated: *Strategic and Tactical-effectiveness Values*	Values to be Allocated: *Coordinate and Competing Values*
Political Recruitment	What size regular and reserve forces? Who shall serve? How recruited?	Preparedness Military effectiveness	Representativeness Political equality
Political Socialization	What type military education and training? What rules of military justice? How administered?	Discipline Loyalty Expertise	Individual liberty Pluralism, tolerance of dissent Avoidance of militarism
Interest articulation and aggregation; Political Communication	How much political activity by military personnel is acceptable? What kinds of information should be classified?	Professional commitment Thorough and accurate intelligence Advantage over enemy	Freedom of expression and association Informed public

TABLE 2—*Continued*

Political Functions Performed in the Political System	National Security Issues Relevant to Each Function	Values to be Allocated	
		Strategic and Tactical-effectiveness Values	*Coordinate and Competing Values*
Decision Making	How much authority to the chief executive? What size defense budget? Goals? Weapons systems?	Speed of decision making Flexibility of response Credible deterrance Cost-effectiveness	Accountability of policy makers to public Domestic welfare and prosperity Arms control Development of internatl. law and organization
Implementation	How much autonomy should military commanders in the field have? What "strings" attached to military aid?	Combat effectiveness Control Flexibility	Political accountability Diplomatic cooperation

Hypothesis: "If a foreign-policy course of action favored by the President requires the commitment of a substantial number of American troops in its implementation, the President will seek advance endorsement of the decision by Congress."

Hypothesis: "Once Congress has condoned, although never formally sanctioned, a reduction of its authority relative to that of the President for engaging in various kinds of activities in the foreign-policy process, the President will resist relinquishing authority to Congress even if the rationale under which the authority was originally asserted has become outmoded by changing circumstances."

Hypothesis: "The greater the tension within the society stemming from concern about an external threat to the nation, the greater will be the influence on defense policies of military leaders and of defense contractors whose resources and skills are salient to coping with the threat."

Hypothesis: "The greater the tension within the society stemming from concern about a threat to the nation:

'a. the lower will be the level of tolerance by the general public of individuals and groups whose words, deeds, or ethnic origins seem alien to established national-policy objectives;

'b. the greater will be the tendency of politicians to seek to suppress dissent from policies that purport to cope with the threat;

'c. the more limited will be the range of individual action and expression regarded as constitutionally protected by the courts.' "

We do not argue here the plausibility of the cited hypotheses or the comprehensiveness of the issues identified here. These normative and empirical questions are illustrative only. Which specific questions are pertinent and which hypotheses are interesting and plausible will vary somewhat from one political system to another and from one time period to the next. However, in any national political system and in any time period, the task of analysis of national security politics may be described as that of predicting probable outcomes, given the values at stake (that is, the type of issue), given the groups and structures actively identified with various value priorities, and given the political resources of competing groups and structures. Lowi's useful effort to reconcile the divergent theories of the "pluralists" and of those who argue the existence of a "power elite" in American politics, by demonstrating that power configurations vary with the types of issue, is illustrative of the analysis that is needed to "flesh out" the conceptual framework.[25]

[25] Theodore J. Lowi, "Making Democracy Safe for the World: National Politics and Foreign Policy," in *Domestic Sources of Foreign Policy,* ed. James N. Rosenau (New York: Free Press, 1967), pp. 295–331.

In the light of the far-reaching changes in values and beliefs that American and other societies have been experiencing in recent years, it is important that an analytical framework be sensitive to the *dynamics* of national security politics as well as to the types of variables most relevant to explaining or predicting a particular policy outcome. Elsewhere I have commented at some length on the relationship between changing environmental demands and supports on the one hand and changes in U.S. national security policies on the other, with particular reference to the impact of American involvement in Vietnam.[26] Conceptually, the relationship between changing environments and changing national security policies can be depicted as a cybernetic one (Figure 1). As changes occur in the external

Figure 1. Changing Environment and Changing National Security Policies: A Cybernetic Process.

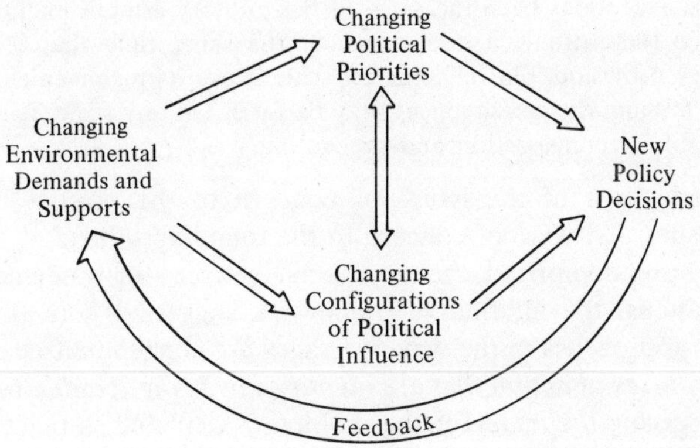

and domestic environments of a nation-state, the perception of such changes leads to a restructuring of priorities on the part of various participants in the political process, both in terms of national security values (sought as goals or because such values are believed to be instrumental to national security) and in terms of coordinate and competing values (for example, health, welfare, democratic values). Such environmental changes also have the effect of making some kinds of political resources more salient than they were previously and some less salient, thereby contributing to changes in the political influence of various groups within the system. The overall effect of such changes is likely to be new policy decisions, which represent an authoritative reallocation of values and which feed back into the environment as outputs from the political system.

[26] John P. Lovell and Philip S. Kronenberg, eds., *New Civil-Military Relations: The Agonies of Adjustment to Post-Vietnam Realities* (Rutgers, N.J.: Transaction Books, 1974), Chap. 1.

I do not wish to make exaggerated claims for the novelty of the conceptualization of national security politics suggested here. Most of the ideas will be familiar to readers conversant with political analysis in general as it has developed in the past two decades. Moreover, the normative and empirical issues that have been identified in the past several pages are for the most part similar if not identical to ones that classically were of concern to persons involved in the study or the practice of American "civil-military relations."

The agonizing choices that often have to be made between the demands of national security and the demands of democratic values, for instance, are familiar themes in traditional writings. For example, James Madison, writing anonymously in *The Federalist* No. 41, observed:

> . . . that the liberties of Rome proved the final victim to her military triumphs, and that the liberties of Europe, as far as they ever existed, have with few exceptions been the price of her military establishments. A standing force therefore is a dangerous, at the same time that it may be a necessary provision. On the smallest scale it has its inconveniences. On an extensive scale, its consequences may be fatal. On any scale, it is an object of laudable circumspection and precaution.[27]

Although most of the issues of concern to the present author are similar to issues that were of concern to the founding fathers of the United States and have comprised the traditional concern of students of civil-military relations, the alternative framework suggested here differs from most earlier approaches in the way the issues are conceptualized and *therefore in the courses of action that are identified as being feasible or desirable means of resolving the issues.* If the problem is depicted as one that necessarily pits the armed forces against the civilian sector of society, then solutions to the problem are likely to be defined exclusively in terms of constitutional checks upon the military (in the formal-legalistic approach) or in terms of taking steps to maximize the professionalism of the military (as advocated by modern analysts such as Huntington). In contrast, the alternative framework suggested here begins not with an image of structures in conflict (military versus civilian), but rather with an assessment of issue areas in which national security values are at stake (competing with other values), reserving to empirical inquiry the question of which individuals, groups, and institutions support which value preferences. Because parties to political conflict are not identified on an *a priori* basis, simple formulas for resolving conflict cannot be prescribed in advance. Rather, the solution that is appropriate will depend upon the distinctive distribution of values and power and upon a combination of other factors peculiar to each situation.

[27] Alexander Hamilton, James Madison, and John Jay, *The Federalist,* ed. Benjamin F. Wright (Cambridge, Mass.: Belknap Press of Harvard University Press, 1961).

What I have presented thus far is not really a theory, of course. Rather, the discussion simply represents an effort to reconceptualize familiar, but important, analytical and policy issues. However, adequate conceptualization is a prerequisite to sound theorizing and to sound policy-making. In earlier sections of the paper I have identified what seem to me to be severe limitations of both traditional and most modern approaches to the analysis of civil-military relations (or, as I would prefer to say, to the analysis of national security politics). In this vital area of concern, we can ill afford to retain a conceptual apparatus that leads us to pose the wrong questions and to employ unreliable solutions.

2

The Constitutional Framework of Civil-Military Relations

ELMER J. MAHONEY

Today, with the American military establishment under unprecedented domestic critical assault and all those who exercise military power driven to the defensive, it is instructive to explore the role of the armed forces within the constitutional system. With rumblings echoing from all strata of society, it is clear that we have a national divisiveness centered, in large part, on our long involvement in war and in preparations for war. Beyond doubt, among the alleviations necessary for our nation's return to unity and good health is the need to seriously reconsider the whole problem of the role of the military in our democratic scheme of government.

To begin at the beginning is to place in proper historical perspective the issues that have given rise to our present discontent. To reexamine our past is to hope that out of our national experience we can fashion a fulcrum on which the military and civilian components of government can be balanced effectively in the future.

In the beginning it was commonplace to accept war as a reality of national life. At the time of the drafting of the Constitution, the memory of colonial wars and bloody revolution was still fresh and the society to be served was still hemmed in by hostile powers. While recognizing the need for avoiding war at this critical stage of our national existence, the Framers had the good sense to acknowledge that the best way to guarantee peace was to be prepared for war.

The need of the new nation to have a strong military arm constitutionally mandated was not to be denied. But also embedded in the consciousness of the Framers were the struggles in England and the American colonies to overcome and contain the exercise of arbitrary military power. England's experience pointed up the dangers of embodying the powers both to declare and to wage war in one office, and history sanguinely orchestrated that British monarchs who held such powers had plunged the American colonies into calamitous conflicts.

To avoid this risk the Framers assigned the power of decision over war and peace to the Congress, except in situations of extreme emergency, leaving the President, as Commander-in-Chief, to conduct military operations. In the constitutional scheme, intent and design are manifest. The awesome power of changing society from a condition of peace to a state of war was given to the Legislature; the supplementary power of commanding the armed forces and using the implements of war was assigned to the Executive. Emergency situations, in which the Chief Executive was authorized to respond militarily without legislative consent, were recognized and provided for in the fundamental charter.

The dichotomy of the country's need for military strength coupled with fear that the power given and the instruments created could be inherently destructive if arbitrarily used was to be solved by adherence to the principle that the military arm of government must be subordinate to the civilian arm and by various aspects of the checks and balances system.

In deference to the country's need for military strength, no fewer than a third of the express powers given the federal government had to do with the armed forces.[1] Congress was given the power to declare war; grant letters of marque and reprisal; make rules concerning captures on land and water; raise and support armies; provide and maintain a navy; make rules governing the land and naval forces; provide in part for the militia and call it forth under stated conditions; and build forts, magazines, arsenals, and dockyards.

To emphasize the national government's general responsibility for national defense, the Constitution provides that the states are forbidden, without congressional consent, to "keep troops, or ships of war in time of peace," or to "engage in war, unless actually invaded, or in such imminent danger as will not admit of delay." [2] The war power that has developed from these grants of constitutional authority staggers the imagination by its scope and variety.

The Founding Fathers' distrust of the armed forces is manifested clearly in various provisions of the Constitution that sought to establish civilian supremacy over the military, a principle deeply rooted in the nation's traditions. The President, the nation's highest elected civilan officer, was made Commander-in-Chief of the army and the navy and of the militia of the several states when called into the actual service of the United States.[3] Only Congress, the elected representatives of the people, could declare war and raise and support armies and maintain a navy.[4] Further strictures were imposed by the provision that no appropriation of money

[1] Art. I, Sec. 8.
[2] Art. I, Sec. 10, Cl. 3.
[3] Art. II, Sec. 2.
[4] Art. I, Sec. 8.

for military purposes "shall be for a longer term than two years." [5] Control of the militia, a citizen-type military body, was divided between the national and state governments.

Not only were specific restraints on the military written into the document to keep the military subservient to civilian authority, but the grand design of separation of powers and checks and balances, which characterizes the whole Constitution, was employed to contain the exercise of military power. Controls over the armed forces were divided among President, Congress, and the states so that no one instrument of government could gain sole domination of the military. This maneuver was consistent with the Founding Fathers' basic philosophy of dividing authority as a deterrent to the establishment of despotic government.

WAS THE CONSTITUTIONAL DESIGN WELL-CONCEIVED?

Was the Framers' scheme the best possible and most enduring way of restraining arbitrary military power? How has the system of countervailing authority worked out in practice? At least one scholar, whose views on the military are highly respected, answers these questions in the negative, arguing that such division of constitutional authority has produced paradoxical results.

> The very aspects of the Constitution which the framers and later commentators have cited as establishing civilian control are in fact those which hinder its realization: civilian control would be more easily achieved in the twentieth century if the framers had been less eager to achieve it in the eighteenth century. Objective civilian control is maximized if the military are limited in scope to professional matters and relegated to a subordinate position in a pyramid of authority culminating in a single civilian head. The military clauses of the Constitution, however, provide for almost exactly the opposite. They divide civilian responsibility for military affairs and thereby foster the direct access of the professional military authorities to the highest levels of government.[6]

That civilian control of the military breaks down at times is manifest. But is it because the design is faulty or because the civilian officials fail to exercise the constitutional power given them? One can safely depart from this dialogue by noting the overriding democratic purpose common to all plans. No matter what the design, its success is going to depend on how

[5] *Ibid.*

[6] Samuel P. Huntington, "Civilian Control and the Constitution," *American Political Science Review,* Vol. 50 (September, 1956), p. 682.

strongly the electorate demands adherence to time-honored democratic principles, how faithfully civilian officials exercise their constitutional powers, and how humbly the military accept their subservient role. Uninformed and lethargic public opinion, civilian timidity and vagueness, and crass military careerism and professional parochialism are detriments to a workable system of civilian control. When these factors are multifariously present in society, civil supremacy has no chance of working out according to design.

Nor is there much hope that civilian control of the military will be anything but a continuing problem in a society in which civilian officials find it difficult, if not impossible, to dismiss a general. The Lavelle episode in Vietnam is a case in point, one of many that could be cited. General John D. Lavelle allegedly violated the rules of engagement laid down by his civilian superiors, by conducting unauthorized air warfare over North Vietnam. Who brought him up short for his violations? Not his civilian or military superiors, but an Air Force sergeant whose conscience would not permit him to falsify reports on bombing raids to make the forays look legal.

The Senate Armed Services Committee, after hearings, administered a mild rebuke to General Lavelle, but found his superiors, both military and civilian, blameless. The Secretary of Defense, at the time of the hearings, said he was satisfied with the existing system of command and control but later installed a system of inspection to insure that civilian directives would be carried out. The lesson seems obvious: where political timidity and confusion prevail, military power is bound to go unchecked.

As early as July 1970, the Fitzhugh Commission Report informed the President that there were serious defects in the military command and control system. The Commission said the system "inhibits the flow of information to and from the combatant commands and the President and the Secretary of Defense even in crisis situations."

Admittedly, many civilian officers exercise their powers hazed over by a mist that makes it difficult to know what is going on in the field, although it is the essence of their authority to know. If the command and control system is defective, then it is their immediate job, certainly in time of war, to design one that works. Difficult? Yes, but not impossible. It would be an act of democratic statesmanship for modern surrogates of the Commander-in-Chief to give back as rain what they have received as mist.

Lavelle's military superiors testified under oath that they did not know of his twenty-eight unauthorized sorties in North Vietnam. But why did they not know? By the canons and traditions of the armed services all senior commanders in the chain of command are responsible for the combat actions of their subordinate commanders. There are no valid grounds for senior commanders being ignorant of what is going on in the commands under their control.[7] Concerned citizens can only feel uncomfortable that they did not know and outraged that a supine Congress accepted their ignorance. In the same vein it would be difficult to file a brief on behalf of the Commander-in-Chief's civilian aides, whose constitutional duty it was to uphold the principle of civilian supremacy. In the face of such irresponsibility at the top, it is small wonder that a lowly 23-year-old sergeant with a conscience had to report the dereliction to his congressman.

If the constitutional design for civilian control is valid in conception but is not working in practice, what can be done about it? The answer is to be found in an aroused and informed electorate and stronger, more tough-minded civilians in both political branches, who have a deep-seated understanding and appreciation of the principle of civilian supremacy. There is not that much wrong with the present system that faithful adherence to the letter and spirit of civil supremacy will not correct. The power to control is there, but the civilians have failed to use it and the electorate has not held them accountable for their omissions. Under our constitutional system, for the good of all of us, it is imperative that the civilians control the military because it is increasingly apparent that there is no mechanism by which the military control themselves.

MILITARISM VERSUS DEMOCRACY

One needs no more awareness than a rough idea of the military-industrial complex, about which President Eisenhower warned in his Farewell Address, and the size of the annual military budget to conclude that, despite the constitutional restraints, the military have achieved awesome power in our society. D. W. Brogan, a twentieth-century Alexis de Tocqueville, a Scot who knows this country better than most natives, acutely discerned in 1957 that the ". . . transformation of an America nominally at peace into one of the world's two great military powers is perhaps the single greatest and most ambiguous change in America. Over the past thirty years, the armed forces have gradually become one of the most important of American social institutions." [8]

[7] In the aftermath of World War II, a U.S. military commission held Japan's General Yamashita responsible for the atrocities committed by his subordinates in the Philippines as the war was winding down. Even though the General testified that at the time he took command he did not know and had no way of knowing (with all communications disrupted) what was going on in the territory, he nevertheless was held responsible for his subordinate commanders' actions and sentenced to death. The Supreme Court upheld the decision of the military commission. See *In Re Yamashita,* 327 U.S. 1 (1946).

[8] D. W. Brogan, "Unnoticed Changes in America," *Harper's Magazine* (February, 1957), pp. 29–30.

The expanded role of the military is a necessary concomitant of our national involvement in almost constant war and preparedness for war. There is only a blurred line, hardly distinguishable, between military and civilian affairs today. Even when the line can be seen, it is hardly significant. This is true because we have allowed our military leaders to become much more than planners of military strategy and tactics and commanders of combat units in the field. Beyond soldiering, we have allowed them to assume roles that require the qualities of the statesman, diplomat, business executive and lobbyist. Among other things, our military leaders now

> . . . are required to understand, to communicate with, and to evaluate the judgment of political leaders, officials of other executive agencies, and countless specialists; they must make sound judgments themselves on matters which affect a wide variety of civilian concerns. They are called upon to evaluate the motivations and capabilities of foreign nations and to estimate the effects of American action or inaction upon these nations. And above all, the new role of military leaders requires of them a heightened awareness of the principles of our democratic society.[9]

Democracy is threatened by assigning military leaders nontraditional roles to play. The danger lies in the impossibility of their playing these roles under constitutional rules as we once knew them. Their assignments sometimes put them in positions where the rules are blurred and shifting. Within this context, we give them a nearsighted professional goal—national security—with ill-defined powers to achieve it. We permit them to perform functions that are, in some cases, constitutionally conflicting. Herein, perhaps, lies the greatest danger. Even men of good will could get lost in the maze and lose sight of the fundamental values of the democratic society they are supposed to protect.

In a pervading military atmosphere, there is less toleration of unorthodox views, dissenting opinion, and open debate. Astigmatic concentration on security enhances fear of disloyalty. The open society tends to become less open and individual freedoms become more restricted, as demand for swift action replaces concern for sober deliberation.

When the specter of war hangs over a society, its members want their fears dispelled in a hurry. When fear is rampant and security is at stake, there is a natural tendency to surrender the power of decision to the military. The armed forces are geared to act immediately; civil government can only act after ponderous deliberation and time-consuming compromise. When emotion replaces logic it is very easy for the electorate to look to the military for leadership and to accept its decisions. Little thought is given

[9] John W. Masland and Laurence I. Radway, *Soldiers and Scholars, Military Education and National Policy* (Princeton, N.J.: Princeton University Press, 1957), p. vii.

to the fact that the price for doing so might be forfeiture of some of its democratic freedoms.

Playing multifaceted roles not only adds to the power and prestige of our military leaders but also widens the horizon of their ambitions. No longer does the ambitious officer contemplate a 20-year professional career followed by early retirement in California or Florida. There are board rooms of great business corporations to be populated, civil offices within the federal bureaucracy to be filled, always on an indispensable-need basis, embassies to be lived in, and cabinet posts to be assumed as progressive steps in a two-stage career. For a few, there is the White House itself, a goal that our history tells us is not beyond the reach of military dreamers.

The last military man to occupy the White House gave us much to think about on leaving it. In his Farewell Address, Dwight Eisenhower pointed out that we are now committed to a vast armament industry and a huge defense establishment, spending ever-increasing billions of dollars annually. He emphasized how all-pervading the influence of this monolithic military-industrial complex was bound to be and its potential for misplaced power. He then warned:

> We must never let the weight of this combination endanger our liberties or democratic processes. We should take nothing for granted. Only an alert and knowledgeable citizenry can compel the proper meshing of the huge industrial and military machinery of defense with our peaceful methods and goals, so that security and liberty may prosper together.[10]

The threat of militarization comes not only from the military but also from civilians who wear the mantle of civil office and seek unfettered power.[11] War and defense are omnibuses of power that encourage not only generals and admirals to hop on for the ride but also bureaucrats, industrialists, labor leaders, scientists, and many others.

Historically, our fortunes have been good. Unlike some other so-called democracies, we have never had a military caste in our society, and for the most part our military personnel have been respectful of constitutional restraints. But the point to remember is that keeping the military within constitutional bounds is harder than ever, because there is no longer a clear demarcation between official military and civilian conduct. When militarism threatens to take over, the whole process of democratic government hangs precariously in the balance. What we must prevent is military usurpation taking place even once. The saving grace is the hope that, while developing the varied skills and mustering the resources for the country's defense, the military will, at the same time, heighten their awareness of the need

[10] *The New York Times* (January 18, 1961), p. 22.

[11] John McCloy, *Hoover Commission's Task Force Report on National Security Organization*, p. 59.

to be good citizens, dedicated to time-honored constitutional principles. "For it is by 'civilizing' the military that much can be done to prevent militarizing the civilians." [12]

The Founding Fathers saw the inherent dangers of ill-defined military power and took elaborate constitutional steps to restrain it. No less for them as for us, short-term security is hardly worth it, if in the long run the ultimate price paid is a lessening of individual freedoms and a weakening of the constitutional fabric.

THE PREROGATIVE THEORY OF PRESIDENTIAL POWER

When the Constitution was presented for ratification, Alexander Hamilton defended the propriety of making the President the Commander-in-Chief of the armed forces by predicting that his constitutional assignment would amount "to nothing more than the supreme command and direction of the military and naval forces, as first general and admiral of the Confederacy." [13] Hamilton, prescient in most matters, could not foresee the tremendous reserve of power inherent in the President's various roles.

Actually Hamilton's forecast was accurate enough up to the Civil War period, at which time Abraham Lincoln gave new dimensions to the presidential office. In his resolve to keep the Union from disintegrating, Lincoln "linked together the presidential power to take care that the laws be faithfully executed with that of Commander-in-Chief to yield a result approaching constitutional dictatorship." [14] Under this brace of assumed power, among other things, Lincoln, without statutory authorization, suspended the writ of habeas corpus, blockaded the Southern ports, called 40,000 volunteers into the armed forces, and paid out two million dollars from unappropriated funds in the Treasury.

That civilian personal and property rights were dealt with arbitrarily by the President is unassailable. The Civil War was one of the great turning points in American constitutional development and Lincoln's precedents made the case for future wartime Presidents to use an initiative of indefinite scope in meeting the knotty problems that a great war produces. The Framers of the Constitution could not have foreseen this development, which has posed new and complex problems for the preservation of the separation of powers principle and individual liberties.

[12] James MacGregor Burns and Jack Walter Peltason, *Government by the People*, 5th edition (Englewood Cliffs, N.J.: Prentice-Hall, Inc., 1963), p. 607.

[13] Alexander Hamilton, *The Federalist No.* 69, Modern Library Edition (New York, N.Y.: Random House, 1937), p. 448.

[14] C. Herman Pritchett, *The American Constitution*, 2nd ed. (New York, N.Y.: McGraw-Hill Book Company, 1968), p. 372.

World War II was a "total" war, with uncertain outcome and the danger of external attack and internal treachery very real. The President and his military leaders faced unprecedented situations and, like Lincoln and his generals, met them by resorting to unprecedented extensions of military authority. The spectacular case of the Nazi saboteurs landing on our shores and the enforced evacuation of Japanese-Americans from the West Coast are cases in point.

That "total" war means essentially presidential government was supremely exemplified by President Franklin D. Roosevelt's message to Congress in 1942. When Congress refused to repeal a provision in the price control act that protected farmers, the President demanded that the lawmakers act within a month or he would. The President proved himself a good poker player; Congress meekly repealed the provision. According to one noted authority, Roosevelt's demand on Congress amounted to "a claim of power on the part of the President to suspend the Constitution in a situation deemed by him to make such a step necessary." [15]

The doctrine of the presidential actions taken by Lincoln and threatened by Roosevelt—sometimes called the prerogative theory—was that when emergencies arise the President had the same power that John Locke once argued that kings had, the power "to act according to discretion for the public good, without the prescription of the law and sometimes even against it." [16]

These two wartime Presidents took actions that went beyond their express or reasonably implied constitutional authority. Indeed, on occasions, they took action that violated the Constitution outright, always with the assertion that they were acting for the public good.

How do we equate such actions with the belief that ours is a government of laws and not of men? The simple answer is that the two cannot be reconciled. The power of the President to be a Draconian lawgiver in time of emergency is incompatible with the rule of law. This incompatibility derives from the nature of each. According to one analyst: "Only recurring and predictable situations can be brought within the rule of law. Great emergencies are not recurring, nor are they predictable; if they were they would not be emergencies." [17]

As Locke indicated, many problems arise for which there is no relief within the recognized law; therefore power must be found to act for the public good. He thought it proper that this emergency power should reside

[15] Edward S. Corwin, *Total War and the Constitution* (New York, N.Y.: Knopf, 1947), p. 64.

[16] Edward S. Corwin, *The Constitution and What It Means Today,* 10th ed. (Princeton, N.J.: Princeton University Press, 1948), pp. 84–85.

[17] Rowland Egger, *The President of the United States* (New York, N.Y.: McGraw-Hill Book Company, 1967), pp. 19–20.

within the Executive Office and should be exercised, on occasion, in defiance of the existing law.[18]

That President Lincoln was beholden to Locke can be seen during the Civil War emergency. After Chief Justice Taney, riding the circuit in Baltimore, held that Lincoln's suspension of the writ of habeas corpus for civilians suspected of disloyal action was unconstitutional, the President defied the ruling and defended his action in Lockian terms in a message to Congress.

While the use of emergency power and the rule of law cannot be reconciled, the clash between the two has the effect of limiting the use of executive emergency power. When the presidential prerogative is used, the rule of law "puts the burden of proof in its invocation on the President who attempts to exercise it."[19] The Executive's decision-making leverage is always relative to the credibility of the emergency in the minds of the electorate and other branches of government with the constitutional power to check his actions. A President would be inviting disastrous consequences, if he attempted to flout the rule of law, when no real and apparent emergency existed. President Truman found this out when he took over the steel mills during the Korean War. The Supreme Court held he had no inherent emergency powers within his office to seize private property, but could do so only when authorized by Congress.[20]

It is to be recognized that the rule of law is not to be set aside by every claimed emergency. Emergency power will not be sanctified as higher law by applying it unrelentingly to conditions in which its mandates cannot logically be expected to triumph. It was the logicality of his multifarious "illegal" actions that made Lincoln's conduct generally acceptable at the bar of public opinion and brought him history's favorable verdict.

A President must always work within the parameters established by the confrontation between emergency power and the rule of law. He must perceive that when he uses the prerogative he operates outside the law as most men know it. His action bears the stamp of illegality unless and until the various bars of judgment—legislature, courts, public opinion, history—retroactively sanction his conduct. In the temple of his mind, he must solve the dilemma of conflicting moral duties: to uphold the law as it now exists or to seek a higher order of law for the good of the country. As one observer has noted:

> . . . The moral duty of the President to keep within the law ends at the point where the legal order itself hangs in the balance. Lincoln understood

[18] John Locke, *The Second Treatise of Government,* J. W. Gough (ed.) (New York, N.Y.: The Macmillan Company, 1956), pp. 81–82.

[19] Egger, *op. cit.,* p. 23.

[20] *Youngstown Sheet and Tube Company* v. *Sawyer,* 343 U.S. 579 (1952).

this when, in his message of July 4, 1861, he accepted the moral obligation to preserve the Union even if he had to break the law to do it. In the final analysis, this is the only ground upon which Lincoln's conduct in his great emergency, or the conduct of any President in any great emergency, can be brought within the bounds of political viability.[21]

THE POWER TO DECLARE WAR

The Constitution gives Congress the sole power to declare war, but, as was argued before the Supreme Court in 1863, "war is a state of things and not an act of the legislative will." [22] Theoretically, this is an awesome power; practically, it has been more ministerial than discretionary. Congress' declarative power may be, and frequently has been, rendered meaningless by circumstances that allow no choice. The President, through his powers as Commander-in-Chief, chief formulator of foreign policy, and Chief Executive can shape events to eliminate the choice.

Our history reveals that several times we have been factually at war without an express declaration. The undeclared war with France from 1798 to 1800 and our recent involvement in Vietnam show the range of such wars, and there have been several like instances in between. Generally, *ex post facto,* Congress has been only too willing to acknowledge by joint resolution that war has been thrust upon us, as in the declaration that followed the Japanese surprise attack on Pearl Harbor. In such matters, Congress has expressly or implicitly approved the waging of a war for which the only prior constitutional justification was the President's power as Commander-in-Chief.

The extent of the President's power to wage war without a congressional declaration remains a much-argued issue, as is evidenced by the aberrations growing out of our involvement in Vietnam. It is a rarity for Congress to declare war in advance of hostilities. The usual thing is for the President to ask Congress to recognize that a state of war exists. In the Korean War in 1950, presidential discretion alone, exercised in answer to a United Nations Security Council's request for aid, took the United States into a large scale *de facto* war. In the Vietnam War, the Tonkin Gulf Resolution was regarded by President Johnson as tantamount to a declaration of war by Congress.

Congress may, of course, authorize presidential action by a declaration of war, but clearly its authorization may take other forms. The Gulf of Tonkin Resolution is akin to the congressional delegation of power given to President John Adams to stop French vessels on the high seas, to Presi-

[21] Egger, *op. cit.,* p. 23.

[22] This was the view of Richard Henry Dana in his argument before the Supreme Court in *The Prize Cases,* 2 Bl. 635 (1863).

dent Eisenhower to use troops in Lebanon and in Formosa, and to President Kennedy to use armed forces in connection with the Cuban missile crisis. In our history, both Congress and the President have made it clear that it is the substance of congressional authorization, and not the form the authorization takes, that determines the extent to which Congress has exercised its portion of the war power.

That Congress, as a coordinate branch of government, has a constitutional role to play is beyond challenge. But how to play it without endangering the security of the country; or, alternatively, how to represent the public will and exercise an effective check on the President, without denying him the supporting authority to do his constitutional duty, are the critical questions. Emergency situations invariably produce concentration of powers in the presidency. Occasionally, the President assumes the role of constitutional dictator to the point where it seems that Congress has abdicated its constitutional rights and responsibilities. Recently, Alexander Bickel, Yale law professor and constitutional law expert, told the Foreign Relations Committee of the Senate that President Johnson's decision to send troops to Vietnam "amounted to an all but explicit transfer of the power to declare war" from Congress to the President.[23]

Admittedly, within the constitutional system power has to shift somewhat to meet emergencies; that it focuses on the President with his multifarious leadership roles and constitutional responsibilities is not surprising. But, in recent years, there is fear that Congress has all but defaulted on its constitutional prerogative, that its powers have been usurped so completely that it is helpless. Some hold the belief that the President, in the exercise of the total powers of his office, can wage war almost without limit. Buttressing this notion is the record of our post-World War II hostilities in Korea and Vietnam and the invasion of Cambodia and Laos. In the light of our Indochina involvements it would seem fair to conclude that undeclared wars, initiated by the President, have shifted from emergency measures into instruments of foreign policy.

This development strains, indeed violates, the separation-of-powers principle and is in defiance of specific provisions of the Constitution. How it got to be that way in a fast-moving and volatile world, perhaps, is best explained by citing the relative ease and speed of one-man action, keeping all counsel secret, compared with the snail's-pace deliberations and open debate that characterize the legislative procedures.

In the internecine struggle for power the President has a decided advantage over the Congress. As Commander-in-Chief, constitutionally charged with the conduct of military operations, he can create or respond to confrontations that make hostilities inevitable. As formulator and enforcer of foreign policy, many of his decisions and actions can be concealed

[23] *The Washington Post* (July 27, 1971), p. 2.

until it is too late to do anything about them. Thus innovative actions are established *de facto,* and if their constitutionality is unchallenged and undetermined, they serve as precedents to support the legitimacy of conduct later on.

Many of the President's claims to legitimacy as a user of the war powers are constitutionally sound. Beyond doubt are his constitutional powers to repel invasion or resist sudden attack on our territory, without a declaration of war by Congress. Reasonably implied within the fundamental charter are his powers to protect American lives and property interests abroad and to carry out military commitments required by laws or treaties. In today's international situation, where war is a mere missile flight away, the nation has no choice but to recognize that, constitutionally and expeditiously, the President has unlimited power to wage a retaliatory war under the circumstances of a great power attack. It is a matter of survival to recognize that the President has the power to respond to the challenge of total war at any given time. There are no built-in constitutional safeguards against the possibility of the President abusing his power. Here one must rely entirely on his conscience and judgment and his own regard for his place in history.

None of these uses of the President's war powers are seriously challengeable. What has caused the gauntlet to be dropped is the use of war as a bald instrument of foreign policy, without congressional consent, or with a psuedo-consent achieved by false representation and artful wording of the statement of facts that required it. The presidential message to Congress that elicited the Gulf of Tonkin Resolution does not merit high marks for purity of motives and truthfulness of contents. To use war as an instrument of foreign policy and then argue for its constitutional legitimacy strains the credulity of many constitutional scholars. Yet, with a historical record of progressive extensions of presidential authority to back him up, Assistant Secretary of State Nicholas Katzenbach, as a representative of the Administration, told the Foreign Relations Committee of the Senate on August 17, 1967, that declarations of war are "outmoded" in the international arena.

Katzenbach's claim is long on historical support but short on constitutional warrant. If one accepts his thesis, it is easy to embrace the implied corollary that the Chief Executive can initiate hostilities at his own discretion without a declaration of war by Congress. The chief support for Katzenbach's claim is precedent.[24] To many constitutional scholars, view-

[24] A 1966 study listed 162 instances where the President used the armed forces outside the country without congressional approval. Many Americans can recall President Truman sending troops to Korea in 1950; President Kennedy's abortive Bay of Pigs invasion of Cuba; and President Lyndon Johnson's order to the armed forces to occupy part of the Dominican Republic in 1965.

ing the constant swelling of presidential war powers during the last three decades, this is just another way of saying that the habitual exercise of unconstitutional power makes it constitutional.

Leaving the threat of big-power missile warfare aside and focusing on the "limited" wars now in vogue, there is much to be gained by Congress asserting its prerogative to declare war, chief of which would be informative dialogue on the worthiness of the particular war at hand. That Congress, either instantly or by ultimate effect, can halt any war to which it does not subscribe, by withholding the funds necessary to support it, is generally acknowledged. Conjointly, it is admitted that this is solution by sledgehammer and that the consequences make it too drastic for practical employment.

While the institutional characteristics of Congress do not give it free rein in dealing with requirements of national policy that call for speed and secrecy in times of crisis, there is much it can do to reassert its constitutional authority in the "limited" war sphere. Typical is a bill introduced by Senator Javits to make "rules respecting military operations in the absence of a declaration of war." While recognizing and affirming the power of the President to initiate hostilities without a declaration of war under the circumstances directly and inferentially sanctioned by the Constitution, the bill seeks to restore Congress' role as a policy-maker in the undeclared-war sphere. The bill would require the President to report promptly to Congress all unauthorized hostilities and prohibit their continuance beyond 60 days from their initiation, except as may be provided by Congress. To avoid undue delay in its consideration, Congress, under the bill, is compelled to take prompt committee action and to reach a final vote of both Houses within 30 days. The Javits bill became law in 1973.

The Javits proposal would seem to satisfy the demands both of the constitutional purists, concerned with maintaining checks and balances as a part of the constitutional design and of those who worry about the risks of unduly restricting a President in his foreign policy implementations. It cites and acknowledges the President's unfettered use of emergency powers. What it implicitly denies is that war as an instrument of foreign policy can be included, as some claim, within the President's authorized emergency powers. At base what it seeks to do is restore Congress to its rightful place in matters of war and peace, by regulating deviations from well-established constitutional rules.

Realistically, there are few significant issues involving war that can be resolved by solitary presidential action. The President needs the wholehearted support of Congress and the confidence of the American people. The essence of presidential power is one of leadership, the ability to enlist public support for national policy. Consensus engendered by deceptive secrecy and seductive action are slender reeds to lean on. Such support risks loss of faith and credibility and invites divisiveness. Congress' role in matters of war and peace must be much more than a mere sounding-board and a pseudo-automatic supplier of funds for presidential policy. A vigorous Congress, providing meaningful dialogue on all aspects of national policy and checking the use of war powers when the consensus indicates such need, can do much to maintain the constitutional system according to the grand design of the Framers, heal the country's divisiveness, and restore faith in national leadership.

THE PRESIDENT AS COMMANDER-IN-CHIEF

In addition to the Commander-in-Chief aspects of his job noted earlier, the President as head of the armed forces has a multiplicity of other powers to exercise and roles to play. Although a civilian, he is constitutionally the Number One member of the armed forces,[25] and as such he is the legal, administrative and ceremonial head of all the military services. His powers of appointment and dismissal of high-ranking general officers and admirals, his authority, if he wishes to exercise it, over defense strategy and emplacement of military forces, and his policies of internal management of the military services put him in position to shape and control the nation's ultimate coercive machinery. It is at his disposal to enforce the national laws and treaties, to protect the states against domestic violence and invasion, and to defend the country against its external enemies.

As he must have able professional advisers and subordinates to help him carry out his duties, one of the most vitally important functions of the President as Commander-in-Chief is his power of appointment and dismissal. He appoints, with the consent of the Senate, all officers of the armed forces, though Congress determines the grades to which appointments may be made and may specify the qualifications of the appointees. This means that within his power of selection rests the responsibility for determining which of our professional military leaders will boss our military forces and plan the over-all strategy for the defense of the country. The President has an unlimited power to dismiss the "top brass" in time of war, as when President Truman relieved General MacArthur of his Far Eastern command in 1952, "but in time of peace Congress has provided that dismissal shall be only in pursuance of the sentence of a general court martial." [26]

[25] President Lincoln's civilian assassins were tried by a military tribunal for the military crime of killing the Commander-in-Chief while in actual command of the armed forces of the nation. The military tribunal's jurisdiction over the civilians was never challenged before a civil court.

[26] Pritchett, *op. cit.*, p. 378.

While Congress has the constitutional power "to make rules for the government and regulation of the land and naval forces," the President, in subordination to the congressional power, has broad internal management powers that permit him to act effectively. He may set up rules and regulations as administrative directives that significantly affect the way of life in the armed forces. Presidents Truman and Eisenhower used their authority as Commander-in-Chief to issue directives against racial discrimination within the armed services. These important first steps toward eliminating segregation in the Army, Navy, and Air Force were taken before the Supreme Court handed down its monumental segregation decision in *Brown* v. *Board of Education*.[27]

The President has charge also of defense plans and disposition of military, air, and naval forces. Usually he delegates the power of decision over such matters to his civilian and professional subordinates, but he may involve himself in military movements, strategy, and operations should he deem it desirable. President Washington took personal command of the troops in the field to suppress the Whiskey Rebellion in 1792. No other President has assumed field command, but there are many examples of personal involvement by the Commander-in-Chief in strategic decisions. "One need think only of President Lincoln's telegraphic orders and personal visits to his generals in the field, or President Roosevelt in the chart room of the White House mapping the grand strategy of World War II, or President Johnson personally approving the targets to be bombed in North Vietnam, to appreciate the tremendous potential of the President's role." [28]

Not only does the President use the war machine to defend the country from its external enemies, he may use it also internally to enforce the public law of the United States (national laws and treaties) and to protect the states against invasion, insurrection, and domestic violence. Early Supreme Court decisions underscored the fact that the President is not accountable in the courts for his emergency use of the armed forces within the country.[29] The Supreme Court has said the decision as to whether there is a need for the use of force to thwart a threatened invasion, or to suppress domestic violence, or to see that the laws be faithfully executed belongs exclusively to the President.[30] It is a "political" question which the courts will not undertake to decide.

When the President uses the armed forces outside the country, neither the courts nor the Congress is likely to stand in his way. A modern example of such use would be President Johnson's unhindered sending of military

[27] 347 U.S. 483 (1954), 349 U.S. 294 (1955).

[28] Pritchett, *op. cit.*, p. 378.

[29] *Martin* v. *Mott*, 12 Wheaton 19 (1827), and *Luther* v. *Borden*, 7 Howard 1 (1849).

[30] *The Prize Cases, op. cit.*

forces to the Dominican Republic in 1965. The courts, to preserve the separation-of-powers principle of our constitutional system, readily acknowledge that judicial restraint is necessary and they have no power to examine the presidential decision. Congress, mainly through its control of the purse-strings, could check the President's action and, on occasion, has threatened to do so. Usually, Congress is long on threats and short on restrictive action. When the debate has ended and the votes are counted, they reveal that the lawmakers are reluctant to cramp the President's discretion in the external employment of the armed forces.

To note the Supreme Court's restraint in certain aspects of military power is not to say that the judiciary has retired from the arena where military authority is concerned. Not all of the questions raised are political in nature. War and its aftermath produce many clashes between military authority and civilian rights. Most of these conflicts raise justiciable questions to which the courts supply ready answers. The underlying premise of the questions: What the allowable limits of military discretion are and whether they have been overstepped in a particular case are judicial questions of the greatest import.[31] Prudent answers to these issues, occasionally, decide the meaning of freedom in an open society.

Although it is important to emphasize the role the Supreme Court plays, at the same time it is to be noted that its role is a limited one. As one close observer has pointed out, the Court has had before it

> only a tiny fraction of the President's significant deeds and decisions as commander in chief, for most of these were by nature challengeable in no court but that of impeachment—which is entirely as it should have been. The contours of presidential war powers have therefore been presidentially, not judicially, shaped; their exercise is for Congress and the people, not the Court, to oversee.[32]

The futility of the judiciary as a restraining force was admitted by Mr. Justice Robert H. Jackson who noted that the Supreme Court had no power equal to the use of the war power in the hands of nefarious men. "The chief restraint upon those who command the physical forces of the country, in the future as in the past, must be their responsibility to the political judgments of their contemporaries and to the moral judgments of history." [33]

[31] *Sterling* v. *Constantin,* 287 U.S. 378 (1932).

[32] Clinton Rossiter, *The Supreme Court and the Commander in Chief* (Ithaca, N.Y.: Cornell University Press, 1951), p. 126.

[33] Dissenting opinion of Mr. Justice Robert H. Jackson, *Korematsu* v. *United States,* 323 U.S. 214, 248.

CONCLUSION

The principle of civil supremacy is not based on sentiment, accident, or the intuitive genius of the Founding Fathers. It simply reflects history's bitter lesson that civilian control of the military is essential to the maintenance of a democratic society. Distrust of military power is but one aspect of the general suspicion that the Framers had about the totality of governmental power in a free society. It grew out of an awareness that all power tends to be self-aggrandizing. To head off tyranny, they took the precaution of checking power with power, by designing a system that diffuses control and responsibility among several organs of government. Among the various arrangements of the Constitution are those designed to keep military power subordinate to civil authority.

For most of our history it was traditional in peacetime to avoid large standing armies, all but disband the navy, and treat military problems with disinterest. Today, given the realities of the contemporary world, large and permanent military establishments with all the up-to-date, sophisticated weapons systems spawned by modern science and technology are necessities. The world leadership position of the United States has so expanded the scope of military affairs that there is no longer a clear-cut cleavage between military and civilian spheres of activity. Not only the military class, but virtually all segments of society—bureaucracy, labor, business, science, the press—are in a position to affect the national security.

As military aspects of problems are brought to the fore, generals and admirals are asked, or allowed, to play non-traditional roles. They are invited, or permitted, to pass judgment on issues that in the past have not been thought to be within their jurisdiction. At the same time, their civilian superiors find it more difficult to secure the information they need to exercise control of military affairs. In many cases it is the military who decide what information must remain top secret and what rules of engagement to follow in a war. Congressmen, civilian superiors in the Defense Department, and the general public are at a disadvantage in exercising civilian control. Military usurpation of civilian authority tends to thwart self-government by depriving those in authority of the challenges that promote efficiency, the dialogue that produces refined judgment, and the awareness that allows the correction of official error.

One of the direst threats to a free society is surveillance of political dissent by the military. In the era of war protests and student unrest that characterized the decade of the 1960s, the military, in the interest of national security, breached the stronghold of personal privacy—a barrier the late Clinton Rossiter thought should be "an unbreakable wall of dignity . . . against the entire world." The Pentagon admitted, under pressure, that it had dossiers on 25 million American "personalities." [34] These included persons loosely described as "considered to constitute a threat to security and defense," as well as Congressmen, political leaders, journalists, and other citizens who attended antiwar rallies.[35]

As our laws provide for military aid to civil authority, it must be conceded that military involvement in certain types of information-gathering is a valid exercise. Any agency of government that has a police function must have information about people and forces that threaten public order and national security. Indeed, certain intelligence is essential to the performance of its assigned duties. What is of concern are excesses charged to the military and their means of carrying out their task. Of equal concern is the unanswered question: Why did not the civilan superiors in the Defense Department do something about the excesses when they were building up? Left to his own estimates, more than likely, no general in combat ever has enough reserves and no chief of military intelligence ever has enough information. In the latter case, it is possible that astigmatic concentration on professional purposes overshadowed the need to avoid violations of personal liberties. If the important goal was to get the information, the means of doing so, under the pressure of threats to public order, could easily seem unimportant.

After public exposure of the extent of military zeal, the Secretary of Defense shifted the Defense Intelligence Agency from the control of the Joint Chiefs of Staff to his own office. If the public is comforted by this action, it is still concerned with the delay in exercising civilian control and other questions. It is tempting to infer that this information-gathering reflects a purpose to establish improper military influence over civil society. But when this notion is balanced against the thought that most military involvement in civil affairs is undertaken on the direct order of the President and his civilian Cabinet officers, a different conclusion is possible. If blame must be assigned, civilian officials must receive the lion's share, because no matter how it got started, civilians had the authority and responsibility to rein it in or stop it.

Democratic freedoms are in jeopardy when the military, because they either arrogate power to themselves or exercise it at the direction of civilian superiors, act as watchdogs over civilians. The magnitude, scope, and use of their surveillance suggest that the trustees of military power can get shockingly out of touch with their own democratic traditions. Official surveillance of political dissent is always abhorrent, because in an open society it has a chilling effect on the exercise of basic freedoms. Surveillance by the military is the most dispiriting of all, because of the overwhelming resources they command.

[34] *The New York Times* (March 8, 1971).

[35] *Ibid.*

Remembering that professional military men are also citizens, what role should the military play in a democratic society? A strictly professional one, with a willingness to maintain a clear line of demarcation between civilian and military authority and a sincere dedication to the spirit and letter of the civil supremacy principle and other values of our democracy. This in no sense means that the military mind is to be turned off and its voice silenced. The military view has relevance to almost every conceivable national policy. In the mix of opinion that should be solicited before policies are determined, the military input has its place.

When power is entrusted there is always the danger that it will be abused. When assessing the risk of military power, perhaps one may find more to fear from civilians than from their military subordinates. When creeping militarism besets society, more often than not it is the fault of civil officials who have the constitutional power to act but fail to do so. Reflection indicates that Vietnam was in no sense an aberration of the military but a product of civilian policy contoured by three successive Presidents, aided mainly by civilian intellectuals drafted into public service. As our involvement passed from adviser to combatant, the record shows that the strongest objection to a land war in Asia came from the military. The tones of bellicosity that one notes in the Pentagon Papers are mainly attributable to civil officials in the Defense Establishment.

Fear is a product of darkness and ignorance. It feeds on itself and, if prolonged, produces divisions in society. An uninformed electorate dealing with internal and external threats to its security is more than likely to turn to the military for quick solutions, with no regard for the cost in terms of individual freedoms. A strong President, with a high regard for the values of our constitutional system and with bureaucrats and Congressmen sharing his views and following his lead, is the best prescription for dispelling fear and avoiding repressions. The best deterrent to national divisiveness is a President who keeps his electorate reasonably well-informed, consistent with national security. Abating the anxieties of society, without resorting to authoritarian action, is largely a matter of strong national leadership that closes the credibility gap between the government and governed.

No President is going to be in a constitutional bind in a true emergency and no court is going to deny him the power to deal with it. As Abraham Lincoln and Franklin D. Roosevelt have demonstrated, the President's emergency powers are always equal to society's felt necessities. If his moral judgment is correct, the President will be sustained at the bar of public opinion and the "rule of law" that he flouted will give way to a new one that absorbs his derring-do.

Granting the President his emergency powers, there is still a constitutional role for Congress to play in most matters of war and peace. There is much to be gained by a Congress that asserts its prerogatives and provides adequate checks against the President's unbridled use of war powers.

3

Civil Rights Versus Military Necessity

ELMER J. MAHONEY

When trying to determine the proper role of the military in a free society, one is reminded that democratic government has within it the seeds of its own destruction. Forces necessary to protect it may also be used, unwittingly or otherwise, to destroy it.

Inherent in any free society is the eternal task of maintaining order and national security without destroying liberty. A military establishment is, of course, an indispensable instrument of government, but the range of its power must be contained lest the delicate harmony between liberty and order be disrupted. Achieving this delicate balance is an age-old problem; each generation must enter the lists to maintain it. Preserving the harmony is made more arduous by the fact that the one institution indispensable to the nation's security is, at the same time, the one organ of government that exercises a kind of power not easily absorbed by an open society.

Embedded in our Constitution are the powers of national defense; revered in our heritage are the freedoms guaranteed by the Bill of Rights; ever before us is the question: Is the present exercise of military power compatible with the preservation of our basic liberties? The exercise of war powers to keep us safe and the guarantee of personal freedoms to uphold human dignity are necessities in an open society. Each of the three coordinated branches of our national government has a role to play in determining the dimensions of these powers and rights. The purpose of this exercise is to assess the role the Supreme Court has played and the dimensions it has supplied in balancing military necessity against guaranteed individual rights.

It is consoling to note that in our own hemisphere only Canada and the United States have avoided rule by the military throughout their national existences. Our military leaders, to their credit, never have aspired as a matter of philosophy to change the traditional relationship between the civil government and the military establishment. But without the support of philosophic purpose and ambitious design, there can be both perceptible and imperceptible changes in the civil-military relationship that threaten basic liberties. Invariably, these encroachments are defended in the name of military necessity or national security. One of the misfortunes of war is that military necessity and the guaranteed rights of the individual are not compatible. Our history reveals that in the crucible of war many civil rights are curtailed and such abridgment is frequently supported by public opinion.

Individual rights are not absolutes; they are relative to the rights of others and society as a whole. Their application must be governed by the circumstances under which they are exercised. But it is well to remember that military power is a means to an end and substantive civil rights are ends in themselves. They are essential to our well-being as free men. How to give the military the power it needs to protect the commonwealth without unnecessarily trampling individual rights is one of the eternal balancing tasks of a democratic state.

HABEAS CORPUS

Habeas corpus, every man's guarantee against arbitrary arrest and detention by his government, is one of the basic rights guaranteed to an individual in a free society. It normally pertains to a court order directed to an official of the government who has a prisoner in custody to bring him before the court to determine the reason for his detention. The writ of *habeas corpus* may be used also by prisoners in penal institutions to reopen their cases on the grounds of illegal detention because of constitutional rights denied before or during their trials.

Under our Constitution, however, this right can be denied under certain circumstances. In Article I, section 9, the Constitution provides: "The privilege of *habeas corpus* shall not be suspended, unless when in cases of rebellion or invasion the public safety may require it." Rebellion and invasion, or the threat thereof, are emergency situations in which martial law, "the law of necessity," usually pertains and the privilege of the writ of *habeas corpus* is suspended. In its most absolute form martial law recognizes the necessity for military officers to replace civil officials and to assume control over the civilian population. When *habeas corpus* is suspended, civil or military authorities are permitted to hold persons in jail indefinitely without placing a charge against them or bringing them to trial.

While the Constitution is clear that the privilege of *habeas corpus* may be suspended, it is not clear as to who may suspend it. This became a critical question in our Civil War, when President Lincoln, of his own authority, declared martial law and suspended the writ in several border states.

One civilian who was adversely affected by this action was John Merryman, a Southern agitator residing in Maryland. Because of his activities on behalf of the Confederacy, he was arrested on order of the military commander of the district and imprisoned in a federal fortress.

On May 25, 1861, he petitioned Mr. Chief Justice Roger B. Taney, sitting in the circuit court in Baltimore under statutory authority, for a writ of *habeas corpus*. When the writ was issued the military commander detaining the petitioner refused to honor it, saying that he was authorized by the President to suspend *habeas corpus*. The Chief Justice thereupon issued a contempt citation against the commander and sent a United States marshal to serve it. When the marshal reported that he had been denied admittance to the fortress, Taney contented himself with writing a full account of the case, which he ordered sent to President Lincoln.

In his report, Taney indicated that the President's action in suspending the writ was unconstitutional and concluded that it now remained for the President, in fulfillment of his constitutional duty to see that the laws are faithfully executed, to carry out the judgment of the court.[1]

Lincoln countered with an opinion of his own addressed to Congress in which he upheld the constitutionality of his action and continued to exercise the power that Taney said he did not have. Merryman was soon turned over to the civilian authorities, however, and indicted for treason.

Up to the present, the Supreme Court has never decided who, constitutionally, may suspend the writ of *habeas corpus*. Although Taney was the Chief Justice of the United States at the time the Merryman case was decided, his opinion was rendered as a circuit judge, deciding a case in a lower federal court. He ruled that only Congress had the power to suspend the writ, when the public safety required it, because the clause is located in Article I of the Constitution, a section devoted mainly to legislative powers. He reasoned that if the Framers had intended the President to have the power also, they would have conferred it on him in plain words in Article II, the section devoted principally to executive powers.

Lincoln, in his July 4, 1861, message to Congress, noted the silence of the Constitution on the question of suspension but argued that "the provision was plainly made for a dangerous emergency," and that he could not believe "the framers . . . intended that in every case the danger should run its course until Congress could be called together, the very assembling of which might be prevented . . . by the rebellion." He countered Taney's taunt about the faithful carrying out of the laws by arguing it would be better to violate a single law "to a very limited extent" than to have all laws go unexecuted and "the Government itself go to pieces" through failure to suppress the rebellion. Lincoln denied, however, that he had violated any law, a view supported by his Attorney General, Edward Bates.

The Attorney General's formal opinion stressed the separation-of-powers principle, holding that the executive was not subordinate to the judiciary but was a coordinate department of government. Moreover, he argued, the President was duty-bound to defend the Constitution, a function

[1] *Ex parte Merryman,* 17 Fed. Cas. 144, No. 9487 (1861).

the courts were too weak to perform. Citing the Supreme Court's opinion in *Martin* v. *Mott* (1827)[2] to buttress the concept of the President's discretionary power in discharging his duties, he concluded that the President could suspend the writ of *habeas corpus* on his own authority.

In the final analysis, when the legal arguments are stripped away, both Lincoln and Taney are revealed as seminal men. Each appreciated individual civil rights and each wished to preserve the substance of what was best in society. But how to order the priorities? To Lincoln, holding the nation together was of such transcending importance that he was willing to abate individual rights in order to achieve his goal. To Taney, civil rights and the rule of law were the core of our nation's well-being and, if necessary, dissolution of the Union was not too great a price to pay in order to preserve them.

In the Habeas Corpus Act of 1863, Congress gave *ex post facto* approval of the President's actions by providing that he was authorized to suspend the writ "during the present rebellion," but without pinpointing what part of the Constitution authorized him to do so. In its enactment, Congress tried not only to legitimate indisputably what the President had done but also sought to safeguard personal freedoms by adhering somewhat to accepted civil processes.

The law required that political prisoners held in custody by the military be brought before a federal grand jury and, if they were not indicted, be released on taking an oath of allegiance. In theory, Congress aspired to replace executive warrant with legislative authority and executive discretion with civil judicial process as a basis for the detention of prisoners.

What do we have as constitutional guidance if this problem should arise again? Would we follow the views of Lincoln or of Taney? Semantics and constitutional logic aside, the case is a great watershed in constitutional development for what Lincoln did, not what Taney said he could not do. Any future occupant of the White House will know that in like circumstances, if supported by Congress and a consensus of public opinion, he can do as Lincoln did and no court will stop him. As one close observer of our political system has said: "The law of the Constitution, as it actually exists, must be considered to read that in a condition of martial necessity the President has the power to suspend the privilege of the writ of *habeas corpus*. The most a court or judge can do is read the President a lecture based on *Ex parte Merryman*." [3]

[2] 12 Wheat. 19 (1827). In this case the Supreme Court, in upholding the President's order calling out the militia under statutory authority during the War of 1812, emphasized that the Chief Executive was not judicially accountable for his emergency use of the armed forces. A later Court in *Luther* v. *Borden,* 7 How. 1 (1849) reemphasized the view that no court could question a presidential order calling out the militia.

[3] Clinton Rossiter, *The Supreme Court and the Commander in Chief* (Ithaca, N.Y.: Cornell University Press, 1951), p. 25.

MILITARY TRIALS OF CIVILIANS

When a person's life and liberty are jeopardized by government action it behooves a democratic government to see to it that this jeopardy is fair, reasonable, and according to time-honored tradition. The fundamental importance of this proposition is eloquently underscored by one observer who said: "The quality of a civilization is largely determined by the fairness of its criminal trials." [4] Another noted that "the history of American freedom is, in no small measure, the history of procedure." [5]

It was no accident that most of the provisions of the Bill of Rights are procedural. It simply reflects that among the threats to liberty is that from the government itself. The procedural safeguard in our Constitution "rests upon two underlying assumptions of democracy, the integrity of the individual and government by law rather than men." [6] Procedure is the distinguishing difference between equal rules of the game for all men and rule by whim or caprice. "Steadfast adherence to strict procedural safeguards is our main assurance that there will be equal justice under law." [7]

It is commonplace to note that civil courts and procedural safeguards are indispensable to our system of government. It is equally apparent that military judicial procedures are something less than what pertains in a civil court. Military rules and tribunals are the antithesis of laws made by the elected representatives of the people and courts presided over by civilian judges. We tolerate the former only out of direct necessity. A democratic society must always be concerned about the potential evils of summary criminal trials.

During the Civil War, President Lincoln directly challenged the regular civil courts. In his September 24, 1862 proclamation, in addition to suspending the writ of *habeas corpus* he ordered that all persons "guilty of any disloyal practice affording aid and comfort to rebels" should be liable to trial and punishment by "courts-martial or military commission." "Of all the arbitrary executive practices in which Lincoln found it imperative to engage, certainly the most dubious and judicially assailable was the trial of civilians by military commissions." [8] At no time did Congress by lawful enactment sanction such trials. The only constitutional authority invoked to warrant such procedures rested on the President's power as Commander-in-Chief.

Ordering civilians to be tried by military tribunals put the President on

[4] Eugene V. Rostow, "Introduction" to Edward Bennett Williams, *One Man's Freedom* (New York, N.Y.: Atheneum, 1962), p. ix.

[5] Mr. Justice Felix Frankfurter, *Malinski* v. *New York,* 324 U.S. 401 (1945).

[6] Leo Pfeffer, *The Liberties of an American* (Boston, Mass.: Beacon Press, 1956), p. 158.

[7] Mr. Justice William O. Douglas, concurring opinion in *Joint Anti-Fascist Refugee Committee* v. *McGrath,* 341 U.S. 123 (1951).

[8] Rossiter, *op. cit.*, p. 26.

a collision course with the civil courts, but the Supreme Court did not get around to denying his power until the war was over. The Court had a chance to negate his action in 1864 in *Ex parte Vallandigham,*[9] but took refuge in a technicality to avoid a decision on the substantive issue. The justices declined to accept the case on the grounds that the military commission which tried Vallandigham was not a "court" within the constitutional and statutory meaning of the term.

That the Court was avoiding the real issue is beyond doubt. If it had been willing to clash with the President, a procedural avenue was open to it. It could have changed Vallandigham's petition for *certiorari* to a request for a writ of *habeas corpus.* The latter was returnable by the whole Court or by any one justice until overruled by his brothers on the bench. Under *habeas corpus* the case would have been properly before the Court as an original suit brought by a citizen under a claim that he had been denied his constitutional rights by a lower federal court.[10]

A similar case, but one destined to have a definitive judgment from the Supreme Court, was that of Lambdin P. Milligan. In this case, which was decided one year after hostilities had ended, the Court ruled that trials of civilians by military commissions in areas where civil courts were open and functioning were unconstitutional.[11]

Milligan had been arrested in Indiana in 1864, tried before a military tribunal, and convicted of conspiracy to release and arm rebel prisoners. At the time of his arrest and trial, the circuit court in Indianapolis was open and could have tried him under procedures outlined by Congress in the Habeas Corpus Act of 1863.

At the war's end, Milligan sought a writ of *habeas corpus* from the federal circuit court in his district to test the validity of his trial and conviction by a military tribunal. The circuit court disagreed on the propriety of issuing the writ, but certified the question of law to the Supreme Court.

Against a background of intense conflict between President Johnson and the Congress over reconstruction, the Supreme Court rendered its decision in December, 1866. The Court held that Milligan should be released because the President has no constitutional power to establish military commissions for trial of civilians in areas where the civil courts are open and functioning.

A majority of five justices, speaking through Mr. Justice Davis, stated further that Congress also was without constitutional power to establish military commissions to try civilians in areas remote from the theater of war, when civil courts were functioning where the crime was committed.

The minority justices, with Chief Justice Chase as spokesman, agreed

[9] 1 Wall. 243 (1864).

[10] A later Supreme Court took this step in *Ex parte Grossman,* 267 U.S. 87 (1925).

[11] *Ex parte Milligan,* 4 Wall. 2 (1866).

that Milligan should be released, but dissented from the majority's narrow strictures on military authority. They insisted that Congress had the power, though not exercised, to authorize military tribunals, like the one set up in Indiana.

Ex parte Milligan is usually considered a landmark decision. Many students of constitutional law, taking their cue from Mr. Justice Davis' righteous tone and language, regard it as one of the great defenses of personal liberty. The truth of the matter is that no President since Lincoln has been deterred by it from doing what he thought was necessary to preserve the common good. While it has been urged on the Supreme Court several times in the hope of curtailing some emergency use of presidential power in a martial situation, it has never succeeded. What it amounts to in American jurisprudence has been ably summarized by Clinton Rossiter in these words:

> . . . *Ex parte Milligan* is sound doctrine in forbidding the presidential establishment of military commissions for the trial of civilians in areas where the civil courts are open—but it is little else. Its general observations on the limits of the war powers are no more valid today than they were in 1866. Here again the law of the Constitution is what Lincoln did in the crisis, not what the Court said later.[12]

CIVIL RIGHTS IN WORLD WAR I

World War I renewed the old confrontation between constitutionally guaranteed personal rights and military necessity. Woodrow Wilson, like all wartime Presidents, was elevated to a position of dictatorship by the exigencies of war. But unlike Lincoln, in the early stages of the emergency, Wilson did not have to rely solely on his power as Commander-in-Chief.

The war was officially begun by a congressional declaration and, from the beginning, Congress delegated much of its legislative power to the President for the duration. If Wilson wore the mantle of the dictator, it was because Congress had granted him unprecedented powers, with many wartime statutes void of standards to guide his discretion. While he could, and did, use his power as Commander-in-Chief, the fact remains that his authority was already buttressed by the powers given him by Congress. He was never required to dictate a course that was not sanctioned either by constitutional mandate or legislative approval.

The Supreme Court came into the wartime picture mainly through the enforcement of two wartime statutes: the Espionage Act of 1917 and the

[12] Rossiter, *op. cit.*, p. 39.

Sedition Act of 1918. Each of the acts imposed certain limitations upon speech and press and branded certain broadly defined utterances and actions as seditious and made them illegal.

The Court sustained the validity of the laws in six cases[13] that came before it at war's end. In all six cases, the Court had to determine the degree of individual freedom that was compatible with war's felt necessities. In all six cases military necessity prevailed.

The most celebrated of the six was *Schenck* v. *United States* in which Mr. Justice Holmes introduced the "clear and present danger" test. This case involved an appeal from a conviction in a lower federal court on charges of violating the Espionage Act by circulating antidraft pamphlets among prospective inductees and members of the armed forces. Schenck's contention was that the law under which he was convicted denied him free-speech rights guaranteed by the First Amendment.

The Court, with Mr. Justice Holmes delivering the opinion, unanimously upheld the constitutionality of the law and the petitioner's conviction thereunder. Holmes, with an underlying appreciation of the delicacy of his task, pointed out that free speech is never an absolute right and the circumstances under which it is used can modify its application. That which might be freely said in time of peace could be a hindrance to the country's effort to protect itself and, under the circumstances of war, could be properly restrained.

The opinion indicated that as free speech and military necessity are weighed in the balance, it becomes a question of proximity and degree. The test in every case, said Holmes, "is whether the words used are used in such circumstances and are of such a nature as to create a clear and present danger that they will bring about the substantive evils that Congress has a right to prevent."

The Espionage Act was a criminal law which, for conviction, required proof of intent. Heretofore, where the common law had applied, courts had attempted in speech cases to establish intent by allowing evidence to show the degree of proximity between the utterance and the resulting illegal action. Under this rule of "proximate causation" to prove intent, a direct and immediate relationship between the utterance and the illegal act must be shown. Under this doctrine, general statements, remote from illicit conduct, were not illegal.

Holmes, an expert on the common law and under the pressure of coming up with a sensible guideline to distinguish the rights of the individual

[13] *Schenck* v. *United States,* 249 U.S. 47 (1919); *Frohwerk* v. *United States,* 249 U.S. 204 (1919); *Debs* v. *United States,* 249 U.S. 211 (1919); *Abrams* v. *United States,* 250 U.S. 616 (1919); *Schaefer* v. *United States,* 251 U.S. 466 (1920); *Pierce* v. *United States,* 252 U.S. 239 (1920).

from the collective rights of an endangered society, used the rule of "proximate causation" as a building stone upon which to lay his "clear and present danger" test.

Two juridical questions arise in cases like Schenck's. One, was the act unconstitutional on its face? Two, if not, was the accused guilty under the law? The first question must be answered negatively, if it is found that Congress has used reasonable means in exercising its war powers. Basically, Congress has a right and a duty to control or punish utterances that could trigger dangerous or illicit actions. The most troublesome aspect of the second question was that of establishing intent.

Holmes' test was to be used mainly to test the sufficiency of the evidence to spell out the element of intent. Under the "clear and present danger" standard, involving the highly complex interrelated issues of proximity and degree, Schenck's conviction was upheld. To Holmes, when the nation is at war and the speech of the individual is designed to interfere with the drafting of men into the armed forces, the gap between utterance and action virtually disappears. The speech itself is the action which Congress has a right to prohibit.

If the rule of "proximate causation" had been used, the defendant's defense that there was no evidence that anyone responded to his pleas by refusing induction into the army or by deserting therefrom probably would have been sufficient to bring acquittal.

The essence of Holmes' test is that speech becomes punishable as action only under circumstances that indicate there is a clear and immediate danger that the utterance will bring about harmful action to society. If no clear and immediate danger is likely to be triggered by the utterance, the speech does not amount to action and the law forbidding the conduct has not been violated.

World War I again demonstrated that the political branches of government in spelling out war's felt necessities need not fear the Supreme Court. Wartime is not the time to look to the Court as the jealous guardian of basic individual liberties. This is, perhaps, as it must and should be. If President and Congress are supported by a strong consensus of public opinion, there is no power within the Court equal to the force generated under "military necessity."

Libertarians, with a nod toward Holmes and Brandeis, could take heart in the knowledge that the Bill of Rights was not superseded by congressional enactments but only trimmed to the core in application. The justices did what their sense of logic and awareness of the temper of the times told them they must do under the exigencies of war. Still, at least some of them did it with a spirit that acknowledged that individual rights glow, albeit dimly, even in time of war.

DRAFTING MEN INTO THE ARMED FORCES

Although men had been drafted into the armed services during the Civil War, the authority of Congress to use this means of raising armies was not seriously challenged until the Selective Draft Act of 1917 went into effect. Under this law, all male citizens aged 21 through 30 were subject to conscription into the armed forces. Exemptions were extended to those holding public office, ministers of religion, and ministerial students. Those objecting to service on grounds of conscience supported by religious convictions were conscripted but were assigned to noncombatant roles.

The Supreme Court unanimously upheld the validity of the law, overruling claims that Congress had acted beyond its constitutional authority.[14] The Court held that our national lawmakers had neither encroached on the states' power over the militia nor violated the establishment of religion clause of the First Amendment. Further, they had not subjected the draftees to "involuntary servitude" in violation of the Thirteenth Amendment. The Court's basic reasoning was that the authority to conscript men into military service was reasonably implied in the constitutional mandates to Congress "to raise and support armies" and "to declare war."

Down through the years the Supreme Court has been unrelenting in its support of Congress' right to draft men into the armed services. Its support has held in peacetime, wartime, and during undeclared wars. The troublesome area of the draft law's application has been the "conscientious objector" clause.

Numerous challenges to the draft, some tied in with the legality of the war itself, were raised during the Vietnam conflict. In one such case,[15] the potential draftee applied for exemption on the grounds that he had conscientious scruples against participating in any war and on his conviction that killing was morally wrong. He admitted that his attitude was based on his personal philosophy, embodying his moral and ethical beliefs, but was not "religious" in the traditional sense.

His entitlement to exemption was upheld by the Supreme Court, holding that the proper criterion was whether the objection to war stemmed from moral, ethical, or religious beliefs about what was right or wrong and whether such beliefs were held with the strength of traditional convictions. According to Justice Black's reading of it, the draft law actually exempts "all those whose consciences, spurred by deeply held moral, ethical or religious beliefs, would give them no rest or peace if they allowed themselves to become a part of an instrument of war." [16]

[14] *Arver* v. *United States* (Selective Draft Law Cases), 245 U.S. 366 (1918).
[15] *Welsh* v. *United States,* 398 U.S. 333 (1970).
[16] *Id.*, p. 344.

In 1971, in two long-awaited decisions,[17] the Supreme Court ruled that young men were not entitled to draft exemptions as conscientious objectors if they objected only to the Vietnam conflict as an "unjust war" and did not oppose all wars. The Court held that Congress had acted constitutionally when it ruled out "selective" conscientious objection by authorizing exemptions only for those men who were "conscientiously opposed to participation in war in any form." Mr. Justice Thurgood Marshall, speaking for the Court, said that the ruling neither favors religious denominations that teach total pacifism nor does it infringe the freedom of religion of those who believe that only "unjust" wars must be opposed.

Justice Marshall declared that the rule against selective conscientious objection was essentially neutral in its treatment of various religious faiths and that any "incidental burdens" felt by particular draftees were justified by the government's interests in procuring the manpower necessary for military purposes.

Mr. Justice William O. Douglas, the lone dissenter, said: "I had assumed that the welfare of the single human soul was the ultimate test of the vitality of the First Amendment." He argued that whether an individual's abhorrence of killing was the product of religious faith or individual conscience, the First Amendment's guarantee of freedom of religion should shield him from conscription into a war that he believed to be unjust.

The draft, against the background of our military involvement in Indochina, produced the unique case of an entire state going to the Court to challenge the legality of an undeclared war. Massachusetts, under the mandate of a legislative enactment, tried to go into the Supreme Court to contest the President's power to wage war in Indochina without a formal declaration by Congress.

The Court, dividing 6 to 3, refused to entertain the challenge.[18] Exercising its power to ignore a legal complaint without giving its reasons, the Court in a single sentence announced it was denying the state permission to file its suit directly in the Supreme Court. The fact that three justices wanted to hear the case showed a growth of concern over the legal issues involving the Vietnam War.[19] Justice Douglas, never timid about tackling cases with political overtones, filed a fifteen-page dissent, rejecting the federal government's argument that any Supreme Court involvement would embarrass the nation.

[17] *Gilette* v. *United States* and *Negre* v. *Larsen,* 401 U.S. 437 (1971).

[18] *Massachusetts* v. *Laird,* 400 U.S. 886 (1970).

[19] When the legality of the Vietnam War first appeared as a peripheral issue in earlier cases, Justice Douglas stood alone in insisting the Court answer legal questions raised by the conflict. He was later backed by Justice Stewart. Finally, Justice Harlan cast his vote to support a hearing on the legality of the war.

While the draft has not perished by judicial condemnation, it seems likely that its unpopularity in recent years will cause its demise by political action. From the signs now observable, future manpower needs of the armed forces are likely to be filled on a voluntary basis, making a legal draft unnecessary.

THE EVACUATION OF JAPANESE-AMERICAN CITIZENS

Immediately after the Japanese attack on Pearl Harbor, a tremendous pressure built up to take action against over 100,000 persons of Japanese ancestry living on the West Coast. On February 19, 1942, President Franklin D. Roosevelt, as Commander-in-Chief, in response to military, congressional, and public-opinion pressures, issued an executive order endowing the Secretary of War "and the military commanders whom he may designate" with broad discretionary authority to establish "military areas" from which "any or all persons" might be excluded in order to prevent espionage and sabotage.[20]

Under this authority the Pacific Coast states and a part of Arizona were proclaimed military areas and all persons of Japanese extraction, 70,000 of whom were American citizens, were evacuated from these areas. On March 21, 1942, Congress enacted a statute ratifying the executive order and authorizing its continuation.

Officialdom explained this enforced removal of 70,000 full-fledged United States citizens from their homes on the ground of "military necessity." Military authorities said that if there should be a Japanese invasion of the Pacific Coast states, the presence of thousands of disloyal or unpredictable persons of Japanese ancestry might easily produce confusion that the enemy could use to advantage. In addition, the military claimed time was of the essence. There was no time for individual examination to distinguish loyal and disloyal Japanese-Americans. Once again, the exigencies of war brought "military necessity" into conflict with due process of law, raising issues of the gravest importance for the Supreme Court.

As usual, the ponderous pathway to the Court, with characteristic delays, gave the Court a period of grace before it had to provide answers. The first case arising out of the evacuation program was *Hirabayashi* v. *United States*,[21] which the Court decided on June 21, 1943.

Gordon Hirabayashi, an American-born citizen of alien Japanese parents and a senior at the University of Washington, was tried and convic-

[20] Executive Order 9066, 7 Federal Register 1407.

[21] 320 U.S. 81 (1943).

ted in a federal district court for violating two orders issued by the military commander of his district. One order directed him to report at a certain time to a civil control station to register for evacuation. The other set a curfew requiring all persons of Japanese ancestry to be in their residences between 8:00 P.M. and 6:00 A.M. His sentences for the two offenses were to run concurrently.

The Supreme Court had a choice. It could review the conviction on both charges, forcing itself to consider the legality of the order commanding Hirabayashi to report to the control station and possibly requiring it to consider the constitutionality of the entire program of evacuation. Or it could limit itself to reviewing one count and, if it upheld his conviction, could then ignore the other count, as the two sentences ran concurrently.[22] The Court took advantage of this circumstance to limit its review to the curfew violation, clearly a less drastic interference with personal liberty than coerced evacuation from one's home.

Without dissent, the Court found the general's curfew order valid and sustained Hirabayashi's conviction. Chief Justice Stone's opinion held that the combined used of presidential-legislative war powers were constitutional and clearly authorized the curfew order issued by the commanding general. To Hirabayashi's contention that a curfew regulation discriminating between "citizens of Japanese ancestry and those of other ancestries" violated the Fifth Amendment, he replied that "the actions taken must be appraised in the light of the conditions with which the President and Congress were confronted in the early months of 1942." [23]

Stone emphasized the grave character of the national emergency which had confronted the nation at that time and the possible disloyalty of a segment of the Japanese-American population. Under the circumstances, he said, the curfew did not violate the Fifth Amendment, which contains no equal protection clause.

The Court, Stone thought, ought not challenge the conclusion of the military authorities that the war power be interpreted as broadly as possible. He concluded: "In this case it is enough that circumstances within the knowledge of those charged with the responsibility for maintaining the national defense afford a rational basis for the decision which they made. Whether we would have made it is irrelevant." [24]

Justices Murphy, Douglas, and Rutledge wrote separate concurring opinions, of which Murphy's was the most blisteringly critical. He thought the curfew regulation smacked of such arbitrary treatment that only the

[22] *Brooks* v. *United States,* 267 U.S. 432, 441 (1925). The concurrent sentence doctrine came under attack by a later Supreme Court in *Benton* v. *Maryland,* 395 U.S. 784 (1969).

[23] *Hirabayashi,* op. cit., p. 93.

[24] *Id.,* p. 102.

"critical military situation" on the Pacific Coast kept it marginally within the Constitution.

The decision indicates that when faced with the combined powers of President and Congress, the Court is not likely to find the application of such powers lacking in constitutional validity. Thus, when the act of Congress followed the President's order the Court could say: "We have no occasion to consider whether the President, acting alone, could lawfully have made the curfew order in question or have authorized others to make it."[25] By accepting the estimates of the political branches as to the extent of their war powers and by confining its review to the unadorned issue of the reasonableness of the curfew order, the Court put its stamp of approval on the government's action.

The constitutionality of the exclusion order, then in effect for over two-and-a-half years, finally came before the Supreme Court in December, 1944 in *Korematsu* v. *United States*.[26]

Korematsu, a Japanese-American, had been convicted in a federal court for remaining in his home despite General DeWitt's evacuation order. He cited Bill of Rights protections contained in Amendments IV through VIII as deterrents to what the military had done to him, but to no avail. All of these claims were rejected by the Court, which upheld the evacuation program as a valid exercise of presidential-congressional power.

In his opinion, Mr. Justice Black carefully separated the exclusion order from the detention program, the validity of which was to be decided by the Court on the same day, and went on to justify the decision on the former.

In tone, the opinion reflects the thought that the evacuation program was an accomplished fact and there was little the Court could do about it. In substance, Black argued: The military leaders believed that the evacuation program was necessary to abate the danger, and the immediacy of action was justified by the shortness of time. He denied that the evacuation was based on racial prejudice, emphasizing that he believed the military authorities had rendered their judgment strictly on the military factors of security against invasion, espionage, and sabotage. He concluded: In time of war we must trust our military commanders. "We cannot—by availing ourselves of the calm perspective of hindsight—now say that at that time these actions were unjustified."[27]

The crux of Black's argument was "military necessity." It induced the Court to accept the military commander's judgment as to the scope and gravity of the danger and likewise persuaded it to accept that extent of constitutional power as needed to protect the nation.

[25] *Id.*, p. 92.
[26] 323 U.S. 214 (1944).
[27] *Id.*, p. 224.

In arriving at its decision, it is to be noted that the Supreme Court was not marching to a different drumbeat from that heard by the rest of society. Many public figures, including Earl Warren, whose records indicate a deep regard for human rights, were marching to the same beat.

Justices Murphy, Roberts, and Jackson put vigorous dissents to the *Korematsu* decision on the judicial record. Murphy cited the constitutional brinksmanship the Court was playing and felt the exclusion program was racially inspired. "He had apparently bothered to read the military and congressional reports on the evacuation and had been shocked by the evidence of naked prejudice that ran like angry veins of poison through its entire history." [28] To Murphy, the whole military scheme was blatantly unconstitutional; to uphold it was to legalize racism.

Justice Roberts' dissenting opinion matched Murphy's in bitterness. Roberts thought it a clear case of convicting a citizen as punishment for not submitting to imprisonment in a concentration camp, solely because of his ancestry, without evidence or inquiry into his loyalty. Korematsu, he believed, had been under contradictory orders,[29] which in fact "were nothing but a cleverly devised trap to accomplish the real purpose of the military authority, which was to lock him up in a concentration camp." [30]

Justice Jackson's dissent was the most curious of all, estimating that war was an extra-constitutional aberration beyond constitutional controls. Jackson did not challenge the necessity of the relocation plan, because he was convinced that no court would have the practical power to obstruct it. He insisted, however, that the military, judging the security situation in its own terms, should not then come before the Court and attempt to have it canonized as constitutional doctrine. Under the circumstances of war, the best the judiciary can do, Jackson intimated, is to recognize that "we cannot confine military expedients by the Constitution," but neither should we "distort the Constitution to approve all that the military may prove expedient." [31]

In *Ex parte Endo*,[32] decided the same day as the *Korematsu* case, the

[28] Rossiter, *op. cit.*, p. 50.

[29] Korematsu was forbidden by military order to leave the zone in which he lived. He was also forbidden by another military order, after a fixed date, to be found within that zone, unless he was in an assembly center located in that zone. The earlier order made Korematsu a criminal if he left the zone in which he resided; the later order made him a criminal if he did not leave. Professor Rossiter explains the contradictory orders as follows: "The general had the Japanese-Americans 'coming and going.' One order forbade them to leave the area, another to remain in it. The result, fully intended, was to force them to report to the evacuation stations. This is what Korematsu would not do. In effect, he was punished for sitting in his own home." Rossiter, *op. cit.*, p. 48, footnote 43.

[30] *Korematsu, op. cit.*, dissenting opinion of Mr. Justice Roberts, p. 232.

[31] *Id.*, dissenting opinion of Mr. Justice Jackson, p. 244.

[32] 323 U.S. 283 (1944).

Court held that an American citizen of Japanese ancestry whose loyalty to the United States had been established could not be held constitutionally in a war relocation center but must be unconditionally released.

The litigant in the case was Mitsuye Endo, an American citizen of demonstrated loyalty who worked as an employee in the California Civil Service. In 1942 she was evacuated from her home in Sacramento to a relocation center near Tule Lake, California, and still later to another relocation depot in Utah. By the time the Supreme Court passed on Miss Endo's petition for a writ of *habeas corpus*, the military areas had been disestablished and the relocation camps were being broken up.

Justice Douglas' majority opinion followed a narrow channel, carefully avoiding any hazards which would force the Court into ruling upon the constitutionality of the confinement program in its entirety. Instead he ruled merely that the War Relocation Authority had no authorization to subject persons of undoubted loyalty to confinement or conditional parole.

Douglas avoided the embarrassing constitutional questions arising out of the presidential-congressional action in authorizing the relocation program by pointing out that neither the executive order nor the statute anywhere specifically authorized detention. He found that the illegal detention had resulted from an abuse of powers by the War Relocation Authority.

In steering his way to the decision, Douglas heeded no signal to discuss a related constitutional question: Could a citizen charged with no crime be forcibly detained under orders of military authority in other than an immediate combat or danger area? The shoals in constitutional law marked by *Ex parte Milligan,* where this question had been in part an issue, were avoided by distinguishing the *Milligan* rule from the present case.

In the earlier case, Douglas said, the civilian had been detained by military authorities; Miss Endo's confinement had been at the hands of civilian officials. The distinction might be challenged as hair-thin, because Miss Endo's confinement had in fact taken place under direct orders from the military and it was obvious that she would not have been in the relocation center at all except for military coercement. Besides, she was in the hands of civilian detainers without any proceedings in a civil court.

Justices Murphy and Roberts wrote short but bitter concurring opinions, the latter taking pains to castigate the Court's majority for steering around the great constitutional issues that he felt the case presented. Both justices made it clear they felt the Court's reasoning left much to be desired.

Murphy, adhering to the racial theme which he had pursued so vigorously in the earlier *Korematsu* case, flatly stated that the detention program was "not only unauthorized by Congress or the Executive," but that the *Endo* case was but "another example of the unconstitutional resort to racism inherent in the entire evacuation Program." [33]

[33] *Id.,* concurring opinion of Mr. Justice Murphy, p. 307.

Roberts stressed the absurdity of the Court's position, which claimed that neither the President nor Congress had sanctioned the detention of Miss Endo. He felt that by silence and inaction, when they might have spoken and acted against it, they sanctioned it. He charged that, although the President could have, he never used the powers of his office to alter the detention program and Congress, although it might have, never failed to appropriate the funds needed to maintain the Relocation Authority.

In the "calm perspective of hindsight"—which Justice Black disdained in *Korematsu*—what conclusions can be drawn from the three Japanese-American cases? Legal scholars approach unanimity in the belief that our highest court blundered seriously in deciding the cases. In the clash between "military necessity" and the citizen's "due process" protection, the former came off a going-away winner. The Court indicated that when the President and Congress jointly exercise the "war powers" there is not much it can do to protect the citizen's constitutional rights. It went further than this, much to the chagrin of Justice Murphy. Instead of making its own determination of the security situation on the West Coast, it accepted the military commander's evaluation that called for wholesale infringement on the citizen's Bill of Rights guarantees. In the process, the Court wrote on the record much that makes such a denial a matter of constitutional law. Many scholars consider this the Court's most serious dereliction.

By the Court's pronouncements it now appears that a citizen, solely because of his racial extraction, may be legally uprooted from his residence, segregated from his community, forcibly evacuated to a concentration shelter, and kept there against his will, until his loyalty has been ascertained.

More than a little evidence has emerged to indicate what Justice Murphy feared—that the racial antagonism against Japanese living along the Pacific Coast played a part in the military program to evacuate them. The commanding general who ordered the evacuation testified before a committee of the House of Representatives: "A Jap's a Jap and it makes no difference whether he is an American citizen or not. . . . I don't want any of them." [34]

There is little or no evidence in the record to sustain the proposition that a large part of the Japanese-American group was disloyal. In fact the record tends to prove that there were no overt acts of espionage, sabotage, or disloyal conduct. It appears that the handful of radical Japanese-Americans who were likely to cause trouble were well-known to our intelligence agencies at the beginning of the war and could have been easily weeded out. In fact, this is what was done with Americans of German and Italian extraction living in the United States.

[34] Robert E. Cushman, "Civil Liberties in the Atomic Age," *The Annals of the American Academy of Political and Social Science,* Volume 249, January, 1947, p. 57.

Did time permit a weeding out process on the West Coast? The military said "no," but the answer does not concur with events. The record reveals that the first evacuation order was promulgated four months after Pearl Harbor; additional orders were still being issued eight months after that date. In all it took eleven months to complete the evacuation program. As Justice Murphy was moved to state in his dissenting opinion in *Korematsu*: "It seems incredible that under these circumstances it would have been impossible to hold loyalty hearings for the mere 112,000 persons involved—or at least the 70,000 American citizens—especially when a large part of this number represented children and elderly men and women." [35]

One scholar proclaimed the whole evacuation program "an abuse of power and an appalling violation of the constitutional rights of citizens." [36] In 1947 President Truman's Commission on Civil Rights concluded that the evacuation was "the most striking mass interference since slavery with the right to physical freedom" and recommended that the evacuees be compensated for their property losses.

One final conclusion seems warranted. All those who looked upon the Bill of Rights as everyman's guarantee against arbitrary treatment by his government had less to believe in after the war. Certainly 70,000 loyal citizens would be justified in concluding that "due process" had lost some of its meaning.

THE NAZI SABOTEURS

Echoes of the *Milligan* case were heard in the summer of 1942 when the Supreme Court reassembled from its summer recess to review the case of the Nazi saboteurs.[37] The eight saboteurs, transported by a German submarine, had landed on our shores, buried their uniforms, and proceeded in civilian dress to various parts of the country with the apparent intent and materials to commit acts of sabotage against our war industries. They were all native-born Germans who had lived in the United States at one time or another and had returned to Germany, where they had been trained as saboteurs.

About ten days after their arrival they were apprehended by the FBI and ordered by the President to stand trial before a military tribunal, on charges of violating the laws of war. Two army officers were designated to defend them.

The defense attacked the presidential orders which subjected the defendants to trial by military commission and denied them access to the civil

[35] *Korematsu, op. cit.,* dissenting opinion of Mr. Justice Murphy, pp. 241–242.
[36] Cushman, *op. cit. supra* note 34 at p. 57.
[37] *Ex parte Quirin,* 317 U.S. 1 (1942).

courts. Counsel admitted that the accused parties had come ashore in partial uniform from an enemy submarine but claimed they had no intention of committing sabotage but had undertaken the mission to escape from the Nazi regime. The lawyers denied that the defendants were belligerents and, relying heavily on *Ex parte Milligan* as a precedent, claimed a right to trial in a civil court.

When the case before the military tribunal was well along, to the surprise of most close observers, the Supreme Court consented to hear arguments for a writ of *habeas corpus*. After proceedings that lasted two days, the Court, without Justice Murphy's participation, voted unanimously to uphold the military tribunal's jurisdictional power to try the case.

The Court found that the President was legally empowered to establish military tribunals in cases of this kind by virtue of both constitutional and statutory authority. It held that the petitioners were belligerents and that the offenses charged were indeed offenses against the law of war. Because of this finding, the Court explained, the constitutional mandates of grand jury indictment and jury trial were not applicable.

The Court disposed of the *Milligan* precedent by citing the factual differences in that case and the one at bar. Milligan, a citizen and resident of the United States, had never resided in a rebellious state, was not a member of the armed forces of the enemy, and as a non-belligerent was not subject to the law of war. Thus in no way, said the Court, did the circumstances of involvement encompassing the petitioners match the factual conditions pertaining to Milligan.

Crucial in the case was the determination of the status of the invaders. Were they belligerents or civilians seeking asylum? This important issue was decided by the President and his military tribunal and, by agreement of the parties, was not before the Court; nevertheless, the justices could have considered it, if they had wished to do so. It is curious that the facts essential to the jurisdiction of the military commission were not at issue. With the key question already decided, the Court confined its review to the President's power to create the commission and apply the law of war to the case. The petitioners thus went before the Court stamped as belligerents by military authority, and the justices treated this decision as final. Once again in the crisis of war, the Court demonstrated that it was not about to substitute its own judgment for that of the military.

In its decision the Court was fortified by both history and legal precedent. But if the key jurisdictional issue had been decided already, why did the Court bother to grant a hearing? Beyond the ready answer that several constitutional aspects of the President's war powers had to be clarified, various speculations are possible. "Perhaps, . . . the justices were interested in impressing upon the totalitarian world the extraordinary degree to which the American constitutional system threw safeguards around accused persons—particularly since their speedy disposal of the appeal did not interfere in the least with Draconian military justice." [38] Perhaps they were honoring the notion that any trial—military or civil—under American auspices must be fair and that judicial review was necessary to guarantee the result.

It just might be, however, that the Court at this time found it necessary to reassert the power of civil courts to inquire into the jurisdiction of presidentially established military commissions. As one commentator has noted: "The Supreme Court stopped the military authorities and required them, as it were, to show their credentials. When this had been done to the Court's satisfaction, they were allowed to proceed." [39]

Was anything gained by this exercise? Beside returning the corpse of Lambdin P. Milligan to its sarcophagus, the benefits were minimal. Civil libertarians, viewing any check on the military as wholesome, might have been slightly comforted. Others regarded the Court's review "as little more than a ceremonious detour to a pre-determined goal intended chiefly for edification." [40] Perhaps Clinton Rossiter summed it up best when he noted "the whole affair was a shadow play without blood or substance." [41]

MARTIAL LAW IN HAWAII

The specter of *Ex parte Milligan* revisited the Supreme Court in 1946 in two cases[42] arising out of the declaration of martial law in Hawaii during World War II.

On December 7, 1941, the day following the Japanese attack on Pearl Harbor, the Governor of Hawaii suspended the writ of *habeas corpus,* declared martial law throughout the islands, and turned over the governing of the territory to the Commanding General, Hawaiian Department. The Governor's action was based on authority granted him by Section 67 of the Organic Act of the Territory of Hawaii.[43]

President Franklin D. Roosevelt approved this action two days later, thereby assuming full constitutional responsibility for the initiation of mil-

[38] Alfred H. Kelly and Winfred A. Harbison, *The American Constitution,* 4th ed. (New York, N.Y.: W. W. Norton and Company, 1970), p. 850.

[39] Robert E. Cushman, "The Case of the Nazi Saboteurs," *American Political Science Review,* Vol. 36 (1942), p. 1091.

[40] Edward S. Corwin, *Total War and the Constitution* (New York, N.Y.: Alfred A. Knopf, Inc., 1947), p. 118.

[41] Rossiter, *op. cit.,* p. 116.

[42] *Duncan* v. *Kahanamoku* and *White* v. *Steer,* 327 U.S. 304 (1946).

[43] 31 Stat. 141, p. 153.

itary government in the territory. This was no mere abstract transfer of power from the civilian to the military side of the house. The military assayed to perform and, in fact, did perform all acts of government necessary to maintain the islands as an organized entity. The criminal and civil courts were replaced by military tribunals and the normal civil procedures: grand jury indictment, trial by jury, rules of evidence, subpoenaing of witnesses, and the issuance of writs of *habeas corpus* were prohibited.

To responsible military leaders, focusing on the necessity of protecting the islands from invasion, this severe subjection of civilian affairs to military control undoubtedly seemed imperative, but to the civil officers of the territory it came off as an extravagant and unnecessary denial of constitutionally protected civil rights.

Civil officials made a strong case for mitigating the strictures of the military regime. They argued that any real danger of invasion of the islands evaporated after the Battle of Midway in June, 1942. They pointed out also that other symbols of danger were not manifest. There were no known acts of sabotage, espionage, or other disloyal conduct by Japanese in Hawaii. They stressed that the civil courts of the territory were ready to resume their normal functions and requested the army to permit them to do so. Despite continued criticism, which increased in fury as the war turned more and more toward an inevitable Allied victory, martial law continued in the islands until ended by presidential proclamation on October 24, 1944.

It was against this background early in 1944 that two civilians—White and Duncan—were able to petition the territorial district court for writs of *habeas corpus*. White, a Honolulu stockbroker, was serving a four-year prison term, after having been convicted by a military court in August, 1942 of embezzling stock. Duncan, a civilian shipfitter employed in the Honolulu Navy yard, had been convicted in March, 1944 of assaulting two armed sentries in the yard and was serving a six-months sentence.

The territorial court, in each instance, found that the civil courts always had been able to function but for the military orders closing them and consequently there was no military necessity for the trial of petitioners by military tribunals. It, accordingly, held the trials void and ordered the release of the prisoners. These holdings were appealed in tandem to the circuit court, which reversed them. The Supreme Court granted *certiorari* and, after hearings, handed down its decision on February 25, 1946.

Deciding the cases on the narrowest possible ground—the construction of the statute—the Court, by a 6 to 2 vote, held that the prisoners had been unlawfully tried and punished by the military courts, because Congress in granting the Governor power to declare martial law had not meant to supersede constitutional guarantees of a fair trial by processes well-established, when such rights were capable of being protected by civil courts.

Justice Black's majority opinion did not reach the constitutional issue but, as noted, was based on the construction of an act of Congress. Justice Murphy concurred in the result but insisted it should have been based on constitutional grounds. He emphasized the "open court" rule reached in *Ex parte Milligan,* which held that the military lack constitutional power in either war or peace to try civilians, when the civil courts are capable of functioning.

Justices Burton and Frankfurter, in dissent, thought that the strategy and tactics of war are largely a matter of executive discretion under the Constitution. They looked upon the Hawaiian Islands as a potential battlefield and argued that the Constitution intended the President's discretion to be complete and supreme in this area. Their conclusion was that the original declaration of martial law was clearly justified and that the President and his military commanders should be allowed a reasonable period in which to decide when and how to restore the battlefield to peacetime controls.

Of more than passing interest is the part of the opinion in which they seemingly addressed the Court's majority. They felt the majority in denouncing, from the safe vantage point of 1946, the military decisions made early in the war might be establishing a precedent "which in other emergencies may handicap the executive branch of the government in the performance of duties alloted to it by the Constitution. . . ." [44]

However much one might credit the dissenters' views with respect to constitutional theory, there is little to be said for the notion as a practical matter. Our constitutional history tells us they were unduly alarmed about the possibility that a Supreme Court decision might hamper the constitutional power of the President to meet future martial emergencies. Future Presidents, faced with such emergencies, are more likely to follow the conduct of past Presidents rather than a Supreme Court decision in determining what is constitutionally possible to meet the difficulty.

Several aspects of *Duncan* v. *Kahanamoku* are worth noting. Most surprising was the Court's unwillingness to base its decision squarely on *Ex parte Milligan* as a controlling precedent. Only Justice Murphy espoused the *Milligan* rule in full application.

The majority's reluctance probably was due to the criticism that had been levied against the *Milligan* decision in recent years. Many legal scholars have argued that the "open court" rule pronounced by the *Milligan* Court is so amorphous that it might endanger the security of the nation, if adhered to in the future. They believed "that the exigencies of war on occasion may leave little room for so large a play of civilian authority in a

[44] *Duncan* v. *Kahanamoku, op. cit.,* dissenting opinion of Mr. Justice Burton with whom Mr. Justice Frankfurter concurred, p. 357.

possible field of military operations as the *Milligan* case insisted upon." [45]

Another aspect to note is the timing of the Supreme Court's decision. As in the *Milligan* case, the Court's ruling came after the dust of battle had settled. Judicial notice was undoubtedly taken of the fact that Duncan and White got their writs of *habeas corpus* only after the practical necessity for military government in Hawaii had ceased. One can only wonder what the Court would have decided if the petitioners had gotten their cases before the Court before October 24, 1944.

Still another intriguing development was the unusual willingness of the Court to look behind the testimony of the military authorities as to the necessity for establishing and maintaining military rule and to decide the facts for themselves. This they had refused to do in the earlier wartime case of *Korematsu* v. *United States*. In that case they had accepted at face value the military authorities' estimates of the danger that lurked on the West Coast of the United States. In *Duncan* v. *Kahanamoku* they accepted nothing, preferring to substitute their own judgment for that of the military.

Finally, it is to be noted that the Court based its ruling on the construction of a statute and not, as Justice Murphy insisted, on constitutional grounds. When the Court spells out the meaning of a constitutional provision it is expounding constitutional doctrine that not even Congress can change by its law-making authority. When it interprets an act of Congress it is proceeding on a lower level of meaning. It is construing congressional intent, that can be overridden by Congress by further use of its statute-making power. A case, then, that had all the ingredients for a constitutional *tour de force* was in the end only a vehicle for statutory interpretation.

CONCLUSION

Military necessity versus individual rights is a study in the realities of constitutional law. At this time in our constitutional history, it is commonplace to recognize that the "necessity" of using the war power is always equal to war's felt needs or, short of war, to the dangers which seem to beset the country.

In moments of real or imagined danger, as judged by the political branches of government, military power can be expanded to equate with the estimated peril. Constitutionally, the dimensions of the war power are most likely to be presidentially determined. At best they will be established by presidential-congressional action. The Supreme Court is likely to be supine while war is in progress, virtually accepting at face value the military's estimate of the danger.

[45] Kelly and Harbison, *op. cit.*, p. 848.

In each of our past "total" wars, the President, either through his own claimed powers or with the help of Congress, has established a pseudo-dictatorship, always with strong popular support. In each instance there have been restrictions on individual rights in the name of military necessity, blatantly emphasizing the inner conflict between the ideals of democracy and the crisis requirements of national security. Balancing personal rights against national security so that each value gets its due is a vexing problem at all times but especially so in time of conflict.

In crisis periods, if these are the weights the Supreme Court must put on the scales, it is not surprising that the beam tips in favor of national security. In the process of balancing, the Court, like the political branches of government and also like a plurality of people, sees our survival as a free nation as the weightiest factor of all. To the Court, as Earl Warren has pointed out, "the issue is not individual against society; it is rather the wise accommodation of the necessities of physical survival with the requirements of spiritual survival." [46]

One of the misfortunes of war is that national security and guaranteed individual rights are not compatible. Our history reveals that the Supreme Court, under the shield of military necessity, rather consistently upheld governmental repression of personal rights during periods of war.

The Court has been unrelenting in its support of the right of Congress to draft men into the armed forces and, by strict interpretation of the exemption clause, has largely favored the government's claims for enforcement of selective service.

Even the bastion of *habeas corpus* can be constitutionally threatened in time of emergency. The "clear and present danger" test as used by the Court has not been a very formidable barrier to arbitrary instrusions on freedom of speech. Nevertheless, the Court never has held that constitutionally guaranteed individual rights are superseded in wartime. They have been bent and reshaped in the crucible of war, but always with an acknowledgement of their spirit.

It is not likely, however, that 70,000 loyal Japanese-American citizens evacuated from their homes on the West Coast during World War II found much spiritual solace in the Court's decisions. Nor were libertarians heartened by the Court's handling of the case of the Nazi saboteurs. To them, the Court's review smacked more of calculation than inspiration. Only in its decision on martial law in Hawaii did the Court produce a redemptive counterweight to its other World War II civil rights pronouncements. Civil rightists were encouraged by the Court's findings and its willingness to make its own determination of military necessity rather than accept at face value

[46] Earl Warren, "The Bill of Rights and the Military," in Edmond Cahn (ed.), *The Great Rights* (New York, N.Y.: The Macmillan Company, 1963), p. 109.

the estimates of the military. They can be forgiven for wishing it had all come about before the dust of battle settled.

Today, as always, the electorate, no less than the Court and political branches of the government, must remain vigilant in awareness and dedicated to the need to preserve the values of our Constitution, lest in our striving to be safe we surrender our ability to be free. Each war demonstrates the remarkable flexibility of our governmental system and requires free men to profess an act of faith in America. If survival is the supreme test, then our constitutional system has met the challenge to date. The sobering thought for the present is that, beyond doubt, we will have to take the test again.

4

Civil-Military Relations and the Formulation of United States Foreign Policy

ROCCO M. PAONE

The military today performs an important functional part in the input process of our foreign-policy planning. Traditionally, this segment of leadership has rarely been permitted an involvement in the foreign-policy formulation process, a policy often allowing significant voids in United States foreign policy. Since World War II, however, it has been assigned responsibilities of making inputs into the conversion mechanism of our foreign policy. In the thinking of an increasing number of critics who feel that the pendulum has swung too far, the influence of the military seems over-emphatically reflected; consequently they see a danger that the natural concern of the armed forces with military might gives our national policy an undue stress on force. Concomitantly, they fear that the military's legal control over the most violent means of destruction in existence will give it a preponderance of power not appropriate in a democratic society. Serious discussions among congressional and other leaders on the influence of the military on United States foreign policy have therefore been taking place.

The role of the military as an institutional mechanism in the foreign policy formulation process is the major topic of this study. When asked, some seven years ago, "What single quality is most needed in today's leaders, both military and civilian?" Lieutenant General Thomas Harrold, former Commandant of the National War College, replied, "Broad knowledge of the world today." The military man, he asserted, must have "knowledge of the major political, economic, and social forces at play in the world, and how these forces affect the United States and his profession."

This statement still applies to the military because it indicates a new era in military education that reflects the impact of revolutionary developments in United States foreign policy, the close association between military programs and foreign and domestic policies, and last but not least, radical advances in contemporary weapons technology. Today's milieu of international environmentalism requires that military officers be prepared not only to organize and manage a missile program, direct the diplomatic functions of a military advisory group, relate military programs to political climates, and advise civilian authority on certain aspects of foreign policy[1] but also that the military protect this nation against the varied threats of conventional, nuclear, and limited war. The young officer must be prepared to exercise as well such "old-fashioned" but necessary attributes as discipline, honor, courage, and command ability. What has occurred is not a change in the responsibilities of the military but rather several new dimensions to these obligations.

The political leadership has had in this same era to acquire more than a passing knowledge of the intricacies of firing systems and military offensive and defensive deployment tactics, while recognizing the close affinity between strategic military planning and national political policy. However, attempts to institutionalize the government's decision-making process in foreign affairs to include these considerations have been wasteful and overly time-consuming and still leave much to be desired.[2] At present, probably as a result of the Vietnam conflict, military relations with political leaders as well as much of the public has reached a very low ebb, despite the fact that the military advised the nation's political leaders not to involve United States military forces in a limited war in Southeast Asia.[3] In civil-military relations on a high governmental level, the civilian leadership has pursued an "independent"course in the policy-making process.

Not until the era of World War II did the political leaders of the United States fully comprehend the practical necessity for an intimate relationship between military and foreign affairs. The Congress reflected its awareness of this understanding when in 1947 it created the National Security Council, which provided machinery for an executive assessment of foreign and national security policies in the light of military capabilities. The President was thereby afforded another source of advice from heads of the major executive-branch agencies. Though the work of the National Security Council has disappointed many, the machinery of the Council has given the military a much greater peacetime opportunity to influence United States foreign policy.[4]

The Secretary of Defense often seems most important in foreign-policy

[1] Gene M. Lyons, "The New Civil-Military Relations," *American Political Science Review,* Vol. LV, No. 1, pp. 58–61.

[2] Roger Hilsman, *The Politics of Policy Making in Defense and Foreign Affairs,* New York: Harper and Row, 1971, pp. 3–11. For a more intensive study of the apparatus of foreign-policy making see Burton M. Sapin, *The Making of United States Foreign Policy,* New York: Frederick A. Praeger, 1966, pp. 135–142.

[3] *Ibid.,* p. 54.

[4] R. M. Paone, "Foreign Policy and Military Power," *Military Review,* November 1964, p. 10.

formulation. Whenever he visited Vietnam during the course of the war there, the Secretary of State, the President, and our allies anxiously have awaited his recommendations for changes of action or policy.

As the President's principal military advisers, the Joint Chiefs of Staff, who generally represent the professional military men, frequently have direct access to the White House. The degree of influence of the military in foreign policy, however, is dependent upon such variables as the President's desires and the possible courses of action, as well as the personalities and abilities of the Secretaries of Defense and State and the Chairman of the Joint Chiefs of Staff. A strong Secretary exerting civilian control can demonstrate successfully to the President the *sine qua non* of our national security over the objections of the Joint Chiefs, although the latter are permitted to have some direct access to the President.[5] The Secretary of Defense can also veto the suggestions of the Joint Chiefs. The dynamic executive ability of the former Secretary McNamara was often reflected in the clarion cry for "civilian control." Generally, Presidents Kennedy and Johnson supported his contentions against those of the professional military.[6] [The disclosure of expanding military intelligence activities in seemingly political matters in various regions of the world and the publication of the so-called Pentagon Papers have created an even greater demand today for civilian control.]

Despite its vast impact on U.S. foreign affairs since World War II, military policy certainly does not control foreign policy. "Political" considerations have often been difficult for the military to comprehend. At the same time the enhanced position of the military in the conversion mechanism of foreign policy coordination has intensified the growth of clandestine intelligence organizations that apparently contrive their greatest successes in secrecy, at times producing a Congressional boomerang and a popular suspicion that too much "cloak-and-dagger" work is involved in foreign policy. Today a number of Congressmen fear the loss of democratic control over the realities of national security, as in the U-2 affair, the Bay of Pigs venture, and the involvement of intelligence agents, including Army agents, in Laos and Cambodia and in Chicago during the Democratic National Convention of 1968. The recent appointment of the Assistant Secretary of Defense for Administration (ASDA) as chief coordinator of Department of Defense intelligence has only partially allayed these fears.[7] The Deputy Assistant to the ASDA for intelligence, a military

[5] *Ibid.*

[6] Hilsman, p. 5.

[7] A thorough analysis of the intelligence community is found in G. F. Mauk, "Department of Defense Intelligence Resource Management," a thesis presented to the U.S. Army Command and General Staff College in partial fulfillment of the requirements of the degree of Master of Military Art and Science, Ft. Leavenworth, Kansas, 1971, pp. 18, 88–94.

officer of three-star rank, is in a position to influence the ASDA greatly in matters of Defense intelligence.

The fear that the intelligence community may exceed its proper bounds is not altogether unjustifiable. The shadowing of controversial youth leaders and a number of rather liberal congressmen does arouse suspicion as to the "normality" of military intelligence conduct.[8] The Central Intelligence Agency, in the process of policy implementation, on occasion has had under its jurisdiction airplanes and their pilots, naval vessels and their crews, and some army troops and artillery, as well as guerrilla training centers. The exact amount of money available to the intelligence agencies is secret, because the CIA is free from regular auditing and accounting procedures.[9]

TRADITIONAL POLITICAL-MILITARY RELATIONSHIPS

Because military organization and philosophy are not deemed democratic, the traditional civilian attitude toward the military has often been one of disdain, distrust, and even fear. Early pioneers of American democracy recalled only too well the exalted position of the military in the autocratic society of Mother Europe. They were adamant in their desire to subordinate the military in all matters of national significance, even though the military often constituted the means of achieving the objectives of national policy. This attitude is reflected in the constitutional provisions giving the President control over the armed forces.

Generally the military establishment was eschewed in national policy planning, and often it was conceived as a straw man to be whipped for the continuing Indian wars or excesses in government spending. Sometimes military leaders, particularly those of the army, were transferred to prevent any concentration of power. Many of our political leaders had acquired some military experience and therefore often felt that their knowledge of military affairs equalled that of the careerists.

Yet Americans have generally had a profound regard for the military hero (including the professional) and on six occasions have elected him to the Presidency, although the military as such has never been the instrument of his victory.[10] Military men in the White House have created no more than the usual effect on the formulation of national security policy and collectively have been more "peace minded" than other Presidents. The

[8] *Army Times,* "Military Spying Spurs Intelligence Shakeup," January 13, 1971, p. 6.

[9] Hilsman, p. 63.

[10] *Ibid.*, p. 51.

United States has never embarked upon war (except possibly with the Indians) under a "military" President. Thus Americans may feel that the election of war heroes to the highest office will not destroy the constitutional civilian control over the military—something that can be realized in few countries throughout history.[11]

Perhaps the most significant exception to the shunning of military figures in national security was Admiral Alfred T. Mahan, whose concepts of a new horizon for United States foreign policy were well tailored to the ideas of Theodore Roosevelt, Senators Lodge and Beveridge, and other expansionists. Mahan's thinking actually formed much of the blueprint—an unofficial one to be sure—for United States foreign policy at the turn of the twentieth century.

CHANGING ROLE OF THE MILITARY

Today it is a generally accepted dictum that diplomacy without power—political, military, economic, psychosociological—is feeble and that power without adequate diplomatic direction is futile and often counterproductive. It is an age-old dictum of international relations that the ultimate arbiter in diplomatic relations is military force, although we do not stress this point today. Ideally, the various elements of power and diplomacy should be mutually supporting. Yet it was not until the end of World War II that the United States accepted this harmonious combination theorem as a basic ingredient in the machinery of foreign-policy planning. Despite the present ebb tide of military popularity in the United States, as far as national security is concerned, military and nonmilitary factors are so clearly interrelated that they may be thought of as inseparable.

What motivated the post World War II appreciation of the role of the military in the formulation of United States foreign and national security policies? One reason certainly is the confidence the country has acquired in its ability to maintain civilian control of the military. The military, most of us now agree, "can be trusted," despite the renaissance of some popular suspicions due to the prolongation of the Vietnam war. Another reason lies in the revolutionary change in the direction of United States foreign policy in the late 1940's and the 1950's—i.e., from flexible "isolation" to world-wide entanglements. Still perhaps another stimulation to the trust in the military may be found in S. E. Finer's recent work, *The Man on Horseback:* The American people have reached a highly developed political culture and realize that the military has accepted a complete adherence to the principle of civil supremacy. According to Professor Finer, the military tends toward

[11] Paone, p. 10.

the constitutional and not the unconstitutional as in those states where the level of political culture is low. We also may feel that civilian leadership is sufficiently strong to defeat any unconstitutional moves of the military.

The military often has not presented a united front on military policy, even though their major differences may be reduced to an unrefined contrast between dichromatic doctrines. Some of these differences have been noted in a number of published "Pentagon Papers" and in the author's discussions with several flag officers.

After prolonged serious disagreements on priorities, the Air Force and the Navy have come to realize that there is a major function for each in the development of air strategy, and the Army now admits that flexible response requires both tactical and strategic power, even though it is committed to the development of a large tactical force. Despite a number of accusations to the contrary, civilian authorities have not abdicated responsibility for the creation of national security policy; there is little basis for the idea that the military controls government policy. It is generally accepted that General Matthew Ridgeway virtually vetoed the plan for a United States intervention in Vietnam in 1954. It was not the military who decided to make the recent conflict there an American one. In fact the military has generally opposed any limited land war on the Asian mainland.[12]

The new concept of political-military relations includes the old spectre of military responsiveness to the policies of the political administration leaders. It requires as well a greater degree of civilian expertise in military, economic, and scientific affairs to render the political leadership capable of proper decision-making. It would also admonish the Secretary of Defense and members of the Senate and House Military Affairs Committees against a too-quick development of a "military mind" in relating the power aspects of foreign-policy problems. As the military too must have a much greater knowledge of political, economic, and scientific endeavors, a trend has developed toward "militarization" of the civilian and "politicization" of the military. Some officers have urged a depoliticization of the military and the return of that group to a more meaningful professional attitude.[13]

Because of the immediate access of defense policy to congressional and public inquiry, which is often effected by the military, the civilian leadership has endeavored to develop a much wider knowledge of military programs and concomitantly exert a stronger control of the military even on the operational level.

The military has had to be brought into the inner sanctum of official

[12] Hilsman, p. 54.

[13] Frederick C. Thayer, "Professionalism: The Hard Choice," *U.S. Naval Institute Proceedings,* Annapolis, Maryland, June 1971, pp. 39–40. Also see Lawrence B. Tatum, "The Joint Chiefs of Staff and Defense Policy Formulation," *Air University Review,* May-June 1966, pp. 40–55; July-August 1966, pp. 11–20.

policy planning, formulation, and execution. Through regular institutional channels military recommendations are fused into foreign and national-security policy planning and execution. The realization that a nation as powerful as we are has been virtually paralyzed by the enormity of its weapons technology has forced a greater dependency of the political leadership on the military; as a result recommendations by the military are generally sought before the creation of United States foreign policy rather than after.

MACHINERY FOR CIVIL-MILITARY COOPERATION

With the ascendancy of the United States to a leading position in world affairs during the post-World War II era, a number of agencies for the pursuit of civil-military cooperation in the formulation of United States foreign policy were created. These include, among others, the National Security Council (NSC), the International Security Affairs Office of the Department of Defense, the Bureau of Politico-Military Affairs of the Department of State, the Politico-Military Policy Division (OP61) of the Office of the Chief of Naval Operations, and a similar office in the Joint Staff of the Joint Chiefs of Staff, commonly known as J-5. Both the Army and Air Force also have political-military divisions within the organization of offices of the respective Chiefs of Staff.

These agencies are the major focal points of institutionalism in the political-military functionalism forming United States foreign policy. Not one of these agencies makes policy; each, however, is generally given the opportunity to make inputs and present reactions to policies and programs under consideration by the President and can do so from both working and high-level vantage points. The President, however, is not bound to accept the recommendations emanating from these offices, nor does he have an absolute requirement to utilize them, although in other than crisis decisions he generally does.

It has become evident that President Eisenhower made many of his decisions by "calling in Secretary Dulles and a number of his trusted cronies." [14] Nevertheless, under him the National Security Council stepped away from being an organization of voices resplendent in wings of a conspicuous void and became a *bona fide* advisory body, achieving the same level of importance in executive planning as the Cabinet. Through the work of the Council the President can know the tenor of military thinking, even if the recommendations of the military are unacceptable to that body. The Chairman of the Joint Chiefs of Staff who attends all Council meetings has

[14] Interview with Mr. John Eisenhower, February 15, 1966.

a direct channel to the President. Mr. Kennedy did not utilize the services of the Council as profusely as had his predecessor until the latter part of 1962, although he generally sought the advice of a number of key individual members of that group.[15] President Kennedy streamlined much of the work of the NSC by creating an *ad hoc* committee for sudden emergencies, consisting of several key members of the NSC and several men outside the Council whose judgment he valued highly. This committee played a major role in deciding action related to the Cuban missile crisis in October 1962.[16]

President Johnson pursued a policy similar to that of Mr. Kennedy until the last two years of his administration, when he permitted the NSC to have a more active role in matters of foreign policy. Actually, Mr. Johnson generally used his "Tuesday luncheon" meetings with his top advisors as "the principal form of deliberation" and thus preempted the functions of the National Security Council.[17] Although it may be too early to assay the contributions of the NSC under President Nixon, under the White House Advisor for National Security Affairs the staff of the Council has been reorganized with a senior flag officer as a Deputy and "has never been so busy." It is generally felt by individuals who have served several administrations that through the NSC there is at present a more orderly approach to the problems of national security than has existed since the creation of the Council.[18]

The military has acquired a political role in the formulation of foreign policy that has created a dilemma between the partisan tenets of its professional creed and the necessity to participate effectively in the contemporary political process. The recommendations and reactions of military leaders are eagerly sought by the President and Congressional leaders for their respective advantages. Quite naturally, this new position has accentuated the politicization of the military.

THE INTERNATIONAL SECURITY AFFAIRS OFFICE OF THE DEPARTMENT OF DEFENSE

Although the Department of State did not establish its politico-military affairs staff until 1961, the Department of Defense has had its International Security Affairs (ISA) office since 1950. This office, of all the units under

[15] Vincent Davis, "American Military Policy: Decision Making in the Executive Branch," *Naval War College Review*, May 1970, Newport, Rhode Island, p. 8.

[16] Elie Abel, *The Missile Crisis*, Philadelphia, Pennsylvania: J. B. Lippincott Company, 1966, pp. 33–34, 44, 65.

[17] *Time*, February 14, 1969, "Kissinger: The Uses and Limits of Power."

[18] This idea of greater orderliness is refined somewhat by Edward A. Kologziej, "The National Security Council: Innovations and Implications," in the *Public Administration Review*, November-December 1969, pp. 573–585.

the Secretary of Defense, is the one most directly related to political-military cooperation in the formulation of both foreign and national security policies.

Charged with the development and conditioning of Defense policies in international political-military and foreign economic affairs, including the planning and direction of the Military Assistance Programs, this office coordinates relations between the Departments of Defense and State in the political-military area. This point is somewhat illustrated by the number of direct telephone lines between the counterparts of this office and the Bureau of Politico-Military Affairs of the Department of State.[19] This aspect of harmony, it must be emphasized, is reflected in the institutional structure, not necessarily in the ideas and personalities involved.[20] Currently ISA, with a staff of almost 300 people that includes approximately 150 professional or project officers of which some 75 are military officers, is composed of the following major units: Policy Plans and NSC Affairs; Director of Military Assistance and Sales; International Logistics Negotiations; and three regional offices that include Europe and NATO Affairs; East Asia and Pacific Affairs; Near Eastern, African and South Asian Affairs; Inter-American Affairs; and Foreign Trade, Disclosure and Military Rights Affairs.[21] Each office is headed by a Deputy Assistant Secretary.

Often called the "little Department of State," the International Security Affairs Office examines national policy or proposed policy for the Department of Defense in political-military terms, i.e., arms control, collective security arrangements, and foreign aid, as the Department of State, via its Politico-Military Staff, translates the same policy into the diplomatic steps to be taken. The International Security Affairs staff offers military considerations to a political policy, as the Bureau of Politico-Military Affairs of the Department of State scrutinizes the diplomatic ramifications of a proposed military policy. ISA also functions as a coordinator of research in the foreign-affairs recommendations made by the appropriate offices of the three services and by the Joint Staff of the Joint Chiefs of Staff.

The working relationships of the Assistant Secretary of Defense for International Security Affairs permits him to cut across many service and State Department lines. Transactional communication between the regional offices of ISA and the country desk officers of the Department of State[22]

[19] Personal observation.

[20] Interview with Mr. Jonathan Moore, Special Assistant to the Assistant Secretary of Defense, ISA, September 15, 1966.

[21] Thomas J. Bigley, "The Office of International Security Affairs," *U.S. Naval Institute Proceedings,* Annapolis, Maryland, April 1966, p. 64. Also see present organizational chart, "Office of the Assistant Secretary of Defense" (International Security Affairs).

[22] Conversations with Mr. Willard Mitchell, Policy Planning Staff, ISA, October 13, 1971.

has resulted in a focusing, increased under President Nixon, of a "great deal of power and influence on the Assistant Secretary which is readily transmitted through the Secretary of Defense to the National Security Council." [23] With the usually reliable information given him by ISA, the Secretary of Defense very often has played a leading role in the formulation of U.S. foreign and national security policies.

The Department of Defense policies in regard to foreign affairs are submitted to the President via the National Security Council Staff, composed of military and civilian specialists (about fifty substantive individuals) under the direction of the President's Adviser for National Security Affairs. In many Washington circles it is asserted that, despite all the organic institutionalism for political-military relations in foreign policy formulation, this NSC staff often "runs the country." The Director of this staff usually sees the President daily and generally without appointment, whereas the Secretaries of Defense and State (before Dr. Kissinger became Secretary of State) spend much less time with the President, which lends support to this contention.[24]

BUREAU OF POLITICO-MILITARY AFFAIRS OF THE DEPARTMENT OF STATE

The Department of State has been dealing with political-military problems through its Political-Military staff, created in 1961, and earlier via the regional bureaus, the Policy Planning Council, and other groups within the Department. The Deputy Undersecretary of State for Political Affairs had worked with senior Defense officials and the Joint Chiefs of Staff, but on a so-called "required" basis that proved inadequate. The Department required a regular organization that could view political-military problems on a worldwide basis and simultaneously provide a focal point for the political-military activities of the Department's regional bureaus. Some State staff was needed to review the total national defense effort and the major lines of policy being executed by the Department of Defense in terms of their foreign policy implications. Certainly, it would also be much more convenient to have one central point of contact within the State Department accessible to the Defense Department.[25] It would be somewhat unfortunate

[23] Bigley, p. 70.

[24] According to *Time* in "Kissinger: The Uses and Limits of Power," February 14, 1969, the Director of the National Security Council Staff saw the President "an average of 90 minutes a day, apart from formal meetings of the National Security Council."

[25] Interview with Mr. Seymour Weiss, Director for Combined Policy, Politico-Military Staff, Department of State, September 15, 1966.

if the Defense people decided to construct a submarine base in Upper Strata when State has made known publicly that the United States will not construct a submarine base in that country or to have State announce that we will reinforce our troops in South Vietnam as Defense redeploys the armed forces there. Today any unusual redeployment of troops is reviewed by the Bureau of Political-Military Affairs of the Department of State for any possible diplomatic implications.[26]

To promote further political-military coordination between Defense and State, an exchange of officer personnel was inaugurated in 1960. Military officers are working in the Bureau of Politico-Military Affairs, and Foreign Service Officers are on duty in the Department of Defense's International Security Affairs office. The normal tour of duty is two years. On a long-term basis, the Department of State presently also assigns foreign service officers to the war colleges, the political-military sections of the services, and other military educational institutions as advisors, students, liaison officers, and faculty. Political advisors are assigned to major United States military commands, and military officers attend the Foreign Service Institute of the Department of State. To accentuate the institutionalism currently recognized in political-military relations, both the Undersecretary of State and the Deputy Secretary of Defense serve on four of the five Standing Committees of the National Security Council.

ANATOMY OF DECISION-MAKING

Now the question arises, What about the mechanism of decision-making? Certainly this machinery requires the most thorough political and military coordination. Let us suppose that as the implementation of the Nassau Agreement begins to take shape, our national plans for Polaris forces are changed to require another Polaris submarine base abroad. While this requirement seems to be an uncomplicated military matter, it is in reality fraught with political and economic ramifications and does implicate an important question of national policy. In foreign affairs, as the student of international relations so well knows, nothing is devoid of complications. If some element seems simple, the search for its complex ramifications should be all the more intense.

Such a decision as the location of a submarine base must be viewed from various directions. Will the proposed site be in an area consistent with over-all political-military policy or national policy? How much will it cost and which country will construct it? Another significant factor is the domestic political climate, i.e., the attitude of Congressional leaders. At least

[26] *Ibid.*

as important as the other elements are the international security situation and the Department of State views.

After the proposal is accepted by the NSC, the Director of its staff will issue a directive to the Departments of Defense and State, via the Deputy Secretary of Defense and the Undersecretary of State, to explore relations with the country of the proposed site and the feasibility of constructing the submarine base there. The Assistant Secretary of Defense, ISA, probably would be given the responsibility of guiding the proposal through the agencies involved. Will that country accept the submarine base? What compensation will be required? What would be the effect of the base on our allies and the multilateral force agreements question? What will be the reaction of other major powers? Once Defense and State have weighed and reviewed these questions, additional help probably would be requested from the Joint Staff of the Joint Chiefs, the Politico-Military Division of the Department of the Navy, the Defense Intelligence Agency, and other groups, including the Central Intelligence Agency.

The input from all these agencies will produce a "working-level" paper, which will be refined into a Defense Memorandum. The "working-level" paper is reviewed and, if need be, amended by the National Security Council Staff and dispatched to Defense and State and other agencies involved for finalization on an Undersecretary level. Although the proposal to construct this submarine base seems peculiarly a military concern, it must be approved by State. If it is not, then it is written in such a manner as to indicate the views of both Defense and State. Needless to say, a number of *ad hoc* committees of working-level diplomatic and military personnel confer to work out differences of opinions. Personnel in J-5 of the Joint Chiefs of Staff, OP61 of the Navy, and the Bureau of Political-Military Affairs of State will have made inputs into the "working-level" paper. As they do not see the full spectrum of all inputs until the Undersecretary "go-round," they are generally afforded a second opportunity for comments when this takes place.

Although this process is often cumbersome and time-consuming, it does reflect the practical necessity for a multi-directional approach to a problem and certainly reflects the functional institutionalism of political-military relations in the formulation of national policy.

Let's follow the refined proposal further. Rewritten and even further refined by the National Security Council Staff, sometimes in such a way as to reflect predominantly the desires of the Director of the Staff, it is sent to the President as a Defense Memorandum.[27] The President may request additional views from the NSC, the Joint Chiefs of Staff, various members of his cabinet, or from his Advisor on National Security Affairs. It is the

[27] Interview with several members of the National Security Council Staff, October 1971.

President's prerogative to accept those recommendations he thinks are best suited to the national security policy, regardless of their source.

Having accepted the Defense Memorandum as presented or recommended, the President thereupon orders action via a National Security Action Memorandum, which is a crisp summary of the President's decision coupled with an assignment of duties and orders. The Department of State will open negotiations with the other government to receive the Polaris submarine base, while representatives of Defense assist with discussions on a technical level. The Department of State in this case is regarded as the Captain of the team; Defense, at least in theory, knows this as the final negotiations are completed.

The pathway just described is the usual one pursued in political-military considerations of United States foreign policy. Neither the Department of State nor the Department of Defense is autonomous in this function; both, working for the Chief Executive, have been institutionally drawn together in many aspects of United States foreign policy formulation.

IN RETROSPECT

This study has dealt with the organization of the flow of political-military considerations in the formulation of United States foreign affairs. Whereas an orderly, functional institutionalism does exist that seems reasonably effective and practical, although at times too slow and repetitive, some factors have yet to be mentioned. One is the human element. All kinds of hindrances develop if the human factor does not reflect cooperation. The ability to persuade without a resultant aggravation or agitation is an indescribable factor that cannot be measured in the contrivance of political-military equations, even though it is essential to the effective action of that conversion mechanism. Without it the system will crack and perhaps even break down.

Another consideration is the personal make-up of the President himself. An elastic flexibility within which foreign policy formulation may fluctuate exists because the President need not follow the pathways of political-military efforts emphasized in this paper. In crisis decisions he cannot use them. At other times he may order that nongovernmental studies be made, as well as independent ones within government agencies.

A suggestion that a Polaris submarine base be constructed in Upper Strata can be studied from many directions, but what of critical problems that have to be solved quickly—if not yesterday? Where does the organization for political-military considerations fit into the much faster tempo of solving this type of crisis? Is there no structure for this type decision-making?

The Cuban crisis of late 1962 is a vivid point of illustration. Here the President and his chief advisors personally immersed themselves in the problem of Soviet missiles located 90 miles from our shores. Mr. Kennedy quickly formed an executive *ad hoc* committee of the National Security Council composed of the Secretaries of Defense and State, the U.S. Ambassador to the UN, and General Taylor, Military Advisor to the President, and added several other key men, i.e., Dean Acheson, John McCone, Robert Kennedy, and McGeorge Bundy.[28] The "Rump Parliament" met twice daily and for several days sat in virtually continuous session. Discussions led by Robert Kennedy, Mr. Bundy, and Mr. McNamara naturally centered on both defense and diplomatic considerations. State, it is generally regarded, was more heavily represented than Defense and somewhat more volatile.

The President—there is no doubt here—was in charge, and after all the issues were identified and comprehended he made the decision. He did not utilize the full spectrum of Defense and State we have outlined. He did, however, make use of the principle of coordination that was seeded into political-military functionalism. He did not have time to be tied down to advice except that which emanated from high-level and personally trusted advisors. This certainly was no time to become a "prisoner of staff reports."

Even with changes of administrations and within administrations, the conversion mechanism for the flow of political-military considerations in foreign affairs does exist on working and executive levels and is readily available to policy-makers. More significantly, whether the decision must be reached quickly or within a reasonable allotted time, there is a specific acknowledgement that it can be made only after necessary political-military inputs have been considered. Presidents Johnson and Nixon reflected this in their "crisis" decisions related to the invasions of the Dominican Republic and Cambodia respectively.

How the contrivance of political-military considerations in foreign policy formulation is utilized by the President is his prerogative. We are aware that all the groups involved in this multiplex machine are concerned with foreign policy; no one office makes it. The President and his political men, from his Assistant Secretaries on up, are the actual policy-makers. They all, however, depend upon coordination and cohesion generally across departmental lines for the refinements that are ultimately consolidated into a recommendation to the President.

[28] Abel, pp. 33–34.

5

The Defense Budget and Civil-Military Relations

ROBERT A. BENDER

LOGIC AND THE DEFENSE BUDGET

"In May, 1946, the President decreed that in Fiscal year 1948 military activities could have one third of the funds remaining after the fixed charges had been met." [1]

In practice this "remainder method" came to mean that the defense budget should be whatever remained after both fixed charges such as interest on the debt and the cost of domestic programs had been subtracted from probable federal government revenues. And, lest the reader suspect that President Truman was unique in this rather arbitrary method of establishing a defense-budget ceiling, it should be noted that, save for the two Korean War years, President Eisenhower used this same approach throughout the fifties.[1A]

To many observers this seat-of-the-pants calculation of so vital a matter as the limits of national defense was both irrational and irresponsible. First, it was irrational in that the resulting figure often bore no necessary relation to the goals and strategy of our foreign policy. For example, in the spring of 1950 both the JCS and the State Department offered overwhelming evidence (in National Security Council Paper #68) of sharply increased Soviet strength and urgently recommended a corresponding increase in ours. The Administration, however, stubbornly maintained the existing defense ceiling until finally the Korean War outbreak forced its

[1] Samuel P. Huntington, *The Common Defense* (New York: Columbia University Press, 1966). Once one has studied this superb and all-inclusive volume on the military during the Truman and Eisenhower years, there is no escaping its overwhelming influence in any attempt to write further on the subject. I am therefore constantly indebted to Prof. Huntington for both my approach and treatment of this period of budget making.

[1A] see Table 1 for budget statistics during these and succeeding administrations.

hand. Equally unresponsive to changes in the international situation was the Eisenhower Administration in the latter fifties. Despite the Laotian, Hungarian, and Lebanese crises and the alarming appearance of Sputnik, no serious change in the level of defense spending was forthcoming.

Indeed the record of the Eisenhower years suggests that, rather than develop a budget to support a particular strategy, one can do quite the reverse. The strategy of "massive retaliation" as proclaimed by Secretary of State Dulles was almost certainly the product of the administration's open commitment to a stable level of defense spending, although it could perhaps be somewhat justified as an attempt to make the fullest use of the new atomic technology. Reliance on air-atomic or tactical nuclear response to enemy action made possible an enormous reduction of conventional—especially Army—forces and a corresponding stabilization of the budget at roughly $40 billion in the middle fifties. On the other hand, this approach to international affairs meant we had but one response to any possible threat to our own or our allies' security—atomic devastation.

> It could well be asked whether in an open society in which rationality is encouraged and there is a demand for political accountability, massive retaliation would, in fact, be a response to any but the most direct and provocative of communist actions. In this context, Dulles' doctrine lacked credibility.[2]

Equally lacking in credibility was the Administration's insistence that it was getting—in Secretary of Defense Wilson's immortal words—"a bigger bang for a buck"; instead it seems clear that the Administration's concern for an "economy budget" led it to adopt an almost certainly useless strategy.

On the other hand, criticisms of the arbitrary ceiling limit as irrational and irresponsible are borne out by the frequent Executive appeal to fallacious or irrelevant economic contentions.

First and foremost of course was the claim of the necessity to limit defense spending in order to balance the budget, quite as if matching government income and expenditures each time the earth travelled around the sun had a peculiar merit. As any college student who has passed an elementary course in economics knows, a balanced federal budget makes sense *only* when the private sector of the economy is behaving precisely as we want it to, i.e., providing full employment, relative price stability, and reasonably rapid growth. Otherwise a government surplus to dampen inflation or a government deficit to stimulate growth or employment is economic common sense. Furthermore, in the unlikely event we should economically wish a balanced budget, more defense spending would easily be accommodated

[2] Gene M. Lyons, "The Pressures of Military Necessity," in *Contemporary American Foreign and Military Policy*, Burton M. Sapin (ed.), (Glenview, Illinois: Scott, Foresman, and Company, 1970).

either by lessening government spending elsewhere or, if that proved economically unwise, by raising taxes. The fact that both these measures, of course, are apt to be politically inexpedient only suggests the nature of the "balanced budget" argument, i.e., an appeal to public ignorance rather than to economic merit.

A second argument, that "our resources are limited: we can spend just so much on defense," is simply irrelevant, as John Galbraith made clear in his *Affluent Society*.[3] Whereas Ghana or Bolivia could scarcely support our defense effort because of (among other things) a lack of resources, our present limits have to do only with our willingness to commit resources to defense, not with our ability to do so. Indeed, especially considering that 6% of our work force and some 25% of our productive capacity is presently unused—or unemployed, we could obviously vastly increase our defense effort with no strain whatever on our resources. Again the question is political, not economic.

A third concern voiced frequently as a reason for defense limitations is that additional government spending will cause inflation. The answer to this of course is that it will cause more "demand-pull" inflation *only* if there is little unused productive capacity in the economy. If there is much unused capacity as in 1940-41, even enormous increases in government spending will simply increase the level of production. "Cost-push inflation," of course, has no necessary relation whatever to government spending.

The final two economic arguments so often used to disguise political expediency in this field we will consider together. One, frequently voiced by President Eisenhower as being a deliberate Soviet aim, is that we will spend ourselves into bankruptcy through continued large defense budgets. The other argument, one that we have heard officially only recently, is that we must continue our high level of defense spending to maintain full employment and prosperity. Taking these together, of course, leaves one agasp at the unique ability of military spending to bring on both bankruptcy and prosperity. And yet our point is not only that one argument must be wrong, but rather that both are absurdities. As with the argument of limited resources, there is no need whatever to face "bankruptcy" (a most imprecise term) as a result of any remotely realistic defense budget, provided we are willing to make sacrifices elsewhere. As for the second argument, government spending on defense or the SST just to maintain full employment can easily (economically speaking) be replaced by government spending on other worthwhile public services.

On the one hand, the specious nature of these arguments should make it clear that they were nothing more than rationalizations of a desire to keep

[3] John Galbraith, *The Affluent Society* (New York: New York Library, Inc., 1958), Chapter XII, "The Illusion of National Security."

defense expenditures stable and preferably low. On the other hand, that such specious arguments could be used and widely accepted suggests that *perhaps there is no clearly rational way to estimate what should be spent for our defenses,* especially when that defense is not put to any wartime test of its efficacy. Indeed, the imponderables of the defense question make the appeal to the political possible, perhaps even inevitable. For politics is, after all, a method "for resolving through the interplay of power, those questions that do not lend themselves to intellectual resolution." [4] Hence, while criticizing these administrations for indulging in economically nonsensical justifications and dubious military strategy, it is necessary to see their behavior in political terms, that is, as designed to meet the minimum demands of the various groups represented in the administration, without unduly disturbing a reasonably passive electorate.

POLITICAL ACCOMMODATION AND NATIONAL SECURITY

It always seems shocking to a novice in the study of pluralistic American democracy that defense policy and the level of defense spending should be a product of the interplay of interest groups. That this is true of the general American public even today—despite the continuous interest-group hassles of the late forties and fifties—is obvious from the outraged reactions to the recent CBS television program, *The Selling of the Pentagon.* Liberals were furious that the Pentagon should be "propagandizing"—especially with tax money—as any interest group does. Conservatives, on the other hand, were furious that the Pentagon had been accused of behaving like an interest group.

The reasons for this lack of public understanding are not hard to find. First, it is well nigh unthinkable to the average citizen that national security should represent less than the national interest or that it should in any way be the plaything of parochial interests. Then, of course, ever since Madison denounced "factions," any good American has known that interest groups are but conniving, self-seeking aggregations—all, that is, save those he himself identifies with. And finally, the struggle of those interest groups to determine national strategy and defense spending takes place in only a very limited degree where we would expect it—in the public spotlight of Congress. Rather it is in the relative privacy and seclusion of the Executive Branch that the critical battles occur. Here, writes Professor Huntington, "just as agricultural policy is the product of conflict, bargaining, and com-

[4] Quoted in Michael H. Armacost, *The Politics of Weapons Innovation* (New York: Columbia University Press, 1969).

promise among the interested groups in Congress, military strategy is the product of conflict, bargaining, and compromise among the interested groups in the Joint Chiefs of Staff and in the National Security Council." [5] It is again here that "The conflicts between budgeteers and security spokesmen, between the defenders of military and nonmilitary programs, among the four services, and among the partisans of massive retaliation, continental defense, and limited war, are as real and as sharp as most conflicts of interest groups in Congress." [6]

What follows is another equally critical and equally unexpected factor in the formulation of the defense budget. The President, in contrast to popular myth, must act largely the part of the judge among conflicting interests and contentions rather than that of a dynamic leader and decision-maker. For one thing, he must keep peace within his own executive home, which is made up of leaders and representatives of the many and varied interest groups that add up to his "national constituency." This means compromises and concessions to produce consensus. To an extent his leadership depends on his personality, his popularity, and his preferences. Second, and probably just as important, in the field of foreign and military policy, as nowhere else, he is dealing in imponderables of enormous consequence. In short, he has neither the power (save in a "productive crisis"), the knowledge, or the self-assurance (foolhardiness?) to act without the general consent of his political family in this field. He needs them quite as much as they need him.

To be sure, Congress does enter into the making of the defense budget. The committees concerned with military affairs generally consider strategy-making not their business. We should, said one Congressman, but in no way do concern ourselves with "policy determination." [7] Or again, to quote the Chairman of the Senate Armed Forces Committee, consider Senator Richard Russell's famous remark, "God help the American people if Congress ever starts legislating military strategy." [8] The reason is simple: no particular Congressman has any overwhelming constituency interested in strategy as such. With "force make-up," things are quite different. Here many groups—National Guardsmen, military contractors, veterans, and patriotic groups—have vested interests in maintaining or if possible expanding the activities of their particular favorites. Thus, for example, the National Guard Association was powerful not only in pursuading Congress in 1958 "to appropriate funds for 400,000 Army Guardsmen (instead of the 360,000 asked by the Administration) but also in obtaining language

[5] Huntington, *The Common Defense,* p. 154.

[6] *Ibid.*, p. 146.

[7] L. A. Dexter, "Interviews with 100 Congressmen," in *The Components of Defense Policy*, D. B. Bobrow (ed.), (Chicago: Rand, McNally and Company, 1965).

[8] *New York Times,* March 15, 1953, p. 17.

making maintenance of 400,000 men mandatory upon the Executive Branch." [9] Yet save for rare occasions when virtual unanimity permits such action, all Congress can do is appropriate more funds, leaving the decision to spend them or not in the hands of the Administration. To quote the possibly exaggerated lament of the House Armed Services Committee in 1962, "more and more the role of Congress has come to be that of a sometimes querulous but essentially kind uncle who complains while furiously puffing over his pipe but who finally, as everyone expects, gives in and hands over the allowance. . . ." [10]

Consequently, never from World War II until 1969 did the Administration receive essentially less overall money than it requested, both for the reasons just suggested and because public opinion during the entire period was willing to support greater funds for defense.[11]

The first step then—setting the over-all levels of defense spending and the general strategy—has always been pretty much a product of political accommodation within the Administration. The next step has been to allot the funds among the services in accordance with the general strategy. As prior to the Korean War we were thinking of war readiness in terms of mobilization of the World War II type of forces, defense funds were almost evenly divided among the major services. Once the strategy had shifted in the fifties to deterrence via primarily air-atomic power, however, the lion's share went to the Air Force; hence, throughout the latter fifties the Air Force steadily received approximately 47% to 49%, the Navy 28% to 29%, and the Army 23% to 25% of the total defense funds.[12] At this level too the ceilings tended to become "arbitrary" because, regardless of changing needs, each service got its "regular cut," so to speak. Once the proportions were allotted, each service was responsible for spending its share to help carry out the over-all strategic goals under the very loose coordination of the JCS. Thus during both the Truman and Eisenhower presidencies, the defense budget became simply the combined budgets of the services.

This method of handling the defense budget was to have some surprising bearing on civil-military relations. For one thing, there was curiously little reaction by the military against the arbitrary budget ceilings, even when they were lowered after World War II and the Korean War. The reasons appear to be several. For one thing the military were overwhelmingly

[9] Martha Duthick, "The Militia Lobby in The Missile Age: The Politics of the National Guard," in *Changing Patterns of Military Politics,* S. P. Huntington (ed.), (New York: Free Press of Glencoe, Inc., 1962).

[10] Quoted in Jack Raymond, *Power at the Pentagon* (New York: Harper and Row, 1964).

[11] *New York Times,* August 14, 1969, p. 14:3. Also see the Chapter on Public Opinion and The Military.

[12] See Table 1.

conservative and generally accepted as true the economic arguments earlier noted.[13] Second, once a decision on the over-all level of defense spending had been reached within the Administration, it would have done the military little good to have appealed to either Congress or the public for, as we have said earlier, there was no way to force the Administration to spend more than it wished to. To suggest that the military, by not openly protesting these ceilings, were thereby demonstrating their respect for "civilian supremacy" seems far less pertinent than to suggest that they had fought their battle in the only available arena and lost. Last, the JCS, the only body that could have contested the over-all defense level, was scarcely a sufficiently unified body to do this. The primary concern of each of its members was the welfare of his own service rather than the total picture, a fact that explains General Taylor's comment that "The Joint Chiefs of Staff as a body took no part in the formulation of the 1960 budget—nor had they in previous years." [14]

On the other hand, sharp and unequal cuts in the appropriations of a single service brought notable reactions. As Professor Wildavsky notes, in any budgetary process ". . . marked departures from the commonly held notion of fair shares would generate opposition." [15] It did. When, for example, Army funds were sharply and disproportionately cut from $16.3 billion in 1953 to 8.9 billion in 1955 in the shift from mobilization strategy to deterrence, the result was an appeal over the heads of both the Administration and an unsympathetic Congress to the public. Army Chief of Staff General Matthew Ridgeway in 1955 (after his retirement), General James Gavin in 1958, and Ridgeway's successor General Maxwell Taylor all wrote books scathingly denouncing the doctrine of "massive retaliation" and the reduction of conventional (Army) forces.[16] However, in view of the remarkably dignified and intellectual nature of their appeal and the fact that their arguments slowly but surely won the day (General Taylor was brought from retirement to become President Kennedy's military advisor), the whole episode probably represented a gain for civil-military relations.

On the other hand, a distinct loss resulted from the brief but explosive "Revolt of the Admirals" in 1949 against Secretary of Defense Louis Johnson's cancellation of the flush-deck carrier. What so piqued the Navy was that both Congress and the Administration had already approved the car-

[13] My personal observation at the Academy suggests that this is certainly true of the senior officers. Just last spring, for example, a military Head of Department asked my confirmation of his conviction that all government spending was inflationary.

[14] Maxwell D. Taylor, *The Uncertain Trumpet* (New York: Harper, 1969), p. 69.

[15] Aaron Wildavsky, *The Politics of the Budgetary Process* (Boston: Little, Brown and Company, 1964), p. 154.

[16] Taylor, *op cit.;* Matthew B. Ridgeway, *Soldier* (New York: Harper, 1956); James M. Gavin, *War and Peace in the Space Age* (New York: Harper, 1958).

rier, and Secretary Johnson's economy move represented a unilateral withdrawal of funds already voted; hence, the Navy appealed over the head of the Administration to a sympathetic Congressional committee. Fortunately for the Navy, Johnson was already unpopular for other reasons and resigned the following year. Even so, the funds were never restored.

The real problem came at the service level. Individual service budgets were also thought of as ways of keeping spending down rather than as a method of positive control over what each service did with its allotment, as long as it was within the limits of the general strategic plan. The trouble was that the over-all strategy concepts were extremely vague. As General Taylor said of the Eisenhower formal strategy guidance papers, "The basic National Security Policy document means all things to all people and settles nothing." [17] The consequence was that each service was able—indeed, encouraged—to base "its planning and force structures on a unilateral view of priorities and how a future war might be fought." [18] Finally, each service presented its claims for new funds to the Administration and Congress alike in categories such as personnel, construction, and the like, which tended to obscure such goals and priorities as each service was setting. General Taylor's comment summarizes the resulting confusion nicely: "It is not an exaggeration to say that nobody knows what we are actually buying with any specific budget." [19]

MILITARY COMPETITION FOR THE BANG IN THE BUCK

With these conditions—that is, the inability of the services to react "upward" against the intense pressure of the Administration for low budget ceilings and the lack of clearly defined boundaries of each service's activities, it was inevitable that the services would attempt expansion "outward" and equally inevitable that severe friction, indeed, virtual open warfare, between the services would follow.

It is not our intention to recount these struggles, save to say that they covered every possible point of contention—strategy, appropriateness of weapons and weapon systems, control of weapon systems, and always, funds. Nor are the varieties of competition important, save to say it was carried on in Congress among committees, subcommittees, and individual Congressmen, on TV where the Army and Navy each had regular programs,

[17] Taylor, *op. cit.*, p. 83.

[18] Alain C. Enthoven and Wayne K. Smith, *How Much is Enough* (New York: Harper and Row, 1971), p. 10.

[19] Taylor, *op. cit.*, p. 70.

in newspapers with constant service news releases about their own merits (or leaks about the other services' failings), by columnists, in the comic strips (where the Air Force was dominant with its *Steve Canyon* and *Terry and the Pirates*), and by the Air Forces Association, the Navy League, the Army Association, the National Guard, the Reserves, the military contractors for each of the Services—through any and all media. From personal memory of the times while a faculty member at the Naval Academy, one recalls only a steady stream of rancorous, interservice arguments, fortunately interrupted now and then by the far less heated and considerably more thoughtful disputations on interservice football supremacy.

Our concern here is, however, with the effect of this on civil-military relations. It was not apparently a question of public reaction against the military as a whole, for the public throughout the period was willing to support heavier defense spending. However, "interservice rivalry, outside groups often argued, was the source of many evils in the Department of Defense. Interservice harmony, the elimination of duplication (rational organization), reduced costs, and greater unification were often seen as directly related." [20] More important was the reaction of President Eisenhower, who was "determined to eliminate the public impression that service rivalry was pervasive and harmful." [21]

The next step of course was the Reorganization Act of 1958, which gave "the Secretary of Defense the authority to determine the force structure of the combatant commands—and to transfer, reassign, abolish, and consolidate combatant functions." [22] Thus the excesses of interservice rivalries played a part in eliminating their very cause by helping to produce Defense Department integration with—for the first time—real military as well as real financial power in the hands of the Secretary of Defense. Here at last was a serious attempt to bridge the gap between civilians setting arbitrary ceilings at both national and service levels on military spending—from the top down, so to speak—and the services planning their individual strategies and military force requirements from the bottom up. And, although the power to do this was available in 1958, it was not until Robert McNamara became Secretary of Defense in 1961 that the attempt to bridge this gap was made.

The word "attempt" is used advisedly, for the aim was no less than to deal rationally with one of "those questions that do not lend themselves to intellectual resolution." To begin with the fundamental question of the over-all fiscal confines of the defense effort, working on the assumption that "the United States is well able to spend whatever it needs to spend on

[20] Huntington, *The Common Defense,* p. 416.
[21] Armacost, *op. cit.,* p. 234.
[22] Enthoven, *op. cit.,* p. 2.

national security," President Kennedy authorized Secretary McNamara to determine and provide for security needs "without arbitrary budget limits, but to do so as economically as possible." [23] In theory this was a complete departure from arbitrary budget ceilings. In practice, of course, President Kennedy was no more free than his predecessors from political pressures when it came to the spending of well over half the Federal budget. However, what is suggested here is a reversing of the priorities. Defense needs would come first, a proposition supported by the sharp escalation of defense budgets in the first few Kennedy years. Now other programs would come from the "remainder."

Then too, the improvement in clearly stating the over-all strategy that the Department of Defense was to support was but a matter of degree. Rather than the formal but vague statements of national security policy of earlier days, Presidents Kennedy and Johnson preferred the more pragmatic approach of issuing specific policy declarations on particular problems. Draft Presidential Memorandums, initiated by the Secretary of Defense, also dealt with fundamental policy assumptions and conclusions on specific programs such as General Purpose Forces and Research and Development (some 16 in all by 1968); these as well as the Presidential declarations were circulated throughout the Department of Defense to assure common understanding on all major questions. They were helpful, to be sure, yet the only overview of national defense strategy came from the Department of Defense itself in its annual "posture statement" that accompanied the yearly presentation of the defense budget to Congress. These, "under Secretary McNamara became an exceptionally articulate analysis of the world situation, United States foreign policy objectives, military strategy, and force structures comparing favorably with the military portions of the old BNSP papers," and were assumed to have "tacit Presidential consent." [24] A better approach, perhaps, and certainly one that gave the President more flexibility, but for planning purposes it was hardly a military blue print.

Third, the strategic plan was broken down into its component parts or programs, some nine functional commands such as strategic retaliatory forces, continental defense, and so on. Priorities were determined among these, and for each program an attempt was made to establish a concrete goal. For example, the goal of strategic retaliation was "assured destruction" of 20% to 25% of the Soviet population and 50% of her industrial capacity. Finally, a study of alternate ways of accomplishing these goals was made.

[23] Robert S. McNamara, *The Essence of Security* (New York: Harper and Row, 1968), p. 87, 88.

[24] K. C. Clark and L. J. Legere, *The President and The Management of National Security* (New York: Frederick A. Praeger, 1969), p. 240.

Again there was nothing terribly new here. Unified commands had steadily developed during the fifties and, if priorities among them were not formally stated, the Administration had made its emphasis clear, for instance, by enormously increasing the air-atomic deterrent power of the Air Force while cutting funds for conventional Army forces. Although the attempt to state the goals of each program in precise terms was new with Secretary McNamara, some areas—such as continental defense—defied any exact definition even under McNamara. Finally, the search for alternative ways to achieve these goals was hardly novel, for this was precisely what the struggles between Army's *Jupiter* and the Air Force's *Thor*, or the Army's *Nike* and the Navy's *Talos,* had been about. However, what was new, distinctly new, was *who* was going to determine which alternative to choose and upon what *basis*. The *who* of course was Secretary McNamara and his staff, originally with the aid of his Department of Defense comptroller and his experts, and after 1965 with a separate Systems Analysis Office as well. The *basis* was cost-effectiveness.

The individual service would now find that the approval and support of its own military experts, its own scientists, and its own intelligence agency were no longer enough to gain the Secretary's approval for its programs. Nor would the additional approval of the JCS necessarily carry the day. Finally, the services would no longer find the Secretary a mere referee to work out a satisfactory compromise among competing service programs. Now a single Defense Intelligence Agency would furnish common data to all. Supervision of all Research and Development was in control of a common Department of Defense Director of Defense Research and Engineering. Individual service proposals for accomplishing particular programs were of course still offered, but now these had to be offered in terms of fully and carefully determined costs along with the expected military results calculated as precisely as possible. These were then subjected to Systems Analysis Office, which exercised one of several choices. One, it could play the role of "devil's advocate," to use Senator Jackson's description, and seek out every imaginable flaw in the Service's proposal. Two, it could submit alternative plans from the same and/or other services. Three, it could make its own independent study of the question if it hadn't already done so. Secretary McNamara and his staff then determined which alternative offered the greatest return per dollar of investment; that is, they chose what appeared to them the most efficient and economical way to accomplish the particular goal. For all programs the means thus chosen and their estimated costs were projected for a five-year period, the complete process being known as the Planning-Programming-Budgeting System (PPBS). The defense budget now, far from the old combined-service budgets, was a clear quantitative statement of a unified defense plan devised and developed along standards set by the Secretary of Defense. The budget was his method both of assuming active leadership in defense planning and of exercising a goodly measure of postive control in its execution.

The reaction of the military was predictably one of outrage. Curiously, it was not aimed particularly at the claim of economies or more efficiency, or such further "centralizing" tendencies as the setting up of a common Communications or Supply Agency. When Secretary McNamara reported a $14 billion saving in the first five-year program,[25] the great defender of the traditional military, *New York Times* military analyst Hanson Baldwin, admitted that McNamara had "certainly instituted some much needed management reforms, effected some economies, and added considerably to our ready strategic strength and our conventional war and general support forces," partly by bringing to a halt "the proliferation of unneeded weapons, and the expenditure of billions on projects that turned out to be 'duds' or duplications of others." [26] Rather, the anger of the military was aimed overwhelmingly at the predominately civilian-staffed Systems Analysis Office run by the "Whiz Kids" who "complete with slide rules and computers, brushed aside the factor of professional judgment or scientific hunch." [27] Air Force Generals T.D. White and Curtis LeMay denounced "defense intellectuals" who lacked "sufficient worldliness or motivation to stand up to the kind of enemy we face" and who "posed as 'Experts' in a field where they had no experience," proposing "strategy based on hopes and fears rather than upon facts and seasoned judgment." [28] Admiral Rickover felt the "social scientists who have been making the so called cost-effectiveness studies have little or no scientific training or technical expertise." [29] Armed Forces Management early in 1963 warned McNamara that "your staff is in revolt! . . . when you refute with generalities the technical recommendations of military officers . . . it is extremely risky business, no matter what the management motives." [30] In 1969 it was still pointing out that "under the mailed fist of the McNamara regime all decisions were made at the Secretary's level with the Director, Defense Research and Engineering, and the Assistant Secretary for Systems Analysis flanking as advisors. In fact the services were, on occasion, treated in almost cavalier fashion. . . ." [31] The point of course was that neither Secretary McNamara nor his staff—in their own opinion—were ignoring military judgment at all but were merely put-

[25] McNamara, *op. cit.*, p. 102.

[26] Hanson Baldwin, "Slow-down at the Pentagon," in *Defense, Science, and Public Policy,* Edwin Mansfield (ed.), (New York: W. W. Norton and Company, 1968), pp. 63, 65.

[27] *Ibid.*, p. 63.

[28] Quoted in Enthoven, *op. cit.*, p. 78.

[29] *Ibid.*, p. 78.

[30] Editorial, *Armed Forces Management,* June 1963, p. 11.

[31] Editorial, *Armed Forces Management,* October 1969, p. 35.

ting it in its proper place. Comptroller Hitch himself admitted that there "was no reliable quantitative data for military worth," that "mathematical models and computations" were "in no sense alternatives to or rivals of good intuitive judgment, (but) they supplement and complement it." Indeed "systems analysis is simply a method to get before the decision maker the relevant data. . . ." [32] To McNamara and his staff the relevant data included considerably more than the "purely military." Colonel Ginsburgh of the Air Force, even while criticizing the assault on "military professionalism," saw this point and admitted that with the new and ever-changing technology the scientist, the engineer, and the industrialist had all become the military's "partners," especially when the military could no longer claim the advantage of experience in atomic warfare.[33] Systems Analysis Chief Enthoven would add more "partners," for instance, when determining as complex a question as the number of American divisions that ought to be stationed in Europe; experts on the balance of payments problem; experts to make "political and psychological judgments" on the reactions of Europeans, friend and foe alike, to our troops there; experts on the extent of the Soviet threat, the deterrent value of our strategic nuclear power, and the like.[34] In short, rarely were questions purely military; professional military judgment was but one of many factors in the equation, all of which one did one's best to reduce to the common language of "cost-effectiveness" to make a rational judgment possible. Secondly, even if a question were of a purely military nature, the Secretary would still need an independent staff of experts responsible *only* to him to analyze the problem from *his* point of view, to offset the partisan nature of the Services (and the JCS), precisely as the President needs his Executive Office advisers to offset the frequently partisan nature of the Cabinet. What Secretary McNamara and his group felt they were doing, then, was providing a relatively unbiased overview of the national interest. Controversy was to be expected, said Secretary McNamara, if the Secretary of Defense were "to place the interest of the many above the interest of the few. And yet it is the national interest, after all, which he has sworn to serve." [35] Or as Enthoven put it, "he (the Secretary of Defense) is the only one in a good position to shape the program in terms of the whole—in terms of the national interest." [36]

Whether or not one agrees that Secretary McNamara and his staff served the national interest better than previous arrangements had, it is

[32] Charles Hitch, "The Case for Cost-Effectiveness Analysis," in *Defense, Science, and Public Policy, op. cit.,* p. 86.

[33] Robert A. Ginsburgh, "The Challenge To Military Professionalism," in *Components of Defense Policy, op. cit.,* pp. 132–3.

[34] Enthoven, *op. cit.,* p. 82.

[35] McNamara, *op. cit.,* p. 104.

[36] Enthoven, *op. cit.,* p. 336.

clear that they saw the defense policy and spending problem in exactly the same interest group terms earlier noted. Moreover, the reaction to Secretary McNamara's use of the budget to curb the autonomy of parochial interests was about of the same decibel level as would be the reaction to withdrawing the determination of federal farm policy and spending from the hands of the agriculture committees of Congress—made up as they are so heavily from representatives of farm states and districts—and placing it in the hands of a group of efficiency experts. The nation might well be better off, but the farmers would never believe it.

The Nixon administration has obviously picked and chosen from its predecessors. On the one hand, reminiscent of the Eisenhower days, national defense policy is apparently determined again by the National Security Council, which now, however, makes decisions on the basis of "cost-benefit studies" of alternative defense policies. These studies are rather rough estimates worked out by a Defense Program Committee consisting of the Secretary of Defense, the JCS, the heads of the CIA and the Budget Bureau, and chaired (of course) by Presidential Assistant Henry Kissinger. The final choice of policy by the NSC from the alternatives proposed by the committee naturally sets the defense budget ceiling, quite as with President Eisenhower.[37]

On the other hand, clearcut policy statements on either general or specific matters are not to be found, thus perhaps going all previous administrations one better. The Nixon Doctrine is probably surpassed in vagueness only by the current Defense Department's annual posture statements, which one columnist terms, "long on vague philosophy and extraordinarily short on facts." [38]

The practice of "fair shares" in dividing defense money among the services is carefully observed by the Nixon Administration, indeed to a degree unmatched since the Truman days, and is again dignified by the term "balanced forces." Each service gets approximately the same amount, allegedly the price Secretary Laird had to pay to maintain peace within the Department.[39]

Thirdly, autonomy as to how each Service spends its allotment of funds once again is the order of the day. The management techniques

[37] Even these rough cost-benefit analyses appear to have disappeared. Joseph Kraft (*Washington Post,* Nov. 9, 1971, p. A19) points out that Dr. Kissinger's "committee has been allowed to wither on the vine. Half a dozen of the analysts connected with it have resigned. . . ." Instead the President has simply "backed the big spending program of Defense Secretary Laird."

[38] Robert Kleiman, *New York Times*, March 2, 1971, p. 31. Also see appended charts offered by the current D.O.D. to illustrate its new approach to the defense problem (Figures 1 and 2).

[39] Elizabeth Drew, *The Atlantic Magazine*, May 1970, p. 4ff; also see Table 1.

introduced by Secretary McNamara have been "liquidated," writes one columnist.[40] The Systems Analysis Office has been retained but "emasculated," adds another. Secretary "Laird has virtually demolished the internal management capacity of the office of the Secretary of Defense." [41] Both claims appear to be well supported by Robert Moot, Comptroller of the Defense Department, who rather proudly notes that "each Service is responsible for completely designing its own program and submitting it to the Secretary of Defense for decision." Concerning resulting disputes over these programs between the individual Services and the staff of the Secretary of Defense, he goes on, "Frankly, the staff has not prevailed very often and the Secretary definitely favors the Service position whenever he can. . . .[42] we are reversing a trend toward centralization that was in operation for nearly eight years." [43] Perhaps enough said.

Finally, a word more ought to be added on the over-all budget ceilings. Again, as in the Eisenhower days after the "conclusion" of a war, a return to a "normal" level of defense expenditures is in order. A Gallup Poll of October 1970 showed "49% of the public favoring further cuts in military spending with only 34% favoring the present level of expenditures." [44] Worse still, so conservative and cautious a source as *Fortune* made a strong case for budget reductions of more than $17 billion.[45] The general civilian discontent with high military spending was of course mirrored in Congress, especially in the Proxmire Committee hearings of 1970 and the more recent organization of the "Members of Congress for Peace Through Law."

The administration's handling of the potentially explosive civilian-military rift, however, has been nothing short of remarkable. On the one hand, it has made much of its defense reductions, announcing almost at once, for example, its lowering of its sights from a "2½ war strategy" of the Kennedy and Johnson days to a "1½ war strategy" today. This change clearly implied enormous reductions, but as "the 2½ war strategy" was the vaguest sort of concept, suggesting the ultimate condition we might have to prepare for, reducing it to an equally vague if "smaller concept" meant nothing in practice.[46] Perhaps even a bit shocking was its "Defense Budget Hoax," a not terribly inept term for the new national budget bookkeeping, obviously designed to give the public a sharp impression of vastly decreased defense spending. Although President Johnson in 1968 began counting trust

[40] Kleiman, *op. cit.*

[41] Joseph Kraft, *Washington Post,* November 22, 1970, p. B7.

[42] Address by the Honorable Robert C. Moot, Assistant Secretary of Defense (Comptroller) to the U.S. Naval Postgraduate School, July 30, 1970, p. 9.

[43] *Ibid.*, p. 11.

[44] Chalmers Roberts, *Washington Post,* 18 October 1970, Outlook Section.

[45] *Fortune,* August 1969, p. 69.

[46] Elizabeth Drew, *op. cit.*

Figure 1. Nixon Strategy for Peace: Strength, Partnership, Negotiations*

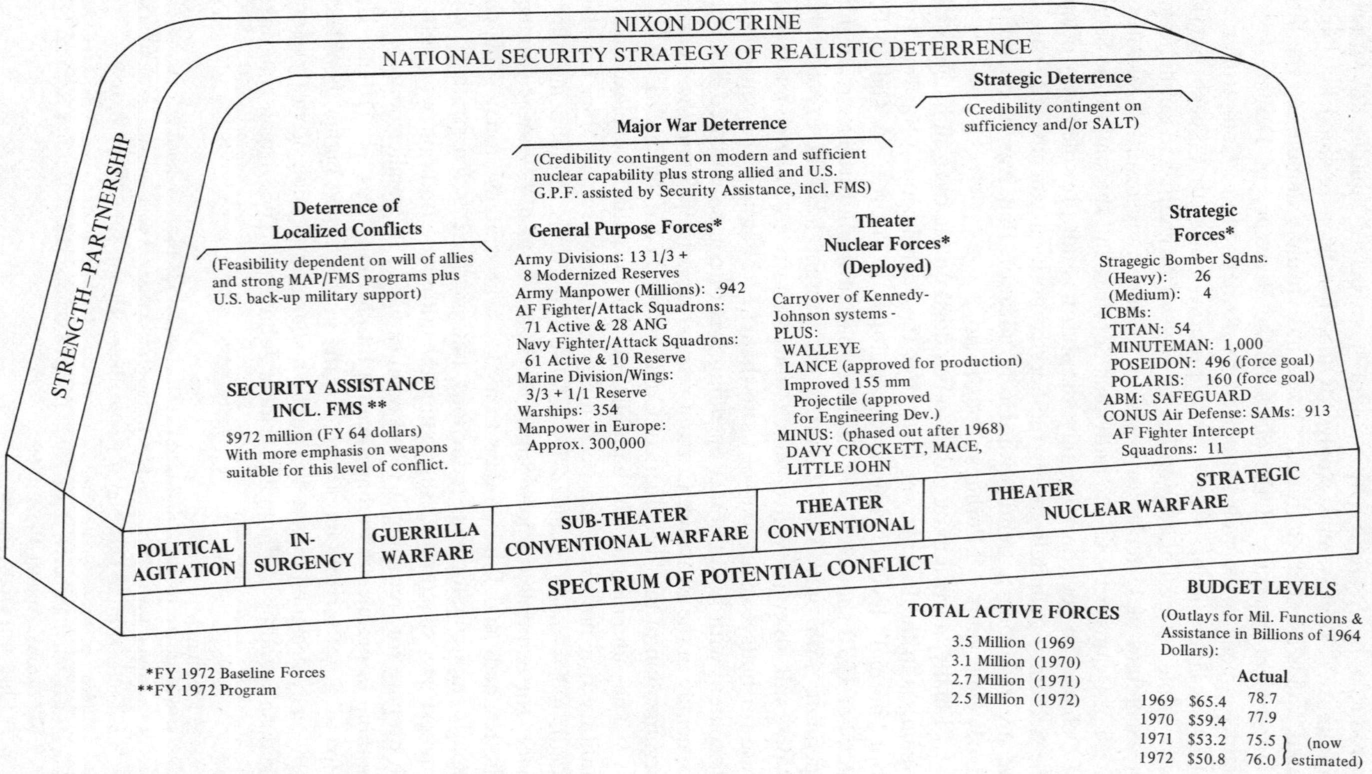
NIXON DOCTRINE
NATIONAL SECURITY STRATEGY OF REALISTIC DETERRENCE
STRENGTH–PARTNERSHIP
Strategic Deterrence
(Credibility contingent on sufficiency and/or SALT)
Major War Deterrence
(Credibility contingent on modern and sufficient nuclear capability plus strong allied and U.S. G.P.F. assisted by Security Assistance, incl. FMS)
Deterrence of Localized Conflicts
(Feasibility dependent on will of allies and strong MAP/FMS programs plus U.S. back-up military support)
General Purpose Forces*
Army Divisions: 13 1/3 + 8 Modernized Reserves
Army Manpower (Millions): .942
AF Fighter/Attack Squadrons: 71 Active & 28 ANG
Navy Fighter/Attack Squadrons: 61 Active & 10 Reserve
Marine Division/Wings: 3/3 + 1/1 Reserve
Warships: 354
Manpower in Europe: Approx. 300,000
Theater Nuclear Forces* (Deployed)
Carryover of Kennedy-Johnson systems -
PLUS:
WALLEYE
LANCE (approved for production)
Improved 155 mm Projectile (approved for Engineering Dev.)
MINUS: (phased out after 1968)
DAVY CROCKETT, MACE, LITTLE JOHN
Strategic Forces*
Stragegic Bomber Sqdns.
(Heavy): 26
(Medium): 4
ICBMs:
TITAN: 54
MINUTEMAN: 1,000
POSEIDON: 496 (force goal)
POLARIS: 160 (force goal)
ABM: SAFEGUARD
CONUS Air Defense: SAMs: 913
AF Fighter Intercept Squadrons: 11
SECURITY ASSISTANCE INCL. FMS **
$972 million (FY 64 dollars)
With more emphasis on weapons suitable for this level of conflict.
POLITICAL AGITATION
IN-SURGENCY
GUERRILLA WARFARE
SUB-THEATER CONVENTIONAL WARFARE
THEATER CONVENTIONAL
THEATER
STRATEGIC
NUCLEAR WARFARE
SPECTRUM OF POTENTIAL CONFLICT
TOTAL ACTIVE FORCES
3.5 Million (1969
3.1 Million (1970)
2.7 Million (1971)
2.5 Million (1972)
BUDGET LEVELS
(Outlays for Mil. Functions & Assistance in Billions of 1964 Dollars):
Actual
1969 $65.4 78.7
1970 $59.4 77.9
1971 $53.2 75.5
1972 $50.8 76.0
(now estimated)
*FY 1972 Baseline Forces
**FY 1972 Program

*Compare projected budget levels with actual figures, or those *now* estimated.

Figure 2. Foreign Policy Objective of Lasting Peace and Freedom Through National Security Strategy of Realistic Deterrence and a Foreign Policy Strategy of Vigorous Negotiation*

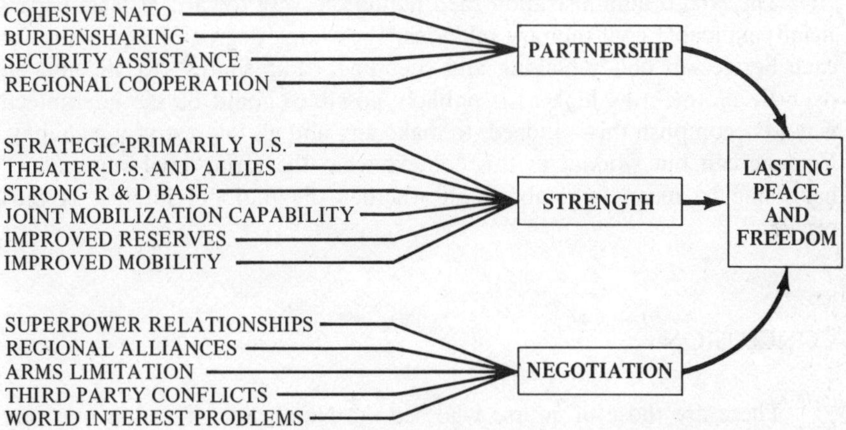

*This chart was offered to the author by Defense Department officials as clearly showing–in simplified fashion, of course–the *new* approach of the Nixon Administration. One is tempted to add to the stated goals the words: "along with promoting virtue, motherhood, and the flag."

funds—such as Social Security contributions, which last year were in the neighborhood of $50 billion—as part of the over-all federal budget, today they are included in that portion of the budget devoted to "human resources." On the other hand, "defense expenditures" in the budget no longer include "the national debt interest attributable to war. . . , Veterans' Administration costs (including pensions), and the cost of Selective Service"; indeed, these too are now considered government expenditures devoted to "human resources." The not-surprising result of this juggling of figures is the claim that defense expenditures have now been reduced from roughly 80% to 50% of the federal budget.[47] Actually, the amount of Defense Department spending reduction between 1968 and mid-1972 will apparently be about $2 billion,[48] hardly warranting the contention that Secretary Laird has been making for some time that defense economizing is "near the bone." [49]

In short, whereas the Eisenhower administration pushed reductions a public did not insist on, thereby setting off an interservice war, the Nixon administration has avoided this by doggedly fighting—with apparently considerable success—publicly demanded defense reductions. Little wonder a Defense Department official, when asked about the Services' attitude

47 T. Braden and F. Mankiewicz, "The Defense Budget Hoax," *Washington Post*, October 27, 1970, p. A3.

48 Kleiman, *op. cit.*

49 Chalmers Roberts, *op. cit.* The phrase is Roberts', not Laird's.

toward Secretary Laird in view of the spending reductions, replied: "They know he is doing the best he can for them." [50]

The Nixon administration then points the way toward at least superficially amicable civil-military relations.[50A] A large degree of autonomy for each Service in policy-making and spending, "fair shares" to all, and an over-all allotment as high as is publicly possible should be the guaranteed way to accomplish this—indeed, to make any and all interest groups happy. Yet one can but wonder in this context what the term "civil supremacy" has come to mean, and above all whether the national interest is thus served.

CONCLUSION

There are those of course who see the Nixon line of action not only as acceptable but indeed wise. Professor Wildavsky, for example, argues that decisions claiming merit in terms of the national interest are almost invariably "my preferences" or "the interests of those with whom I identify." [51] Furthermore, he sees a "comprehensive approach" to a national budget as impractical—simply too complex, beyond man's capability for establishing and working out priorities. Hence he concludes that distributing "fair shares" to the various interest-group claimants in terms of whatever pressures they can bring to bear, short of sheer fraud or force, may well be the most efficient as well as the *only* way.[52]

Morris Janowitz, an eminent scholar of military affairs, puts the matter far less enthusiastically in his *The Professional Soldier*. He seems to feel, nonetheless, that allowing the Services to battle it out among themselves for weapons and funds is a "good thing" in that it prevents a unified military assault on American public opinion, one that might well prove dangerous to the precept of civilian supremacy.[53] It is curious to note that Colonel Ginsburgh, seeing this same interest-group scramble among the Services, feels it is partly a deliberate civilian "divide-and-rule" tactic, and partly the fault of the Services' own shortsightedness. His solution is the creation of "military generalists," professional men capable of seeing the "whole military picture," who could thereby both placate the Services (who would

[50] Personal interview, March 1, 1971.

[50A] See Figures 1 and 2.

[51] Wildavsky, *op. cit.*, p. 175.

[52] *Ibid.*, p. 148.

[53] Morris Janowitz, *The Professional Soldier* (New York: The Free Press, 1960), Chapter VII.

apparently recognize their superior background and hence accept their decision) and convince the political authorities of their unbiased over-all military knowledge (thereby guaranteeing the nation of the critical military guidance it needs and assuring the military its proper place in the scheme of things!).[54]

Professor Huntington occupies a somewhat middle ground. Although he sees in the interest-group struggle the "price of reasonable content and consensus," he finds the struggle requires direction and leadership. This he believes Secretary McNamara provided, as had earlier strong figures in the previous administrations, such as Dean Acheson.[55] Somewhat along the same line of thought is Charles Schultze's suggestion that the Secretary of State provide each year a "Posture Statement" of our foreign policy goals and needs to provide, if not guidance, at least a counterbalance to the military influence of the Defense Department.[56]

Another approach to the problem is to try to bring Congress further into the picture, to make it possible for Congress to take a positive, active role in both the formation of strategy and the determination of the means to carry it out. Senator Proxmire gets to the heart of this approach by proposing a "zero-base" budget each year, that is, consideration of each request from "scratch" rather than merely a determination of whether to have, say, more or fewer aircraft carriers.[57] Thus, for example, rather than decide if more or fewer carriers were necessary, Congress could get at the question of whether carriers were needed at all, forcing the Navy to justify them in terms of current needs and strategy. Others, as Richard Barnet, suggest setting up congressional committees on national priorities, a sort of permanent joint committee to consider defense needs *in relation to other national needs* rather than as separate entities.[58] It is, however, somewhat difficult to take these proposals seriously, other than as a protest against what their proponents see as the pro-military bias of the executive branch as a whole. Our point here is that Congress is far more beset by interest-group struggles than is the executive, and the idea of the national interest emerging from unbiased, disinterested, nationally oriented reviews by Congress is beyond this writer's imagination.

Indeed many conclude that an independent board of review of defense

[54] *Components of Defense Policy, op. cit.*, p. 136–8.

[55] *Ibid.*, p. 89–91.

[56] *National Priorities,* by Kenneth Boulding and others (Washington, D.C.: Public Affairs Press, 1970), Compilation of statements at the hearings of the Senate Subcommittee on Economy in Government of the Joint (Congressional) Economic Committee chaired by Senator Proxmire.

[57] *Ibid.*, p. 129.

[58] Richard Barnet, *The Economy of Death* (New York: Atheneum, 1969), p. 138.

policy and needs is in order. Professor Sherer of the Economics Department of Michigan University modestly proposes an academic review board of presumably objective "physicists, engineers, economists, political scientists," at least for the field of weapon needs and development.[59] The National Planning Association, in addition to a proposed Special Presidential Assistant for "Plans and Priorities" and a Joint Congressional Committee on national goals, calls for a "Citizens Committee on National Goals and Priorities."[60] More civilian "think tanks" such as the Rand Corporation might well provide such independent judgment, yet Professor Lyons warns us that they are apt to become captives of the particular Service that hires them. Finally, John Galbraith's solution is a panel of eminent scientists to report to Congress on the need and wisdom of defense spending. He adds, one trusts with tongue in cheek, that all such clearly biased fellows as Edward Teller are, of course, to be excluded from such a panel.[61]

Professor Galbraith's comments suggest the real problem with boards of "experts," be they in the executive or legislative branch, independents, or any special group, from Plato's guardians to modern efficiency experts. To repeat Professor Wildavsky, "experts"—unfortunately—tend to be those who agree with our preferences, who side with those with whom I identify. Or to quote Paul McCracken, Chairman of the present Council of Economic Advisors, the great question of national security, "whether more of it is worth what it costs, meaning the sacrifice of other objectives that would be necessary to obtain it—is not a question to be decided by technicians [!]."[62]

Who then should decide? Who should determine the proper military policy and the size and content of the budget to support it? Dr. McCracken answers in a way guaranteed to warm the heart of every student of democracy. ". . . we have to rely on the judgment of government officials who were chosen by the people in the belief that they have that good judgment, and reasonably represent the peoples' standard of values."[63]

Splendid. Unfortunately, in the 1964 elections, if there was one thing that distinguished Lyndon Johnson from his Republican opponent it was Johnson's insistence on a reasonable, moderate view on Vietnam as opposed to Goldwater's extreme aggressiveness. Yet after his reelection Johnson soon adopted all Goldwater's proposals. President Nixon, in his campaign of 1968, promised "secret plans" to end the war shortly and honorably, a promise scarcely fulfilled. In short, elections can be misleading, even if one should agree with Dr. McCracken that soundness of judgment on things military is a critical part of an election.

59 *Components of Defense Policy, op. cit.*, p. 165.
60 *National Priorities, op. cit.*, p. 87.
61 *Ibid.*, p. 120.
62 *Ibid.*, p. 21.
63 *Ibid.*, p. 21.

TABLE 1. MILITARY SPENDING (IN BILLIONS OF DOLLARS).* SOURCE: DEPT. OF DEFENSE, JAN. 29, 1971.

	Fiscal Year	Total Defense Budget		Army	Navy	Air Force		Office of Secretary of Defense	
F.D.R. and H.S.T.	1945	79.7	Height of WW II	49.7	30.2	—		—	"Unification" begun
	1950	12.0	Back to normalcy	4.0	4.1	3.6	←Truman "fair shares"	0.2	
	1951	20.7	Rearmament	7.5	5.6	6.3		0.4	
	1953	47.7	Height of Korean War	16.3	11.9	15.1		0.4	
Eisenhower, Dulles, and the stable fifties	1954	44.0		13.0	11.3	15.7	Emphasis on air force and air-atomic power	0.5	
	1955	37.8	Stabilized budget resting on massive retaliation strategy	8.9	9.7	16.4		0.5	
	1956	38.4		8.7	9.7	16.7		0.6	
	1957	40.8		9.1	10.4	18.4		0.6	
	1958	41.2		9.1	10.9	18.4		0.7	Reform of Secretary of Defense's position
	1959	43.6		9.5	11.7	19.1		1.0	
	1960	42.8		9.4	11.6	19.1		1.1	
Kennedy	1962	48.2	End of massive retaliation; emphasis now on balance	11.4	13.3	20.8	increase of conventional forces	1.9	Increasing power and personnel in OSD; also Def. Dept. Supply Agency, Communications Agency, and Intelligence Agency
	1963	50.0		11.5	14.0	20.6		1.9	
Johnson	1964	51.2		12.1	14.5	20.5	PPBS approach to distributing funds	2.6	
	1965	47.4		11.6	13.4	18.2		2.9	
	1966	55.4	Vietnam War	14.8	16.0	20.1		3.3	
	1967	68.5	Escalation	21.0	19.3	22.9		4.3	
	1968	78.0		25.2	22.1	25.7		4.2	
	1969	78.7	Vietnam high	25.0	25.5	25.9		4.4	
Nixon "deescalation of the war"	1970	77.9	"Cutting to the bone"†	24.7	22.5	24.9	Nixon "fair shares"	4.9	
	1971 est.	75.5		23.0	22.0	23.8		5.6	
	1972 est.	76.0		21.0	21.3	22.9		6.2	

* Civil defense and military assistance not itemized.
† Estimated 1973 military budget $81.5 billion (*Washington Post*, December 12, 1971, A1).

Still, in a democracy, public opinion should in the last analysis be the determinant of *great* policy questions. And surely the size alone of the military budget puts it in this category. It is with perhaps this in mind that Professor Huntington suggests that the stimulation of public discussion *before* major military policy decisions are taken would greatly improve the entire process.[64] Charles Schultze puts it negatively in arguing that "perhaps the most important reason for the increasing military budgets is . . . that some of the most fundamental decisions which determine the size of the budgets are seldom submitted to outside review and only occasionally discussed and debated in the public arena."[65] An enlightened public opinion, one helped and encouraged by our political leaders to see and understand the problems of foreign policy, and to draw and make known its conclusions—this is clearly what democratic theory calls for. And yet, if there is one clear impression to be drawn from the *Pentagon Papers,* it is that the Johnson Administration in no way took the public into its confidence about enlarging the Vietnam War. Nor do President Nixon's "bombshell" decisions on Cambodia or China suggest any desire to enlighten public opinion and then to be guided by its choices. The immediate future, in short, offers little encouragement that this most promising avenue of improvement is to be taken.

[64] *Components of Defense Policy, op. cit.,* p. 93.
[65] *National Priorities, op. cit.,* p. 45.

6

Midshipmen Political Characterization and Academy Socialization

CHARLES L. COCHRAN
and LUIS R. LUIS

Academy graduates in all the services attain flag rank out of proportion to their numbers. Flag-rank officers set the standards for the military and largely determine the lenses through which the military perceives the civilian world. The influence of academy graduates can be expected to increase as the size of the ROTC contribution declines with the contraction of the officer corps in the post-Vietnam era. Further, a much higher percentage of academy graduates can be expected to remain in the service after they have completed their obligatory tour of five years than will either ROTC or OCS graduates.[1] For all these reasons, the attitudes of academy students at the outset of their careers at the academies is an important and fertile field of study, enabling us better to understand and to project expected attitudes in the officer hierarchy.

The content of this study is concerned with the student entering Annapolis. The entering plebe (freshman) is a collection of characteristics, some of which will be changed during his social and educational experiences in the institution, while many will remain the same or be reinforced. Social science theory has generally developed three basic positions concerning the role of the college experience in the sociopsychological development of the individual.

> 1. In college the individual acquires habits (including value-orientations) that are socially adaptive in postcollege life. . . . In one version of this view, college experience serves mainly to reinforce habits acquired earlier; in

[1] *Report of the President's Commission on an All-Volunteer Armed Force* (Washington: Government Printing Office, 1970), p. 77. The report indicates that approximately 80% of academy graduates remain in the service beyond their obligatory tour of five years. In contrast the report indicates that fewer than 50% of the ROTC scholarship graduates and fewer than 25% of the OCS graduates stay beyond their obligatory tour.

another version, the discontinuity between precollege and college environments is stressed, indicating that entirely new habits must be learned. In either event, measurable and permanent changes in behavior are expected to occur during the college experience.

2. The college is one of several successive social environments through which individuals may pass between adolescence and death . . . what behavioral changes take place during college years are not seen as having any long-range effect, except insofar as an individual's having gone to college (or to a particular college) may help determine his place in adult society.

3. The individual's life in college is part of a transition from family life to adult participation in the wider social system. . . . Behavior in this period is neither carried over from childhood nor socially adaptive in adulthood. Its function lies more in extinguishing childhood habits than in specific preparation for adult life. College experience, then, prepares a new *tabula rasa* for socialization in the adult role system of a complex society.[2]

These three positions are not mutually exclusive, and as Robert Levine points out, either position may be accurate for a given type of college environment.[3] The first view, stressing the reinforcing effect of the college experience with some elements of the necessity of learning entirely new habits, appears to be particularly appropriate for the role of the Naval Academy experience, on the basis of similarity between the academy students and those examined in other studies.

One study by Davie and Hare of an eastern men's college, "IVY," emphasized that there was a great deal of continuity between the student's college training and his earlier experience in the home. The findings indicated that particularly for men from the upper- and upper-middle classes the college experience is both continuous and compatible with the precollege home life and postcollege life in that college completes the socialization process begun at home to prepare the student for an appropriate position in life.[4]

[2] Robert A. Levine, "American College Experience as a Socialization Process," *College Peer Groups,* Theodore M. Newcomb and Everett K. Wilson (eds.) (Chicago: Aldine Publishing Company, 1966), p. 110.

[3] *Ibid.,* p. 111. Unfortunately the distinction between the first view stressing the reinforcing effect of the college experience and the second position is not a crisp or clear one. For example, Philip E. Jacob concluded in his study that "When all is said and done, the value changes which seem to occur in college and set the college alumnus apart from others are not very great, at least for most students at most institutions." A good case could be made that his views support either of the first two positions. Philip E. Jacob, *Changing Values in College: An Exploratory Study of the Impact of College Teaching* (New York: Harper & Row Publishers, Inc., 1957).

[4] J. S. Davie and A. P. Hare, "Button-Down Collar Culture: A Study of Undergraduate Life," *Human Organization,* 1956, Vol. 14, pp. 13–20. Research by Theodore M. Newcomb suggests that as the college student and his noncollege peer are both undergoing the same socializing process under different conditions, the college environ-

Qualification

The study is based partly on the assumption that the academy will generally reinforce attitudes fostered in the home and will be primarily a continuous experience that would not greatly change the students' outlook. This assumption should be qualified by acknowledging that studies have shown that some educational institutions may produce significant behavioral changes.

Nurses-training programs, medical internships, Bennington College, and British Officer Training schools, among others, have been shown to effectively change the values and attitudes of young people. Quite possibly the academy is such an institution. Professor Levine has developed an empirical model of such institutions.[5] Clearly, new values are inculcated in the "professional socialization" of a midshipman, but it is unclear how directly this process is related to social attitudes. A longitudinal study of Academy students is needed to determine the nature of the relationships.

If one is to classify the upper- and upper-middle classes on the basis of income, then plebes at the Naval Academy would generally be considered to be in that category when compared with students from the private universities, as Table 1 indicates.

TABLE 1. FAMILY INCOMES OF PRIVATE UNIVERSITY STUDENTS COMPARED TO NAVAL ACADEMY PLEBES (1970)

Estimated Parental Income	Academy Plebes	Private University Freshmen
Less than $4,000	1.4%	2.6%
$4,000– $5,999	2.4	3.8
$6,000– $7,999	6.2	6.7
$8,000– $9,999	11.8	10.2
$10,000–$12,499	19.7	15.9
$12,500–$14,999	16.7	14.4
$15,000–$19,999	21.3	15.8
$20,000–$24,999	10.5	10.3
$25,000–$29,999	4.0	5.5
$30,000–$34,999	1.9	3.7
$35,000–$39,999	1.5	2.4
$40,000 or more	2.7	8.7

ment is not necessarily responsible for most of the changes that do occur. Theodore M. Newcomb, "Research on Student Characteristics: Current Approaches," *The College and the Student,* Lawrence E. Dennis and Joseph F. Kauffman (eds.) (Washington: American Council on Education, 1966), p. 107.

[5] Levine, *op cit.,* pp. 113–17.

The academy students are from upper-middle-class families on the whole and are likely to see the academy experience as leading to careers as gentlemen and scholars in the naval officer corps. At the same time they expect to learn the proper role of an officer and conform their behavior to that expected of an officer.

There is evidence that many college students, including midshipmen at the Naval Academy, choose institutions and peer groups that are highly compatible with their own preferences or represent goals with which the student identifies.[6] In fact, plebes entering the Naval Academy do not exhibit a random distribution of ascribed characteristics. First of all, it is an all-male institution, which sets it apart from most institutions of higher learning in the country. Also, the range of ages is considerably narrower than at most colleges, as an entering plebe must be between the ages of 17 and 21. Perhaps the most significant distinction between the academy student and his average counterpart at the private universities is in the area of scholastic and leadership qualities exhibited in high school. Table 2 illustrates the comparative academic records.

TABLE 2. AVERAGE GRADE IN HIGH SCHOOL—ACADEMY PLEBES AND PRIVATE UNIVERSITY MEN

Average Grade	Academy Plebes	Private Universities
A or A+	15.0%	10.1%
A−	21.7	13.3
B+	29.5	19.6
B	20.3	23.8
B−	9.7	16.6
C+	2.4	11.8
C	1.4	4.6
D	0.0	0.1

The Naval Academy as an institution had an entering student body with a higher average grade than that of the highest norm group, the private universities.[7]

The responses to the question concerning grades are supported by

[6] See Everett K. Wilson, "The Entering Student: Attributes and Agents of Change," pp. 71–106, in Newcomb and Wilson, *College Peer Groups.*

[7] The private universities are taken as the highest-scoring category. While the Naval Academy student is superior when compared to the norm, it does not rule out the possibility that some private universities might have as high a grade distribution, and perhaps higher.

cross-checking that response with a question concerning class standing. Once again the Academy reported the highest rankings (Table 3).

TABLE 3. ACADEMIC RANK IN HIGH SCHOOL (MEN ONLY)

Rank	Academy Plebes	Private Universities
Top Quarter	80.5%	56.6%
Second Quarter	15.9	29.8
Third Quarter	3.4	12.8
Fourth Quarter	0.3	1.4

Academy students compiled this impressive record while attending, for the most part, schools in which an unusually high percentage of the students were college bound[8] and where the scholastic competition would have been keen.

The achievements of academy students while in high school, compared with students from private universities, suggest that Naval Academy students as a whole not only have excellent academic potential but are high achievers as well. Plebes were more likely to have excelled in areas where excellence can be measured by the individual's performance, such as earning a varsity letter or being elected president of an organization (Table 4).

TABLE 4. SECONDARY-SCHOOL ACHIEVEMENTS (MEN ONLY)

Achievement	Naval Academy	Private Universities
Elected President of Student Organization	40.1%	23.4%
Varsity Letter	79.1	45.2
Scholastic Honor Society	56.7	33.4
National Merit Recognition	17.0	7.5

Of major significance in Table 4 is the high score of academy students in these areas. The non-letter winner or the non-honor-society member is the exception rather than the rule. Plebes come to the Naval Academy with a record of having excelled in comparative areas.

The service academies undoubtedly attract students who are unusually

[8] Approximately 78% of the Naval Academy students and private university students estimated that at least 50% of their high school classmates were going to college, which was higher than any other norm group.

competitive and have a high academic potential. Further, as the academy actively recruits this type in its selection program, it is probably fair to say that recruitment policy is at least as important in determining the composition of the student population as the self-selection process of students.

The student body at the Naval Academy is in many respects rather homogeneous. At Annapolis they will be constantly exposed to like-minded peers, which will serve to reinforce many values brought to the institution. Because of the unique purpose of the Naval Academy, however, the effect of the peer-group influences may differ from those at other colleges, and it is reasonable to expect a greater degree of socialization in the values of the military profession than at other institutions.

Variables Analyzed

This paper presents the results of a statistical study of a 173-item questionnaire administered to entering plebes in the summer of 1970. The questionnaire or "Student Information Form" prepared by the American Council on Education (ACE) was given to first-time students at 425 institutions of higher education.[9]

The study whose results are reported here concerns in particular the responses to the question: "How would you characterize your political views at the present time?" There were five possible political self-characterizations: far left, liberal, middle of the road, conservative, and far right. In this study the determinants of political behavior as measured by the five answers to the question are identified and analyzed.

The potential determinants of plebe political characterization were represented by the answers to 72 questions in the "Student Information Form." These potential determinants were selected as being *a priori* the most plausible of the 173 items in the survey. Included among these variables were political-attitude questions, socio-economic characteristics of the respondents, and a large number of other attitudinal questions. The 72 items were classified according to the divisions in the ACE survey into six mutually exclusive categories:

A. Personal and family characteristics (e.g., family income, grades, race, religion) (15 variables).
B. Direct questions concerning the involvement of the government in several areas of activity (15 variables).
C. Attitudinal questions on college issues (9 variables).
D. Attitudinal questions on noncollege issues (15 variables).
E. Questions concerning life goals (10 questions).
F. Items relating to the respondent's precollege activities.

[9] American Council on Education, *National Norms for Entering College Freshmen*, Fall 1970, p. 6.

Political Characterization

Naval Academy plebes identified themselves as being more conservative than any other norm group reported by the American Council on Education. The norm group most closely approximating the Academy's political characterization was "technical institutions," while the most liberal norm group reported in 1970 was "private universities," followed by "four-year Catholic colleges." Table 5 illustrates the comparison of the political identification of the norm groups.

TABLE 5. COMPARISON OF MIDSHIPMEN POLITICAL IDENTIFICATION WITH THE MOST CONSERVATIVE AND MOST LIBERAL GROUPS

Political Characterization	Academy	Technical Institutions	Catholic Colleges	Private Universities
Far Left	0.3%	1.4%	3.4%	4.6%
Liberal	28.4	32.4	43.0	43.7
Middle of the Road	37.0	38.8	36.9	36.9
Conservative	32.6	26.0	15.8	15.0
Far Right	1.7	1.4	0.9	0.8
Totals	100.0	100.0	100.0	100.0

Naval Academy responses might be expected to be close to those from four-year technical institutions because the Academy educates engineers to a large extent (approximately 40% of its graduates) and natural science majors (approximately 30%) and is considered to be a technical institution by the ACE.

The distribution of political self-identification at the Naval Academy into the five categories is approximately symmetrical. The distributions of all other norm groups reported by the ACE are more skewed, indicating that the proportion of students to the left of the political spectrum is greater elsewhere than at the Naval Academy. Figure 1 compares the distribution at the Naval Academy with that of private universities.

Assuming that political polarization to either extreme of the characterization scale is directly related to activism, the distribution in Figure 1 may be interpreted as indicating that the proportion of entering students at the Academy who are political activists is smaller than it is elsewhere. Using this criterion it may then be stated that midshipmen are less politicized than their counterparts at all other colleges and universities.

Figure 1. Distribution of Political Characterization at the Naval Academy and at Private Universities

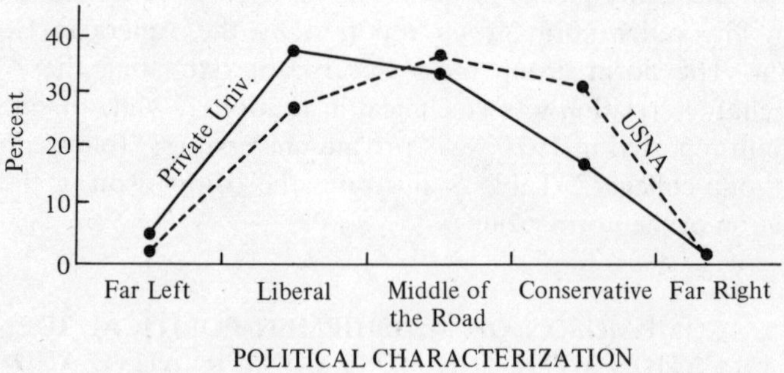

Political Characterization	USNA	Priv. Univ. (male)
	%	%
Far left	.3	4.6
Liberal	28.4	43.7
Middle of the Road	37.0	36.9
Conservative	32.6	15.0
Far Right	1.7	.8

Attitudes Determining Political Characterization

By means of a statistical analysis of the 72 potential determinants of political characterization, those variables with the greatest predictive power were selected for further study. For the method used, see the Appendix. Table 6 ranks the 24 best predictors and classifies them into the six categories, A to F, in which the items in the ACE's "Student Information Form" were divided. Only types A, B, C, and D are included, since E & F variables proved to be too weak a predictor. The variables in the table provide a base for the following analysis: Responses to individual items can be examined in terms of (a) the direction of their relationship to the political spectrum, (b) the intensity with which the particular attitude is held, if the item or variable is attitudinal, and (c) how central the attitude appears to be in the determination of certain political attitudes. In what follows an analysis is made of selected variables cross-classified by political characterization.

The variables were selected by utilizing two criteria. First, the variables with the highest predictive power were included. Then to insure the inclusion of variables with low predictive power whose analysis may help to clarify the nature of midshipmen political characterization, other relevant variables that have been found significant in the literature were included.

TABLE 6. DETERMINANTS OF POLITICAL CHARACTERIZATION RANKED IN TERMS OF PREDICTIVE POWER

Rank	Variable	Type of Variable
1	Laxity of college officials in dealing with student protests	C
2	Legalization of marijuana	D
3	Right of college officials to ban extremists from speaking on campus	C
4	Abolition of the death penalty	D
5	Military involvement in Southeast Asia	B
6	Role of students in college curriculum	C
7	Religion	A
8	School desegregation	B
9	Federal role in elimination of poverty	B
10	Gun control	B
11	Development of ABM capability	B
12	Abolition of college grades	C
13	Concern of courts for rights of criminals	D
14	Widening of opportunities to attend college	D
15	Compensatory financial aid for the disadvantaged	B
16	Compensatory education for the disadvantaged	B
17	Right of college officials to clear student publications	C
18	Having a diversity of friends	B
19	All-volunteer armed forces	D
20	Federal control of television and newspapers	B
21	Having beliefs similar to those of other students	D
22	Right of college officials to regulate behavior off campus	C
23	Liberalization of divorce laws	D
24	Size of "Generation Gap"	D

The first group of variables to be analyzed are collectively referred to as "conventional values." Political conservatives tend to hold very conventional social and political attitudes as a general pattern.[10] By accepting the prevailing values of the external social order, an individual acquires an anchor with which to stabilize his own identity. The stability of such an individual is related to the stability and the traditional values which are seen as an essential part of the social order. Thus, the conservative's view that

[10] See Hans Jurgen Eysenck, *The Psychology of Politics* (London: Routledge & Kegan Paul, 1968), pp. 143–169. Also L. Harned, "Authoritarian Attitudes and Party Activity," *The Public Opinion Quarterly*, XXV, 3 (Fall), 393–399. And Fred I. Greenstein, "Personality and Political Socialization: The Theories of Authoritarian and Democratic Character," *The Annals of the American Academy of Political and Social Science,* 1965 361 September, 629–641.

nonconformists are a threat to the basis of society is manifested in hostile and aggressive attitude toward those whose behavior or values differ from the prevailing standards. At the same time the rigid support for those in authority or the strict adherence to those conventional middle-class values of society may reflect a lack of self-esteem in one's own being and the need for approval and affection through the vigorous defense of the values of the social group.

The results of the questionnaire agree with our expectation. Those who agree with the conventional attitude and are reluctant to question established authority correlate strongly with conservatism. Those who challenged such views tend to identify with liberals.

TABLE 7. "MOST COLLEGE OFFICIALS HAVE BEEN TOO LAX IN DEALING WITH STUDENT PROTESTS ON CAMPUS" VARIABLE: ABSOLUTE NUMBERS AND PERCENTAGES (IN PARENTHESES) OF RESPONSES

	Attitudes			
Political Characterization	Disagree Strongly	Disagree Somewhat	Agree Somewhat	Agree Strongly
Far Left	2 (11.7)	11 (0.7)	0	0
Liberal	10 (58.8)	77 (54.6)	139 (34.1)	89 (16.6)
Middle of the Road	4 (23.5)	50 (35.4)	166 (40.7)	185 (34.5)
Conservative	1 (5.8)	13 (9.2)	102 (25.0)	242 (45.3)
Far Right	0	0	0	19 (3.5)
Totals	17 (100.0)	151 (100.0)	407 (100.0)	535 (100.0)

Table 7 indicates that a large majority of midshipmen agree that "most college officials have been too lax in dealing with student protests on campus." While 85.6 percent of the plebes indicated agreement with the statement, 50.7 percent of the freshmen at private universities agreed, if we compare the norm group with the most dissimilar pattern of answers. Sixty-one percent of the students in all institutions agreed with the statement.

The statement just analyzed predicts political characterization better than any other single statement. The polarization of views at the extremes of the political spectrum is particularly striking. All 19 of the respondents who characterized themselves as "far right" agree strongly with the statement, and all midshipmen in the "far left" category disagreed with the statement.

The third important conclusion from Table 7 is the nature of the "consensus" on this particular issue. In all three central political categories, including "liberals," a majority of the respondents agree with the statement. The proportion of agreement increases as we move toward the right in the political spectrum. The direction of the relationship between the subjective valuation of the statement concerning laxity of college officials and the subjective political characterization is the expected one. Those who agree that officials have been too lax are more likely to be in the right half of the political spectrum than the reverse.

It is noteworthy that among these variables reflecting statements of attitudes and values with high predictive power, the first, third, and sixth were related to conventional middle-class values and to submissive attitudes toward the idealized moral authority of the in-group. The California F scale[11] designed by Adorno and others conceived of the authoritarian personality syndrome as comprising nine variables. Among the nine variables are conventionalism, authoritarian submission, and power and "toughness." These three characteristics are reflected in some of the most highly significant responses. The trait of conventionality or conformity to traditional values and submission to in-group authority and, conversely, rejection and condemnation of those who violate conventional values, has been frequently correlated with conservatism.[12]

Those who would strongly agree that "college officials have been too lax in dealing with student protests" are in fact expressing displeasure with college students who violate conventional values, which are their own values, while believing that more authority should be exerted to support traditional values. The results here would tend to confirm earlier studies.

The cross-tabulation of political identification with the right of college officials to ban extremists from speaking on campus in Table 8 is in the same vein.

[11] See T. Adorno *et al., The Authoritarian Personality* (New York: Harper, 1950).

[12] See Herbert McClosky, "Conservatism and Personality," *The American Political Science Review,* 52 (March 1958), pp. 27–45. Fred I. Greenstein, "Personality and Political Socialization: The Theories of Authoritarian and Democratic Character," *Annals of the American Academy of Political and Social Science,* 361 (September 1965), pp. 81–95. Samuel P. Huntington, "Conservatism as an Ideology," *American Political Science Review,* 51 (June 1957), pp. 454–473.

TABLE 8. "COLLEGE OFFICIALS HAVE THE RIGHT TO BAN PERSONS WITH EXTREME VIEWS FROM SPEAKING ON CAMPUS" VARIABLE: ABSOLUTE NUMBERS AND PERCENTAGES (IN PARENTHESES) OF RESPONSES

	Attitudes			
Political Characterization	Disagree Strongly	Disagree Somewhat	Agree Somewhat	Agree Strongly
Far Left	3 (1.3)	0	0	0
Liberal	103 (47.4)	98 (30.9)	76 (21.9)	40 (17.2)
Middle of the Road	72 (33.1)	133 (41.9)	139 (40.1)	67 (28.8)
Conservative	38 (17.5)	82 (25.8)	127 (36.7)	115 (1.1)
Far Right	1 (0.4)	4 (1.2)	4 (1.1)	10 (4.3)
Totals	217 (100.0)	317 (100.0)	346 (100.0)	232 (100.0)

The response to this statement lacks the clear consensus apparent for the first statement. The midshipmen response to the statement more closely approximates that of the average college student than the private university student. In this case 51.8% of the midshipmen agreed with the statement, while 40.6% of the students in technical institutions and only 25.3% of the private-university freshmen agreed.

The direction of the relationship between the two variables is as expected. Of those who agree the greater proportion are in the conservative and far-right category, while those who disagree are grouped to the political left.[13] Once again those on the right prefer the use of authority to prevent those who might threaten traditional values from speaking on campus. Those on the left meanwhile give more support to the value of thinking and acting freely without social restraints.[14]

[13] Sixty-three percent of the respondents who identified as being far left or liberal agreed with the statement while 33% of the respondents identifying as conservative or far right agreed.

[14] This conforms with the findings of Gilbert Abcarian, "Radical Right and New Left: Commitment and Estrangement in American Society," in *Public Opinion and Politics,* Wm. Crotty (ed.), pp. 168–187.

The same desire to maintain the status quo is strikingly reflected in the cross-tabulation of political characterization with the statement "marijuana should be legalized." Table 9 shows this cross-tabulation.

TABLE 9. "MARIJUANA SHOULD BE LEGALIZED" VARIABLE: ABSOLUTE NUMBERS AND PERCENTAGES (IN PARENTHESES) OF RESPONSES

	Attitudes			
Political Characterization	Disagree Strongly	Disagree Somewhat	Agree Somewhat	Agree Strongly
Far Left	0	1 (0.3)	0	2 (3.6)
Liberal	113 (19.6)	62 (24.4)	106 (47.3)	36 (65.4)
Middle of the Road	211 (36.6)	117 (46.0)	73 (32.5)	9 (18.7)
Conservative	237 (41.1)	73 (28.7)	42 (18.7)	8 (14.5)
Far Right	15 (2.6)	1 (0.3)	3 (1.3)	0
Totals	576 (100.0)	254 (100.0)	224 (100.0)	55 (100.0)

Polarization and consensus are both illustrated strongly by the response to the statement on marijuana. For instance, 25.3% of the midshipmen agreed with the statement, while comparative figures for the students at technical institutions and in private universities are 32.5% and 53.3% respectively. The average private university student again was clearly the most liberal in the study, and the average technical institution student was the most conservative.

At the Academy liberals are almost equally divided between those who agree and those who disagree with the statement on marijuana, although the latter are the majority. The direction of the relationship between the political and the attitudinal variables is again as may be predicted: in the distribution of those who agree with the statement, the proportion of individuals in the political left is dominant, while the opposite is true of those who disagree.

The question of the legalization of marijuana does not appear to be related to a personality trait but is rather an issue in which certain positions are in "vogue" among liberals and conservatives.

It is usually accepted that conservatives, more than liberals, are concerned with the frailty of man and would be inclined to use strong sanctions to punish those who violate the laws and norms of society. Conservatism correlated in the predictable direction with the statement that "the death penalty should be abolished."

In Table 10 it can be observed that 47.6% of those who disagree strongly are conservatives, while 44.7% of those who agree strongly are liberals. There is also a symmetry between those conservatives who disagree somewhat (35.7%) and those liberals who agree somewhat (35.1%). This may be interpreted as indicating that agreement is correlated with liberalism and disagreement with conservatism.

TABLE 10. "THE DEATH PENALTY SHOULD BE ABOLISHED" VARIABLE: ABSOLUTE NUMBERS AND PERCENTAGES (IN PARENTHESES) OF RESPONSES

	Attitudes			
Political Characterization	Disagree Strongly	Disagree Somewhat	Agree Somewhat	Agree Strongly
Far Left	1 (0.4)	0	0	2 (1.0)
Liberal	44 (18.8)	85 (21.6)	98 (35.1)	89 (44.7)
Middle of the Road	66 (28.3)	162 (41.3)	107 (38.3)	74 (37.1)
Conservative	111 (47.6)	140 (35.7)	73 (26.1)	32 (16.0)
Far Right	11 (4.7)	5 (1.2)	1 (0.3)	2 (1.0)
Totals	233 (100.0)	392 (100.0)	279 (100.0)	199 (100.0)

Another characteristic difference between liberals and conservatives is to be found in the area of social responsibility. Liberals tend to have a higher sense of duty to assist their fellow man in areas of social welfare even when there is nothing to be gained by those rendering the aid. Conservatives are more likely to stress individual responsibility.

A number of statements statistically significant in predicting political characterization express sentiments widely recognized as related to attitudes toward social responsibility. In all but a few cases, liberals agree with these statements far more frequently than do conservatives. Table 11 illustrates the point.

TABLE 11. ATTITUDES TOWARD SOCIAL RESPONSIBILITY

Statement	Percentage Agreement		
	Liberals & Far Left	Conservatives & Far Right	Predictability Rank
Government should be more involved in school desegregation.	51.7	29.1	8
Government should be more involved in the elimination of poverty.	75.7	51.3	9
Courts protect the criminal too much.	54.5	73.5	13
All should have a chance to go to college.	35.4	24.4	14
Government should be more involved in compensatory financial aid for the disadvantaged.	37.9	23.7	15
Government should be more involved in compensatory education for the disadvantaged.	62.4	42.6	16

If the significant variables are ranked in order of predictability, these statements of attitudes toward social responsibility form a cluster in the middle third of that listing. Since the dispersion is in agreement with known fact this is another indication that these significant variables associated with political characterization possess the properties of a valid measure of liberalism and conservatism. A comparison of the attitudes of midshipmen in the area of social responsibility with those of private university students reveals a pronounced difference (see Table 12).

This contrast might have been expected on an *a priori* basis: students preparing themselves for a career in the military, where traditionally little emphasis has been placed on the problems of society, would not be expected to be concerned with questions of social welfare as students preparing themselves for other careers. The statistics give us some indication of just how great the difference in outlook is.

Just three statements in the questionnaire were related to the role of the military, and all three met the criteria of significance for our purposes. The statements in decreasing order of predictability are shown in Table 13.

TABLE 12. ATTITUDES TOWARD SOCIAL RESPONSIBILITY

Statements	Agreement	
	Naval Academy	Private Universities
Federal govenment should be more involved in school desegregation.	41.1%	54.5%
Federal government should be more involved in eliminating poverty.	65.6	82.2
Courts protect criminals too much.	64.8	49.3
All should have a chance to go to college.	31.3	48.5
Government should be more involved in compensatory financial aid to the disadvantaged.	30.0	49.4
Government should be involved in compensatory education for the disadvantaged.	51.1	65.4

TABLE 13. ATTITUDES TOWARD THE MILITARY

Statements	Agreement	
	Naval Academy	Private Universities
Government should be more involved in military involvement in Southeast Asia.	33.4%	11.1%
Government should be more involved in development of ABM.	81.6	20.9
The Army should be voluntary.	50.6	76.7

It is interesting that by the summer of 1970 there was a consensus among all students, including Naval Academy students, that we should not increase our commitments in Southeast Asia. There was a strong correlation between those who responded that the commitment should be increased and conservative identification. The largest disparity between Academy students and those at the other end of the spectrum occurs for the statement approving the development of military weaponry. More than four fifths of the Naval Academy students agreed that the commitment to develop an ABM should be increased, while a little over one fifth of private university students agreed. The idea of a volunteer army has wide appeal although again a smaller proportion of midshipmen favor this idea.

These results are in conformity with other studies of political ideology of the right and left.[15] The far right sees the nation weakened and dishonored through policies of compromise and "appeasement" that are heading in the direction of national destruction. In contrast the belief of the far left is that the United States should withdraw from economic, political, and military intervention into the affairs of other states. It holds that the United States must reform its own social and political institutions before it can act constructively in world affairs.

Liberals and conservatives would not go so far. Conservatives would emphasize the need to be prepared militarily and respond forcefully to threats to the position of the United States. Liberals would emphasize, on the other hand, the need for caution because a "hair-trigger" response might ensnare the nation in extended and unnecessary commitments with unfortunate results for both ourselves and our allies. An increased concern with military strength is seen as one moves to the right.

In addition to the clusters of variables dealing with social welfare issues and military and foreign policy posture, a third group of items dealt with the issue of authority versus individual freedom or, depending on the perception of the individual, "order versus anarchy." We have already analyzed some of these items, i.e., the alleged laxity of college officials in dealing with student protests, the right of college officials to ban extremists from speaking on campus, and increasing the role of students in the college curriculum. In fact, five of the first six variables, in terms of their strength as a predictor of political characterization, are in this category.

TABLE 14. ATTITUDES TOWARD INDIVIDUAL OR GROUP CONTROL

Statements	Agreement	
	Liberals and far left	Conservatives and far right
Government should be more involved in gun control.	38.0%	21.7%
College grades should be abolished.	34.5	20.2
College officials should regulate student publications.	36.9	56.4
Government should control television and newspapers.	8.8	18.9
College officials have a right to control students off campus.	18.1	31.2

[15] See especially, Daniel Bell (ed.), *The Radical Right* (New York: Doubleday, 1963).

At least five more variables or statements related to individual or group control or discipline were significant according to the criteria adopted. They are shown in Table 14.

It is noteworthy that ten of 24 statements that proved to be significant deal with the general concern for order and discipline versus lack of control. It has long been recognized that conservatives are inclined to stress duty and order over individual rights, and the results presented above bring forth further evidence on this matter.

When midshipmen responses on the five statements in Table 14 are compared with the responses of freshmen at private universities, further evidence is obtained of the relatively more conservative positions taken by the students at Annapolis. Only first-year students at junior colleges are consistently more conservative than plebes.

The category of statements on interpersonal relationships also appeared to help predict political characterization. How the individual views himself in relation to his friends and other students and in relation to his parents and the "older generation" is indicative of political attitudes.

Four variables concerning interpersonal relations met the statistical criteria for ability to predict political characterization. They are shown in Table 15.

TABLE 15. ATTITUDES CONCERNING INTERPERSONAL RELATIONS

Statements	Agreement	
	Liberals and far left	Conservatives and far right
It is essential or very important to have friends different from me.	65.8%	50.4%
My beliefs are similar to those of other students.	56.2	45.9
Liberalize divorce laws.	54.6	41.8
There is a generation gap with parents.	9.4	4.7

All the interpersonal items were on the lower end of the ranking in terms of predictability, but they were statistically significant nonetheless. Compared to students at private universities, the percentage of plebes that agree is uniformly smaller in all the statements, which tends to substantiate what other tests have indicated, that conservatism is more characteristic of people who prefer the friendship of those who share their perception of society.[16]

[16] McClosky, *op. cit.*, p. 36. Also Giuseppe Di Palma and Herbert McClosky, "Personality and Conformity: The Learning of Political Attitudes," *American Political Science Review* (December 1970), pp. 1054–1073.

It is interesting that Naval Academy students are less open to a liberalization of divorce laws than are Catholic college students (47.2% versus 43.5% for the Naval Academy plebes), who for obvious reasons would be expected to disagree with the proposal. Those who identify as conservative are less inclined to experience a generation gap at least in part because their attitudes are in greater conformity with those of their parents. Liberals would be expected to experience a generation gap because they prefer some changes that their parents are reluctant to accept. Academy students might experience less of a generation gap with their parents because their parents are pleased by their enrollment at the Academy where more attention is given to academic matters, discipline, and training. Conversely the greater generation gap experienced by students at private universities, along with every other category of four-year institution, is in large measure a reflection of parental misgivings over lack of discipline and required application to studies in most institutions. Generally one could infer that parents would agree with earlier statements concerning the alleged laxity of college officials in handling student protests. The Academy relieves parents of some anxieties concerning their sons' activities while in a college environment. This contrast also indicates that the academy experience tends to reinforce goals from the home environment. One study conducted at West Point concluded that a high percentage of the cadets chose that military academy because of its discipline in contrast to the student disorders at other institutions.[17]

TABLE 16. CURRENT RELIGIOUS PREFERENCE

Religious Preference	Number in group	Far left	Liberal	Middle of the road	Conservative	Far right
Protestant:						
Reformation*	300	0.0%	26.7%	37.0%	34.6%	1.7%
Pietistic†	247	0.0	21.4	37.2	39.3	2.0
Other	104	0.0	23.1	37.5	38.5	0.9
Jewish	5	20.0	40.0	0.0	40.0	0.0
Roman Catholic	397	0.3	34.0	37.8	26.2	1.8
Other religions	22	0.0	50.0	31.8	18.2	0.0
No religious preference	40	2.5	32.5	32.5	30.0	2.5

* (e.g., Episcopolian, Lutheran, Presbyterian)
† (e.g., Baptist, Methodist)

[17] In a questionnaire, over 41.3% of the plebes at West Point indicated that "turmoil on college campuses was a factor that increased their desire to pursue a military career." Captain Gary Spencer, "A Social-Psychological Profile of the Class of 1973" (West Point: Office of Research, 1969), p. 11.

One of the main results of this study is that it reveals the lack of significance of personal and family characteristics in determining political characterization of midshipmen, except for the influence of religious preference. The only variable relating to personal and family characteristics (e.g., family income, grades, race, father's education) analyzed in this study that was found to be a statistically significant predictor of political characterization was "current religious preference."

For purposes of simplifying the analysis, the data on religious preference has been collapsed from 17 categories down to seven. Table 16 summarizes the data grouped under the more comprehensive categories.

Table 16 illustrates in general terms the importance of religious preference as an indicator of political characterization. The results clearly indicate a tendency for all three Protestant groups to be more conservative than the non-Protestant groups. If one excludes the small Jewish sample, it is remarkable that there is relatively little deviation in the proportion of each group identifying themselves as moderate, including those who claim no religious preference. The major contrast is in the number of Protestants who identify as conservative and the increased number of non-Protestants who identify as liberal.

These results conform with the general results in the data compiled by the American Council on Education. The University of Michigan's Survey Research Center has also concluded that Jews have been consistently more liberal than either Catholics, Protestants, or any other ethnic group on virtually all issues. And, also nonsouthern white Protestants tended to be more conservative than nonsouthern white Catholics.[18]

CONCLUSIONS

The Naval Academy attracts students primarily from upper-middle-income families. In this regard the midshipmen have financial backgrounds very similar to private university students. The plebes also possess a commendable record of scholastic accomplishments in high school that is superior to the other norm groups, as well as an unusually high level of competitive leadership demonstrated in their secondary school performance.

All this leads to the conclusion that these students are very similar to those cited in earlier studies in which the college experience is continuous and compatible with both precollege and postcollege life patterns. Their college experience tends to reinforce their previous ideas on their appropriate place in society. Certainly the Academy tries to encourage the belief

[18] John P. Robinson, Jerrold G. Rusk, and Kendra B. Head, *Measures of Political Attitudes* (Ann Arbor: University of Michigan Survey Research Center, Institute for Social Research, 1963), pp. 54–62.

that upon graduation a midshipman will be prepared for "responsible leadership." In short, as the Academy experience will not be discontinuous, social attitudes will not change greatly in four years.

The object of the study was to identify the variables that explain midshipmen political characterization and compare this characterization at the U.S. Naval Academy with the results obtained at other colleges and universities. The study was successful in identifying variables that generally separate conservative students from liberal students.

The evidence presented in this study indicates that student self-identification along a liberal-conservative continuum is generally very accurate as judged by other scholars who have examined the characteristics of liberal-conservative perceptions. The items that most effectively distinguish between liberals and conservatives tend to cluster around four attitude patterns. These four areas of disagreement reflect a scale of different values between liberals and conservatives in areas in which neither side can empirically demonstrate the superiority of their position.

First, among the variables with some of the highest *tau* rankings (see Appendix) were statements that refer to attitudes toward *conventional values,* especially those dealing with college issues. Thus conservatives, and particularly individuals on the far right, associate themselves more strongly with conventional moral values than those on the left of the political spectrum. Conservatives are more likely to react favorably to the strong use of *authority* by those in positions of leadership and to believe that some problems could be solved by a stronger use of authority. At the same time they are more inclined to reject those who oppose this authority.

Second, the set of attitudinal statements dealing with *social responsibility* generally displayed the second-greatest ability to separate individuals at different ends of the political spectrum. Proportionally more of those who identified themselves as liberal or far left were uniformly in favor of collective action on the issues of assistance to those in poverty, school desegregation, and rights of the accused than were individuals on the right of the political spectrum who stressed individual responsibility.

Third, statements on the *role of the military* are also good predictors of political characterization, although on this general issue, except for the attitude toward involvement in Southeast Asia, there is clearly more of a consensus among Academy students. Conservatives clearly show a greater concern for military strength than do liberals.

Fourth, the psychological forces affecting *interpersonal relations* are also good predictors of political characterization. Statements included in this category were concerned with diversity of friends, similarity of beliefs, divorce, and the generation gap. Here conservatives appeared to be set more apart from their college colleagues in that their ideas conformed more closely to those of their parents, and they acknowledged that their beliefs were less likely to be like those of their college colleagues. They were also less likely to think it important to have friends with ideas different from their own, which suggests some isolation from their contemporaries.

Another significant aspect of this study was the determination of the 25 variables independent of political characterization as tested by the chi-square statistic. The conventional wisdom is challenged by the finding that no relationship exists between political identification and certain of these variables. All the personal and family characteristics such as family income, grades, and race, except "current religious preferences," were not significant predictors of political characterization. It is particularly noteworthy that the size of home town, the social characterization of the home neighborhood, and social status were independent of political characterization. A tentative interpretation of this is that social, economic, and geographical mobility in America is so high that we have literally attained a "mass society" in which these socioeconomic and geographic characteristics are no longer so significant as they once were. Because political and social attitudes are, by contrast, learned attitudes they are, like religion, usually shaped by the environment of the particular home. This connection explains to some extent the significance of religion and the lack of significance of other personal factors.

The Academy produces a large proportion of the elite of the officer corps for the Navy, just as the private universities produce a large proportion of the civilian elites. As expected, the distribution of the political characterization of Academy midshipmen is centered to the political right of the distribution for private university freshmen. Compared to the other groups of colleges and universities identified by the American Council on Education, midshipmen attitudes most resemble those of technical institution students, politically the most conservative group in the ACE classification. The distribution for midshipmen appears to be centered near the middle of the political spectrum and to be symmetrical on both tails.

Identification of the determinants of political characterization at the Naval Academy and their comparison with similar results at all other universities and colleges enhance the understanding of military behavior in relation to political and social issues. The importance of these traits is reinforced by the fact that Academy graduates tend to become, in position disproportionate to their numbers, the future leaders of the Navy. The analysis of their present political characterization should shed some light on the views and attitudes of the next generation of military leaders. As the results are strikingly similar to responses at West Point and Colorado Springs, the conclusions hold valid for all three services.

The results of this study also suggest that the recruitment and self-selection process largely determines the outlook of the student body, as most of the student body has a particular orientation upon arrival. It may be questionable to attribute the political outlook of academy students or graduates to the socialization process of the academy. Rather, to a considerable degree, conservative students may be attracted in disproportionate numbers to the academies and merely have their predispositions reinforced by their experience there.

This study suggests the degree of variance from other norm groups in outlook. Other recent studies have examined the longitudinal effect of social and political attitudes development on adult social and political behavior.[19] These studies indicate that there is significant stability in personality factors over an individual's life. Particularly significant for our interest is that it was found that ethnocentrism, authoritarianism and political economic conservatism were strong predictors of the basic orientations of political belief over more than two decades.

APPENDIX

Test Design

The initial step in the statistical analysis was to construct tables of cross-classifications between the values of the political characterization variable and the values of each of the 72 potential determinants. Once these tables of cross-classifications were completed, several test statistics were utilized to measure what, if any, association existed between the variables in each table.

First the chi-square statistic was employed to test the null hypothesis of independence between each one of the potential determinants (see Table 6, page 123) and political characterization (for example see Table 7, page 124. Potential determinance was a simple dichotomy of yes or no. Thus each chi-square table tested a table of 2 columns and 5 rows. Whenever the null hypothesis was rejected at the 5% level of significance or better, the alternative hypothesis of a significant association between the variables was accepted. Table 1A summarizes the results of the chi-square tests by type of variable.

As Table 1A indicates, 47 of the 72 potential determinants showed a significant association at the 5% level of significance or better. Moreover, most of the significant relations (34 of them) reached the .5 level of significance or better. The variables in category C have the highest levels of significance, although categories B, D, and E also show a high proportion of variables related to political characterization.

[19] J. Block, *Lives through Time*. In collaboration with Norma Haan (Berkeley: Bancroft Books, 1971). See also Jeanne N. Knutson, "Long Term Effects of Personality on Political Attitudes and Beliefs," a paper delivered at the 1973 Annual Meeting of the American Political Science Association.

TABLE 1A. CHI-SQUARE STATISTIC BY TYPE OF SIGNIFICANT VARIABLE

	Level of Significance				
Type of Variable	0.5%	1.0%	2.5%	5.0%	Total of Sig. Variables
A	1	0	0	1	2
B	11	0	1	1	13
C	7	0	1	0	8
D	9	1	1	0	11
E	5	1	0	2	8
F	1	2	0	2	5
Total	34	4	3	6	47

The chi-square test results indicate that a large number of potential predictors show some association with political characterization. However, the chi-square test means only that chances are better than 95 out of 100 that the two variables involved are *not* independent. Further analysis is needed. It indicates in fact that the relationship is strong enough to be meaningful and is 95% sure that it could not be due to mere chance.

The 47 variables found to be significantly associated with political characterization by the chi-square test were next analyzed by means of Goodman and Kruskal's *tau*.[1] This statistic gives the percentage error reduction in predicting the distribution into categories of a variable when other information is known over a simple random distribution.[2] For example, suppose we have a sample of 1200 midshipmen distributed randomly into

[1] See, for instance, Hubert M. Blalock, *Social Statistics* (New York: McGraw-Hill, 1960), pp. 232–234.

[2] Goodman and Kruskal's *tau* was calculated according to the following formula:

$$tau = \frac{(E_2 - E_1)}{(T - E_1)}$$

where we have a contingency table of N rows and M columns and Y_{ij} represent the elements (number of items in each cross-classification) of the table, and $T = Y_{ij}$ (sample size); $S_j = Y_{ij}$ (column totals); $T_i = Y_{ij}$ (row totals);

$$E_1 = \left(T - \frac{S_j}{T}\right) S_j$$

and

$$E_2 = \left(T_i - \frac{Y_{ij}}{T_i}\right) Y_{ij}$$

the five political identification categories in the "Student Information Form." Based on our knowledge of this distribution alone we can attempt to identify the political identification of each midshipman. But with so little information we would expect to make a considerable number of errors. A measure of the average number of errors we would be likely to make in this procedure is then calculated. Now suppose that the midshipmen's religious affiliation is known, and we try to predict their political characterization based on this additional information. Goodman and Kruskal's *tau* serves as a measure of the percentage reduction in our prediction error when we include this additional information. The advantage of this statistic is that it enables the ranking of the potential political characterization determinants as to their effectiveness. The criterion of effectiveness is ability to predict. Those variables that greatly reduce prediction error will have high ranks, while the ones that reduce prediction error only slightly will rank lower.

In order to limit the number of determinants studied to those with high explanatory power, an arbitrary level for the *tau* statistic of a 1% reduction in error was utilized as a cutoff point. Those variables that reduce the error in predicting political characterization by less than 1% were eliminated from further consideration. Except for one variable,[3] all the variable with *tau* values better than 1% were also statistically significant at the .5% level or better of the chi-square test statistic.

[3] Family income was a variable that was not statistically significant at even the 5% level of the chi-square test. Yet further analysis indicated that its *tau* value was 1.396%. Nonetheless, family income was excluded from the list of variables to be analyzed.

7

Vietnam and United States Military Thought Concerning Civil-Military Roles in the Government

JOHN R. PROBERT

With the increasing unpopularity of U.S. intervention in Vietnam and a concurrent demand for additional resources to solve pressing domestic problems came a decline, in the early seventies, in military prestige, pronounced antimilitarism throughout the country, and disillusionment in the armed forces. Military men reacted to these developments with a variety of proposals for changes in civil-military relationships within the government. This chapter was designed to determine the nature and significance of these proposals.[1]

[1] To acquire a representative sample of military proposals, some 75 periodicals, the overwhelming majority of them published by the military or related organizations, were surveyed. Some 70 of these periodicals are included in the *Air University Library Index to Military Periodicals.* These periodicals are the principal vehicles for the expression of responsible, but generally unofficial, military points of view. Occasionally, a statement by a military man will come out in a newspaper, in book form, or as an article in a popular magazine, as Marine General David M. Shoup's "The New American Militarism" in *The Atlantic* for April, 1969. For this reason, an attempt was made to include significant articles from other than military or military-related publications.

With one or two exceptions, the articles all appeared during the years 1968 to 1972. These years were chosen because it has been during this period that most of the impact of the Vietnam War and subsequent developments on relationships between the civilian and the military in governmental processes has been reflected in the writings of military men and those closely associated with them. In all, some 25 relevant articles have been analyzed. They have varied from three to 70 journal pages in length and were authored overwhelmingly by officers, most of them in the upper ranks. Some few were written by civilians, who were, in almost every case, presently or formerly, closely associated with defense institutions. It is believed that these articles comprise a representative sample of authoritative, post-Vietnam military opinion on the nature of future civil-military relations in U.S. national governmental processes.

This study attempts to analyze and categorize these various views on the correct

PAST AND PRESENT CIVIL-MILITARY RELATIONSHIPS IN THE AMERICAN GOVERNMENT

For the American military, Vietnam served to make crystal clear a problem of long standing, namely, how to square traditional professional ethics with the new requirements of formulating and implementing national security policy. In an earlier day, the responsible civilians in our government had been accustomed to make and carry out our foreign policy with little military participation. When peaceful means failed, matters were left to the military almost in their entirety. The military professional ethic precluded political activity, especially in domestic affairs but also clearly in the making and conduct of foreign affairs. Though this attitude denied the validity of von Clausewitz, it obtained as established American practice through World War II.

The atomic bomb changed the context in which such a precedent had operated, and in fact made the precedent untenable. In a world in which the two major powers possessed atomic weapons, war pressed to the unconditional surrender of one of those powers, or even an ally, was too dangerous. Escalation could precipitate a war of annihilation. Wars persisted, however—most pointedly, the cold war. Contending nations strove by any means short of nuclear holocaust to bend opponents to their will. A nation had to be prudent and gradual in its application of a variety of means of pressure on the enemy. Wars could not be fought all-out; they were not fought by strictly military means. Under such circumstances, war could not be left to the generals. The world began to realize that victory in war could consist simply in denying the enemy the achievement of his objectives and did not necessarily include his capitulation.

It is now clear that the military voice must be heard in peacetime, and the civilian voice in wartime. Modern conflict management, in an age of cold war, requires a meshing of all the various kinds of expertise and all the elements of national power to maintain national security. Yet the professional ethic with its nonpartisanship and its apolitical view persists. Civilian supremacy is acknowledged; our democratic institutions must be safeguarded by circumspect political activity on the part of the military.[2]

The simplistic past having given way to the complex present in American civil-military relations within the government, what are the various

---

nature of intragovernmental relationships between the civilian and the military and to assess their impact upon currently prevailing modes of civil-military relationships in the U.S. Government.

[2] See Robert J. Gard, Jr., Colonel, USA, "The Military and American Society," *Foreign Affairs,* 49, #4 (July, 1971), pp. 698–710, for an excellent statement of this dilemma of the present-day military.

kinds of political activity in which a military man might conceivably engage? Which kinds would appear logically consistent with our democratic system; which inconsistent? And what are the present arrangements?

Huntington has defined five possible roles for the military in politico-military affairs: the advisory, the representative, the executive, the advocatory, and the substantive. The first three he considers nonpolitical and hence, by implication, acceptable forms of activity within the professional military ethic. The last two he has labelled as unqualifiedly political and, again by implication, proscribed by the professional ethics of the military profession.

In the *advisory* role, the military man makes available to the civilians his military expertise, advising them on the military implications of proposed policies. He is contributing his special skills and knowledge of weapons and weapons systems, of the likely effects of particular strategies and tactics upon the enemy, neutrals, or the home front. Naval officers, explaining just how a naval quarantine would work in the Cuban missile crisis, appear an apt example.

The *representative* role finds the military man advancing the interests of the military in intragovernmental councils within the executive branch. In this instance the military man is partisan in the sense that he is advancing points of view held by the military and considered by them advantageous to the armed forces and the nation.

Pursuing the *executive* role, the military man implements governmental decisions.

The *advocatory* role, in its mildest form, calls upon the military officer to explain and defend publicly, or in Congress, the policies of the administration.

A different form of advocacy would be an attempt to convince the public of the wisdom of military policies at variance with those of the government in power. This second form of the advocatory role verges on the fifth role of the military, the *substantive*. In this role the military man is attempting to overturn established military or other policy of the administration by engaging in overt political activity. This role is forbidden to American military men on active duty but has been played increasingly by those in a retired status.[3] Examples would be Generals Matthew Ridgeway and Maxwell Taylor as they sought to change, after retirement, administration policy on the composition of defense forces.

Under present practice, the first three of the roles, when played by the

[3] Samuel P. Huntington, "The Challenge of Defense of Political Science," (the author, mimeographed, undated), pp. 10–11, as quoted in William R. Treacy, "Politico-Military Involvement—A Functional Imperative," *Military Review,* 49 (April, 1969), p. 35 and Samuel P. Huntington, *The Soldier and the State* (Cambridge Mass.: Belknap Press, 1957), p. 374*ff*.

active-duty military, are entirely consistent with the maintenance of our democratic institutions and the principle of civilian supremacy. Most authorities, to include Huntington, agree on this. The substantive, they also agree, is clearly not, and it is, in fact, prohibited by regulation.

It is in connection with the advocatory role and its various forms that the difficulties arise. Military issues in an age of vast military forces and budgets are inevitably political issues. Vietnam, the TFX instance where a huge contract for airplanes was awarded with evidence of political pressures and the loan guarantee for the Lockheed Company, where political influence was brought to bear to save a large defense contractor from bankruptcy, are cases in point. Political administrations have turned increasingly to military men holding responsible positions for defense of politico-military decisions. Increasingly, military men have explained and defended those decisions.

In a democracy, administrations change inevitably. What appeared to be "explaining" and "defending" to one administration becomes "selling" to its successor, as in the instance of the Joint Chiefs of Staff at the time of General MacArthur's dismissal. The central issue is: When does "explaining" and "defending" become "selling" and hence the politicization of the military man? Where is the fine line dividing professionalism from politics to be drawn?

Though there is considerable evidence that the rule is not always followed, the present standard appears to be that the high military officer limits himself to defending and explaining administration policy before Congress and selling clearly established administration policy in public speeches. He may survive taking a position opposed to that of the administration if it is clearly elicited by a Congressional committee. Advocacy of any position not sanctioned by the administration in any other forum is taken on at considerable peril. Recently, incumbent senior military officers have invariably espoused publicly the administration's positions on civil-military relationships in the policy-making apparatus and the level of armaments.[4]

In summary, then, the advisory, representative, and executive roles are clearly acceptable. The advocatory role may be played currently to explain and defend and even to sell. It may also be used to advance positions opposed to those of the administration if such testimony is elicited before Congress. It may not be used with impunity to advance such opposing positions to the general public in speeches. And the substantive role is prohibited categorically.

[4] Earle G. Wheeler, General, USA, Chairman, JCS, "Policy, Power Mesh in Formula of Global Strategy," *Armed Forces Management,* 14 (June, 1968), pp. 42–4, and Thomas H. Moorer, Admiral, USN, Chairman, JCS, "Directions 71," *Commander's Digest,* 10, #12 (23 June 1971), p. 4ff and 10, #13 (July 29, 1971), p. 4*ff*.

CURRENT MILITARY OPINION ON CIVIL-MILITARY RELATIONSHIPS IN OUR NATIONAL POLICY-MAKING PROCESSES

Current military opinion on the kind of civil-military relationships that should characterize our national governmental processes almost universally proposes changes from the status quo. There are the inevitable problems of understanding the status quo and agreement as to what it is. These will be developed as we examine the range of views. It is not a complete spectrum of Huntington's roles of the military. No one really proposes that the military assume the substantive role, for example. On the other hand, one proposal, that of General Shoup, implies the existence of an already far too pervasive role for the military.

Let us start with the advisory role and General Shoup's view of it, proceed next to the views of those who feel the military is too frequently overridden by civilian command, and then take up the views of the defenders of the status quo as they see it. The positions of those who think the military must perform the representative role more effectively will follow in our discussion, and finally, we will come to the views of those who espouse a form of the advocatory role. The views do not fall neatly into the various role categories, but those categories are useful for purposes of rough classification.

Critics of Performance of the Advisory Role

General David M. Shoup, former Commandant of the U.S. Marine Corps, sees the United States as carried away on a tide of rampant militarism. He traces its roots to the nucleus of high-ranking, aggressive, ambitious professional military leaders. Their dominance he ascribes to their "sheer skill, energy and dedication." As he puts it, "It has been popular to blame the civilian administration for the conduct and failures of the war rather than to question the motives of the military. But some of the generals and admirals are by no means without responsibility for the Vietnam miscalculation." [5] What the General is saying is that present government arrangements afford the military too much influence, given their great abilities and dedication and the extent of militaristic feeling present in the general society, a contention he develops at some length in his article.

The General does not specify his solution to this problem, but presumably he would reduce the military to a minimal role of an advisory and executive nature. One cannot imagine him going beyond this in the present

[5] David M. Shoup, General, USMC (Ret.), "The New American Militarism," *The Atlantic,* 223 (April, 1969), p. 56.

state of the world's affairs. At no point does he suggest that the military should be completely divorced from the policy-making process, as some civilian critics have,[6] but he clearly implies a roll-back of military influence.

With some nostalgia, Colonel Robert J. Gard, Jr., in the July 1971 issue of *Foreign Affairs,* has referred to the simplistic situation of bygone days where "civilian authorities conducted politics and diplomacy without military participation; the military conducted war to victory without civilian intrusion." [7] But this is by no means Colonel Gard's prescription for proper civil-military relations. As mentioned earlier, he is actually a proponent of a modified professional ethic for the military where it actively but circumspectly participates in policy formulation and execution, as it must in these days of fully integrated national security policy.

A more extensive advisory role appears the next gradation of participation. All the military sources covered assumed the advisory role as an intrinsic part of the military function in our government. There was some feeling that the military could be better qualified for its advisory role, especially in the area of international politics and the internal politics of other nations. The rationale here is that the officer trained in external politics will better perform not only the advisory role but also the executive role in foreign countries.[8]

Another point of view holds that "since national security issues cannot be taken out of politics, military leaders must be trained accordingly." [9] The military and the political are so intertwined and national security policy-making so vital to a nation very much involved overseas that every segment of the society must play a part in policy-making. Of course, this position implies support of strong representative and executive roles as well. The line of separation between the advisory and representative roles in particular is indistinct.

Ward Just ascribes to the Army a determination to train its officers for political input to decision-making. The Army, he maintains, through circumspection or limited knowledge about the political side of things, did not have enough to say about Vietnam. This it intends to remedy.[10] Here again, the point of view seems to go beyond the advisory role and to extend strongly into the representative.

[6] See William A. Williams, "Officers and Gentlemen," *New York Review of Books,* XVI, #8 (6 May 1971), p. 7.

[7] Gard, *op. cit.,* p. 698.

[8] Donald B. Vought, Lt. Col., USA, "Soldiers Must be Statesmen," *Military Review,* 48 (October, 1968), p. 79.

[9] J. L. Miles, Lt. Col., USMC, "The Fusion of Military and Political Considerations: Threat or Challenge to the Military," 52 (August and September, 1968), p. 52.

[10] "Soldiers," *The Atlantic,* 226 (October-November, 1970), p. 77.

Opposition to "Civilian Command"

Those officers who complain about what they call "civilian command" are taking exception to the executive or implementing role the military has been required to play. Just reports encountering such complaints among Army officers.[11] A *New York Times* article ascribes the view to senior Air Force officers in Vietnam "disheartened by the restrictions placed on their conduct of the air war over North Vietnam."[12] General Krulak, U.S. Marine Corps (Ret.), complains of it in the same speech in which he extols civilian supremacy.[13]

It remained for Captain Samuel P. Ingram to express fully the military viewpoint on civilian control of military operations in Vietnam. His rationale is probably his own, but he certainly speaks for many in his criticisms. Captain Ingram sees the real nub of the problem of civil-military relations growing out of Vietnam as the question of "how much civilian control should be imposed on our military leaders in the prosecution of a war?" He contends there is no provision in the Constitution for either command or control of the armed forces by anonymous, untrained civilians who are not directly responsible to the electorate. His position is: "In the conduct of a war, let the tactical details of military operations be decided by military leaders without restriction, properly holding them responsible for the outcome."[14]

Defenders of the Status Quo

The defenders of the status quo in its entirety are few in number. Others defend the status quo by and large; but they do not all see the status quo as comprised of the same set of relationships, and they have, inevitably, qualifications. Some propose characteristics that appear to be recent innovations and therefore not part of the traditional status quo. Admiral Moorer and General Wheeler, the present Chairman of the Joint Chiefs of Staff and his immediate predecessor, in their public utterances take no exception to the civil-military relationships characterizing our decision-making and implementation in the national security area. Nor, basically, does General Maxwell Taylor, the immediate predecessor of General Wheeler as Chairman of the Joint Chiefs of Staff. General Taylor, for example, rebuts the charge that "our allegedly excessive political commitments are the

[11] *Ibid.*

[12] Saturday, May 14, 1966, p. 8.

[13] Victor H. Krulak, General, USMC (Ret.), "The Low Cost of Freedom," U.S. Naval Institute *Proceedings,* 96, #7 (July, 1970), p. 71.

[14] Samuel P. Ingram, Captain, USNR, "Civilian Command or Civilian Control?" U.S. Naval Institute *Proceedings,* 94, #5 (May, 1968), pp. 26–31.

results of excessive military influence in the decision-making process of foreign policy." He maintains that from his own experience the armed forces "in my time have never asked for more political commitments—rather they have been a force for restoring some kind of balance between liabilities undertaken and means of fulfillment." [15] In an earlier speech, however, General Taylor had set forth his idea of what the existing set of civil-military relationships in the national security area had become. He stated that prior to the present, war was something for generals, and generals stayed out of politics. Now, though, he added, because of the fear of World War III, the military is closely checked and made by civilians to keep options open and to practice gradualism to prevent any misunderstanding by the enemy. For this and a variety of other reasons, increased civilian control is here to stay. And its necessity he apparently accepts.[16]

Again, a civilian analyst of military policy, commenting on civil-military relationships in national security policy-making and its execution, exhorts the military to continue to press its case. It must not withdraw into isolation but must "forge the best posture, given the resources available." [17]

It was pointed out that a number of the defenders of the status quo added qualifications to this position, even though they were generally in agreement with the state of things. Those who generally agree with the existing system, even though they had some reservations, have been cited through representative examples in the preceding section. We now turn to those whose exceptions are basic. At the outset the exceptions of General Taylor to the existing system will be covered in fairness to his over-all observations.

Critics of the Military's Representative Role

"What is needed," General Taylor has said, "is a better method in our foreign policy-making process to assure a hearing for all sides of the issue before undertaking obligations which may set in motion a train of events which, in the end, may become the responsibility of the soldier. But in such a case, one must accept the soldier at the national council table, whereas the legitimacy of the military presence there is being challenged today as another example of excessive military influence." [18] General Taylor is calling for improvements that are not entirely clear. In an earlier speech he

[15] Maxwell D. Taylor, General, USA (Ret.), "A Seat for the Soldier at the National Council Table," *Armed Forces Journal,* 107 (November 1, 1969), p. 2.

[16] ———, "Post-Vietnam Role of the Military in Foreign Policy," *Air University Review,* XIX, #5 (July-August, 1968), pp. 50–58.

[17] Stanley L. Harrison, "Military Challenge in the 1970's," *Marine Corps Gazette,* 55, #1 (January, 1971), pp. 28–31.

[18] Taylor, "A Seat for the Soldier, etc.," *op. cit.,* p. 2.

insisted that the military in playing its representative role of support for civilian control must show it does not think only in terms of force and defends the national and not just the military interest.[19]

Like General Taylor, the former Deputy Assistant Secretary of Defense for Education Edward L. Katzenbach, Jr., takes the military itself to task for its improper performance of the representative role. He contends that because they feel that others are making their decisions, the military feels no need to concentrate on its own professional business. If they did so, in their war college studies particularly, they would be more effective in the national councils.[20]

Navy Captain Paul R. Schratz (Ret.) also faults the military itself for its failure properly to perform the representative role. He prescribes improvement of the JCS organization by the development of an accepted body of professional doctrine by the Joint Staff, use of the Joint Staff as the primary planning body by all services, better administrative efficiency in the Joint Staff, restoration of the prestige of professional military opinion, and retention of an ability for self-analysis and constructive self-criticism. He concludes that either doctrine and strategy must be integrated in the top echelons of military thought or professional opinion from the man in uniform must certainly wither.[21]

Colonel Fred C. Thayer, USAF (Ret.), continues in this vein. He maintains that only if the military gets on with the task of developing an over-all expertise that transcends the parochial boundaries of the services will it be able to maintain its necessary professional autonomy and still influence sufficiently the formulation of national policy.[22]

Finally, Army Colonel Robert J. Gard, Jr., cited earlier, and Anthony Hartley, military writer, contend that relaxation of the strictures of military professionalism on participation in the policy process and effective performance by the military of the professional military representative role will make for the correct level of influence in the policy process. In somewhat the same terms, a civilian writer on military subjects calls for a more articulate presentation of the military viewpoint in the broadest contexts in administrative circles if we are to have effective foreign policy-making in the future. The military is too preoccupied with intramilitary matters, too ingrown and inflexible in approach, too specialized. It has semantic problems,

[19] Taylor, "Post-Vietnam Role of the Military," *op. cit.*, p. 58.

[20] "The Demotion of Professionalism at the War Colleges," U.S. Naval Institute *Proceedings*, 91, #3 (March, 1965), pp. 33–41.

[21] "The Ivy-Clad Man on Horseback," U.S. Naval Institute *Proceedings*, 91, #3 (March, 1965), pp. 42–49.

[22] "Professionalism: The Hard Choice," U.S. Naval Institute *Proceedings*, 97, #2 (June, 1971), pp. 36–40.

and has over-quantified relying on an excess of data rather than relevant conclusions so that there is no real communication.[23]

While most of the criticism of the military performance of the representative role has been self-criticism, not all has been. From a Foreign Service Officer who has worked extensively with the military comes the contention that foreign policy-making should be done in partnership rather than with dominance by the civilian. He claims the military mind brings an indispensable element and complement to policy-making and implementation.[24] Again, two Army officers call for political involvement upon the part of the military in the representative process. Their advice is carefully qualified so that they advocate not doing for one administration that which they, as military officers, might regret should its opponent get into office. They also point out that in a democracy military leaders are frequently called upon to make public statements and that as they are public servants, they must not make statements that conflict with the position of the current administration. While they realize political involvement threatens military objectivity, they are aware that noninvolvement may be perilous as well, as witness the Nuremberg trials. Hence they suggest, finally, some basis for the advocatory role.[25]

The Advocatory Role

The advocatory role must be played with extreme circumspection by the military man. There are numerous instances in the past when it was not and the individual suffered. Admiral Denfeld was one instance; General MacArthur was another and a more prominent example.

When the military or a part of it feels imperiled or subjected unfairly to opprobrium, or when it feels national or international affairs are developing in a manner decidedly disadvantageous to the nation, it is tempted to turn to the advocatory role, or even to the substantive.

Our survey revealed no published calls for the practice of the unambiguous advocatory role. In three instances, however, what was proposed came very close indeed. The first was at best an oblique approach involving a call upon the part of General Taylor to the armed forces to do something about assuring the support of the home front for foreign policy, the legitimacy of the military role in a democratic society, and the indispensability

[23] Herman S. Wolk, "The Military-Civilian Defense Team—Time for Constructive Self-Analysis," *Air Force and Space Digest,* 52, #2 (February, 1969), pp. 52–55.

[24] R. J. Barrett, FSO, "Thoughts on the Military Mind," *Air Force and Space Digest,* 51 (May, 1968), pp. 66–67.

[25] S. H. Hays, Colonel, USA, and Thomas A. Rehm, Lt. Col., USA, "The Military in the Free Society," U.S. Naval Institute *Proceedings,* 95, #2 (February, 1969), pp. 26–36.

of military power as part of national power in support of our foreign policy.[26] Admiral Moorer has done approximately the same thing.[27] This call for action is political in its effects. High-ranking military men have engaged in this kind of activity traditionally. With circumspection, it appears to be a proper kind of activity. But great care is necessary to keep it non-partisan and non-self-seeking over the long term. As military and foreign policy has changed, military men, in retrospect, have seen the extent to which they have lent themselves to politicization. The prestige of the military is not enhanced thereby, and it is extremely difficult to determine how public statements during one administration will be viewed by the next or the one after that. Still, the concerned military man cannot and probably should not remain inactive in all instances.

A substantial portion of today's military sees itself under attack as it has seldom, if ever, been before. The war in Vietnam, domestic pressures, and contemporary philosophies are the causes. From this military point of view, the country is coming apart at the seams and the military is the only place where the old true virtues of unselfishness, honor, and patriotism persist. The world, as the military traditionally sees it, a world of power politics, would be overrun and enslaved if it were not for American military might. Furthermore, there is an enemy within seeking to destroy the military through malevolence, ignorance, misunderstanding, and wishful thinking.

Such a view of the military's position in the United States, the threat to it, and the threat to America is presented in one outstanding article included in the survey.[28] The author advocates an activist program for the military as its bounden duty. In addition to putting its own house in order, the military must speak out, not in generalities, not blandly, but confronting critics directly. And the military must not stop with refutation and rebuttal but produce a positive set of answers on the nation's security needs with consideration of the "nation's domestic political and fiscal realities." "To honor the oath we have taken [as military officers] we must speak for ourselves," says the author.

This appears to be a clear instance of a call to the advocatory role that could lead to the kind of political activity that would do great harm to the professionalism of the military ethic. The diagnosis of the domestic and international ills of the country is the military's; the prescription for its cure is to be the military's. If it is at considerable variance with the incumbent administration, you have a basic problem. Even if it is not at variance with the incumbent administration's views, it may be with the next.

[26] Taylor, "Post-Vietnam Role etc.," *op. cit.*

[27] Moorer, *op. cit.*

[28] Robert J. Hanks, Captain, USN, "Against All Enemies," U.S. Naval Institute *Proceedings*, 96, #3 (March, 1970), pp. 23–29.

CONCLUSION

In conclusion, this survey of military opinion has revealed no clarion call for a disavowal of the traditional military professional ethics of civil-military relations within the United States government. There is dissatisfaction with some of the present arrangements because they conflict with real or imagined relationships in the past. Harkening back to the days when the civilian and the military, for good or bad, operated in distinct spheres, they seem to want to turn the clock back but know that this cannot be done. There is widespread recognition of the increasing interrelationship of the civilian and the military and the constraints of the nuclear age.

With full awareness of the pitfalls which line the way, what is proposed, with some diffidence, is a broadened representative role for the military and an advisory role played more ably by military officers better educated in national and international politics. It follows that if officers are better educated in the politics of other countries, they will probably perform the executive role abroad with greater effectiveness.

With some chagrin over what is considered undue supervision of purely military kinds of activity, and exhortations to military and civilians to realize the degree to which we must hear and heed the military viewpoint, the broadest role proposed for the military, with one exception, is the customary advocatory one played by high-ranking military men. In this role, strong military forces as basic to the pursuit of an adequate foreign policy are the traditional ingredients, to which has been added, because of the current antimilitarism in some sectors of American society, a rationale for the legitimacy of the military role in our democratic society. This last, new to American life in this generation, is not without precedent in the last.

Above all, there is much self-criticism, a healthy self-evaluative reaction to a thought-provoking, traumatic military, and indeed, national experience. It might be added that there is a need for as much introspection in the other elements of our society as the military has exhibited in its reaction to Vietnam.

8

The Press and National Security

Lt. CHARLES R. D'AMATO

This chapter focuses on a currently explosive issue: the relationship of a free press to the "national security." Specific relations between the press and the working military will be touched upon and their several perceptions of each other's role in American democracy examined. However, the central concern is not so much with the military as an institution as with "military," "security," and "national interest" considerations as defined and implemented by the executive branch as a whole.

It is not particularly productive to examine press-military relations in isolation, for several reasons. First, though the military plays important roles in the policy-making process and, indeed, attempts to use the private media as well as its own large information outlets to push its point of view, this is true of all agencies within the executive bureaucracy and a normal part of policy-making behavior. The Pentagon's methods of using the media to enhance its position in policy debates are typical of all the executive agencies.

Second, as most of the executive bureaucracy was in agreement as to the directions of policy in the last decade, the policies espoused by the military were not unique to the military and in some cases were not original with the military. It would be a mistake to assume the military made policy in the decade of the 1960's, although, to be sure, it had dominating influence over Presidents at times when those Presidents were desirous of military solutions.[1]

Third, within the executive there has been a general consensus on how to handle the media and unspoken but very definite assumptions on the

[1] In fact, argues Lawrence Radway, military leaders have a smaller voice in the formation of American foreign and defensive policy today than they had in the 1950's. "To be sure . . . the military executive still plays a prominent role. . . . But to the extent that the foreign policy of the United States has relied heavily on military force in recent decades, it has reflected . . . the judgement of successive Presidents, their principal political associates, a majority of Congress, and a majority of the . . . people. It has not been the result of inordinate military power." *Foreign Policy and National Defense* (Glenview, Illinois: Scott, Foresman, 1969), pp. 80–81.

questions of providing timely information via the press to the public. Again, this has not been an information policy unique to, or original with, the Pentagon.

Fourth, given the recent behavior of the Nixon administration in its response to the "Selling of the Pentagon" TV documentary by CBS—once epitomized in attacks by Spiro T. Agnew—and the attempt to restrain the printing of the *Pentagon Papers* by the *New York Times* and the *Washington Post*, poor press-military relations merely reflect the more critical White House-press relationship. As will be discussed below, however, the media and the military have developed an extremely strained relationship and highly antagonistic images of each other, which should certainly be a cause for concern.

The period under scrutiny is 1961–71, during which time rather profound changes have occurred in the perceptions and values of the press, altering the press-executive relationship and raising significant issues for American democracy and security. We begin with a case study of the Bay of Pigs episode. So much has been written about that invasion by both the principal government actors and the members of the American press that it is possible to put together a nearly complete picture of information—suppression, military fiasco, press-executive recriminations, and recantations and confessions; all the while, sitting squarely in the middle of these events, is the classic problem of "responsible" news judgment.

The propriety of the withholding or release of information by the press thought to be in the interest of national security has been a central and unresolved problem for the nation, particularly since World War II. The fundamental issue concerns the tension between, on the one hand, the requirements of an open society for free, broad, and timely discussion of the significant problems of the day and, on the other, the necessity to conduct effective foreign policies in a world of many systems, some of which utilize suppression and censorship to advantage in their external strategies. The view of many has been that the two ideals of liberty and security are, at least partly, mutually exclusive. Samuel Huntington, for example, has summed it up: "The tension between the demands of military security and the values of American liberalism can, in the long run, be relieved only by the weakening of the security threat or the weakening of liberalism." [2] Does the press owe its primary allegiance to the ideals of truth and full discussion, even though its disclosures may seem to effect adversely foreign policies? Or does loyalty to country sometimes require suppression of information judged vital to the "national interest"? If so, who is to determine the limits of permissibility and what set of standards will be invoked?

How can the people best control their government? Bernard Cohen's

[2] Samuel Huntington, *The Soldier and the State* (N.Y.: Vintage, 1957), p. 456.

examination of attitudes of editors and foreign affairs journalists has revealed a general sense of their responsibility to provide enough information to allow the public to form rational opinions and make intelligent judgments about the issues of the day. He found that the reporter conceives of his role as a supplier of information culled from the executive branch and from abroad to the public, which in turn "communicates its preferences to the Congress." The Congress is then able to act on the issues and exert pressure on the executive. Thus the "better the job that the press does in providing the information, the better the capacity of the people to make intelligent judgements," and, presumably, the more effective is Congressional power. Furthermore, the press views itself as a representative of the people in holding the executive accountable for its actions.[3]

In contrast to Cohen's findings on the attitude of newsmen toward newsworthy information, many responsible members of the press during the months preceding the Bay of Pigs debacle attempted to draw the line between suppression and exposure of vital information. The Cuban situation did not raise the problem frequently cited today, the increasing difficulty an editor encounters in selecting coherent and important information from the flood of available material. On the contrary, there was a clearly defined, important story, the details of which grew over a period of about six months. A number of reporters and editors knew the facts, knew their importance, and in what they considered the interests of national security, chose to suppress them. In some cases, they were asked to suppress them; in some other cases, they were warned to suppress them. In a few cases, the story or some part of it was printed, and those men were later accused of jeopardizing the national interest.

The following sections of this chapter will examine (1) how the media treated early information, (2) what was happening at the policy-making and operational levels of the invasion plan, and (3) what the effect of (1) was on (2).

PRESS COVERAGE OF THE BAY OF PIGS AFFAIR

Early Stories

In March 1960, the American government was sufficiently disenchanted with Fidel Castro that President Eisenhower ordered the CIA to train a force of Cuban exiles for possible use against his regime. The first indication in the world's press that something of this nature was happening came seven months later, on October 30, 1960. Clemente Maroquin Rojas,

[3] Bernard Cohen, *The Press and Foreign Policy* (Princeton: Princeton Univ. Press, 1963), pp. 20–23.

a leading Latin American commentator and director of the Guatemalan newspaper *La Hora,* stated in a front-page editorial that:

> . . . in Guatemala an invasion of Cuba is well under way, prepared not by our own country, so poor and so disorganized. . . . The issue here involved is simply that of giving all possible facilities to the enemies of Fidel Castro . . . for a jump to their country.[4]

The story was broken shortly afterwards in the United States by Ronald Hilton, director of the Hispanic American Institute at Stanford University. In an editorial in the *Hispanic American Report* he was entirely accurate:

> There is now widespread belief in [Guatemala] that the C.I.A. is sponsoring a similar invasion [similar to Castill Armas' military campaign] of Cuba from Guatemala. Reliable observers in Guatemala say that without doubt there is in Retalhuleu a large and well-fortified base where Cuban exiles are being trained to invade Castro's fortress.[5]

He continued that these "responsible" Guatemalans believed Castro had been informed about the base, and he called for a U.S. press investigation of the question, warning against "having another U-2 incident." *The Nation, The Los Angeles Mirror,* and the *St. Louis Post-Dispatch* were the only publications to follow up this story in print during the next two months.

The Nation published editorials November 19, December 3, and December 10, 1960, repeating Hilton's story in full and calling on the media to check these reports in Guatemala so that "public pressure . . . be brought to bear upon the Administration to abandon this dangerous and harebrained project." [6] On December 3, in an editorial entitled "A Black Day—If We Are Found Out," *The Nation* quoted an exchange of remarks between Mr. Lyman Kirkpatrick, then Inspector-General of the CIA, and a questioner after a speech by Kirkpatrick before the Commonwealth Club of San Francisco. Kirkpatrick was asked: "Professor Hilton of Stanford University says that there is a CIA-financed base in Guatemala where plans are being made for an attack on Cuba. Professor Hilton says it will be a black day for Latin America and the United States if this takes place. Is this true?" The reply is quoted as: "It will be a black day if we are found out." [7] No newspaper repeated this story.

[4] *La Hora,* Guatemala, Guatemala, October 30, 1960, p. 1.

[5] Ronald Hilton, *Hispanic American Report,* Stanford University, Hispanic American Society, Vol. XIII, No. 9, p. 583. An analysis of developments in Spain, Portugal, and Latin America during September, 1960 (appeared in early November).

[6] "Are We Training Cuban Guerrillas?" *The Nation,* Vol. 191, no. 17, November 19, 1960, pp. 378–379.

[7] *The Nation,* Vol. 191, no. 19, December 3, 1960, pp. 425–426. A subsequent version by Douglass Cater may be more accurate: "It will always be a black day for the U.S. whenever the C.I.A. gets caught," in "Is All the News Fit to Print?" *Reporter,* Vol. 24, no. 10, May 11, 1961, p. 19.

The Los Angeles Mirror reported Dr. Hilton's charges, and subsequently in the *The Nation*, on January 7, 1961, Don Dwiggins (the *Mirror's* Aviation Editor) repeated them on the basis of his own investigation. In the two subsequent issues of the *Hispanic Report,* Dr. Hilton reiterated his claims and lambasted the American press for not investigating them "seriously," (excepting only the *St. Louis Post-Dispatch*).[8] He went further to say that there were operations originating in Florida sponsored by the CIA:

> Given the necessary modus operandi of the Central Intelligence Agency, it is difficult to report accurately on its part in the affair. Yet we have from reliable and trained observers in Florida the location of the U.S. government airports and equipment used in flying potential guerrillas to Guatemala, and a description of how the pickups are made.

The *Post-Dispatch* brought to light other developments in Guatemala; newsmen were having trouble with both the Guatemalan and American authorities there. Richard Dudman, the *Post-Dispatch*'s reporter there, wrote in November that he had found no evidence to substantiate the rumors of CIA training of exiles. But the *Post-Dispatch* editorialized that something was wrong: "What is going on in Guatemala? Who is trying to conceal what, and for what purpose?" The editorial asserted Dudman was unable to send any dispatches out of Guatemala, and had to go to neighboring El Salvador to file his story. He apparently told his editors that he could relate only "some of the truth."

By February, 1961, according to reliable sources, most of the working American press in Latin America knew what was happening but were under pressure to keep it out of print. For example, *Time* magazine on January 6 said reporters in Guatemala had found President Ydigoras Fuentes' contention that only Guatemalans were being trained and only for defensive purposes, to be true: "reporters found that the facts supported Ydigoras." Then on January 27, *Time* reversed its position, saying that the Frente is making impressive preparations: guerrilla training camps in Florida and Guatemala, . . . the mystery field at Retalhuleu, . . . and the inactive U.S. Marine Corps Opa-Locke air base in Florida." The implication was, however, that it was a Cuban endeavor solely, that the only U.S. aid was financial, that it was doled out by "Mr. 'B', the C.I.A. agent in charge." [9]

After these two articles, *Time* devoted its Cuban space only to what

[8] *Hispanic American Report,* events during October, pp. 669–670 (released early December).

[9] *Time,* Vol. LXXVII, no. 2, January 6, 1961, pp. 32–34, no. 5, January 27, 1961, p. 26.

some others in Latin America had been speculating about invasion plans. It wrote nothing of what it knew of the concrete plans. There was never any implication of U.S. control. Yet sometime in early 1961 Robert Rosenhouse of *Time,* in Guatemala, was having a heated argument with U.S. Ambassador Bell. Rosenhouse said he was going to attempt to have the story of the CIA base printed. Bell told him that if he did, he would not only not be working for any news agency but he could not guarantee Rosenhouse physical safety in Guatemala. Rosenhouse was apparently not the only one.[10]

Despite these several initial stories, the American public was almost totally uninformed of the events until the *New York Times* broke a story by Paul Kennedy on January 10, 1961. Because of the possible influence of the *Times* on other newspapers' policies and its possible influence on U.S. government policies, it is necessary to go into some detail about its handling of the Cuban story.

The New York Times

The *Times* knew of the stories in the *Hispanic American Review* and *The Nation.* Mr. Clifton Daniel, managing editor of the *Times,* in an address to the World Press Institute, St. Paul, Minnesota on June 1, 1966, implies that the first knowledge the *Times* had of the Guatemalan activity came from *The Nation's* editorial of November 19, 1960;[11] that it was on the basis of this article that Mr. Paul Kennedy was sent from Mexico City to Guatemala to check Dr. Hilton's information. Mr. Herbert Mathews, member of the *Times* editorial board and a Cuba specialist, however, maintains that this was Kennedy's second trip to Guatemala. Dr. Hilton had apparently communicated with the *Times* through Mr. Mathews before anything had been broken in this country and explained what he had discovered. Kennedy was sent down, according to Mathews, but "muffed the job on his first trip. . . . He made the mistake of asking Fuentes, the President of Guatemala, about it." Fuentes denied the story. "Kennedy very foolishly accepted his story without looking, and went back to Mexico City."[12] Following this, the story broke in the *Hispanic American Review* and *The Nation.* The foreign desk then sent Kennedy back, and he dis-

[10] This information was given the writer by sources he considers highly reliable. Mr. Rosenhouse has not been consulted.

[11] Mr. Daniel's speech was reprinted by the *New York Times* in pamphlet form.

[12] The result of this was a November 20 article in the *Times* noting only Ydigoras' admission of the existence of a secret military base at Retalhuleu and that Guatemalans were being trained there for guerrilla warfare with U.S. weapons and with U.S. military consultation.

covered the U.S. activity that was the basis for his January 1961 page-one story.[13]

Mr. Mathews, however, had received information about the CIA project in October, 1960, from Cuban sources (presumably about the same time candidate Kennedy was receiving similar information), but this was given to him "off-the-record." Dr. Hilton maintains the *Times* "called him long distance and displayed a lack of familiarity with the problem." [14] Asked why the *Times* did not report the American CIA control of the operation, Mr. Mathews replied:

> Some of it couldn't be printed because it was sort of underground CIA work and every newspaper's got to respect that kind of information; but when it became so open (later) it was ridiculous not to print it. When any confidential material comes along—and anybody in touch with the Cubans knew all about it—it was simply confidential material. That's a rule of the profession, and you don't break it. No reputable newsman violates it.[15]

Mathews' opinions seem to have been in accord with the general policy of the *Times* at that time. Briefly stated, that policy was that the press cannot take the responsibility for jeopardizing operations vital to the national security, that no such stories should be printed until they are such common knowledge that it becomes "ridiculous not to print it." This is the substance of left-hand editorials (April 16: "The aid that has been given by the United States to the Cuban exiles in training has been too well advertised to be ignored." April 18: "This has been too well publicized to be ignored . . .). Mr. James Reston wrote on April 26, after it was all over:

> Neither the President nor the press could present all the facts with candor, and if they had, the mess would be even worse than it is. In the

[13] Interview with Mr. Herbert Mathews, November 20, 1966. All of his statements come from that interview. For the substance of the second Kennedy story, see the following.

[14] Hilton, report for November 1960 (released early January, 1961).

[15] The rule Mathews describes is interesting in the light of a comment made by Mr. Kirkpatrick in an interview on November 23, 1966: "No reputable newsman would accept an order not to publish it," i.e., confidential material; that, in the final analysis, it is up to the newsman's conscience, not any rule. During the same October, Mr. Daniel made a speech at Chapel Hill, North Carolina, in which he said: "There are still people who think it is unpatriotic . . . to publish news that is in conflict with the opinions and policies of our government. What is the responsibility of the reporter and editor in *that* area? The answer is not simple, but it seems to be that, up until the time we are actually at war or on the verge of war, it is not only permissible, but it is our duty as journalists and citizens to be constantly questioning our leaders and our policy." "Responsibility of the Reporter and Editor," reprinted in Louis M. Lyons, *Reporting the News* (Cambridge, Mass.: Harvard University Press, 1965), pp. 199–200.

> international maneuverings of subversion, limited war, etc., the news is not always fit to print.[16]

The consequence of exposing such secret operations, claims Mathews, are too great even for the *Times* to bear. "If you print it so widely you frustrate such an operation, then you'd be blamed for its failure and no newspaper or individual can take this responsibility, and no newspaper or individual should take it."

Here, then, is a deep respect for the underground operation and a lack of any clear statement or notion of the responsibility of the media to the public it is charged to inform. An analysis of the content of the *Times* reporting on Cuba throughout the period before the invasion shows the *Times* carefully following this policy:

1. Articles reporting Cuban charges in the U.N. of the U.S. invasion preparations were printed, but the charges were editorially scoffed at.[17]

2. Charges made by the Fair Play for Cuba Committee—which were accurate—were printed but buried as obscure articles.[18]

3. Paul Kennedy's article of January 10, on page one, entitled "U.S. Helps Train an Anti-Castro Force at Secret Guatemalan Air-Ground Base," described Guatemala's military

> preparations for what Guatemalans consider will be an almost inevitable clash with Cuba. There is intensive daily air training here from a partly hidden airfield. . . . The United States is assisting this effort not only in personnel but in material and . . . construction. . . . Guatemalan authorities from President Miguel Ydigoras Fuentes down insist that the military effort is designed to meet an assault, expected almost any day, from Cuba.

Kennedy cited that the charges of U.S. direction and financing of the preparations were being made by Ydigoras' political opponents. There was no mention of (1) the role of the CIA; (2) the fact that Cubans were being trained, and (3) that it was linked to events in Florida. There was no editorial on the subject. Furthermore, the following day, January 11, in exactly the same position on page one, an article by Jack Raymond from Washington rebutted Kennedy's assertions: "Guatemala Calls Forces

[16] Mr. Reston, and some other *Times*men, reversed their attitudes later, for reasons to be discussed.

[17] Examples: on January 3, the *Times* stated: "It is incredible to us that the Cubans can believe we are about to invade their island. It is difficult for Americans to understand that others can honestly believe things about us which we know to be false." On January 19 the *Times* again ridiculed the charges: "The United States invasion of Cuba, which the Cuban government so confidently predicted would take place by January 18 at the latest, was a figment of Cuban imagination, as the people of the United States had always known it to be."

[18] Examples in January 6 and March 24 issues.

Defensive: Denies U.S.-aided military preparations are aimed at offensive against Castro," citing Guatemalan sources in both Washington and Guatemala, including Ydigoras: "Guatemalan troops were in training with the help of United States officers at a base in the Retalhuleu area." Again there was no editorial. The same day, the *Times* printed a letter from the Guatemalan ambassador to the OAS, Carlos Aparicio, who reiterated Ydigoras' statements. All this heavily qualified the Kennedy story.

4. Articles on Cuban exile activities were run, but there was no linkage to U.S. support.

5. Reportage appeared of the 36-page State Department pamphlet (written by Mr. Schlesinger) bearing the thesis that Castro had betrayed his own revolution (and designed to prepare the public for the invasion) and Raul Roa's renewed charges in the U.N. of invasion preparations. No editorials.[19]

These were the main characteristics of *Times* coverage until Mr. Tad Szulc's articles beginning on April 7, ten days before the invasion. By then, other publications had begun to break the story.

Other Publications

Once the January 10 *Times* story was released—despite its heavy qualification—a number of other newspapers reversed suppression of certain facts. This was particularly true in Florida. William C. Baggs, editor of the *Miami Daily News,* admits playing down stories of the obvious refugee preparations and, according to Douglass Cater, "held back on the investigation of the larger story until the *Times* broke it in January." [20]

John S. Knight, president of Knight newspapers and owner of the *Miami Herald,* had withheld stories about the camps in both Guatemala and Florida at the request "of the highest level of the United States Government." [21] The day after Paul Kennedy's story, the *Herald* published a story on the Guatemala camp and another one on the Opa-Locke air traffic. An accompanying explanation read:

> Publication of the accompanying story on the Miami-Guatemala airlift was withheld for more than two months by the *Herald*. Its release was decided upon only after U.S. aid to anti-Castro fighters in Guatemala was first revealed elsewhere.

While Florida newspapers were printing details of the invasion preparations (it was still U.S. "aid," not "control"), influential eastern newspapers

[19] *Times,* January 18, 1961.

[20] Douglass Cater and Charles Barlett, *op. cit.* Baggs afterwards was unsure that this was the right course. He did not know how to draw the line de Tocqueville described: "Once you make a decision to withhold the news, it raises the question of how far you go and when you stop."

[21] Presumably President Kennedy. Wise and Ross, *op. cit.*, pp. 34–35.

remained essentially quiet. *The Washington Post,* in March, "spiked a story reporting Cuban dissatisfaction with the C.I.A." Both the *Wall Street Journal* and the *New York Herald Tribune* refrained from mentioning U.S. control until after the affair was entirely over.[22] Walter Winchell on April 9 in his *New York Mirror* column proclaimed that the press should maintain voluntary security. "Everyone," he said, "knew that Cuban patriots were training in Florida. But it took the *New York Times* to put it on the front page where it can be used against our country." Winchell's own newspaper ran an exclusive on a New York City recruiting center three days after his column.[23] It is significant in contrast that in Europe both British and French newspapers were "freely referring to the CIA in the days before the invasion." [24]

Florida in the Weeks Before the Invasion

By the end of March and throughout April 1961, it would be an understatement to maintain that there were "leaks" in Miami. The leakage had become such a flood that the story was almost forced into print. Three veteran reporters who quickly discovered this were Tad Szulc on the *Times,* Stuart Novins of *CBS,* and Karl Meyer writing for the *New Republic.* Novins later described the Miami atmosphere as "highly charged":

> Miami buzzed with the open secret of the coming invasion. Even the names of the CIA agents and their telephone numbers were almost common knowledge. . . . Castro had infiltrated at least a hundred spies. . . . Under these conditions, it was naturally impossible to keep the story out of the news. A few reporters, who for weeks had been performing acrobatic feats to protect the CIA, began to mention the mobilization in dispatches.[25]

Although the CIA categorically denies that any press briefings, either formal or informal, were given by anyone in its employ,[26] Meyer and Szulc maintain that CIA operatives in both Florida and Guatemala were very interested in projecting a favorable image:

> Newspaper and magazine reporters were briefed by CIA agents, and Miami newspapers even took to submitting stories on the Agency's activities to the CIA for clearance.[27]

[22] Cater, *op. cit.*

[23] According to *The Nation,* in "Operation Cuba," Vol. 192, no. 19, April 29, 1961, pp. 361–363.

[24] Cater, *op. cit.*

[25] Stuart Novins, "The Invasion That Could Not Succeed," *Reporter,* Vol. 24, no. 10, May 11, 1961, p. 22.

[26] Interview with Kirkpatrick, *op. cit.;* interview with Mr. Richard Bissell, November 30, 1966. All references to Mr. Bissell's views come from that talk, unless otherwise noted.

[27] Karl E. Meyer and Tad Szulc, *The Cuban Invasion: The Chronicle of a Disaster* (New York: Praeger, 1962), p. 99.

This still *did not* mean that the press was writing about a U.S.-directed invasion of Cuba. Meyer's story, called "Our Men in Miami," was submitted by Gilbert Harrison of the *New Republic* to the White House for clearance. It was, according to Mr. Schlesinger, "a careful, accurate and devastating account of CIA activities among the refugees," and Harrison asked if it should be published or not. President Kennedy asked him not to publish, and he did not.[28]

Post-Mortems on the Role of the Press

The New York editors of the *Times* later regretted that they had not published everything they knew earlier. Mr. Daniel stated that perhaps the press is sometimes more capable of determining what is and what is not in the national interest than the President is. "My own view," says Daniel,

> is that the Bay of Pigs operation might well have been cancelled and the country would have been saved enormous embarrassment if the *New York Times* and other newspapers had been more diligent in the performance of their duty—their duty to keep the public informed on matters vitally affecting our national honor and prestige, not to mention our national security.[29]

The New York editors disagreed with Reston, who, in delivering the eulogy at Mr. Dryfoos' funeral in the spring of 1963, declared, "in 1961, when we were on the point of reporting a premature invasion of Cuba, his courteous questions and wise judgement held us back." [30] "Mr. Reston believes," says Mr. Daniel, that "it was too late to stop the operation by the time we

[28] Arthur Schlesinger, *1000 Days: John F. Kennedy in the White House* (Boston: Houghton-Mifflin, 1965), p. 261.

Incredibly, it would seem that there was more knowledge of the operation among the important publications than in administrative levels just below the small top executive group privy to the planning. Roger Hilsman, then Director of Intelligence and Research at the Department of State, concludes, "Because of secrecy, men who had knowledge that could have contributed to the making of sound judgements were excluded from making that contribution." *To Move A Nation,* pp. 31, 83.

Edward R. Murrow, new director of the USIA, learned of the plans from a *New York Times* reporter early in April. According to Schlesinger, he was "deeply opposed (p. 259). "It is instructive to note that the prime means by which these high officials became aware of events was the limited stories that did break, lending substance to Cohen's analysis that "one cannot help but be struck by how much real coordination of policy in an otherwise decentralized political system is provided by the institution of the press (p. 224)."

[29] *New York Times,* June 2, 1966, p. 14.

[30] Gay Talese, "The Kingdoms, the Powers, and the Glories of the New York Times," *Esquire,* November, 1966, p. 1881. Talese places the differences of opinions between New York and Washington as part of deeper divisions in the hierarchy of the *Times.*

printed Tad Szulc's story on April 7." However, it is clear that Reston agrees with New York on the question of earlier disclosure. In a *Times* editorial, "Washington: the President and the Press—the Old Dilemma," on May 10, 1961, he stated:

> The trouble with the press during the Cuban crisis was not that it said too much, but that it said too little. It knew what was going on ahead of the landing. It knew that the U.S. Government was breaking its treaty commitments and placing the reputation of the U.S. in the hands of a poorly trained and squabbling band of refugees.
>
> If the press had used its freedom during this period to protest, it might have been influential even in the White House.

Neither is there any disagreement about how the New York and Washington offices felt about the White House—in particular, Mr. Schlesinger—handing out phony information to the media.[31]

The Nation and Dr. Hilton directed their admonishments at the press itself. *The Nation* on May 6 declared that "public opinion has ceased to function, for the government proceeded in secrecy, most of the press abetted it, and the public was faced with a *fait accompli* and invited to rally round the flag." [32] Hilton declared the suppression meant that "newspaper publishers belong to the power elite, and encourage the suppression of news dangerous to that elite. In this, they are abetted by the government, which lets it be known what stories should not be published." [33]

Yet, simultaneously, the White House was indicting the media for seriously jeopardizing the national security. The State Department told 400 editors and columnists in a briefing late in April that their stories had alerted Castro and helped ruin the plan.[34] President Kennedy made two attempts to ask for more self-control. The first was a speech to the Bureau of Advertising of the American Newspaper Publishers Association in New

[31] Schlesinger states erroneously that New York killed Szulc's April 7 story. He also omits from his book the fact that he lied to the *Times* in April regarding the size and type of landing force. On May 10, the *Times* in an editorial entitled "The Right Not to be Lied to," said, "A democracy—our democracy—cannot be lied to. . . . The basic principle involved is one of confidence. . . . Not only is it unethical to deceive one's own public as part of a system of deceiving an adversary government; it is also foolish. Our executive officers and our national legislators are elected on stated days, but actually they must be re-elected day by day by popular understanding and support. That is what is meant by government by consent." It might also have been well for the *Times* to explain its own role, reflected in its January 8 and 19 editorials (see footnote 17).

[32] "What System, Please?" *The Nation,* Vol. 192, no. 18, May 6, 1961, p. 381.

[33] Ronald Hilton, "The Cuba Trap," *The Nation,* Vol. 192, no. 17, April 29, 1961, pp. 364–366.

[34] Fred J. Cook, "The CIA," *The Nation* (special issue), June 24, 1961, p. 530.

York on April 27. He stated that to the daily question of "Is it news?" each editor should now ask himself, "Is it in the national interest?" The second was at the White House on May 9 when he met with nine top news executives to make an appeal for greater self-restraint. He "ran down a list," says Daniel, "of what he called premature disclosure of security information," including Paul Kennedy's January 10 article. He suggested the publishers appoint a representative to be their "adviser on information affecting the national security," who would make judgments and advisements, on the basis of government briefings, as to whether borderline stories should be printed.[35] The group was not interested in such measures. They argued that such steps would be justified only if the President were to declare a national emergency and that "if the situation is critical enough to warrant press control, other wartime measures should immediately be put into effect." [36]

But Mr. Kennedy actually felt quite differently. In fact, he agreed with the *Times*—they should have printed it earlier. During the very same May 9 White House meeting, Kennedy said in an aside to Turner Catledge: "If you had printed more about the operation you would have saved us from a colossal mistake." He reiterated this feeling in a talk with Orvil Dryfoos at the White House on September 13, 1962: "I wish you had run everything on Cuba. . . . I am just sorry you didn't tell it at the time." [37] The reason for Kennedy's attitude is that he had another culprit in mind: he thought he had been deceived by the CIA regarding many vital parts of the operation and felt if the press had blown it open he would have been saved from this deception.

Conclusion

If it was not Dean Rusk's intention to pull the rug out from under the CIA, that was the effect of his eleventh-hour objection to the second air strike. The Secretary clung to the rule of plausible denial and contended the air strikes broke this rule.

In reality, the press itself is guilty of creating the illusion in Washington that plausible denial was even remotely possible at any time. The CIA concludes that the error made by everyone involved was self-delusion in

[35] Pierre Salinger, *op. cit.*, p. 158. Salinger argued that the press should have used more self-restraint. He apparently was unaware of Kennedy's further remarks.

[36] According to the American Society of Newspaper Editors *Bulletin* of June 1961.

[37] Speech by Clifton Daniel, *op. cit.*

regard to the ground rule. Richard M. Bissell, the Deputy Director of the CIA, stated:

> Everyone concerned, certainly including those of us in the CIA, deluded ourselves that if the operation was carried off it would be plausibly deniable by the United States Government. We thought it would be widely believed that the United States had facilitated the sale of weapons to the Cubans and supplied them with some money but that its role was essentially passive. All the policymakers deluded themselves on this point. Given this belief, very great efforts were made throughout the operation to insure that no evidence would appear which would conclusively prove official United States involvement. Serious consideration was never given to planning an action which would have greatly increased the probability of success and which might have been acceptable if it had been realized that plausible denial was realistically out of the question.[38]

Quite clearly, then, if the American press had fulfilled its responsibility to its readers and revealed the information at its disposal, this self-delusion would have been shattered early in the planning stages. This could have been done at any time during the six months prior to the invasion.[39]

"If the Secretary of State knew plausible denial was impossible," says Bissell, "then probably the whole thing would have been organized differently in the United States Government.

> First, the role of the Pentagon would have been greatly increased. Second, probably we would not have wanted the United States to go along at all. The self-delusion allowed the President and the Secretary of State to approve it on the one hand, and on the other to restrict the means available to it.[40]

Ultimate responsibility for failure, of course, rests with the President. It seems certain, however, that if the press had told what it knew, (1) the impossibility of maintaining plausible denial would have been made obvious and (2) a rethinking of the plan would have been forced on the policymakers. Thus, the press, because it abrogated its prime responsibility, can be considered a major factor contributing to the failure of the invasion.

38 *The Washington Star*, July 20, 1965.

39 Asked if this interpretation is valid, Bissell said: "Yes, this could be, you could put this interpretation on it."

It may be objected that "the public," as used in the theoretical justification for a free press, is too general a term to be useful in particular cases, but even granted that influence on policy comes from minuscule segments of the American people, the argument remains unaffected, as the pressure exerted from these points can be highly potent. Concentration of the press on the real nature of the Cuban adventure would have immediately provoked a public policy debate among these interested segments of the population that would, most probably, have drastically altered the operation.

40 *The Washington Star*, July 20, 1965.

We can ask if it is wise to pursue policies which may well be opposed by the American people? Surely no American President worth his politics would risk it, yet secrecy does not allow a careful reading of public sentiment prior to the action. Indeed, public sentiment is normally mute, out of ignorance that a decision is available.

If it is too general to maintain that a sovereign people would have decided whether the operation was in the national interest, it seems reasonable to assume that the Administration would have had, at least, the benefit of the judgment of a larger number of responsible private individuals (both in and out of the press) and other informed officials such as Morrow. The press did not know that the policy-makers were deluding themselves as to their ability to cover their tracks and were making this delusion the touchstone of policy. The press, then, did not have in this case all the necessary information with which to make judgments as to what the public should and should not be told.

THE GROWING PRESS–ADMINISTRATION SPLIT

Cuba made the press acutely conscious of its importance in American affairs with lesser nations and this consciousness was continuously reinforced by the American involvement in Vietnam. If the focus of dissent regarding American foreign policies centered on the CIA in the early 1960's, it swung to criticism of the military as the 1960's wore on, until finally by the end of the decade the President—who had from the beginning, of course, been responsible for the direction of American policies in both Cuba and Southeast Asia—received the heat of criticism. In the meantime both the CIA and the military were tarnished in the eyes of a large number of Americans. As the CIA could not respond to stories pillorying it, attention to the agency waned, but the military could and did answer its critics, helping spiral the level of vituperation and condemnation upward. Highly uncomplimentary images of the senior military (as a band of mindless and dangerous buffoons) and the press (as immature and irresponsible publicity-seekers and worse) emerged, causing a polarization and lack of substantial dialogue of the crucial issues of foreign policy.

"Management" of the news grew into a major issue during the Kennedy Administration, especially when Defense Department officials admitted tailoring information in the interests of national security. Arthur Sylvester, Assistant Secretary for Public Affairs, explained that "In the kind of world we live in, the generation of news by actions taken by the government becomes one weapon in a strained situation. The results justify the methods we used." He later argued the government's right to lie was basic in current cold-war conditions.[41] This raised considerable controversy, straining the Kennedy Administration's press relations. It became increasingly difficult for newsmen to pry information from both Pentagon and State Department officials (who could no longer give interviews without a third person present or unless the official submitted a written report on the interview). However, accessibility to the White House was better than ever before. Kennedy knew how to please and use the media. Thus, criticism of tightening information policies was easily deflected from the President.

Despite Kennedy's adeptness at dealing with the press in Washington, his administration saw continued deterioration in press-mission relations in Vietnam. The credibility of official reporting from Vietnam deteriorated continuously in the eyes of many of the newsmen. As in the Executive bureaucracy, it became more and more difficult for correspondents to get hard information from military and civilian agencies in Saigon. That this was, in fact, a direct Kennedy policy has been verified by William Shannon, who wrote that "it was Mr. Kennedy himself who ordered the ruthless closing down of all sources of information." [42]

After world-wide dissemination of Malcom Browne's (AP) picture of Thich Quang Duc's suicide by fire in a Saigon street, the U.S. Mission heavily censored news and photos coming out of Saigon and made news sources inaccessible to the press corps. It became necessary for correspondents to smuggle stories out of the country with departing American civilians or even American soldiers.

Despite the best attempts by the mission, reportage from Vietnam continued, with a volume of stories coming from the pens of correspondents like Browne, Neil Sheehan (UPI at that time), and David Halberstam (*New York Times*), which disputed official optimism and threw great doubts on the ability of the South Vietnamese to hold up their end of the war. As the image of the Diem regime slowly crumbled, relations between the press and the mission became so bad that they were commonly referred to as the "second war" in Vietnam. John Mecklin, public affairs officer of the mission from 1962 to 1964, maintains that the press achieved a major input into American policy which is "equaled in modern times only by the role of the New York newspapers in precipitating the Spanish American war." [43] Although this is undoubtedly an overstatement, as American policy remained unchanged for another full administration, there seems little doubt the demise of Diem was quickened by the adverse press it received. Indeed Kennedy himself attempted to influence Arthur Sulzberger to remove

[41] William River, *The Opinionmakers* (Boston: Beaçon, 1965), p. 154.

[42] *New York Post*, 4 November 1962, as quoted in James Aronson, *The Press and the Cold War* (New York: Bobbs-Merrill, 1970), pp. 180–181.

[43] John Mecklin, *Mission in Torment* (New York: Doubleday, 1965).

Halberstam from Vietnam. Sulzberger refused.[44] These reporters believed fervently that they were calling the shots as they saw them and more objectively than American officials on the scene. Other reporters disputed the reading of the war that Halberstam *et al.* were making, and this group included, for example, Joseph Alsop, the Hearst people, Marguerite Higgins of the *Herald Tribune*, and the editors of *Time* magazine. *Time* refused to print reports that the war was not going as the administration wished to paint it, and a major story by Charles Mohr (head of the *Times* Far East bureau) that argued that American policy had failed was shelved in New York in favor of an optimistic piece written in the editorial offices. The result of this episode was Mohr's resignation.

The military became increasingly impatient with the press and gradually assumed the attitude that the press was hindering the American effort, standards of "objectivity" in reporting being secondary. The press, in the eyes of the military, was to play a quasi-public relations function. In a now widely told story, Admiral Harry Felt (Commander in Chief, Pacific, 1958–64), confronted by Malcom Browne of AP during a press conference in Saigon, remarked: "So you're Browne. Why don't you get on the Team?"

The respective positions on the proper role of the press were summed up in the *Naval War College Review* recently. Neil Sheehan defended his reportage of Vietnam and criticized the military attitude as follows:

> You think the news media have been unfair to the military. You are right. Undoubtedly the news media have been unfair to the military in many instances. But more importantly, you have been taught to think that there ought to be a partnership between the press and the Government, between the press and the other major institutions in our society. . . . Partnership is bad for the press, it is bad for the Government, and it is bad for the country.[45]

Sheehan went on to explain that, in his view, partnership erodes and finally destroys press independence. Finally, in discussing the proper relationship between the press and the government, he felt "it ought to be a relationship of protagonists, . . . not antagonistic, . . . a relationship of two individuals who talk to each other, but who are independent of each other." Sheehan's position, widely held in the newspaper and television media today, includes an element of fear of the power of the executive branch and its most obvious manifestation, the military. He argues that the executive branch is extremely powerful in its ability to manage news through, for example, control of

[44] See David Halberstam, *The Making of a Quagmire* (New York: Random House, 1968) for a full account of the "second war" of the early 1960's.

[45] Neil Sheehan, "The Role of the Press," *Naval War College Review*, Feb. 1971, Vol. XXIII, no. 6, p. 5.

background briefings and timed release of events and "nonevents"; that the press still uses techniques of reporting developed in the 1920's; and that the result has been a weakening of the press' ability to be an "independent critic and independent force within the society." [46]

A response to this position in the following issue of the Review by S. L. A. Marshall highlights the great gulf in viewpoint between Sheehan and the high military. Marshall candidly remarked:

> To be blunt about it, the military does not trust the average correspondent and it has full reason for mistrust, so long as the correspondent thinks of himself as a protagonist. After all, this is his country and his role as reporter does not make him any less the citizen with a personal responsibility for its keeping.[47]

Marshall quoted General Walton Walker, agreeing that, as for correspondents, "You are Americans first and reporters second." Sheehan's attitude reminded Marshall of his "many-sided and long-suffering experience with the dilletantism and reckless arrogance of American correspondents in the field." [48]

Surely between the roles of teammember and protagonist the chasm is wide indeed. The military has been stung by a wave of antimilitarism on the campuses and a torrent of antimilitary books and articles, such as those by John K. Galbraith, former Marine Corps Commandant David Shoup, and Ward Just.[49] In its defensive reaction against this onslaught (and perhaps in frustration from the Vietnam experience) the military has been led to the conclusion that the press is an albatross around the neck of the country. There is no support, in this view, for the claim that the press has a central or pivotal role to play in our system.

Yet the military has been far from alone in its bitterness and disappointment. President Johnson took this same position the day after he withdrew from the 1968 Presidential race, telling the National Association of Broadcasters meeting on 1 April 1968 that "he felt radio and television had not assisted him in getting his points about the Vietnam war across to the American public." [50] In fact, Johnson later reminisced, he felt it was a

[46] *Ibid.*

[47] Gen. S. L. A. Marshall, "A Reply to Mr. Neil Sheehan," April 1971 issue of the *Naval War College Review,* April 1971, p. 89.

[48] *Ibid.*, p. 7.

[49] Just's series called "Soldiers" in the *Atlantic* during the fall of 1970 is a careful and devastating parody of the career soldier; it drew a raw response from high military officers. Just paints the image of an institution of pompous irrelevancy and men with no central meaning to their lives. He seems to be arguing that there is no essential reason for a military establishment at all.

[50] Quoted by Elmer Lower, president of ABC news, in an address to Phi Delta Phi fraternity, the School of Law, Columbia University, 10 December 1969.

mistake in failing to institute censorship concerning Vietnam so the enemy would be prevented from knowing what the U.S. was going to do next.[51]

A heightening of this already badly strained situation occurred with two episodes, back to back, in February 1971. They were the South Vietnamese drive into Laos, over which the Nixon administration threw a protective cloak in the form of a news embargo, and the broadcasting of a documentary by CBS entitled "The Selling of the Pentagon."

During the Laos news blackout, the White House indicated that correspondents had been thoroughly briefed on the operation and could file their dispatches when the embargo was lifted.[52] Both Congressmen, especially Senator Aiken, and the news media protested the blackout. Harry Reasoner editorialized on ABC Evening News "Comment" that some embargoes are legitimate and in the national interest, but that "this one has a smell about it," that it appeared to be a "managed public relations trick in the guise of security." Aiken claimed everybody, including the enemy, knew about the details of the operation, except the American people, who are "the last to discover what it is their Government is doing." [53]

In a way, ABC executives admitted, for Reasoner to complain over the air about an embargoed Laotian operation is, in fact, a "violation of the spirit, if not the letter, of the embargo." [54] CBS executives admitted that, though they abided by the embargo, there had been "a great deal of discussion on whether the embargo should be honored." [55] ABC officials displayed several attributes perhaps characteristic of the whole national news industry in the current period. First: confusion and skepticism.

> We don't know what to believe anymore. We don't know what the ground rules are, they keep changing—what is permitted and what is not permitted. . . . There's a great deal of confusion about it. . . . How the hell do we know what to do anymore? We cannot accept anything at face value that this administration tells us. . . . We no longer take anything seriously about the war. . . . Frankly, we do not know what to respect anymore. We get less information from the Nixon administration than ever before.[56]

As far as handling embargoes is concerned, ABC is "playing it by ear. . . . We have no written guidelines or critique statements on it."

Coming through very strongly, also, is a heightened awareness on the part of the networks of criticism by the executive. "We are all very aware

[51] *Time* magazine, 28 June 1971, p. 15.

[52] *New York Times*, 4 February 1971.

[53] *Ibid.*

[54] Interview with high-ranking members of ABC television news in New York, 5 March 1971. All further references to ABC officials refer to information received at this time.

[55] Interview with an official of CBS television news, New York, 5 March 1971.

[56] See ff 48 Supra.

of Mr. Agnew," declared one ABC executive. The Vice President lashed out at CBS for showing "The Selling of the Pentagon," a documentary whose line of attack was that the Pentagon's high public relations division sets out "not merely to inform but to convince and persuade the public on vital issues of war and peace." [57] Mr. Agnew, clearly representing the administration, proclaimed it a "subtle but vicious broadside against the nation's defense establishment." [58]

The contents of this program and the reaction of other segments of the press and of the executive branch of government are instructive on the current state of media-executive relations. The program basically agrees with the views of Sheehan that the Pentagon's techniques of controlling, releasing, and tailoring news to its particular desires are far more effective than the media's methods for getting to the heart of controversial and timely stories. George Wilson, the *Washington Post*'s military specialist, is quoted to the effect that the Pentagon has done better at "propagandizing as a whole than the press has done at exposing." The program claims the military is engaged in a continuous and terribly expensive operation to give America a sugar-coated sell that all things military are good for you.

It further complains of the inability of the press to get hard news out of the military, both in Washington and in Vietnam. The upshot, as Roger Mudd explains it, is that democracy as a system becomes choked by a barrage of "misinformation, distortion, and propaganda which make it impossible for people to know what their government is doing, which in a democracy, is crucial."

This also was the theme of a book by Senator Fulbright[59] and has, in fact, been of constant concern to the press ever since the *Washington Post* revealed the existence of the General Starbird and Army Secretary Resor memoranda of February 1969, which set forth the guidelines of a pervasive publicity campaign to "sell" the American public on the antiballistic missile system. It was the revelation of these memoranda which played a significant role in the rejection of that system by Congress.

An interesting part of the reaction of the media to the CBS controversy was the notion that the network had "stood up" to the executive and the military. "CBS had a lot of courage to do that program," ABC executives informed me. The *New York Times* called it "brave," the *Washington Post* "gutty." Apparently a large portion of the news industry fears various forms of reprisal by the executive. The *Wall Street Journal*, for instance, ran a prominent front-page article entitled, "Running Scared—Many in

[57] Text of CBS Reports, "The Selling of the Pentagon," broadcast 23 February 1971.

[58] *Washington Post*, 28 March 1971.

[59] This duplicates the line taken by Senator Fulbright in *The Pentagon Propaganda Machine* (New York: Vintage, 1970).

Broadcasting Fear the Rising Attack From the Government," citing demands by the executive and Congress to see reporters' notes and films:

> Broadcasters see these requests . . . as efforts at government intimidation and censorship. . . . The Broadcasting industry is 'under siege as never before' states Vincent T. Wasilewski, president of the National Association of Broadcasters.[60]

Some ABC executives display almost paranoid uneasiness over army surveillance: "We all know they have dossiers on us. We all know it!" one remarked.

Perhaps the culmination of press reaction to White House "news management" was the remarks by Walter Cronkite, who complained:

> Many of us see a clear indication on the part of this Administration of a grand conspiracy to destroy the credibility of the press. . . . Nor is there any way that President Nixon can escape responsibility for this campaign. . . . He could reverse the anti-press policy of his administration. . . . It attacks on many fronts: often-reiterated but unsubstantiated charges of bias and prejudice from the stump, the claim of distortion or even fakery planted with friendly columnists, the attempts to divide the networks and their affiliates, harassment by subpoena.[61]

If the media is more self-conscious of its role today, it also is less agreeable to giving the executive the benefit of the doubt on national security issues. Despite the supposed fear of "reprisal," it is nearly inconceivable that the press would engage again in the type of voluntary censorship it undertook for Kennedy at the Bay of Pigs.

THE PENTAGON PAPERS

The publication of the *Pentagon Papers,* the subsequent attempt by the executive to use prior restraint in forestalling their full publication, the decisive action by the Supreme Court in supporting the media, and the follow-up coverage by newspapers across the nation mark a culmination of the trends discussed earlier in this paper. From teamwork at the Bay of Pigs, the relationship has moved well beyond the protagonistic and into the antagonistic stage.

The first thing to take note of is the substance and tone of the secret materials themselves. Actually, with all the information provided, there is not much of a general nature that is new; a great deal of the material

[60] *The Wall Street Journal,* 28 April 1971.

[61] Speech to the International Radio and Television Society in New York as quoted in *Time* magazine, 31 May 1971, p. 71.

regarding the bombing pauses, negotiation "attempts," Tonkin Gulf incidents, history of the insurgency in South Vietnam, and history of the Diem regime is common knowledge to specialists in the field of Southeast Asian studies.[62]

What is of considerable interest is the unanimity, excepting the CIA (ironically enough), within the executive branch on (1) the direction of policy toward continued involvement—policy debate turned out to be discussion of narrow options with a premium on imagination—and (2) how to handle information. Information is clearly a tool to further policy, and it was utilized rather effectively. News was leaked to focus attention toward or away from specific ideas or to prepare the public for future actions (usually escalation).[63] Perhaps most serious is the unquestionable series of major deceptions perpetrated on the American people concerning political and military realities in Indo-China. From the origins of the rebellion in the South to the background of covert operations in the North leading to the Tonkin Gulf incidents, the concealment of the deterioration of the Diem regime, and the deliberately concealed decision to introduce ground troops and alter the entire complexion of the American involvement in 1965, precautions were taken to keep the American people ignorant of events. The relevant paragraph indicating President Johnson's wishes that no publicity regarding this momentous decision to introduce offensive American ground troops be made available is worth quoting:

> . . . 11. The President desires that with respect to the actions in paragraphs 5-7, premature publicity be avoided by all possible precautions. The actions themselves should be taken as rapidly as practicable, but in ways that should minimize any appearance of sudden changes in policy. . . . The President's desire is that these movements and changes should be understood as being gradual and wholly consistent with existing policy.[64]

Further troop requests by General Westmoreland and approval of such requests by the President during 1965–66 were not made public, either.

Time magazine gave a very full coverage to the papers, and *Time*'s commentary indicated a fundamental change of attitude toward sensitive information of this kind. Previously, *Time* was inclined to support the administration on national security issues. This was certainly the case in the Bay of Pigs and was true through most of the Vietnam conflict, as the

[62] See, for example, Jean Lacouture, *Vietnam: Between Two Truces* (New York: Vintage, 1966), and George Kahin and John Lewis, *The United States in Vietnam* (New York: Dial, 1967).

[63] See, for example, incidents during the Kennedy and Johnson Administrations in *The Pentagon Papers* (New York: Bantam, 1971), pp. 100, 252, and 338.

[64] *Pentagon Papers, op. cit.*, p. 443, from National Security Memorandum 328 of 6 April 1965.

episode (cited earlier) with veteran reporter Charles Mohr shows. Now *Time* describes the Pentagon Papers as "deeply disconcerting. The records reveal a dismaying degree of miscalculation, bureaucratic arrogance and deception." [65] The magazine calls for an airing of information: "Although complete candor is not always possible, policies that must stand the test of grueling public debate tend to be better policies." [66]

Second only to the deception issue is the question of poor planning and poor reasoning by the policy-makers. The papers reveal a lack of careful deliberation and, as *Time* describes it, the documents "demolished any lingering faith that the nation's weightiest decisions are made by deliberative men, calmly examining all the implications of a policy and then carefully laying out their reasoning in depth." Instead, the impression is one of "harassed men, thinking and writing too quickly, and sometimes being mystified at the enemy's refusal to conform to official projections." [67] The obvious question is, then, what has earned the policy-maker the privilege of making decisions without introducing the problem to the public arena?

What in fact would motivate the executive branch to call for prior restraint of what amounts to ancient documents? Surely documents more than 3 years old can have no relevance to operational problems in Asia. Indeed, the *New York Times* went to great pains to point out editorially that the story was too old to "affect current plans, operations or policy," [68] in which case the story "might have been quite different; and in fact the *Times* would not have endeavored to publish such material." [69] This seems a weak way out, and actually begs the question, for given the evidence in the Pentagon Papers that what was done was against the national interest, one could argue that the only hope for future prevention of military adventure is prior and timely disclosure of plans before they are secreted past the public. And if such is not the case, why bother with recriminations three years after the fact? Either there is disclosure and honest debate, or there is not. This time the media had it both ways. Next time the decision to publish may well be much more difficult.

Given the justification for the present disclosure presented by the *Times,* namely, that it is in the interest of the people of this country to be informed, that the country was not informed early enough for a debate to occur before action was taken, and that this is an "inherent obligation of the responsibilities of leadership in a democratic society" [70] it seems odd to

[65] *Time,* 28 June 1971, p. 11.
[66] *Time,* 28 June 1971, p. 16.
[67] *Time,* 28 June 1971, p. 12.
[68] *New York Times,* 21 June 1971.
[69] *New York Times,* 1 July 1971.
[70] *New York Times,* 21 June 1971.

fall back on the weak argument that the information did not influence current military operations.

Be this as it may, the behavior of the bulk of the American press in quickly following up on the *Times* lead indicates what is in store for future information if it reaches any major portion of the media. Frank Haven, managing editor of the *Los Angeles Times,* said "every major newspaper in the country has been trying to get copies. . . . There's been quite a lot of competition over this and some papers have complained that some have it and some don't." [71]

The major papers did not, apparently pass the information around among themselves, but each (such as the *Times, Post, Boston Globe,* and *St. Louis Post-Dispatch*) received it independently from some part of the Ellsberg distribution system.[72] A number of other national papers, including the 11-paper Knight chain, continued to publish details even as the courts stopped the *Times* and *Post* from publishing, unconvinced that they might be doing any damage to the national security. *Time* magazine polled "two dozen editors across the U.S. asking how they would have played the story had they and not the *Times,* received the Pentagon Papers first." The "great majority of editors" would have done exactly what the *Times* did.[73] Despite this claim, it is true that it was the *Times* that led the media community in the Cuban and Vietnam experiences. It remains to be seen whether other papers will take leads in future cases. Nevertheless, the difference in the general attitude from the early 1960's is striking indeed.

If Sheehan and the authors of "The Selling of the Pentagon" are right that the government has more means at its disposal to deceive and evade than the media has to force candor and enlighten, then the obvious *esprit de corps* engendered in the media is to be welcomed. "Morale at the *Times,*" commented *Time,* "has never been higher. Reston called it 'the best week we've ever had.' " [74] Yet clearly the gulf between the media and its sources of information has not been greater in recent memory. Notwithstanding the necessary independence of the media, it is probable that excess antagonism will be counterproductive for the American people. News sources will become too dry, and timely provision of information on major American policies will be as remote as ever. There are proposals to ease the gulf by building institutions where representatives of the press and the bureaucracies can meet, much in the British manner of a combined committee where sensitive security subjects are aired, resulting in voluntary censorship. This system, however, depends heavily on much mutual trust between the protagonists, and most assuredly that does not now exist.

[71] *San Diego Union,* 20 June 1971
[72] *Ibid.*
[73] *Time,* 5 July 1971, p. 39.
[74] *Time,* 28 June 1971, p. 45.

The opinions of the majority in the Supreme Court decision of 30 June 1971 confirm the general thrust of theory as outlined in the introduction to this article. Justice Douglas opined:

> The dominant purpose of the First Amendment was to prohibit the widespread practice of governmental suppression of embarrassing information. . . . Secrecy in government is fundamentally antidemocratic. . . . Open debate and discussion of public issues are vital to our national health.[75]

Justice Stewart argued in his concurring opinion that "an informed and critical public opinion . . . alone can here protect the values of democratic government." The test, according to Stewart, is whether "direct, immediate and irreparable damage" will be done to the nation. Disclosure of the documents, he found, did not meet that test. And Justice Black, concurring, took direct issue with the contention, supported by Huntington (cited earlier) that liberty and security are mutually exclusive, writing that the "word 'security' is a broad, vague generality whose contours should not be invoked to abrogate the fundamental law embodied in the First Amendment. The guarding of military and diplomatic secrets at the expense of informed representative government provides no real security for our Republic." We come back to the remark of President Kennedy that had information been published earlier the nation would have been saved from a colossal blunder. It is perhaps possible that early disclosure of political and military realities in Vietnam would have forced hard evaluation of the direction of policy, an exercise easily avoided under the cloak of secrecy.

Underlying the current dispute seems to be an assumption that the press has significant power to influence events. One can argue that the press helped develop a public opinion which placed a ceiling on our activities in Indo-China, a rough harness on a President highly sensitive to public-opinion polls. Yet the long-term freedom of action of the executive in Asia throughout most of the 1960's is more striking, given the drumbeat of criticism from the press concerning that involvement. Reston is probably right when he claims that the "influence of the American press on American foreign policy . . . is usually exaggerated." He goes on to maintain,

> No doubt, the press has great influence on American foreign policy when things are *obviously* going badly; it has very little influence, however, when things are going badly but the impending disaster is not obvious and the government is saying, as it usually does, that all is well or soon will be if everybody only has faith and confidence.[76]

[75] *New York Times Co. v. United States,* 403 U.S. (1971) 713, pp. 723–724.

[76] James Reston, *The Artillery of the Press* (New York: Harper and Row, 1966), p. 63. The White House tends to give the media more credit than this. President Johnson told the *Washington Post* its support was "worth two divisions to me." Spiro Agnew in 1969 agreed that "the powers of the networks (are) equal to that (sic) of local, state and federal governments all combined."

The press, too often, is speaking to an attentive foreign affairs elite with not nearly enough electoral power to cause Presidential concern, to a mass public uninformed, unconcerned until the eleventh hour, and so abysmally ignorant on the major foreign policy questions that intelligent guidance from the grass roots is simply out of the question at present.[77]

The challenge, it seems clear, is somehow to bring all the options on major questions in a timely fashion to broad segments of the American public. "Teamwork" among pressmen, bureaucrats, and soldiers in this enterprise would not compromise the independence of the media and, if we have learned the lessons of Cuba and Vietnam, in the great majority of cases it would probably strengthen the democracy, enhance the national understanding and national interest, and thereby strengthen the national security. Clearly, bureaucratic secrecy is at least partly responsible for massive public ignorance. Reston's solution seems reasonable and workable:

> The problem is to present the great issues as a series of practical choices: let the people look at the alternatives as the President has to . . . and try at the end to decide among the hard and dangerous courses. We need simple case-study outlines containing, first, a statement of the facts of the policy question; second, a definition of one course of action, followed by arguments for and . . . against; and so on through definition of a second course, and a third and a fourth. The difficulty with the presentation of foreign-policy news to the people today is that it comes out a jumble of important and trivial things and personalities, so that the people cannot quite get clear the questions for decisions, and end up either by giving up or by choosing up sides for or against the President.[78]

On both sides of the gulf, the antagonists in the administration, the military and the press must make more of an effort to cast aside false images of each other and get on with the business of getting the facts to the people in a sensible fashion. If the American people are incapable of making intelligent choices, the democratic experiment has failed. But if they are capable and the governors yet will not trust them with the choices, the experiment has also failed.

[77] Lloyd Free has demonstrated convincingly that the average American has too little knowledge of external events. In the spring of 1964 the Survey Research Center of the University of Michigan "showed that one-fourth of those interviewed had not heard anything about the fighting in Vietnam," 28% had never heard of NATO, and 38% knew that the Soviet Union is *not* in NATO. 25% did not know there was a Communist government on mainland China. He concluded that only about 25% of the public was "adequately informed." Lloyd Free and Hadley Cantril, *The Political Beliefs of Americans* (New Brunswick: Rutgers, 1967), Chap. 6.

[78] Reston, p. 87.

9

The Reserves and National Guard: Civil-Military Nexus of the United States Armed Forces

JOHN R. PROBERT

This chapter discusses two related theses about the role of the military reserves in civil-military relations in the United States.

The first thesis is that the failure of the Johnson Administration to call the reserves for service in Vietnam was a departure from precedent. The Nixon Administration has returned to precedent, officially stating its policy as involving reliance on the reserves as "the initial and primary source for augmentation of the active forces in any future emergency requiring a rapid and substantial expansion of the active forces." [1]

The recasting of the role of the reserves by the Johnson Administration in July of 1965 as it relied on the draft rather than a reserve call-up to augment our forces in Vietnam appears, over the long sweep of the history of reserves, to be a temporary change, but one that had great significance for civil-military relations in the United States. An examination of the historical precedent for the role of the reserves to July 1965, together with the actual and potential effects of the abandonment of tradition in the Vietnam war, will substantiate this significance and its impact upon U.S. policy.

The second thesis is that the military reserves of the United States, including the Army and the Air National Guards and the various forms of ROTC, are members simultaneously of both the civilian and the military sectors of our national life. For this reason our reserve forces have the potential power to perform unique roles in civil-military relations:

1. As representing a vital portion of the military forces of the U.S., they tend to lessen the requirement for regular forces and to deny them manpower and funds, thereby exercising a constraint on their size. Pos-

[1] Secretary of Defense Melvin R. Laird in a memorandum of 21 August 1970. Subject: "Support for Guard and Reserve Forces," p. 2.

sessed of civilian points of view, and yet part of the military, they modify military thought and action. The founding fathers saw the militia in these terms.

2. Conversely, they can serve as a conduit from the professional military establishment to the civilian sector, conveying military concepts and perspectives about military requirements to civilians and thereby making them more aware and receptive to military needs.

3. They can function as quasi-military pressure groups, free of at least some of the limiting regulations of the military, acting upon Congress, the executive, and state and local organs as well. Because they are not the professional military, they can take issue with it. As civilians, basically, they have political affiliations and expertise derived from their civilian occupations that they can use effectively to secure their aims.

4. The Administration can use its option to call reserves in a crisis to test reactions. The call-up of reserve forces is dramatic and highly visible and has a much more decided impact on the American public than increasing the armed forces by draft. Consequently, the probable public acceptance or rejection of a particular policy move can be ascertained quickly by mobilizing all or significant portions of the reserves.

VIETNAM: CASE IN POINT?

Let us return to the first of our two theses. Had the reserves been relied on in Vietnam, would the war have proceeded in a different fashion? It appears that it would and that an examination of the possible outcome is appropriate here. Of course, some portion of the reserve call-up of January 1968 in connection with the *Pueblo* incident was sent to Vietnam. But the total number of men involved was only about 15,000, and most of them did not go to Vietnam. In May 1968, some additional units were mobilized to bring the total to some 37,000,[2] not a very sizable portion of a Ready Reserve numbering about two million as of January 1968.[3] By contrast, we mobilized 26,000 National Guard and Reserve personnel in the Post Office emergency of March 23, 1970;[4] and we mobilized over 630,000 of the Guard and Reserves in the first year of the Korean conflict. By statute, the President may call one million of the Ready Reserve to active duty for 24 months, simply upon declaration of a national emergency.[5]

[2] *Annual Report of the Secretary of Defense on Reserve Forces, Fiscal Year 1969* (Washington, D.C.: Department of Defense, 1970), p. 1.

[3] *Ibid.*, p. D–4.

[4] *Annual Report of the Secretary of Defense on Reserve Forces, Fiscal Year 1970* (Washington, D.C.:Department of Defense, 1970), p. 5.

[5] Sect. 673, Title 10, USC.

In addition, by the time Vietnam faced us, reserve call-up procedures had undergone testing and improvement. They had been reviewed in Congressional hearings and revised on several occasions, after each preceding reserve call-up since World War II. No substantial reserve call-up is going to proceed without administrative errors, but it is inconceivable that a call-up at the onset of Vietnam would have been in any substantial degree ineffectual.

No civil disturbances plagued the country when the Administration made the decision to rely on the draft rather than the reserves in mid-1965. If the Administration was trying to avoid over-reacting, it could have called the reserves up in installments. Alternatively, it could have called them wholesale for impact. Public opinion probably would not have been overwhelmingly in support of the move, but the Tonkin Gulf resolution of some months earlier was backed overwhelmingly by Congress. There is little doubt that the call-up of the reserves could have been accomplished more quickly, and probably more cheaply, than expansion of the active forces by means of the draft. Though it took six months after Tonkin Gulf for the Administration to react with substantial military support for South Vietnam, no readily discernible reason—the mood of the country, cost, retention of some flexibility, even readiness—prevented the call-up of the reserve.

Although the Ready Reserves were then and are now overwhelmingly comprised of young enlistees, 20% to 30% of them are career reservists, officers and men who are mostly long-term voluntary participants in the reserve program and veterans of previous wars. This hard core—trained, occupying the upper grades, older and wiser, more experienced, and possessed of more varied and developed skills than the short-term enlistees—could have gone to work immediately and with ingenuity and resourcefulness.

The Administration, rather surprisingly, did not immediately move to large-scale expansion of our forces but took ten months to really begin the build-up. By then, it probably wanted to avoid the appearance of all-out intentions concerning Vietnam that the necessary declaration of a national emergency by the President would imply. However, had such a declaration been made in the atmosphere of Tonkin Gulf, with less likelihood of over-reaction in Moscow and Peking, the President would have been free to call up the reserves rapidly or slowly as circumstances dictated.

There was no necessity for the President to make a basic decision on reserves versus draft in August 1964. The crunch did not come until July 1965, when the strategic reserve began to become thin and the uncertainty about the size of the commitment we would have to make in Vietnam to become clear. Even then the reserves could have been called, with a careful watch on overseas reactions; they should have been, considering the precedent of the reserves as the initial and primary augmentation in an expansion. Such a call might have provoked an outcry by reservists and civilians alike.

There certainly would have been more discussion of the whole involvement in Vietnam, especially in the then wider circles of those immediately affected.

The point of this chapter is that no matter what ensued in the face of such a hypothetical call-up, it would have redounded to the advantage of our country. Had there been a hue and cry raised by the public, an agonizing reappraisal by the Administration might have followed, with the possibility of a change in Administration policy. Or the debate might have acted as a catalyst, expanded support, even brought about a consensus, and resulted in resolute and determined prosecution of the war.

If there had been an extensive call-up of the reserves, the progress of the war would undoubtedly have been watched more critically by the general public, with either earlier disenchantment with its prosecution or demands for changed strategy. The reserves, if extensively involved in Vietnam, might have made their own contribution to a change of strategy, possibly by means of the chain of command, more likely indirectly by affecting the home front and Congress.

At home, the draft could have been utilized to reconstitute the strategic reserves, a role for which it appears most suited. At home, too, the dislocations, deprivations, and sacrifices of a large-scale reserve call-up would have provoked discussion, critical reexamination and reevaluation, and the posing of alternatives—in short, all the salutary processes of a democracy at work.

It is unlikely that if we had used the reserves as we traditionally have, we would have as easily slid down the slippery slopes into the quagmire of Vietnam. Hewing to the established reliance on the reserves would have prevented the Administration from becoming extensively involved in Vietnam through means that had only a piecemeal impact on much of our populace.

Vietnam was a politicomilitary misadventure. If the reserves had been mobilized, with the public impact that implies, this mistake might have been avoided. The reserves and the families, friends, and business associates of reservists constitute an independent power center in our pluralistic society. Their interested, influential, and inevitably critical focus on Vietnam was not prompted as it should have been. Had it been, the nation would very likely have changed course earlier. The ineffectual course of the Johnson Administration might have been aborted or, more likely, changed, possibly to an improved military strategy in the field or to greater emphasis on some of our associated programs or to a greater diplomatic effort. It might have become more resolute if public opinion had rallied and backed greater involvement. Had we demonstrated our determination, who knows the Russian and Chinese reaction? It is difficult to believe that the utilization of the reserves in their traditional capacity would have resulted in a more disastrous outcome in Vietnam than we are currently experiencing.

Now let us turn to the second of our two related theses, the proposition that the reserves with one foot in the civilian camp and one foot in the military can perform unique and potentially vital roles in the civil-military relations of our democracy.

THE MILITIA: TRADITIONAL AMERICAN RESPONSE TO THE NECESSITY FOR ARMED FORCES

The Historical Precedent

Even before the minutemen of Lexington and Concord, the first citizen-soldiers of American history were to be found in the colonial militias. Our English forebears in their feudal system had earlier established the dual responsibility of the serf to till the fields and to serve with his lord in the defense of his lands. In the New World, the Indians, French, and Spanish replaced invading Norsemen, Normans, and French, as the frontiersman had continued need to be both provider and defender, now of his own soil. With American adaptations, the British arrangements for organizing groups of civilians to maintain order and repel invasions became the basis of the colonial militias, some of which were precursors of today's Army National Guard units.

In the years after the Revolution, the United States provided by law for the National Guard, of which responsibility for command and authority was given to the individual states. The Guard was national only in the sense that the federal government retained the right to set standards of training and equipment. The right was exercised infrequently and not very thoroughly, and the national government gave little financial support to the militias of the several states.

As small as the state militias were, until 1812 they played a central role in the defense of the nation. The fledgling nation had almost no regular forces. With our defeat in the War of 1812, the ineffectiveness of the militias became obvious; by the time of the Mexican War, the regular Army had expanded and the state militias were used to a very limited extent. This situation persisted through the Civil War and until modern times and the global wars in which the U.S. became involved in the twentieth century. The mass armies with which the wars of the first half of the twentieth century were fought required extensive reserve forces, especially if a nation were unwilling to support large standing forces.[6]

[6] For a brief history of the reserve, see W. F. Levantrosser, *Management of the Reserve Forces* (Washington, D.C.: Industrial College of the Armed Forces, 1967), from which most of this resume comes. For a more extensive history of the National Guard, especially, see W. H. Riker, *Soldiers of the States* (Washington, D.C.: Public Affairs Press, 1957).

From their establishment in colonial days until the present, the militia or National Guard, and later the various Reserves, were without exception to constitute "the initial and primary sources for augmentation of the active forces" in an emergency, to quote again the Laird memorandum referred to in footnote 1. As the reserve forces were never very substantial until after World War II, when we became involved in a major war, there was a necessary and frequently concurrent resort to the draft. But only in the case of Vietnam was there no extensive utilization of whatever reserves existed. Vietnam is, furthermore, an exception difficult to square with the rationale of the precedent. Our reserves were now substantial and, by any previous standard, well-trained and well-equipped.

The Reserves as Economical and Versatile Military Forces

Reliance on the citizen-soldier in our national defense posture was based upon other considerations than precedent. Reserve forces, especially small ones, poorly equipped, were cheap. We were a developing nation, pulling ourselves up by our bootstraps. We could ill afford the tremendous expense of large standing forces. In addition, we had no continuous national security threat, except in the early days of the frontier. Militias were ideal for repelling Indian attacks, quelling domestic disturbances, or dealing on a long-term basis with threats whose nature was frequently indiscernible in the distant future. In fact, with the security of ocean barriers on east and west, the balance of power in Europe, and reasonably secure borders to the north and south, the United States was not preoccupied with external threats either immediate or in the distant future and hence devoted scant resources to meeting them. This international milieu was ideally suited to militias, even to militias starved for funds.

The economic argument still is made for the reserve forces. Secretary Laird in his August 21, 1970, memorandum said,

> . . . in many instances the lower peacetime sustaining costs of reserve force units, compared to similar active units, can result in a larger total for a given budget or the same size force for a lesser budget. In addition, attention will be given to the fact that Guard and Reserve Forces can perform peacetime missions as a by-product or adjunct of training with significant manpower and monetary savings.[7]

Containing the "Man on Horseback"

Economic advantages were not the only appeal reserves had to the framers of the Constitution, especially Washington. Aware of the perils of

[7] Laird, *op. cit.*, p. 1.

the "garrison state" on the one hand and of the need for at least minimal armed forces on the other, General Washington maintained as early as 1783,

> "the only probable means of preventing hostility for any length of time [and] from being exempted from the consequent calamities of War, is to put the National militia in such a condition that they may appear respectable in the Eyes of our Friends and formidable to those who would otherwise become our enemies." [8]

Washington may not have considered any alternative to the militia. The Revolutionary War had been fought successfully upon the basis of such armed forces, and the fledgling nation could afford little else when he wrote. He was particularly concerned with the militia, especially as a deterrent to war, in today's terminology.

Cost and continued readiness, at least in terms of their writings, were secondary considerations for the framers. They saw the threat of the military to our democratic institutions as paramount. The phrases of the Constitution, *The Federalist,* and other writings of the time attest to this. In *The Federalist,* Numbers 24 through 29, Hamilton extensively discusses the dangers of a standing army and the advantages of a militia as an alternative. A standing army may be necessary on occasion, he maintains, but he feels that a well-run and regulated militia will make a large military establishment less necessary and, when needed, less threatening. Standing armies were a thing to be feared. Only if they were carefully circumscribed by controls on their funding were they likely to be contained.

Though armies, or forces in lieu of them, were to be feared, they were also inevitably essential. The dilemma of their day was the dilemma of today, military strength versus democratic safeguards. They saw the reconciling answer in a "well-regulated militia," officered by the states, subject to call by the federal government.

The founding fathers were enamored with the militia not only because the militia provided comparatively inexpensive security against invasion, domestic insurrection, and Indians but also because it appeared to insure the continuance of our democratic form of government against militarism. Down through the years, reliance on the militia continued as a foundation of American national security until eventually, as Hamilton predicted in *The Federalist,* Number 28, we could afford and needed large standing forces. With unusual prescience, he adds that through the medium of the National Guard and Reserves, the safeguard of citizen forces will remain. The re-

[8] From a paper by Washington entitled *Sentiments on a Peace Establishment,* written in 1783 and quoted in G. F. Eliot, *Reserve Forces and the Kennedy Strategy* (Harrisburg, Pa.: The Stackpole Co., 1962), p. 2.

serves were counted upon for initial augmentation of the armed forces in an emergency as well. Hamilton, writing in *The Federalist,* Number 26, says

> It is not easy to conceive a possibility that dangers so formidable [as a military takeover] can assail the whole Union, as to demand a force considerable enough to place our liberties in the least jeopardy, especially if we take in our view the aid to be derived from the militia, *which ought always to be counted upon as a valuable and powerful auxiliary.* [Italics mine.]

Hamilton is stating here his belief that from the citizen-soldier can and will come not only the effective counter-agent to military domination but also the effective deterrent to military or politicomilitary adventurism. By not turning to the reserves as "a valuable and powerful auxiliary" "for augmentation of the active forces" in 1965, did we encourage our ill-fated overextension in Vietnam? If the citizen-soldiers are not a substantial additive to our military forces in a time of large-scale military operations, are we missing a counterpoise, some pluralism at the level of military execution that a democracy ought always to possess? Does the all-volunteer Army, unless we rely upon the reserves, as traditionally, for initial and primary augmentation in the event of emergencies, constitute a threat of militarism in a new form?

The Reserves in a Strategy of Graduated Deterrence

As the balance of terror developed, the U.S. abandoned its reliance on massive retaliation. We had to have forces equal in quality and quantity to a great variety of threats. Increasingly expensive military technology necessitated highly trained and superbly equipped reserves.

In 1961, the Kennedy Administration undertook to develop a military capacity to deal with a variety of threats to the national security. Reliance on massive retaliation alone was discarded. We also forsook the kind of massive mobilization we had relied upon in World War II, as such a force required time to train men prior to their deployment and such time seemed unlikely in future defense situations. A flexible response requiring troops in a high state of readiness made necessary a variety of military forces tailored to a diversity of possible defense situations.

The strategy we evolved came to be known as graduated deterrence. It put tremendous requirements on the military establishment for men, training, and equipment. These requirements cannot all be met through standing forces. Standing forces not only would have entailed exorbitant expenditure but likely would have been less credible as a deterrent. The classic example is the Berlin crisis. By calling up a sizable portion of the reserves in response to Khrushchev's bold threats, we substantiated our resolve as no standing forces could. Large standing forces tend to be offset by large standing forces. The capacity to put into the scales well-trained reserves not only signifies the resolve of the leadership of a nation but also drives home to the populace what is in the balance. Their acceptance of the burden of the risk is unmistakable evidence of a unified nation to the enemy. There were objections to the Berlin call-up from some of the reserves themselves, as well as from various individuals and groups in the general population. If there had been no opposition, the Russians might well have suspected that the call-up was simply a pro-forma exercise. But the objections did not gainsay the fact that the reserves, 150,000 of them, were mobilized and positioned with efficiency and dispatch and that they and the nation, by and large, accepted the strategy and its risks.

The Reserves in the Political Process

The Berlin call-up of 1961 was an important factor in getting Khrushchev to back down, according to George Fielding Eliot.[9] Although the American public, including many reserves, voiced opposition, the complaints concerned mainly administrative shortcomings such as are probably inevitable in any call-up. The strategy basic to calling the reserves was virtually unquestioned.

The Berlin call-up seems to have been the exception rather than the rule, at least in recent years. For example, in 1968, at the time of the *Pueblo* incident, some 15,000 reservists were called in a limited mobilization. The outcry from all quarters—reservists, civilians, and the news media—was loud and varied. The correspondence files in the Pentagon reveal that the call-up was objected to on a variety of grounds: We were not basically threatened; Vietnam was a civil war; committing the reserve decreased our flexibility to meet threats from other quarters and left the home front vulnerable to civil disturbances. Some reservists filed law suits. Pressure was brought to bear on officialdom at all levels by whatever means were available to release those called and prevent any additional call-up.

Here we have a manifestation of the political process at work involving the reserves. Reservists are individuals established in the community. By their affiliation with the reserves, they are concerned especially about foreign policy, which is likely as it develops to affect them directly. Inevitably, they are organized, not only the officers, but also the enlisted personnel, especially the non-commissioned officers and specialist groups.[10] As part of a military organization, they know the benefits of organization. A review of

[9] *op. cit.*

[10] For example, the Reserve Officers Association, the National Guard Association, the Air Force Association, The Fleet Reserve and Naval Reserve Associations, and the Air Force Sergeants Association, to mention only a few.

the record shows they have used their political weight most frequently on those issues where they seek immediate benefits such as larger reserves, retirement pay, hospitalization, or PX privileges; but they do have entree to decision-making centers in their hometowns and in Washington where military policy can be affected. They can use and have used their political power for just such purposes.

Reservists with roots in the civilian communities across the land and reason for a continuing interest in foreign policy can exert strong influence for preparedness. Their concern for a strong defense can be less than unselfish as they strive to keep their reserve positions and enhance their opportunities for promotion. They have exerted such influence, out of whatever motivation, as a glance at any issue of the house organs of the Reserve Officers Association or the National Guard Association will show. They could, though perhaps not so easily because of their predisposition to military discipline and stated policy, exert a restraining influence on possible military or politicomilitary adventurism or error. That they have not, the record will also show. Their interest is strong and immediate, however, and the record shows that they can and will voice opposition. Unlike the 1961 call-up for Berlin, letters to Congressmen originating from objecting reservists were numerous at the time of the 1968 call-up, as the files of the Office of the Deputy Assistant Secretary of Defense (Reserve Affairs) show. Questioning the basic strategy that the call-ups were designed to effect, many of these men did not object simply on grounds of injustice or inconvenience.

As part of a military organization that is basically authoritarian, the individual reservist may be constrained to withhold critical views, more so than a civilian. But he is, after all, only a part-time soldier, and he may be an involuntary one at that. Furthermore, the great variety of reserve units and the kinds of education, training, and vocational pursuit represented in them assure a spectrum of point of view. All levels of society economically and educationally, all geographic areas, all ages from 18 to 60, are to be found in our reserve structure, as can be attested to by any troop list or, for example, some of the studies of reserve personnel.[11] Although the old "society troops" of the pre-World War II years are not quite so representative of the highly influential segments of society as they once were, there are still many business and professional men, both officers and enlisted men, in the reserve. There are currently also in the reserves many students in professional schools, avoiding the draft, educated and critical. There are also many from less influential walks of life. And of particular significance, there

[11] One particularly, done by the Office of the Assistant Secretary of Defense (Manpower and Reserve Affairs) in the Pentagon in 1969, gives a good view of some significant characteristics of personnel in the Ready Reserve.

are substantial percentages of federal, state, and local government employees, as both officers and enlisted men. In our pluralistic society, a sizable reserve structure is likely to be representative of that society and concerned and capable of making its views known and its desires felt.[12] If the complexion of the reserves changes with the lapse of the draft and greater reliance on monetary incentives to man the reserves, this situation may change materially. But for the immediate future, we can expect the reserves to continue to view Administration military policy with a critical eye.

Reserve views could be as constraining on military action as encouraging. Such views should serve a salutary purpose in a society such as ours. As only one of a number of competing pressure groups, the voice of the reserves is not likely to be overpowering. Though certain segments of the reserves, for example the Civil Affairs units in the Army Reserve and their association, the Civil Affairs Association, were vocal in support of a role in Vietnam, they were not called.[13] One would assume that a strongly hawkish sentiment exists in the more influential levels of our reserve structure. The Reserve Officers and National Guard Association journals attest to this. Working closely with Armed Forces committees in House and Senate, the Reserve Officers Association and the National Guard Association have time and again been instrumental in maintaining strong reserves. With no truly objective criteria for measuring what is enough defense force and with active pressure groups on the other side trying to reduce the armed forces, this may be a healthy situation. As high percentages of reserve and Guard officers and enlisted men are government employees, they should and do know how to get things done in government at all levels, where the pressure points are, and how to apply leverage. The Guard is active in politics, as shown by the established practice in many states of patronage appointments to officer slots in the Guard. Although this is more difficult to document, there are close connections between the Guard and certain political factions in a number of states.

Like most other interest groups, the reserve seldom achieves its full aims. The Civil Affairs Association did not with regard to Vietnam. Two of the most powerful, the Reserve Officers Association and the National Guard Association, did not in the case of the proposed merger of the

[12] Before some of our prestige institutions of higher education decided last year to discontinue ROTC, the regular military and the reserves also could expect an input of officers from the upper economic strata, the professions, and the higher levels of intelligence. The certainty of this input is now reduced, although by no means precluded. To the extent that our reserve is composed entirely of the lower economic strata, the less influential vocations, and the less intelligent members of our society, it may be less of a restraining factor in national military policy formulation.

[13] See issues of the Association's journal, titled until the May-June 1971 issue *Military Government Journal and Newsletter,* now the *Civil Affairs Journal and Newsletter,* particularly the issue of June-July 1970 (Vol. 23, No. 6).

National Guard and the Army Reserve by McNamara. Though the total merger was forestalled, a substantial portion of what Secretary of Defense McNamara sought to accomplish was achieved by abolishing hundreds of Reserve units.[14]

Furthermore, influential and articulate reservists and Guardsmen alike find their hawkish bias countered by a preference for reserve rather than active status. Many of those in the reserve structure know that only a reserve status is a good thing. Active duty, particularly for prolonged periods, is disadvantageous to career, family life, educational pursuits, and most especially the pocketbook. Financial incentives primarily in the form of pay for drill periods and summer duty are the most attractive single aspects of the reserve status for our reserves and Guardsmen. Desire to serve the country is a close second. But one of the biggest single disadvantages is the chance of call to active duty. Extended active duty would end the dual income status.

Reservists thus have personal pocketbook reasons, among others, to be critical of call-ups and hence of adventurism overseas. The response of those in reserve status to the call-ups in the *Pueblo* incident referred to earlier is germane here. And it should be remembered that the reserve pressure groups have only after many years, with great difficulty, and fortuitous developments in our foreign policy, succeeded in approaching the reserve force levels they have considered necessary, as the record will show.[15]

Summing up, the reserves are uniquely structured, situated, and motivated to play a role in support of and in restraint upon national security policy that is likely to redound to the advantage of the Republic. No other segment of our society is in the same situation, certainly not the active military forces. But unless the reserves are to be invariably "the initial and primary" augmentation for active forces in a "rapid and substantial expansion," they probably will not be inspired to play their role fully. If they are subject to call, they will be more likely to react in a critical and evaluative way that will be salutary for our policy-making, whether in support of or against the proposed policy. If in support, we should have a result similar to that in the Berlin crisis; if in opposition, perhaps a cautioning effect with secondary looks and reevaluation.

The Reserves' Flexible Response

The flexibility inherent in the reserves has been implied earlier. The term *reserve* connotes flexibility. Reserves are designed to be brought to an

[14] Levantrosser, *op. cit.*, gives the complete account of the Reserve-National Guard merger struggle.

[15] *Ibid.*, and see issues of *The Officer* (Reserve Officers Association journal) and *The National Guardsman* (National Guard Association journal) over the last five years.

active status more quickly than it is possible to create military forces from an entirely civilian base. But the modern reservist concept has been elaborated until its flexibility to meet a variety of changing conditions is much enhanced.

A series of Department of Defense directives, refined over the years to incorporate lessons learned in previous emergencies and mobilizations, provides the administrative basis for a modern reserve system that is capable of being adapted to a wide range of situations.[16] The Selected Reserve Force category, developed several years ago to increase the readiness of reserves with important roles in contingency plans, by adding to the number of drill periods, is a good example of how reserve proficiency can be raised. Secretary of Defense Laird, in his statement before the Senate Armed Services Committee on the 1972 Defense Budget, outlined marked progress achieved in equipping the reserves and in advancing their state of readiness. By the end of Fiscal Year 1971, he maintained, ten reserve brigades will have full equipment allowances. Improved equipment and increased allowances will markedly advance the equipment status of reserve units. In addition, some reserve units will train with active-duty units and others will actually be integrated with active-duty units so that if contingency plans are put into effect, these reserve units will deploy immediately with the parent active units.[17]

The variations possible in the degree of readiness are as broad as the spectrum of readiness and the limits on ingenuity, manpower, and money. Units and individual personnel whose capacities must be available on short notice can be brought to and maintained in a high state of readiness. Others for whose services there is not the same urgent need can be maintained on tap for long periods so that they can, by concentrated training when called to active duty, be brought to the necessary proficiency. The various combinations of drills, active duty, equipment levels, and training, in conjunction with the active forces where possible, ensure great flexibility in reserve response.

The reserve spectrum of readiness utilized in our defense effort has been materially broadened, and we have not seen the limits of it to date. Though those close to estimating the cost of various degrees of readiness by different types of reserve units maintain that the range extends all the way from 50% or less to 90% or 100% of active-forces equivalents, depending upon weapons systems and degree of readiness required, it is apparent the

[16] See, for example, Numbers 1200.7 (2 July 1970), 1205.14 (13 March 1970), 1215.5 (25 August 1969), 1215.6 (25 August 1969), 1215.13 (9 January 1969), 1225.6 (18 April 1970), 1235.9 (13 September 1967), and 1235.10 (27 October 1970).

[17] *Toward a National Security Strategy of Realistic Deterrence* (Washington, D.C.: Department of Defense, 1 March 1971), pp. 102–103.

reserves are potentially remarkably versatile on the readiness score, while remaining basically reserves. The ultimate, one would suppose, in maintenance of reserve status without crossing the none-too-distinct line to active status, must be some of the civilian technicians and aides who are simultaneously members of the Ready Reserve units for whom they work in a civilian capacity.

The Reserves: Stockpiling Essential Skills and Expertise

There are certain types of skills and expertise required by the military on an occasional basis or in the event of emergency which are more likely to be maintained on tap through a reserve program. In spite of the fact that medical personnel are and have been the category of personnel in shortest supply in the Guard and reserves,[18] hundreds of doctors, dentists, and other professional medical personnel find it possible to serve in reserve medical units, on a voluntary basis. Were it not for their reserve status, they would be available in an emergency only by the time-consuming processes of the draft, and then they would not be organized and equipped for almost immediate use. Other professional and skilled personnel of all kinds who find participation in the defense effort possible on a part-time basis would be unavailable if there were no option but an active status.

Nor is this the only advantage of reserve status for many vocational groups. Doctors, engineers, and technicians, but also certain less obvious professionals and technical specialties such as public welfare and public education people, would find it difficult to remain abreast of developments in their areas of expertise as full-time military personnel. On the roles of reserve units, in Civil Affairs and other types of military groupings, they can practice their specialties as civilians and be available simultaneously for call to active duty by the military. Thus they bring into the active military the latest techniques and improvements and retain proficiency while doing it.

The Reserves: Antidotes to the Excesses of Antimilitarism and Isolationism

Neither entirely civilian nor entirely military, reservists can do much to counter those excessive antimilitarist tendencies that result to some extent, from the relative isolation of the active forces.

Reserve forces are increasingly active in their communities with projects of a civic-action nature. A recent Pentagon news release cited 30 units of the Guard and reserves for continuing efforts in support of community

[18] *Ibid.*, p. 135.

projects and domestic actions. These activities ranged from work in public health in areas of poverty and unemployment by an Army Station Hospital in Puerto Rico, to assistance to the mentally retarded by an Air National Guard unit in Steelton, Pennsylvania, and seminars on drug abuse to the youth of the Greater Chicago area by the reserve at the Naval Air Station, Glenview, Illinois.[19]

The active forces of the United States have been characterized recently by high turnover rates and have lived in large numbers in civilian communities. They have, therefore, not been precluded from public service programs and such familiarity and contact with civilian society as to be able to do much to dispel antimilitarism and the adverse effects of such separatism. But the reservists all live in civilian communities, are basically civilians, and can do the job continuously, without obtrusiveness and hence with greater effectiveness.

While it is not usually categorized with the reserves, the Reserve Officers Training Corps is a part of the military reserve, and after obligatory tours of active duty, most ROTC-produced officers end up in the reserve. Although Secretary Laird did not include it in those forces that he counted available for the immediate augmentation of the active forces in an emergency, the ROTC performs many of the functions of the reserves and Guard in the area of civil-military relations and has some unique functions of its own. ROTC can play a crucial role in countering excesses of antimilitarism or isolationism. As it is confined exclusively to institutions of higher education, it enrolls substantial numbers of the future leaders of the country and is in good position to influence many more.

Founded in 1916 upon a base of military instruction at civilian schools that goes back to 1819, with government subsidy beginning with the Morrill Act of 1862, ROTC was created and named by the Military Defense Act of 1916. From the Morrill Act until 1916, the reserve officer training program was limited to land grant colleges.[20]

While the number of colleges and universities now hosting ROTC units is at an all-time high of 374, the number of cadets enrolled has fallen steadily in recent years from 212,416 in 1968–69 to 83,130 in 1971–72 although the decline has apparently slowed. This number does not include enrollments in programs similar to ROTC such as the Navy's Reserve Officer Candidate Program and the Marine Corps Platoon Leaders Class, both of which are for college students but entail no college academic work.[21]

[19] News Release, Office of the Assistant Secretary of Defense (Public Affairs), Department of Defense, 28 April 1971, #371–71.

[20] *What is the Status of ROTC?* (Washington, D.C.: Department of Defense, 1970), mimeographed, p. 243.

[21] *Facts About ROTC* (Washington, D.C.: Department of Defense, 1971), mimeographed, p. 1.

In recent years there have been some marked changes in the kinds of schools hosting ROTC units and the nature of their participation in the program. After anti-ROTC rioting on campuses all over the country, principally in 1969 and 1970, some 15 colleges asked to withdraw from ROTC. Most of them were in the Northeast, including six Ivy League Schools, three of which have been reconsidering their decisions to withdraw. In addition, the number of units at schools where ROTC is compulsory has declined from 112 in 1968–69 to 39 in 1971–72, while the number of units at predominantly black schools has risen from 16 in 1968–69 to 27 in 1971–72.[22] In 1969, the Air Force opened ROTC to women at most of its participating colleges and universities; the Navy followed suit in 1972.[23]

ROTC, it is maintained by both military and civilian leaders, must remain an integral part of the defense structure of the United States. It is simultaneously the source of a large part of the officer corps of the United States armed forces (43% of all new military officers in 1969–70) and much less expensive than reliance on expansion of the service academies or OCS's. But possibly most important as a reason for its maintenance is the balance it brings to the make up of that crucial element in our armed forces, the officer corps.

ROTC provides the citizen-soldier component in the officer corps of our standing forces. Most of the rest come from the service academies and from the ranks. In the case of the latter category, their educations, if not their backgrounds, differ from that of the ROTC officer. The civilian university education of the ROTC officers provides some of the professional skills needed by officers in our armed forces, which cannot or should not be supplied by the officer-education institutions maintained by the services. In addition, officers educated in civilian institutions assure a perception and understanding in the officer corps of the civilian point of view. Retention of ROTC officers beyond their obligated tours has been low in all three services, a fact which has insured a continuous infusion of these essentially citizen-officers into the officer corps of the armed forces.

With the advent of an all-volunteer armed force, the need for a substantial ROTC input to our officer corps will continue. There is little prospect of the abatement of the demands of our armed forces of the future for officers educated in a wide variety of professions, especially the technical and scientific. As the enlisted and officer careerists in the all-volunteer armed forces increase in proportion, as they may be expected to, the importance of a steady infusion of an element of officers educated in civilian universities and possessing recently formed sensibilities to civilian concerns increases.

22 *Fact Book, Selected College Based Precommissioning Programs* (Washington, D.C.: Department of Defense, 1971), mimeographed, pp. 1–2.

23 *What is the Status of ROTC? op. cit.*, p. 9.

The ROTC thus is and will remain an essential part of the reserve structure of the United States military.

CONCLUSION

Not all of the foregoing attributes of the reserves are relevant in each specific civil-military situation. But over time and with changing circumstances, all can serve to enhance the capacity of military forces to meet the needs of the nation.

In summation, reliance on the reserves, early in any emergency and as an integral part of our defense establishment, would appear consistent with the maintenance of the security and the political health of our democratic state. Berlin is evidence of the effective deterrent capacity of such reliance; Vietnam might have been a sequel. The massive reliance of the Israelis on their reserves in their dire peril would appear the example *in extremis.* In our complex and pluralistic society, the reserves and their use for immediate support of the standing forces appears to be a precedent we should nurture and follow.

II

Abroad

Introduction

With the single exception of the Soviet Union, which will be dealt with separately, all the nations examined in this volume fall into the category of Less Developed Countries (LDC's), and about half of them are new states created from crumbling colonial empires. Our central question is: What generalizations can be made about the role of the military in the LDC's of the world? Is there a similar pattern in the functions of the military in all developing states, or are the functions determined completely by the peculiarities of each situation? A closely related question is: How do the functions of the military in these societies compare with the role of the military in developed societies?

It has already been pointed out that it is difficult to categorize neatly "civil" and "military" roles in American society. Our reappraisal of this problem suggested that the traditional conceptual dualism is not appropriate for the contemporary American context: The significant changes that have occurred in recent decades make the traditional formulation inadequate. The other studies included in this book demonstrate that the conventional model is manifestly unsuited for other nations as well.

Joseph Smaldone stresses this view in Chapter Ten, in his analysis of the lack of viable social and political institutions in sub-Saharan Africa. In fact, the conditions he describes are generally present in other states examined in this work. He cites Huntington's statement that:

> . . . military interventions are only one specific manifestation of a broader phenomenon in underdeveloped societies: the general politicization of social forces and institutions. In such societies, politics lacks autonomy, complexity, coherence, and adaptability. All sorts of social forces and groups become directly engaged in general politics. . . .[1]

The political life of most new and many underdeveloped states takes place in an environment marked by a low level of political institutionalization. This situation encourages reliance upon force to effect change. It has been suggested elsewhere that the situation in Latin America and that in East Africa are quite similar even though the Latin American states are not "new".[2] The blurring of the boundary between "civil" and "military" roles results from this low level of institutional differentiation and autonomy.

[1] Samuel P. Huntington, *Political Order in Changing Societies* (New Haven: Yale University Press, 1968), p. 194.

[2] Jonathan Wise Polier, "East Africa: Latin America Revisited?" *The Activist* (Oberlin, Ohio), 4 (1964), pp. 98–100.

Although great differences exist among developing states in terms of their resources for development, institutions, and culture, the boundary between "civil" and "military" is at least as indistinct as in the United States. At the same time political institutions are often relatively underdeveloped when compared to the military. The military is able to intervene in political disputes because it is the most highly disciplined, organized, and technically advanced institution in the society.

Underdeveloped societies are under intense pressure to pursue a thoroughgoing program of modernization. Such programs are bound to cause severe tensions by rending the economic and social relationships that sustained the traditional order. The military may intervene because of its relative strength or to defend its status, frequently finding itself in control of a government without having a comprehensive program for change.

Although military expenditures in developing countries are considerably less than those of the developed countries, it is significant that in the last decade the rate of growth of military spending in the developing countries was appreciably faster than the world average. While military spending has been increasing throughout the world at about 3% to 4% a year, in the developing countries military spending has been increasing at a rate of approximately 7% per year.[3] The arms race has a significant impact on the standard of living and the quality of life in both the developed and the developing countries. The needs of economic development are much more pressing in developing countries, however, which makes it all the more disturbing that those nations find it necessary to put an ever-larger share of their resources in military appropriations. The diversion of even a few dollars for military purposes may keep the very necessities of life from a citizen of a less developed country.

As Pope Atkins indicates in Chapter Eleven, "The Armed Forces in Latin American Politics," the traditional view that the military in Latin American societies are motivated solely to defend the status quo is not valid. That is, the military may be mobilized to perform useful nation-building services with more efficiency and less compromise than their civilian counterparts.

The Latin American military establishments perform a number of roles. Throughout the twentieth century, Latin American governments have been motivated to modernize and professionalize their armed forces in pursuit of several goals, including the development of the army as the symbol of national unity, security in terms of border defense, maintaining law and order and, in the case of the larger states, international prestige. The Latin American military, as in Africa, the Middle East, and Asia, has been used

[3] Report of the Secretary-General, *Economic and Social Consequences of Military Expenditures* (New York: United Nations, 1972). UN Doc. A/8469/Rev.1., pp. 7–13.

in such supposedly "non-military" activities as civic action, the purposes of which have been a mixture of economic and social development.

In Latin America the domestic political roles of the military, including intervention into politics, have been much more significant. The development of military "professionalism" has not been a cure for a high degree of political participation by the armed forces in many states. The military has restricted itself primarily to a role as an interest or pressure group, but everywhere in Latin America, at some point in history, it has been the most important political arbiter by exercising a policy veto, performing a *coup d'etat,* or administering the government directly. The motivations for seizures of power also have been varied, including the pursuit of personal power, the preservation of the status quo, or a sincere attempt at political and economic reform.

Philip Mangano's analysis of the role of the military in North Africa in Chapter Twelve tends to complement and reinforce the conclusions of both Smaldone and Atkins. Mangano points out that the military organizations in these states are generally much more concerned with national development than with national defense. A problem arises when the military as an institution becomes engaged in Civic Action or economic activities, for it may lose its identity as a military unit. This is one reason that the military may choose to oversee the efforts of political leaders, with the understanding that they may intervene again if they deem it necessary. Egypt and Algeria are examples in which military leaders stayed on in civilian posts and became "civilianized." Smaldone refers to a similar occurrence in Zaire, but such cases appear to be the exception rather than the rule.

A second reason that the military may prefer to remain in the background is that it is very difficult for a professional military man to change hats and become an effective Minister of Public Welfare or, for that matter, of Finance or Housing. Although the military may claim to be progressive and reform-minded, in some instances correctly, it is far more frequently a self-serving justification for having taken over a government. Moreover, when the military is not subordinate to an executive or responsible to a constituency, the corporate interest of the officers does not motivate them in the direction of progressive social and economic policies.[4] The positive effects of military rule in the modernization of states tends to be both accidental and incidental to the military's pursuit of political stability, in which the middle-class interest of the military is protected.[5] The military

[4] Eric A. Nordlinger, "Soldiers in Mufti: The Impact of Military Rule Upon Economic and Social Change in the Non-Western States," *The American Political Science Review,* Vol. LXIV, Dec. 1970, No. 4, p. 1134.

[5] Hans Daalder, *The Role of the Military in the Emerging Countries* (The Hague, 1962), pp. 16–20. See also M. J. V. Bell, "The Military in the New States of Africa," in Jacques Van Doorn (ed.), *Armed Forces and Society* (The Hague, 1968), pp. 263–265.

may be most effective in creating conditions in which civilian political leadership is freed from tradition-bound restraints and is provided with the relative stability and security necessary to implement political programs for modernization.

There is general agreement with Mangano's view that although a military regime may begin its tenure with vigor, patriotic zeal, and sometimes attempted reform, it rarely has the political expertise or a comprehensive program for change and inevitably becomes bogged down in the same unyielding economic and social problems with which its civilian predecessors have wrestled. As Smaldone finds, rather than mastering the endemic sociopolitical conditions that retard progress, the military is likely to succumb to them. Thus military regimes tend to have short life-spans and are eventually replaced by new military regimes or civilian political leadership. But, as the conditions remain essentially unchanged, political instability persists.

Richard D'Amato's discussion of the People's Liberation Army (PLA) in Chapter Thirteen points out that the military in China is more completely engaged in the effort to modernize society on the working level than in any other nation. He cites Tilman Durdin's statement illustrating the situation:

> They grow vegetables, raise pigs, operate small factories and state farms, reclaim waste land, spread Mao Thought, act as adjudicators of political orthodoxy in universities, and do manual labor with workers and peasants on dam projects, on farms and in steel mills.[6]

The military during the long civil war was dependent upon close and harmonious relations with the population. At the same time the army had to become independent in that it had to rely upon its own resources, e.g., growing its own food. The effect of the civil war experience and the views of Mao have prevented the development of "professionalism" in the PLA, as this term is understood in other contexts. In the PLA many distinctions between the military and civilian sectors have been consciously blurred. Chinese society, for example, has been militarized in an organizational sense while the PLA itself is described as an "unmilitary army." Underlying all civil-military relations in China, as D'Amato indicates, is Mao's axiom that "political power grows out of the barrel of a gun. Our principle is that the party commands the gun and the gun shall never be allowed to command the party." [7]

There are some fascinating contrasts between this viewpoint and the popular view of the military in the United States. In the United States there is a tendency to attempt to distinguish between what is a military function and what is a civilian function. There is fear that the military may become

[6] Tilman Durdin, "China's Politicized Armed Forces," *New York Times*, 17 February 1972.

[7] Selected Writings of Mao Tse-tung (Peking, 1963), p. 272.

too involved in politics and become a dominant influence in society. There is almost an effort to build a "wall of separation" between civilian and military concerns. Mao has been most critical of the view that sees "political and military affairs in opposition to each other." Indeed, as the political tasks permeate all aspects of the society, the daily activities of the army are totally immersed in politics through its educational, cultural, and even leisure activities. According to Mao this is as it should be. It is only necessary to emphasize the primacy of politics and hence the total political control of the military.

To ensure political control two separate but parallel hierarchies have been developed that extend throughout the PLA. One answers to the Military Affairs Committee of the Party Central Committee. The other is a military organization that reports to the General Political Department of the PLA. After the success of the Civil War and by the middle 1950s "the army had moved well along in the direction of the professional model." Commitment to the revolutionary model by the Party resulted in a campaign against "professionalism" and the arrogant and autocratic behavior of the officers. In the late 1950s the officers were required to spend a month each year as enlisted soldiers. "Political renewal" took several years but ultimately was judged such a success that society was urged to "learn from the PLA."

By the close of the 1960s however, the army had expanded its activity and influence in society very significantly. With increased military influence, Lin Piao, Minister of Defense and Head of the Military Affairs Committee, questioned the whole range of political leadership's policies. The failure of the attempted *coup* by Lin Piao in September 1971 shows that he did not command loyalty throughout the army. It appears that the PLA was divided along generational, doctrinal, and regional lines. The civil-military shake-up that occurred in the aftermath of the abortive coup leaves no doubt that "politics still commands the gun," though the politic rule appears to be more moderate than previously.

In the case of Indonesia the military was not, in the beginning, overly demanding of the government. But the more Sukarno relied on the army for support, the more leverage the military acquired to demand a *quid pro quo*. The fact that it played a major role in gaining independence led it to expect a major continuing voice in the policies of government.

Harry Gilmore's study of civil-military relations in the Soviet Union in Chapter Fourteen must be treated separately. First, the Soviet Union is one of the world's two superpowers and as such is the center around which political, military, and industrial power in the communist world has tended to coalesce. Second, the Soviet Union does not fit the category of a new or developing state. For these reasons, Soviet practice is essential to any comparative study of civil-military relations.

The Soviet experience has served as the prototype for civil-military relations throughout Eastern Europe and, perhaps to a lesser extent, for China's nonprofessional army. The USSR was the only communist state between World War I and World War II and thus the model for new communist states to emulate.

As in the case of China, supremacy over all military and other potentially autonomous institutions derives from the highly centralized Communist Party. Gilmore stresses that the ideological beliefs of Lenin and his successors have been tremendously important in influencing the nature of civil-military relations in the Soviet Union and all other states of the socialist world that have looked to the Soviet Union for direction. The party, as the "vanguard of the proletariat" that achieved power in Russia, has a logical claim to hegemony "over the entire polity and every institution within it." Political officers (commissars) are assigned to military units to provide a system of surveillance that ensures the loyalty of those units. This system parallels the military organization and is responsible to the Main Political Administration (MPA). The MPA in turn is formally subordinate to the Minister of Defense but directly responsible to the Secretariat. These and other methods of control treated in Professor Gilmore's essay have been closely imitated by China as well as other Socialist states.

When the military is relied upon for support in determining domestic policy and leadership, it is in a strong position to win concessions. And it is only too obvious that the military resents what it considers to be outside "interference" in its affairs. The rise and fall of Marshall Georgi Zhukov described by Gilmore shows that the problem of how to control the military is ubiquitous. The tension between the military and the rest of society is not peculiar to the United States. Party control from outside the military makes it difficult to develop the "professionalism" aspired to by some elements of the military.

Professor Gilmore takes issue with the Kremlinologists who see signs of increasing military autonomy in the Soviet Union. Clues cited by other writers,[8] such as cultural pluralism and ideological disillusionment in the society, are discounted by Gilmore. To the contrary, he states that there is no evidence of widespread public support for dissenters in the Soviet Union. He does not contend that the society is monolithic, just that pluralism in the Western sense cannot evolve under present conditions. The government's control of the mass media and the fact that there are no autonomous

[8] Roman Kolkowicz, *The Soviet Military and the Communist Party* (Princeton, N.J.: Princeton University Press, 1967), Chapters IV and V. See also Bohdan Harasymiw, "Application of the Concept of Pluralism to the Soviet Political System," *Newsletter on Comparative Studies of Communism*, Vol. V, No. 1, November 1971, pp. 40–54.

institutions prevent pluralism as we understand it from evolving. The managerial, scientific, and technocratic "elites" differ radically from "interest groups" in Western societies. Various techniques are available to the CPSU to deal with "dangerous" elements in the military, and the CPSU is seen as continuing to dominate, with the attendant tension between military professionals and the Party continuing apace.

In comparing civil-military relations in the United States with those of other states some interesting conclusions may be drawn. As we have seen, the major difficulty for developing states is the internal problem of organizing and mobilizing its forces to modernize. The military may be not only the most convenient but oftentimes the only institution with the ability to impose conformity, if not national unity, on dissident elements in society.

The military is most successful as a symbol of nationhood and national unity in those instances. In the cases examined outside the United States, the military has a proportionally smaller share of the national budget than in the United States, and there are in most cases little or no external threats. The greater involvement of the military in LDC's in domestic questions and results in the professional military playing at least as significant a role in their respective countries as the military does in the United States.

While military involvement in internal conflicts may serve to unite less developed states, external conflicts reflecting internal divisions tend to exacerbate internal conflicts in the United States.

In each case the problem is to control the military as an institution. A common theme found in each chapter is an evaluation of the role of the military in different societies. Changing demands require that old stereotypes concerning the military be discarded and that national priorities be reevaluated.

10

The Paradox of Military Politics in Sub-Saharan Africa

JOSEPH P. SMALDONE

Within the past decade 14 of the 33 independent states of tropical Africa have experienced successful military *coups* and periods of military rule. Abortive *coups* occurred in several others, and virtually every state has been threatened by a military takeover at least once during its brief independent existence.[1] The prominence of the military in African politics

[1] These 33 states are listed in Table 1. The states of Morocco, Algeria, Tunisia, Libya, and the Sudan are treated in Philip A. Mangano's chapter in this book. Throughout this chapter I have used the phrases "sub-Saharan" and "tropical" Africa interchangeably. In addition I have referred frequently to the "new states" of Africa. This designation excludes Liberia and Ethiopia; the former has been independent since 1847 and the latter has been independent since ancient times, with the exception of the brief Italian occupation (1935–41).

Botswana, Equatorial Guinea (Rio Muni and Fernando Po), Gambia, Lesotho, and Swaziland have no national armies *per se,* but rather civil police forces, and thus fall outside the pale of this chapter.

For convenient chronological summaries of African military *coups* and attempted *coups,* see Kenneth W. Grundy, *Conflicting Images of the Military in Africa* (Nairobi: East African Publishing House, 1968), Appendix; Claude E. Welch, Jr., "Violence and Military Involvement in African Politics from Independence through 1968," Appendix B in Welch (ed.), *Soldier and State in Africa* (Evanston: Northwestern University Press, 1970), pp. 270–301; and Marion E. Doro, "Major Events in African States since Independence," in *A Current Bibliography on African Affairs,* 4, 3 (May 1971), pp. 198–205.

Extensive bibliographic references may be found in: Harvey Glickman, "The Military in African Politics: a bibliographic Essay," *African Forum,* II, 1 (Summer 1966), pp. 68–75; Daniel G. Matthews, "Prelude Coup d'etat Military Government: Politics and Government in Nigeria, 1965 to February 1966" (Washington, D.C.: African Bibliographic Center, 1966); "The Sword and Government: a Preliminary and Selected Bibliographical Guide to African Military Affairs," *Current Bibliography Reading List Series* (African Bibliographic Center, V, 2, parts 1 and 2, April 1967); "The In Crowd: a Preliminary and Selected Bibliographical Guide to African Military Affairs," *A Current Bibliography on African Affairs*, I, 3 (1968), pp. 5–9; and Marion E. Doro, "Bibliographic Essay on the Role of the Military in African States," *A Current Bibliography on African Affairs,* 4, 3 (May 1971), pp. 190–197.

appears to be increasing, raising important questions both in Africa and abroad, among laymen and scholars alike, concerning the capacity of military regimes to promote political development and modernization. The purpose of this chapter is fourfold: to analyze the characteristics of modern African institutions and their sociopolitical environments that account for the prevalence of military regimes; to examine the range of noninstitutional factors that have encouraged political intervention by African military officers; to evaluate the performance of African military regimes in their self-appointed political roles; and finally, in the context of the foregoing investigation, to assess the relevance of the conventional concept of "civil-military relations" to the study of modern African politics.

This chapter is not a history of African military *coups,* but rather a study organized around the theme of the paradoxes of military intervention in politics. Frequent reference will be made to the considerable corpus of scholarly literature on this subject. Although sources and interpretations are plentiful, the very nature of the subject precludes definitive conclusions. Most African nations are only about ten years old, and the era of *coups* began only about a half-dozen years ago; as more evidence comes to light, research will undoubtedly provide new perspectives and revisionist critiques of current views. In commenting upon the changing interpretations of recent research on the role of the military in African politics, this paper will on occasion take on the character of a bibliographic essay.

GENERAL CHARACTERISTICS OF AFRICAN INSTITUTIONS

Several factors have combined to make the armed forces of new states potential political agents. These may be classified into (1) features peculiar to military institutions by their very nature and (2) characteristics of the African sociopolitical environment that under certain conditions make it possible, indeed virtually inevitable, for the military to intrude forcibly into the political domain. Earlier studies of African armies stressed the first set of factors, while more recent scholarship has emphasized the nature of the environment in which the military operates and the interaction between the military leadership and institutions and the wider sociopolitical *milieu.*

Peculiar Characteristics of the Military

Several distinguishing features of the armed forces of new states, and of Africa in particular, have been identified by sociologist Morris Janowitz.[2] He shows that the capacity of the military to intervene in politics derives

[2] Janowitz, *The Military in the Political Development of New Nations: An Essay in Comparative Analysis* (Chicago: University of Chicago Press, 1964), pp. 27 *ff.*

in part from its distinctive organizational principle, namely its control of the instruments of physical force. Military technology and organization, based on light infantry battalions and motorized units deployed in and around urban areas, provide ready-made vehicles for political intervention. Military officers, by virtue of their education, training, skills, social origin and status, may be considered part of the "technical-executive intelligentsia" of new states.[3] Professional socialization and indoctrination, *esprit de corps,* patriotism, discipline, and the distinctive nature of the military as a "total institution" regulating all aspects of its members' public life produce a high degree of internal cohesion. Although the military is perhaps the most cohesive social institution in African states, the degree of internal cohesion should not be exaggerated. As we shall see later, the dichotomy between the external appearance of cohesion and internal sources of cleavage is one of the principal paradoxes of African military organizations. But in comparison with other social institutions,

> African armies tend to be the most detribalized, Westernized, modernized, integrated, and cohesive institutions in their respective states. The army is usually the most disciplined agency in the state. It often enjoys a greater sense of national identity than other institutions. In technical skills, including the capacity to coerce and to communicate, the army is the most modernized agency in the country.[4]

Characteristics of the African Sociopolitical Environment

It is impossible to understand the political role of African armies exclusively in terms of their internal structure and social composition. In other words, the basic question asked by Janowitz, "What characteristics of the military establishment of a new nation facilitate its involvement in domestic politics?" [5] provides only a partial explanation for the prominent political role played by African armies. Yet it was typical for scholars to ask such questions in the early 1960s, before the rash of African military *coups* beginning in 1965. Lucian Pye and Edward Shils also sought to explain the role of the army in the political development of new states by reference to the distinctive traits of military institutions. In their view, the unique fitness of the military elite for roles of national leadership made them the logical claimants to political power when the civilian regime faltered.[6]

[3] Edward Shils, "The Military in the Political Development of the New States," in John J. Johnson (ed.), *The Role of the Military in Underdeveloped Countries* (Princeton: Princeton University Press, 1962), p. 23.

[4] Ernest W. Lefever, *Spear and Scepter: Army, Police, and Politics in Tropical Africa* (Washington, D.C.: The Brookings Institution, 1970), pp. 20–21.

[5] Janowitz, *op. cit.,* p. 1.

[6] Lucian W. Pye, "Armies in the Process of Political Modernization," in Johnson (ed.), *op. cit.,* pp. 69–89; Shils, *op. cit.,* pp. 7–67.

Recent scholarship, on the other hand, has emphasized the nature of the sociopolitical structure of African states. In general, this view stresses the relative weakness of the institutional environment, that is, the lack of viable social and political institutions. Samuel P. Huntington, a well-known proponent of this view, regards new states as "praetorian societies" marked by the absence of effective political institutions, the fragmentation of power, and the weakness of authority. Huntington argues, in contrast to Janowitz, that

> Military explanations do not explain military interventions. The reason for this is simply that military interventions are only one specific manifestation of a broader phenomenon in underdeveloped societies: the general politicization of social forces and institutions. In such societies, politics lacks autonomy, complexity, coherence, and adaptability. All sorts of social forces and groups become directly engaged in general politics. . . . Society as a whole is out-of-joint, not just the military. All these specialized groups tend to become involved in politics dealing with general political issues: not just issues which affect their own particular institutional interest or groups, but issues which affect society as a whole.[7]

This view is widely accepted among students of military regimes in the new nations. Fred Greene, for example, refers to the "porous civil-political order" in African states,[8] and Dankwart A. Rustow likewise asserts that the "true explanation [for *coups*] must be sought not in the history of armies or of wars but in the relationship of the military with the remainder of the political structure." [9] The probability of *coups* is related less to the inherent strength of the military than to the weakness and inadequacy of civilian governments.[10]

The strongest statement of this thesis is to be found in the works of Aristide R. Zolberg, who contends that "the most salient characteristic of political life in Africa is that it constitutes an almost institutionless arena with conflict and disorder as its most prominent features" and that constant political disturbances are "characteristic processes which themselves constitute an important aspect of the regime in certain types of political systems." [11]

[7] Huntington, *Political Order in Changing Societies* (New Haven: Yale University Press, 1968), p. 194. This argument is developed in Ch. 4, "Praetorianism and Political Decay," pp. 192–263. See also Amos Perlmutter, "The Praetorian State and the Praetorian Army: Toward a Taxonomy of Civil-Military Relations in Developing Politics," *Comparative Politics,* I, 3 (April 1969), pp. 382–404.

[8] Greene, "Toward Understanding Military Coups," *Africa Report,* 11, 2 (February 1966), p. 10.

[9] Rustow, *A World of Nations: Problems of Political Modernization* (Washington, D.C.: The Brookings Institution, 1967), p. 175.

[10] *Ibid.,* pp. 176–177.

[11] Zolberg, "The Structures of Political Conflict in the New States of Tropical Africa," *American Political Science Review,* LXII, 1 (March 1968), p. 70.

The low level of political institutionalization increases the tendency of regimes to rely upon force as a means to effect changes. Zolberg argues that force has become the major instrument to produce political change in tropical Africa, and that the *coup* itself has become a predominant "political institution." [12]

In seeking to explain the prevalence of institutionalized force in this institutionless arena, we must recall the recent colonial experience shared by most African states. Modern colonial regimes were alien to the environment and structure of African societies. There was a basic incompatibility between the traditional forms of political organization and the style of rule imposed by the European powers. The colonial system attempted to integrate many formerly autonomous cultural and political units, and in the process weakened or destroyed indigenous institutions. The relatively short duration of colonial rule—only about 60 years in most cases—and the relatively brief period of widespread nationalist agitation before independence—only 15 to 20 years—did not provide the time necessary to generate and build a new set of viable political institutions. Nationalist leaders could not produce genuinely mass organizations. In these conditions of a low level of social mobilization and political organization, the departure of the colonial rulers left, in effect, a sort of "institutional void." [13] The incompatibility between modern and traditional political institutions and the failure of the national elite to fashion new ones made the whole system susceptible to crises that provided the military with the occasion to intervene.[14] It is therefore possible to regard African politics somewhat deterministically as a manifestation of what James O'Connell has termed "the inevitability of instability." [15]

Indeed, there seems to be a kind of grim logic to the spate of African *coups*. The apparent absence of "civil order"—the widespread acceptance of basic social and political conventions—is a remarkable feature of the new states of tropical Africa.[16] The low level of political institutionalization

[12] *Ibid.*, pp. 70–87; See also Zolberg, "Military Intervention in the New States of Tropical Africa: Elements of Comparative Analysis," in Henry Bienen (ed.), *The Military Intervenes: Case Studies in Political Development* (New York: Russell Sage Foundation, 1968), pp. 71–98, and "Military Rule and Political Development in Tropical Africa: A Preliminary Report," in Jacques van Doorn (ed.), *Military Profession and Military Regimes: Commitments and Conflicts* (The Hague: Mouton and Co., 1969), pp. 175–202.

[13] Huntington, *op. cit.*, pp. 199–201.

[14] Billy J. Dudley, "The Military and Politics in Nigeria: Some Reflections," in van Doorn (ed.), *op. cit.*, pp. 209–215.

[15] O'Connell, "The Inevitability of Instability," *Journal of Modern African Studies*, 5, 2 (September 1967), pp. 181–191.

[16] J. M. Lee, *African Armies and Civil Order* (New York: Praeger, 1969), *passim*.

frustrates the efforts of a regime to create and maintain political order. The lack of extensive and complex organizational controls throughout society prevents the political system from performing its essential function of providing direction for the polity. Wanting institutional controls, the political system is vulnerable to pressures from within and without. In the absence of clearly differentiated and autonomous institutions to resolve social conflict, conflict becomes politicized and generalized beyond manageable boundaries. The political system, already weak and insecure, becomes further burdened with demands it cannot satisfy and founders in crisis. In these circumstances the military—the most coherent institution in this "institutionless" environment—intervenes to restore order and stability to political life. The lack of organizational control upon the military by the political system seals the fate of the regime and accounts for the relative ease with which governments fall to *coups*.[17] Hence, as J. M. Lee has shown, "the actions of soldiers acquire political significance not from the degree of support which they receive *inside* the security forces themselves, but from the *absence of a political system* which can support a high degree of military discipline." [18]

MILITARY INTERVENTION: THEORY VERSUS REALITY

We now will examine the propositions that the military is a relatively modernized institution in an underdeveloped environment; that its organizational format and skill structure facilitate intervention and the establishment of a military regime; that by social origin and education the officer corps constitutes an elite whose professional ethic and orientation tend to be national and apolitical; and that the "institutionless arena" of political conflict in Africa enables the military to penetrate the permeable political sphere easily. Drawing upon empirical data, we will attempt to arrive at some tentative conclusions concerning the political behavior of African military elites.

The Passive Role in the Early Sixties

Viewed in retrospect, the observations of many scholars in the early 1960s about African armies seem naive. While the military in Latin America, Asia, and the Middle East had made a political *debut* long before, the armies

[17] Van Doorn, "Political Change and the Control of the Military," in van Doorn (ed.), *op. cit.*, pp. 30–31.

[18] Lee, *op. cit.*, p. 175 (italics added).

of Africa remained relatively inactive. Edward Shils, in attempting to explain this apparent anomaly, suggested that African states were not threatened by military intervention "because they have scarcely any military forces."[19] Herbert J. Spiro argued in early 1965 that the most significant feature of African armies in the immediate post-independence period was their *insignificance* and that this condition would probably continue.[20] Other writers were more discriminating in their judgment, distinguishing among types of regimes and their relationship with the military. For example, Morris Janowitz, William F. Gutteridge, and Pierre L. van den Berghe suggested that authoritarian "mobilization" regimes or one-party states tended to exercise effective political control over their armies. Ghana, Guinea, and Mali were thought to be especially immune to military *coups*.[21] Among the few early observers who predicted an active political role for African armies were James S. Coleman and Belmont Brice, Jr., who foresaw military intervention as the likely outcome of failures of African regimes to modernize their societies.[22]

This general underestimation of the political potential of African armies may have seemed logical and justified at the time, but it soon became clear that it was unfounded: *Coups* followed in rapid succession in Zaire (formerly Congo-Kinshasa) and Dahomey in late 1965; in the Central African Republic, Upper Volta, Nigeria (2), Ghana, and Burundi in 1966; in Togo, Dahomey, and Sierra Leone (2) in 1967; in Congo-Brazzaville, Sierra Leone, and Mali in 1968; in Somalia and Dahomey in 1969; in Uganda in 1971; in Ghana and Dahomey again in 1972; and in Rwanda in 1973. During this period there were also several abortive *coups* in these and in other states. African armies had demonstrated that their apparent political disinterestedness was temporary only.

The relatively quiescent posture of the military in the early post-independence years may be attributed to five general factors. First, most African armies were products of the colonial era. They were organized, trained, equipped, and officered by Europeans to serve as instruments of imperial rule and defense. With the coming of independence the role of the military was abruptly reversed and the army became instead the symbol of

[19] Shils, *op. cit.*, p. 54.

[20] Spiro, "The Military in Sub-Saharan Africa," in Wilson C. McWilliams (ed.), *Garrisons and Government: Politics and the Military in New States* (San Francisco: Chandler Publishing Co., 1967), pp. 264–272.

[21] Janowitz, *op. cit.*, pp. 6, 39, 86; Gutteridge, *Armed Forces in New States* (London: Oxford University Press, 1962), p. 67; van den Berghe, "The Role of the Army in Contemporary Africa," *Africa Report*, 10, 3 (March 1965), p. 16 (reprinted also in McWilliams [ed.], *op. cit.*, pp. 278–287).

[22] Coleman and Brice, "The Role of the Military in Sub-Saharan Africa," in Johnson (ed.), *op. cit.*, pp. 402–403.

national sovereignty. This sudden reversal of status created a situation of uncertainty and ambiguity; the military had no well-defined role or purpose. Because of its imperial origin, the military lacked legitimacy as a genuine national African institution. The small size of African armies and meager defense budgets also ensured that the military would have a low social profile.

Second, the social composition of African armies was often marked by large ethnic and regional imbalances. This was attributable both to colonial recruiting practices of favoring the more "warlike" people and to certain accidental factors such as proximity to centers of colonial administration or local attitudes toward military service. Within the officer corps ethnic imbalances later became a source of cleavage when the military became politicized. The effect of these divisions was to neutralize, or at least diminish, the political potential of the military.

Third, African armies remained under expatriate officership even after independence. In the former British colonies less than one fifth of the officer corps was African by independence; in the former French states the figure was about two thirds. The senior officer ranks were almost exclusively European. In the years immediately after independence the rate of Africanization of the officer corps was greatly accelerated, sometimes by force, as in the serious army mutinies in Zaire (1960) and East Africa (1964). This pattern of continued expatriate domination effectively precluded political action by the few junior African officers. It is no accident that within a few years after Africanization had been completed, *coups* occurred in many of these states.

Fourth, the "primacy of politics" was virtually unquestioned by the newly independent African states. Not a single nation in sub-Saharan Africa achieved its independence by means of a "war of national liberation." Everywhere the transfer of power was accomplished peacefully, although not always amicably. [On 25 September 1973 the African Party for the Independence of Guinea and the Cape Verde Islands, which since 1963 has waged a war of national liberation in Portuguese Guinea, proclaimed the independence of the Republic of Guinea Bissau. Scores of states have already recognized this new nation, whose continued existence will constitute an important exception to this pattern of peaceable decolonization.] Kwame Nkrumah's exhortation to "Seek ye first the political kingdom" was a clear affirmation of the efficacy of the political credo. Dynamic nationalist leaders and dominant political parties were the vehicles of independence. As there was no participation by the military in the independence movement, the armed forces did not qualify as similarly legitimate national institutions.

Finally, neocolonial relationships persisted after the formal assumption of sovereignty by African nations. Frequently, the new states were dependent upon Europe for economic assistance, favorable commercial and financial arrangements, and military aid. France negotiated bilateral defense agreements with several of her former colonies. In 1964 French troops landed in Gabon to suppress an attempted military *coup*. Troops were airlifted to the Central African Republic in 1967 to bolster the regime of Jean-Bedel Bokassa, and in the next year a French force came to the assistance of President Francois Tombalbaye of Chad to put down a rebellion in the northern regions. British troops were sent to East Africa in 1964 to quell mutinies in Uganda, Tanganyika, and Kenya. Today there are no British forces remaining in Africa, but French military units are still stationed in Gabon, Chad, Niger, Senegal, and the Ivory Coast. The continued presence of foreign troops in Africa has undoubtedly acted as a deterrent to military *coups*.

Coups of 1965 and After: Causes and Classifications

Since the mid-sixties, when African military elites demonstrated their ability to seize power, students of African politics have offered various explanations for this sudden incursion of the military into politics. Although the study of African military regimes is still in its infancy, several observations and conclusions can be noted at this stage of research.

First, there seems to be no correlation between the "type" or "model" of political system and the likelihood of military intervention. Although some scholars at first believed that the more centralized regimes effectively neutralized the military, subsequent events suggest that authoritarian tendencies and attempts by dominant parties to penetrate the army were factors contributing to the *coups* in Ghana and Mali.[23] It is now generally recognized that single-party regimes (or attempts to create them) often led to widespread political repression and violence, which ultimately prepared the way for the imposition of military rule.[24] Present evidence suggests that one-party regimes are particularly vulnerable to military *coups*[25] and that the recent *coups* may be the beginning of an irregular cycle of regime changes, with charismatic leaders, one-party systems, and military regimes replacing one another in rapid succession.[26]

It is also clear that, in contrast to the assertion of Shils and others that

[23] Lt. General Joseph Ankrah, "The Future of the Military in Ghana," *African Forum*, II, 1 (Summer 1966), p. 11; L. Gray Cowan, "The Military and African Politics," *International Journal*, XXI, 3 (1966), p. 294; *The New York Times*, 22 November 1968, p. 5.

[24] Ronald Matthews, *African Powder Keg: Revolt and Dissent in Six Emergent Nations* (London: The Bodley Head, 1966), *passim*.

[25] Arnold Rivkin, *Nation-Building in Africa: Problems and Prospects* (New Brunswick, N.J.: Rutgers University Press, 1969), pp. 61–76.

[26] Rustow, *op. cit.*, pp. 204–206.

the smallness of African armies acts as a deterrent to intervention, there is no strong correlation between either the absolute or relative sizes of armies and their political behavior. Table 1 summarizes this data and shows that *coups* bear little if any consistent relationship to the size of the army, the size of the total population, the military budget, or the gross national product (GNP). Furthermore, there are neither discernible correlations in these factors among the states that have experienced *coups* nor significant differences between them and the nations in which no *coups* have occurred.[27]

Why, then, have the *coups* occurred? Do the *coups* exhibit any sort of pattern? Can military intervention be predicted? Although the evidence shows that there are often similarities in the socioeconomic conditions in which *coups* are likely to occur,[28] as well as frequently recurring patterns in the politicomilitary strategy of *coup*-making,[29] each instance of military intervention must be examined in its own context. The complexity of conditions, circumstances, and events in each case defies simple mono-causal analysis. As Cowan has observed,

> The military takeovers in Africa were a response to a complicated series of factors. . . . In no case were all, and not necessarily the same, causal factors present in equal degree; to be fully understood, each case must be analyzed within the framework of circumstances surrounding the position of the leader and the party in the country concerned.[30]

Recognizing the complicated nature of African *coups* and the possible combinations of causes, Claude E. Welch, Jr. has identified eight factors that have prompted military intervention: (1) declining prestige of the major political party, (2) schism among prominent politicians, (3) the remote probability of external intervention against new military regimes, (4) "contagion" from seizures of power by the military in other African states, (5) domestic social and/or ethnic antagonisms, (6) economic stagnation, (7)

[27] A statistical analysis of domestic attributes of African states by Roberta Koplin Mapp has disclosed no significant correlates of military *coups:* "Domestic correlates of military intervention in African politics," paper presented at the Canadian Political Science Association meeting, Winnipeg, June 1970. An important review article, which contains a rigorous critique of recent literature and concepts, is Samuel Decalo, "Military coups and military regimes in Africa," *Journal of Modern African Studies,* 11, 1 (1973), pp. 105–127. Although that article appeared after this chapter was completed, it reinforces many of the points made herein and raises several other major issues in the study of African military regimes.

[28] See Dorothy Nelkin, "The Economic and Social Setting of Military Takeovers in Africa," *Journal of Asian and African Studies,* II, 3/4 (1967), pp. 230–244.

[29] See, for example, Rustow, *op. cit.,* Ch. VI, and Edward Luttwak, *Coup d'Etat: A Practical Handbook* (Greenwich, Conn.: Fawcett Premier Books, 1969).

[30] Cowan, *op. cit.,* p. 292. Most scholars agree with this conclusion: See Claude E. Welch, Jr., "Soldier and State in Africa," *Journal of Modern African Studies,* 5, 3 (1967), pp. 312–313; and Greene, *op. cit.,* p. 10.

corruption and inefficiency among government and party officials, and (8) an increasing awareness among military leaders of their capacity to displace civilian governments.[31]

Welch's list is perhaps the most practicable outline. The declining prestige of the dominant party was certainly a contributing factor in the *coups* in Ghana (February 1966), Mali (November 1968), and Uganda (January 1971). Political rivalries that virtually paralyzed the government precipitated *coups* in Togo (January 1967), Zaire (September 1960, November 1965), Dahomey (several since 1963), and the abortive *coup* in Gabon (February 1964). Foreign intervention, as in the cases cited earlier (p. 211), has been the exception rather than the rule; there is no evidence of outside interference in any other instance of military takeover. The improbability of external intervention to restore the old regime insures the new military leadership a certain degree of security.

Whether "contagion" was an active factor in the occurrence of *coups* is difficult to determine. Although at this time there is no direct evidence that contagion existed, the rapid succession of military takeovers between November 1965 and March 1967 suggests that the success of the *coups* may have emboldened disenchanted and ambitious officers to ride the tide of intervention. During this 16-month period there were 12 successful *coups* and several abortive attempts; seven of the successful *coups* occurred in the 3-month period between November 1965 and February 1966 alone (see Appendix). Ethnic antagonism was clearly present in the two Nigerian *coups* (January and July 1966), the two Sierra Leone *coups* in March 1967, the Dahomey *coups,* the Uganda *coup* in January 1971, and the Rwanda *coup* in July 1973. Economic stagnation was prevalent in many cases, particularly in Mali (November 1968), Ghana (February 1966, January 1972), Upper Volta (January 1966), and Dahomey. Alleged corruption and inefficiency among party cadres and government officials is frequently cited as a general cause of *coups*. Finally, the increasing awareness within the officer corps of its potential to influence or to remove political leaders, reinforced by the assumed contagion generated by successful *coups* elsewhere, helps to account for the frequency of military intervention in African politics.

In theory it is possible to distinguish several possible political roles for the military. For example, Samuel E. Finer has distinguished four "levels of intervention" by the military in politics.[32] The first level is that of mere "influence," the ability to persuade the civil authorities to adopt policy favorable to the military. Second, "blackmail" may be employed to exert

[31] Welch, *ibid.*, p. 313 *ff.*, and "The Roots and Implications of Military Intervention," in Welch (ed.), *op. cit.*, pp. 17–34.

[32] Finer, *The Man on Horseback* (London: Pall Mall, 1962).

pressure on political decision-makers. Third, the military may force the "displacement" of the existing regime and install another, more tractable civilian group. Finally, the military may resort to the "supplantment" of the civilian regime and a direct assumption of power.

Once the military has seized power, several alternative outcomes are possible. Dankwart A. Rustow has discerned five possible "sequels" to *coups* in new states.[33] A "back to the barracks" *coup* occurs when the military intervenes to correct what is believed to be a temporary disorder, quickly rectifies the situation, and then withdraws voluntarily to resume a nonpartisan posture. Second, the military may become entrenched as a permanent oligarchy, giving little or no thought to a return to civilian control. Third, a series of *coups* may occur in succession, reflecting deep cleavages within the military leadership and increasing politicization of the officer corps. This situation, which Rustow calls "Praetorianism," results merely in changes of top leadership and encourages further instability. This pattern has evidently emerged in Dahomey, where there have been several *coups* and counter*coups* since 1963. The fourth possible outcome is a "civil-military twilight" in which the military withdraws after having secured certain prerogatives and retains its disposition to intervene again. In this case the military leadership assumes the role of umpire, content to remain behind the scenes but always vigilant and prepared to interfere again. This particular pattern seems likely to become the predominant one in Africa, at least for the near future. Finally, there may occur a genuine revolution under military sponsorship that fundamentally alters the nature and structure of social and political institutions. A new basis for a stable civilian order is thereby created and renders future military intervention both unnecessary and undesirable. While this kind of military government has occurred elsewhere, most notably in Mexico and Egypt, the prospects of this happening in sub-Saharan Africa appear rather remote.

MILITARY REGIMES: THE DILEMMA AND PARADOX

Despite the complexity of causes and motivations for the *coups* in sub-Saharan Africa, it is apparent that the principal problem of military regimes is to create a *national* basis of consensus and a program of political and economic modernization. Military juntas dub themselves with patriotic titles:

[33] Rustow, *op. cit.,* pp. 190–204. Cf. other typologies in van den Berghe, "The Role of the Army," pp. 13–17, and "The Military and Political Change in Africa," in Welch (ed.), *op. cit.,* pp. 254–266; Huntington, *Political Order,* pp. 233–237; Perlmutter, "The Praetorian State and the Praetorian Army," pp. 392–403; Lefever, *op. cit.,* pp. 28–29; Welch (ed.) *op. cit.,* pp. 5–35.

The National Renovation Committee (Dahomey), the National Liberation Council (Ghana, 1966), the National Redemption Council (Ghana, 1972), the National Reconciliation Committee (Togo), the National Reformation Council (Sierra Leone), the National Revolutionary Committee (Congo-Brazzaville), the Provisional Revolutionary Committee (Burundi), the Military Committee of National Liberation (Mali), and the Supreme Revolutionary Council (Somalia). They often attempt to streamline the administrative structure in order to eliminate corruption and regional particularism. Frequently the number of territorial subdivisions is changed to reduce egregious disparities of regional influence on national government. Political parties are banned, constitutions abrogated, national assemblies dissolved, and austerity measures imposed upon the economy. Direct assaults are often made against the tribal structure. The military regime in Sierra Leone, for example, abolished the tribal headman system, and in Dahomey tribal sacrification was declared illegal. But the military cannot achieve national unity by decree, and the quest for political order is often frustrated by the very measures it takes to attain it. In this section we will examine in some detail the problems and paradoxes of military government in tropical Africa.

Cleavages within the Military

In this chapter we have used the term "military" as if it referred to some monolithic and homogeneous organization. This characterization is, of course, an oversimplification. While military institutions in general tend to be more cohesive than their civil counterparts, the external appearance of cohesiveness should not be allowed to obscure certain significant sources of internal conflict and cleavage. First, the "military" includes the army, navy, air force, and other special forces that comprise the defense establishment. Although political intervention has been preempted and monopolized by the army, this does not preclude the possibility of serious opposition from the other branches of the military. The naval and air forces of tropical African nations are nonexistent or extremely small. Nevertheless, their potential role should not be underestimated: a few sorties by a handful of combat aircraft or a naval bombardment of a coastal or riverine capital could well determine the fate of an army *coup* attempt.[34] Even though air and naval forces do not possess the same tactical advantage for political intervention that the army enjoys, the very possibility of their active opposi-

[34] For example, a *coup* attempt in Ethiopia in December 1960 by the Emperor's Imperial Bodyguard was suppressed by the combined actions of the regular army and air force. For general accounts of the abortive *coup*, see Lefever, *op. cit.*, pp. 145–149, and Christopher Clapham, "The Ethiopian Coup d'etat of December 1960," *Journal of Modern African Studies*, 6, 4 (December 1968), pp. 495–507.

tion or collaboration with the civilian regime is a contingency that a cadre of army officers plotting a *coup* must reckon with.

Another source of cleavage within the officer corps can be distinguished. Most *coups* have been the work of colonels and majors, suggesting that certain factors incline this group of middle-rank officers toward political action more than more senior or junior grades. In fact, these middle-rank officers occupy a strategic position in a military organization. The middle level of command and communication is important in two respects. First, its members are few enough to facilitate horizontal communication among themselves. Second, their situation in the vertical command hierarchy is not so high as to isolate or alienate them from junior officers and soldiers. General officers, by virtue of their rank, status, and position, are often implicated in state affairs and may suffer by their association with the high political elite, the very elite segment that *coups* aim to overthrow. Junior officers, on the other hand, lack both the experience and the requisite following to engineer a *coup*.[35]

Not only have middle-rank officers figured predominantly in the *coups*, but within this group it is possible to identify another conspicuous element: staff officers have often played prominent roles in plotting *coups*. These men are specialists in administration and planning; they enjoy access to high military and political circles without contracting the odium of corruption; and they occupy positions in the military hierarchy crucial to the tasks of coordination, communication, and control. While it is essential to admit unit commanders to the conspiracy in order to secure the armed forces and equipment necessary for a *coup*, staff officers are often the brains behind it.

These observations are readily illustrated. The Dahomey *coup* of October 1963 was staged by Colonel Christophe Soglo, the Army Chief of Staff. The major figures in the February 1966 *coup* in Ghana were Colonel E. K. Kotoka, the commander of the 2nd Infantry Brigade at Kumasi, and Major A. A. Afrifa, his Staff Officer in charge of training and operations. A former Lieutenant Colonel and Chief of Staff, Major General Yakubu Gowon, now heads the Federal Military Government in Nigeria. Etienne Eyadema and Sangoule Lamizana, both Lieutenant Colonels and Chiefs of Staff, led *coups* in Togo (January 1967) and in Upper Volta (January 1966), respectively. In January 1966 Colonel Jean-Bedel Bokassa, Army Chief of Staff, led a *coup* in the Central African Republic. General-President Mobutu Sese Seko of Zaire, promoted to that rank from Colonel after his *coup* in September 1960, and later Chief of Staff, seized power

[35] See Hans Daalder, *The Role of the Military in the Emerging Countries*, Publications of the Institute of Social Studies, I (The Hague: Mouton and Co., 1962), pp. 13–14; Karl W. Deutsch, *The Nerves of Government: Models of Political Communication and Control* (New York: The Free Press of Glencoe, 1963), pp. 154–157.

again in November 1965. In March 1967 Lieutenant Colonel Andrew Juxon-Smith seized power in Sierra Leone from Brigadier General David Lansana, who himself had staged a *coup* only two days before.[36]

"Intergenerational" cleavages within the officer corps constitute another source of potential conflict. The rate of Africanization of the officer corps was accelerated greatly in the years just prior to and after independence, and many officers were elevated suddenly into higher ranks and positions. But subsequent expansion of the armed forces has not satisfied the demands of younger officers for more rapid promotion. These junior officers are often better educated than their superiors, more inclined toward progressive views, and impatient with their seniors' conservative outlook. These cleavages increase the probability of a "*coup* from below."

Several examples can be mentioned to illustrate the phenomenon of a succession of *coups,* motivated at least in part by such cleavages. We have already observed the overthrow of General Lansana's two-day regime in Sierra Leone by younger officers. These divisions were apparent also in the two Nigerian *coups* in January and July 1966 and in Dahomey in December 1967 when Major Maurice Kouandete and Captain M. Kerekrou displaced General Soglo. In Ghana there was an abortive *coup* in April 1967 by Lieutenants Samuel Arthur and Moses Yeboah against General Joseph Ankrah's National Liberation Council (NLC). After three years of rule (1966-69) the NLC was dissolved in favor of an elected civilian regime in which the Progress Party of Kofi A. Busia held a large majority. However, on 13 January 1972 Colonel Ignatius K. Acheampong staged a *coup* while Busia was in London for medical treatment. The principal grievances were economic; however, the 40-year-old Acheampong represents a group of officers who lost promotions as a result of the 1966 *coup* that ousted Nkrumah. Lastly, the Mali *coup* in November 1968 was led by Lieutenant Musa Traore, who subsequently became head of state, president of the 14-man Military Committee of National Liberation, and chief of the armed forces. Not only were senior officers placed under arrest, but the original CMLN consisted entirely of captains and lieutenants, with the latter predominating!

Although few would contest the proposition that "it is the officer corps which generally determines the behaviour and attitudes of armed forces," [37] our discussion would be incomplete without reference to another important source of intra-army conflict that has had political consequences, the traditional social and hierarchical division between officers and the rank and file. While in most cases soldiers have cooperated with their leaders in the

[36] Biographical data on many of the new military rulers can be found in Sidney Taylor (ed.), *The New Africans* (London: Paul Hamlyn Ltd., 1967).

[37] Gutteridge, *op. cit.,* p. 40.

execution of *coups,* there have been a few instances of *coups* originating below the commissioned-officer ranks. The most dramatic example is the Togo *coup* of 13 January 1963 in which President Sylvanus Olympio was assassinated. In this instance the *coup* was staged by a combined group of soldiers and disgruntled army veterans led by ex-Master Sergeant Emmanuel Bodjolle in protest against Olympio's "profound contempt for the military." It is probable that violence was not originally intended: a mutiny rather than a *coup* seems to have been the object of the protest. Whatever the intentions, the immediate results of the *coup* were the expansion of the 200 to 300-man army to three times that size, the re-enlistment of some 700 French colonial army veterans who had been demobilized after independence in 1960, and the appointment to command positions of the three veteran NCO's who led the *coup*.

In Sierra Leone it was warrant officers who turned the tables on their superiors in April 1968. Following a year of rule by the National Reformation Council, a group of warrant officers representing the Anti-Corruption Revolutionary Movement arrested almost all military and police officers, established a National Interim Council, and invited ex-Prime Minister Siaka Stevens back from exile in Guinea to head a civilian government. Instances such as these, rare though they may be, illustrate further the complexity of military *coups* and the circumstances in which they occur.

Problems of Military Rule

In addition to internal conflicts, there are other problems inherent in military government. It should be kept in mind that the use of phrases such as "military rule," "military government," or "military regime" does not denote martial law or rule by the army. In fact, the typical "military regime" consists of a ruling council composed of both military officers and civilian officials or an all-military council with civilian policy advisory groups. Although military officers are the dominant political group after a *coup* and the threat of force lends credibility to the intentions of the new regime, the army does not take over the tasks of government and administration below the highest levels. As we will observe later, military *coups* have come increasingly to resemble merely a changing of the guard, in effect just a turnover of personnel.

The organizational and professional qualities that make it possible for the military to arrogate political power are, paradoxically, the very qualities that inhibit its ability to rule effectively. Political leaders specialize in mass ideological appeals and manipulative skills and utilize techniques of negotiation, bargaining, persuasion, and compromise as tools of the trade. Military officers, on the other hand, generally lack the skills of diplomacy and politics, and have no clearly articulated and appealing ideology. As an authoritarian organization based on a rigid hierarchy and a fixed standard of conduct, the military admits of little bargaining; orders are to be obeyed, not discussed and debated. But the problems of national development cannot be solved by commands. Moreover, the smallness of the army and its officer corps, which facilitates communication and control during a seizure of power, becomes afterward a handicap: a handful of men cannot staff or adequately supervise an entire national bureaucracy. In short, the military is not prepared to cope with common political pressures and therefore finds itself groping for support. To compensate for these inherent disabilities, military regimes are forced into accommodation with the civil service. As Edward Shils has pointed out,

> Even though it denounces, purges, and transforms it, the [military] elite will inevitably be forced into a coalition with the civil service. The armed forces themselves cannot replace the civil service; they can only supervise it, check it, interfere with it, and, at best, penetrate and dominate it. To do more would be to cease being an army. . . .[38]

The initial concern of newly-established military regimes is to legitimize their rule, that is, to gain popular acceptance and approval. Here again paradox is evident. The military rarely, if ever, has a comprehensive program of change; it gropes for support and ideas. Lacking a positive program of reform, military governments often follow a negative course: a propaganda campaign to discredit the previous regime. They promise restoration of political freedom, yet they dissolve the representative organs of government, suspend the constitution, outlaw political parties, and enforce their decrees with weapons of war. They promise to achieve economic growth, yet they raise taxes, impose rigid austerity budgets, and sometimes adopt measures more "socialistic" than their predecessors'. They promise a prompt return to civilian rule, but find it increasingly difficult to surrender power. As President Sangoule Lamizana of Upper Volta was forced to admit, "The Army is staying in power because there is no other solution. . . . because if we let go of the reins in the near future it would mean disaster." [39] Facing similar problems, in the wake of civil war, General Yakubu Gowon of Nigeria recently declared the intention of the military to rule until 1976. The problems appear insurmountable; the efforts to solve them are often self-defeating and illusory. It is sometimes with a feeling of fatalism or resignation that African military leaders are impelled to seize power. As General-President Mohammad Siad Barre explained, following his assumption of power in Somalia after President Abdirashid Ali Shermarke was assassinated in October 1969,

> I did this [seize power] with considerable reluctance. I am, after all, a soldier who long shared the view that the military should not interfere in

[38] Shils, *op. cit.,* p. 57.

[39] Cited in "News in Brief," *Africa Report*, 12, 4 (April 1967), p. 36.

> politics and politics should not interfere in the military. We soldiers recognize that we are not good politicians. But there was *absolutely no choice*. . . . After the assassination, the politicians were unable to come up with a successor to Shermarke. The nation was *politically fragmented* and there was *a real threat of anarchy*.[40]

African armies lack a long apolitical tradition like that of the British or American military. The fragility and fluidity of African sociopolitical institutions contrast sharply with the relative organizational strength of the armies that makes the latter likely candidates for positions of power as political order becomes increasingly difficult for a regime to maintain. At times military intervention in politics may occur by design, as a plot by ambitious officers to seize power when the opportunity presents itself. But often it occurs by default, when in the absence of effective political order the army steps in to preserve the state from disintegration. It seems that the political role of the army in the new nations, in Africa in particular, has been institutionalized to such a degree as to constitute not only a precedent for further military intervention in politics, but also a tendency which in the long run could become *a distinct and permanent political tradition*. Recent events suggest that the military, far from remaining aloof from the political arena, may eventually install itself as the permanent, ultimate arbiter of power.

African armies are indeed in a paradoxical situation. We have noted already the internal inconsistency in their ability to seize power and their inability to exercise it effectively. In a larger sense, the very intrusion of the military into the political domain appears to be a paradox. As the cases of Ghana and Mali suggest, a seizure of power by the army may be motivated by a desire to avoid the politicization of its ranks by an authoritarian regime. Thus the appropriation of political power by the military may be the paradoxical outcome of its desire to maintain a position of political disinterestedness! It might be suggested further that the early development of professionalism in African armies paradoxically contributed to their propensity to intervene in politics. The military ethic of selfless national service may have encouraged professional officers to assume power when civilian political elites failed the nation. In such instances, the military might be regarded as carrying its mission of internal security to its logical extreme.[41]

But paradox is the fateful essence of military government. Having intervened against a bankrupt civilian regime, the army suddenly finds it

[40] Al A. Castagno, "An Interview with the Somali President," *Africa Report*, 16, 9 (December 1971), p. 23, italics added; see also Castagno, "Somalia goes Military," *Africa Report*, 15, 2 (February 1970), pp. 25–27.

[41] Jacques van Doorn, "Political Change and the Control of the Military," *op. cit.*, pp. 30–31; Greene, *op. cit.*, p. 11; and the important study by Bengt Abrahamsson, *Military Professionalization and Political Power* (Beverly Hills, Calif.: Sage Publications, 1972).

has bitten off more than it can chew. The inevitable outcome of intervention is that the apolitical military becomes politicized, increasing its vulnerability to further *coups* by disaffected officers who take advantage of the new "rules of the game" to appropriate power by force. If the military does eventually restore a civilian government, it is certain to be a government acceptable to the military leadership and therefore representative of its interests. The new regime, formed under the aegis of the military, becomes necessarily a client of those to whom it owes its very existence. The military therefore assumes a responsibility for the protection of its protégé if it remains faithful; conversely, the military will feel obliged to intervene again if the new regime fails to fulfill its expectations. Having seized power once, the army becomes a protagonist in the political arena of conflicting interests, contracting a deep and perhaps permanent interest in the preservation of a certain style and substance of politics. Believing in its mission of national salvation, it reserves for itself the right to intervene again. In short, the military becomes something of a balancer, ready to tip the scales whenever one political faction upsets the desired equilibrium. Usually content to play the role of referee, the army may again feel obliged to enter the political *mêlée* in order to discipline those whose disreputable performance brings shame upon the nation and to reestablish political order in its own fashion.

African Military Regimes and Political Development

In examining the role of the military in African politics, one must ultimately ask, "Does or can the military make a positive contribution toward modernization and political development?" Although we cannot enter here into a discussion of the numerous theoretical and empirical aspects of modernization and political development,[42] we can on the basis of our foregoing analysis make some tentative observations about the actual and potential performance of military regimes.

Despite the earlier optimism of scholars like Pye and Janowitz, who stressed the modernizing capacity of armies and military regimes, more recent assessments, having had the advantage of observing the behavior of African armies for a longer time and in various roles, have tended to be more cautious, if not pessimistic. The most optimistic of contemporary writers regard military regimes at best as short-time stabilizers that can avert imminent political disaster and serve as temporary custodians of the state until acceptable civilian governments can be formed.[43] The National

[42] See, for example, the excellent "Studies in Political Development" series published by Princeton University Press.

[43] See Lefever, *op. cit.*, pp. 197–198; Gutteridge, "Why Does an African Army Take Power," *Africa Report,* 15, 7 (October 1970), pp. 20–21; W. A. E. Skurnik, "Can the Military Modernize?" *Africa Today,* 15, 2 (April/May 1968), pp. 5–6.

Liberation Council of Ghana, which achieved an orderly transferral of political power to the Progress Party of Kofi A. Busia in 1969 after three years of rule, was widely acclaimed as the most outstanding example of military guardianship. However, the *coup* of 13 January 1972 that ousted Busia seems to indicate that even this view was too optimistic. Indeed, it has been suggested that the most recent Ghanaian *coup* is likely to reinforce military rule elsewhere in Africa by demonstrating the probable failure of such experiments in civilian restoration.[44]

Even if the prospect of civilian failure encourages self-adulation and the prolongation of military regimes, there is little cause for feelings of complacency or superiority among military rulers. The longer the military retains power in the face of overwhelming evidence that it has accomplished nothing substantial, the sooner the population will realize the imperfections of military rule and demand a "second chance" for civilians. The basic incompetence of the military to solve national problems may impel them to hasten the restoration of civilian rule to avoid the stigma of failure. Thus the inherent limitation of the military modernization effort will increase the prospects for a return to civilian rule. As Kenneth Grundy his suggested,

> The common and unfortunate policy, once military rule has been established, has been to muddle through, progressively limiting opportunities for protest and opposition. In this way, military rule itself may unwittingly serve as a catalyst for further revolutionary change. The chances for popular rule may in fact be enhanced *after* the military has had its opportunity to govern. Military rule may indeed be a cleansing experience but not in the way the military leaders had originally intended. . . . Disenchantment with military rule could well be the most positive contribution that military rule can make.[45]

In general, the withdrawal of the military from politics occurs in one of two ways: (1) a return to civilian rule because of popular pressure against military government and/or the desire of the military to retain its professional autonomy and neutrality; or (2) a transformation of the ruling military elite into a *de facto* civilian regime by the progressive reduction of manifest military support and a conscious civilianization of the top army elite.[46] Dahomey and Ghana illustrate unsuccessful efforts to effect permanent withdrawal in favor of civilian leadership, but Sierra Leone's civilian

[44] See the analysis by Jim Hoagland, "Ghana Army Faces Economic Morass," *Washington Post,* 14 January 1972, Sec. A, p. 16.

[45] Grundy, *op. cit.,* p. 32.

[46] Welch (ed.), *op. cit.,* pp. 50–58. See also Welch's elaboration on the theme of military withdrawal from politics in his "Praetorianism in Commonwealth West Africa," *Journal of Modern African Studies*, 10, 2 (1972), pp. 203–221, and "Cincinnatus in Africa: the Possibility of Military Withdrawal from Politics," in Michael F. Lofchie (ed.), *The State of the Nations: Constraints on Development in Independent Africa* (Berkeley: University of California Press, 1971), pp. 215–237.

restoration may prove successful. The remarkable President Mobutu Sese Seko of Zaire has chosen the second alternative. After seizing power in 1965 for the second time, he energetically and consciously effected a metamorphosis of military rule, following the pattern of Ataturk in Turkey and Nasser in Egypt. A new constitution was approved, setting the minimum age of presidential candidates at forty. Nationwide elections were held on 1 November 1970, in which year, coincidentally, Mobutu turned 40, and the General received almost 100% of the vote for a 7-year term as President.

In short, the military appears destined to yield before insurmountable pressures to restore civilian rule. There is little evidence that military regimes can contribute to stable political development or modernization. The relentless problems and unfavorable conditions that confront the leaders of tropical African states cannot be handled better by the military. In fact, intervention may compound and perpetuate instability by adding another dimension to political conflict. One is inclined to agree with the prognostication of Welch, Zolberg, and others that military *coups* and regimes will contribute toward political decay rather than political development.[47]

This chapter suggests that recurring military interventions in African politics are the result of endemic sociopolitical conditions that inhibit the creation of viable institutions to bring these conditions under control. Military interventions have not mastered these conditions; rather, the military has succumbed to them. Military regimes tend to have short lifespans and give way either to new military regimes or to civilian rule. But, because societal conditions remain essentially unchanged, regime instability persists. The military is now an integral part of the political process in many African states and seems likely to remain its ultimate arbiter by vigilant oversight and periodic direct assumptions of power.

CIVIL-MILITARY RELATIONS IN THE AFRICAN CONTEXT

The arguments and conclusions advanced in this chapter have important implications for the conventional conception of civil-military relations in sociological theory. We have argued that the strength of the boundaries between the military and society, and between the military and the polity, ought not to be exaggerated. African armies are not corporate, monolithic, homogeneous institutions. In fact, the most prominent characteristic of

[47] Zolberg, *op. cit.*, p. 198; Edward Feit, "The Rule of the 'Iron Surgeons': Military Government in Spain and Ghana," *Comparative Politics*, I, 4 (July 1969), pp. 485–497; Huntington, *op. cit.*, pp. 199–201; Rustow, *op. cit.*, pp. 187–189; Rivkin, *op. cit.*, pp. 61–76; Welch (ed.), *op. cit.*, pp. 58–59; and "The African Military and Political Development," in Henry Bienen (ed.), *The Military and Modernization* (Chicago: Aldine-Atherton, Inc., 1971), pp. 221–229.

TABLE 1. MILITARY AND FINANCIAL CHARACTERISTICS OF AFRICAN NATIONS*

African Nation	Independence Date	Population (in millions)	Size of Armed Forces	Army	Military Service	Ratio and % of Armed Forces to Population	
Botswana	1966	0.64	1,000 (police)		—	—	—
Burundi	1962	3.525	1,600	1,600	2 years	1:2203	.045%
Cameroon	1960	5.986	4,350	4,000	voluntary	1:1376	.073
Central African Republic	1960	1.55	1,100	1,000	2 years	1:1409	.071
Chad	1960	3.89	2,700	2,500	2 years	1:1441	.069
Congo–Brazzaville	1960	0.98	2,200	2,000	2 years	1:445	.245
Dahomey	1960	2.83	2,250	2,100	18 months	1:1258	.080
Equatorial Guinea	1968	0.29	1,000 (National Guard)		—	—	—
Ethiopia	—	26.0	44,570	40,940	voluntary	1:583	.171
Gabon	1960	0.49	1,050	900	1 year	1:467	.214
Gambia	1965	0.36	580 (police)		—	—	—
Ghana	1957	9.6	18,600	16,500	voluntary	1:516	.194
Guinea	1958	4.075	6,100	5,000	2 years	1:668	.150
Ivory Coast	1960	4.375	3,500	3,100	2 years	1:1250	.080
Kenya	1963	11.9	6,730	6,000	voluntary	1:1768	.057
Lesotho	1966	0.96	1,325 (police)		—	—	—
Liberia	1847	1.16	4,150	4,000	voluntary	1:280	.358
Malawi	1964	4.4	1,150	1,150	voluntary	1:3826	.026
Mali	1960	5.26	3,650	3,500	21 months	1:1441	.069
Mauritania	1960	1.2	1,530	1,400	voluntary	1:784	.127
Niger	1960	4.24	2,100	2,000	2 years	1:2019	.050
Nigeria	1960	57.9	274,000	262,000	voluntary	1:211	.473
Rwanda	1962	3.83	2,750	2,750	2 years	1:1393	.072
Senegal	1960	4.02	5,900	5,500	2 years	1:681	.147
Sierra Leone	1961	2.55	1,600	1,500	voluntary	1:1594	.063
Somalia	1960	2.93	13,500	11,200	voluntary	1:217	.461
Swaziland	1968	0.415	700 (police)		—	—	—
Tanzania	1961	13.9	11,100	10,000	voluntary	1:1252	.080
Togo	1960	1.85	1,250	1,000	2 years	1:1480	.068
Uganda	1962	10.45	12,600	12,000	voluntary	1:829	.121
Upper Volta	1960	5.3	1,800	1,750	2 years	1:2944	.034
Zaire	1960	23.3	50,000	49,000	voluntary	1:446	.215
Zambia	1964	4.43	5,700	5,000	voluntary	1:777	.129

African Nation	Estimated GNP (in millions)	Per Capita GNP (in millions)	Year of Data	Total Budget (in millions)	Year of Data	Defense Budget (in millions)	Year of Data	Defense Budget as % of GNP	Defense Budget as % of Total Budget	Year of Data
Botswana	$ 60	$ 94	1968	$ 19.6	1969–70	—	—	—	—	—
Burundi	160	45	1967	18.73	1967	$ 2.686	1967	1.67%	14.34%	1967
Cameroon	1060	177	1971	127.5	1969–70	21.86	1969	2.54	17.14	1969
Central African Republic	210	135	1968	38.87	1968	4.56	1968	2.17	11.73	1968
Chad	195	50	1971	51.15	1969	6.9	1969	2.42	13.49	1969
Congo–Brazzaville	194	218	1971	64.37	1969	9.46	1969	5.4	14.7	1969
Dahomey	218	77	1971	33.75	1969	4.45	1969	2.23	13.19	1969
Equatorial Guinea	70	241	1968	25.51	1966	—	—	—	—	—
Ethiopia	2550	81	1971	284.	1969–70	40.5	1971–72	1.59†	12.54	1970
Gabon	240	490	1968	72.06	1969	4.25	1969	1.78	5.9	1969
Gambia	32	89	1968	7.48	1967–68	—	—	—	—	—
Ghana	2820	294	1971	460.	1969–70	30.0	1971–72	1.06†	9.65	1970
Guinea	717	176	1971	83.8	1966–67	9.47	1966–67	1.35	11.3	1967
Ivory Coast	1574	360	1971	188.26	1969	22.8	1970	1.58	12.11	1970
Kenya	1650	139	1971	248.	1968–69	24.5	1970	1.55	9.88	1970
Lesotho	80	83	1968	15.28	1968–69	—	—	—	—	—
Liberia	282	243	1971	60.1	1969	4.375	1969	1.79	7.3	1969
Malawi	200	45	1968	49.2	1968	1.313	1968	.66	2.67	1968
Mali	278	53	1971	46.9	1968–69	10.32	1968–69	4.13	22.	1968
Mauritania	200	167	1968	25.5	1968	4.87	1968	2.44	19.1	1968
Niger	360	85	1971	43.75	1969–70	3.69	1969–70	1.12	8.43	1969
Nigeria	9900	171	1971	409.9	1968–69	757.6	1971–72	7.65	—	1971
Rwanda	233	61	1971	13.82	1968	3.21	1968	1.53	23.23	1968
Senegal	745	185	1971	169.43	1969–70	18.06	1969–70	2.51	10.66	1970
Sierra Leone	335	131	1968	48.84	1968–69	2.51	1968–69	.75	5.14	1968
Somalia	180	61	1971	37.8	1967	11.4	1971	6.33	—	1971
Swaziland	130	313	1968	20.44	1969–70	—	—	—	—	—
Tanzania	1300	94	1971	255.	1968–69	26.64	1968–69	2.42	10.45	1969
Togo	210	114	1968	26.51	1969	2.73	1969	1.3	10.3	1969
Uganda	1060	101	1970	189.15	1968–69	16.875	1968–69	1.59	9.22	1969
Upper Volta	250	47	1968	38.38	1969	4.23	1969	1.69	11.02	1969
Zaire	1900	82	1970	370.	1969	84.	1970	4.42	22.7	1970
Zambia	1500	339	1971	586.04	1968	17.64	1966	—	—	—

* *Note on Table 1.* The data contained herein are based on Richard Booth, *The Armed Forces of African States, 1970,* Adelphi Papers No. 67 (London: International Institute for Strategic Studies, May 1970), and *The Military Balance 1972-1973* (London: International Institute for Strategic Studies, 1972). The permission of the Institute to use this data is gratefully acknowledged.

African states whose names appear in bold print have experienced successful *coups*. As noted in the text, there does not appear to be any consistent pattern between or among the states that have experienced *coups* and those that have not. It is important to realize, however, that statistics for African national attributes are notoriously imprecise and inconsistent. In the interest of uniformity, I have relied exclusively upon data compiled by the Institute for Strategic Studies; the lack of comparable data for the same year accounts for the varied estimates between 1967 and 1971 and the few lacunae that occur in the Table. Readers are advised to compare the Institute's data with other sources such as T. N. Dupuy and Wendell Blanchard, *The Almanac of World Military Power*, 2nd ed. (New York: R. R. Bowker Co., 1972), and Robert C. Sellers (ed.), *Armed Forces of the World*, 3rd ed. (New York: Praeger, 1971). Numerous discrepancies occur among these reference works; in some instances the estimates vary by 100% or more! Furthermore, as none of these works cites the original sources of their information, verification is impossible.

In Table 1, the data in the sixth, seventh, and tenth columns are my own, calculated from the raw data in the Table of population size, strength of armed forces, GNP, annual budgets, and military budgets. All figures involving monetary sums are given in U.S. dollars prior to 1973 devaluation.

† 1971.

African armed forces is the existence of significant structural and social cleavages that have been deepened and intensified by their politicization. In this sense, at least, the military has affinities with the civilian political and bureaucratic elite.

As we have observed repeatedly, the African sociopolitical environment is characterized by relatively low levels of institutional differentiation and autonomy. The government is the largest single source of employment and patronage in African states and is popularly viewed as a "job-creating" structure. The lack of institutional coherence makes it difficult for the military to acquire, cultivate, and maintain an identity separate and distinct from the employment opportunities available in the state apparatus. When the government appears on the verge of disintegration and the incumbent regime is powerless to prevent it (or even contributes to it!), the military elite, dependent upon the state for its livelihood and its *raison d'être,* intervenes to assume the burden of national trusteeship. Viewed in this light, military intervention can be regarded at times as a defensive reaction of public servants to perceived threats against themselves. Thus the "characteristic African *coups,*" according to J. M. Lee, "are gestures of frustration by the employees of the state or 'caretaker' actions to preserve the state apparatus in existence." [48] Indeed, it has been argued that the officer corps, essentially middle-class in origin and outlook, intervenes primarily to protect its own class interests and status, using slogans of reform and revolution to legitimize its self-serving action.[49]

An important corollary follows from this lack of civil order and viable political institutions. If the basic premise of civil-military relations theory is the existence of a relatively well-defined and autonomous range of behavioral norms and action within each sphere, the low level of institutional differentiation in the African sociopolitical environment calls into question the applicability of this conceptual distinction. It is difficult to study civil-military relations in Africa precisely because there is no clearly demarcated boundary between military and civilian domains within the context of a common political system.[50] As we have observed at some length, African states possess all the characteristics of praetorian societies: an "institutional void" or "institutionless arena," a "porous civil-political order," the absence of "civil order," a low level of political institutionalization, and a concomitant lack of a pattern of organizational controls throughout the social system. If we are to examine conditions such as these, the conventional distinctions between "civil" and "military" will have to be redefined in such a way as to sharpen our conceptual tools of analysis.

[48] Lee, *op. cit.,* p. 184.

[49] See Eric A. Nordlinger, "Soldiers in Mufti: The Impact of Military Rule Upon Economic and Social Change in the Non-Western States," *American Political Science Review*, XLIV, 4 (December 1970), pp. 1131–1148.

[50] Lee, *op. cit.,* pp. 181–182.

APPENDIX: AFRICAN MILITARY *COUPS*

Burundi	28 November 1966
Central African Republic	1 January 1966
Congo-Brazzaville	4 August 1968
Dahomey	23 October 1963
	17 November 1965
	22 December 1965
	17 December 1967
	10 December 1969
	26 October 1972
Ghana	24 February 1966
	13 January 1972
Mali	19 November 1968
Nigeria	15 January 1966
	29 July 1966
Rwanda	5 July 1973
Sierra Leone	21 March 1967
	23 March 1967
	18 April 1968
Somalia	21 October 1969
Togo	13 January 1963
	13 January 1967
Uganda	25 January 1971
Upper Volta	3 January 1966
Zaire	14 September 1960
	25 November 1965

11

The Armed Forces in Latin American Politics

G. POPE ATKINS

The Latin American region occupies a unique place in the study of civil-military relations. Despite a number of superficial similarities with North American and West European states (such as the constitutional provisions governing military-state connections and the organization of the service establishments), the frequent intervention of the Latin American armed forces in politics is alien to the western liberal tradition. While the Latin American area shares to a considerable degree the challenge of modernization with the rest of the "developing world," a process out of which some patterns of civil-military relations seem to emerge, most of the Latin American states have a long history of independent nationhood which has developed political traditions, institutions, and processes distinct from those of the newer nations of Africa and Asia.[1] Inter-area comparisons of civil-military relations should be encouraged, but as Latin America is an identifiable region upon which to focus a study of the military role in politics it deserves to be analyzed on its own terms.[2]

Any discussion of Latin American politics must consider to what

[1] Morris Janowitz excludes Latin America in his study, *The Military in the Political Development of the New Nations* (Chicago: University of Chicago Press, 1964), because "the forms of military intervention represent more than a century of struggle and accommodation which has produced political institutions different from those found in the new nations." A collection edited by William C. McWilliams, *Garrisons and Government: Politics and the Military in New States* (San Francisco: Chandler Publishing Co., 1967), includes studies on Latin America. While the inclusion of this region is important for comparative purposes, the book's subtitle is consequently inaccurate, as most of the Latin American states are not "new" in the same sense as those of Asia and Africa.

[2] George I. Blanksten appeals to Latin Americanists not to devote their careers "to learning more about Latin America for the sole purpose of learning more about Latin America," arguing that "the more we can apply to other areas what we learn in Latin America, the greater the likely contribution to comparative politics and to political science as a whole." "Political Groups in Latin America," *American Political Science Review*, LIII (March 1959), pp. 106–127.

extent the area may be regarded as a coherent unit for study, other than by mere geographic unity. Do the Latin American states comprise a viable object for comparative analysis, about which valid generalizations can be posited?

To begin with, of the 24 independent states and the remaining dependencies of external powers commonly referred to as Latin America, this chapter's analysis is concerned with a core of 19 Hispanic-American nations (18 Spanish-American states and Portuguese-American Brazil) plus, parenthetically, Haiti.[3] Even among these core states, however, the variety and diversity is considerable; few generalizations apply to all of them. In terms of civil-military relations, consider that Bolivia has experienced 11 violent changes of government over the last four decades (including one each in 1969, 1970, and 1971), as contrasted to Mexico, where no *coups* have occurred during the same period and the probability of such an occurrence is virtually nil. As an additional example, the repressive military government of giant Brazil, in power since 1964, may be contrasted with the highly egalitarian government of tiny Costa Rica, which abolished its army in 1948. On the other hand, one may accurately generalize that one of the most salient features of the history of most Latin American political systems has been a strong military influence in government and politics and a relative homogeneity of types of regimes. Out of today's diversity patterns are discernible in the roles of the armed forces in the politics of some groups of Latin American nations. Military establishments, in turn, are sensitive to developments in other states and have more communication with their counterparts in other states than do civilian political groups. In sum, civil-military relations in Latin America present a varied picture, with essential differences from nation to nation and common denominators among them.

In this interpretive essay, although it recognizes the great diversity in Latin American politics, the emphasis is upon general patterns of civil-military relations in the area, with specific "country" examples given as supporting evidence and major exceptions to the rule noted. The discussion

[3] The remaining western hemisphere dependencies of Britain, France, the Netherlands, and the United States are not included in this study because they lack sovereign status and have not developed patterns of civil-military relations. The four new states emerging in the 1960s—the ex-British colonies of Jamaica, Trinidad-Tobago, Barbados, and Guyana—are also ignored because they currently operate on the periphery of Latin American affairs, and their civil-military relations, which grow out of the context of a district political culture, are in a formative stage. Tiny Haiti is similar to the new states in an ethnic sense and its peripheral regional position, but is culturally distinct from both the new states and the older Hispanic-American politics. However, its civil-military relations have developed over a long period of time (Haiti gained independence from France in 1804) and somewhat resemble those of Hispanic America. The eighteen Spanish American states are Argentina, Bolivia, Chile, Colombia, Costa Rica, Cuba, Dominican Republic, Ecuador, Guatemala, Honduras, Mexico, Nicaragua, Paraguay, Panama, Peru, El Salvador, Uruguay, and Venezuela.

concerns analytical concepts about the armed forces in Latin American politics, the nature of the military establishments, and the political roles they play.

CHANGING CONCEPTS

The variety of forms of military intervention in Latin American politics has long been perceived by scholars, journalists, government officials, and other observers. Beginning in the late 1950s, however, the terms of reference for evaluating civil-military relations began to undergo a radical transformation.

The traditional view regarding the frequent role of the Latin American armed forces as the direct arbiters of domestic politics maintains that the military forces are motivated primarily by praetorian conspiracy, are solely defenders of the status quo, perform few useful social functions, and by their repeated intervention into politics and excessive demands on national budgets thwart political, social, and economic development. The revisionist school holds, contrarily, that the fact of political involvement by the military establishments is an expression, rather than the cause, of underdevelopment and that the armed forces as legitimate, well-organized national institutions may be mobilized to perform useful nation-building and civic-action services.[4]

[4] For reviews and analyses of these schools and many of the individual writers, see Lyle N. McAlister, "Changing Concepts of the Role of the Military in Latin America," *The Annals of the American Academy of Political and Social Science,* vol. 360 (July 1965), pp. 85–98, and his "Recent Research and Writings on the Role of the Military in Latin America," *Latin American Research Review,* II (Fall 1966), pp. 5–36. McAlister was apparently the first to apply the now commonly used terms of "traditional" and "revisionist" in the Latin American context. For his own views as a leading revisionist, see his "Civil-Military Relations in Latin America," *Journal of Inter-American Studies,* III (July 1961), pp. 341–350; and "The Military," in John J. Johnson (ed.), *Continuity and Change in Latin America* (Stanford: Stanford University Press, 1964), pp. 136–160. Johnson's revisionist position is articulated in his "The Latin American Military as a Politically Competing Group in Transitional Society," in Johnson (ed.), *The Role of the Military in Underdeveloped Countries* (Princeton: Princeton University Press, 1962); and *The Military and Society in Latin America* (Stanford: Stanford University Press, 1964). The leading contemporary exponent of the traditional view is Edwin Lieuwen. Of his many works on the subject, the most important are his pioneering *Arms and Politics in Latin America* (rev. ed.; New York: Praeger, 1961); *Generals Vs. Presidents: Neomilitarism in Latin America* (New York: Praeger, 1964); and, more recently, *The Latin American Military,* study prepared for U.S. Congress, Senate Committee on Foreign Relations, 90th Cong., 1st Sess., October 9, 1967. Both positions are critiqued by Martin C. Needler, "The Latin American Military: Predatory Reactionaries or Modernizing Patriots?" *Journal of Inter-American Studies,* XI (April 1969), pp. 237–244.

The recent policy of the United States, the most important external influence on Latin American political systems, has been severely criticized by contemporary traditionalists as allied with the military (unwittingly or as co-conspirators), helping to retard Latin American democratic development. Indeed, U.S. policy moved to a version of the revisionist position during the last days of the Kennedy administration and has remained so in some form to the present. President Johnson's approach reflected a belief in the need for "realism" as well as an optimistic assumption about the military role in the process of modernization and reform. The Nixon administration has also stressed the "new military" in Latin American development, as evidenced especially by Governor Nelson Rockefeller's 1969 report on Latin America, which clearly accepted the military role with favor and optimism. Among other enthusiastic comments on the subject, Mr. Rockefeller said:

> In short, a new type of military man is coming to the fore and often becoming a major force for constructive social change in the American republics. Motivated by increasing impatience with corruption, inefficiency and a stagnant political order, the new military man is prepared to adapt his authoritarian tradition to the goals of social and economic progress.[5]

The Latin American military performance, at least over the last decade, does not generally conform to the traditionalists' wholesale critique. While it is true that all military regimes are authoritarian and many are defenders of the status quo, a number have demonstrated reformist tendencies, seriously addressing the social and economic problems facing their nations. In addition, traditionalists simplistically assign the thrust for personal power as the primary, even exclusive, force behind military officers' behavior, dismissing this behavior as merely personal power-seeking opportunism divorced from ideology, issues, crises, or social conditions. Furthermore, they superficially view "civilian" and "military" governments as mutually exclusive, judging the former as generally good and the latter as necessarily bad. But the military does not act in a political vacuum. Its actions almost always involve civilian allies and urging, and rarely is the military aligned against all other political forces, with one resorting to force and the other to peaceful, constitutional procedures. Nearly all *coups* in the 1960s, for example, were backed by important civilian political groups.[6] Finally, the

[5] Nelson A. Rockefeller, *Quality of Life in the Americas: Report of a U.S. Presidential Mission for the Western Hemisphere* (Washington, D.C.: Agency for International Development, 1969), p. 18. For an earlier, interesting debate between U.S. Foreign Service officers, see the revisionist article by Frank A. Knapp, Jr., "The Meaning of Militarism in Latin America," *Foreign Service Journal* (December 1964), pp. 20–25, and the critique along traditional lines by J. M. Cates, Jr., pp. 25–26.

[6] Jack Davis, *Political Violence in Latin America* (London: International Institute for Strategic Studies, Adelphi Papers Number Eighty-five, 1972).

general indictment of the military as the major force impeding modernization and the implied allegation that the ills of Latin America may be ascribed to military intervention into politics[7] seem to reverse the proper order of cause and effect (no matter how selfish or progressive the motives for intervention may be). The frequency of direct military participation in Latin American political processes is probably the result of the same conditions that impede modernization and democratic development, rather than the impediment itself. In sum, the causal explanations of military intervention are much more complex than traditionalists would have us believe. In the words of one student of civil-military relations in the developing nations, "those who have shared such biases have tended to regard military involvement in politics as a legitimate subject only for the expression of alarm, or for denunciation, but not for serious analytical inquiry." [8]

Revisionists have introduced more scholarly sophistication and objectivity in their critique of the traditionalist approach, but have not answered the persistent questions posed by the armed forces in politics. They correctly insist that military regimes be viewed as part of the total structure and function of society, rather than in terms of villains and heroes, but their stress on military regimes as effective instruments of modernization (even reform-oriented ones) is open to question. The "revisionist" U.S. policy (at least as reflected in the Rockefeller report) especially tends to a simplistic faith in the universal modernizing propensities and effectiveness of the military. In the first place, this undifferentiated view ignores that individual officers or groups may and do act in a predatory manner in a crude thrust for power (although this is not the exclusive motivation) and are still accountable for their actions in personal as well as systemic terms. Secondly, despite a number of extenuating circumstances and the fact that civilian governments often are unwilling to undertake or unable to achieve social reform and economic development, the recent experience of a number of military governments in these areas seriously challenges the proposition that even reform-minded military rule can be an effective instrument for social and economic progress. The record so far shows some achievements, mostly in the economic sphere, but largely only partial success or outright failure.

A normative judgment may be made at this point. One may avoid a blanket indictment of the military role in Latin American politics and accept the need for objective causal analysis of military intervention while remaining anti-militarist and not accepting that which exists as desirable.

[7] Lieuwen said in his *Generals Vs. Presidents* that the military intervene to save their own institutional interests and are, therefore, the "chief impediments to democratic social revolution."

[8] John P. Lovell (ed.), *The Military and Politics in Five Developing Nations* (Kensington, Md.: Center for Research in Social Systems, March 1970), p. 1.

Nor may we remedy that which we consider undesirable by merely denouncing it—it first must be understood in terms of the political system and culture from which it emerges. In general terms, the view of the present writer is to question the desirability of military establishments doing things that properly belong to other agencies. No state organization, especially that which controls the means of physical coercion, should become the dominant social institution. Nevertheless, one must recognize that not all military interventions are "bad" (as, for example, when factions of the armed services overthrow a repressive dictator) and that one may judge that a nation's people are better off under a military government than certain civilian regimes.[9] Although military interventions should not be condemned until the circumstances of the individual case are known, it is preferable that pluralistic societies and civilian-dominated governments be developed.

If the political role of the military develops out of the political environment, a discussion of that environment is necessary to an understanding of civil-military relations. Political violence is a salient characteristic of most Latin American political systems and provides the setting and milieu within which several military roles are played. Political violence means forceful coercion on the part of political groups as a technique to realize political goals. Merely the threat of violence without its actual use may be sufficient. Violence is not the exclusive province of military men, as other political groups (from rioting students to insurrectionary guerrillas) use violent techniques to pursue political goals. Nor do the military act alone with violence; they are usually allied with some civilian political group or move at its urging.

The term most widely used to describe political violence in Latin America is "revolution." As an operational concept, "revolution" is broadly used, referring to at least four types of largely distinct Latin American political phenomena: (1) to describe the national independence movements from colonial masters during the nineteenth century; (2) to denote the *coup d'etat* and its variants, in which a chief executive extends his tenure or is forced out of office; (3) to define social revolutions that fundamentally change the structure and processes of political systems; and (4) to describe political and social change in the sense of long-term evolutionary processes of modernization, reform, and development, not necessarily violent at all.[10]

[9] This normative view is shared with Martin C. Needler, *Latin American Politics in Perspective* (Princeton, N.J.: D. Van Nostrand, 1963), p. 66.

[10] These various meanings of revolution are suggested by George I. Blanksten, "Revolutions," in Harold E. Davis (ed.), *Government and Politics in Latin America* (New York: Ronald Press, 1958); and Rosendo A. Gomez, "Revolution, Violence, Political Morality," in his *Government and Politics in Latin America* (rev. ed.; New York: Random House, 1964). The most important descriptive typologies of violence are those constructed by William S. Stokes, "Violence as a Power Factor in Latin American Politics," *Western Political Quarterly,* V (September 1952), pp. 445–482;

In the western political vocabulary the third type (social revolution) is generally considered to be "real" revolution, with the French Revolution of 1789 and the Russian (Bolshevik) Revolution of 1917 the leading examples. In this sense, Latin America has witnessed very few revolutions, with only those in Mexico in 1910 and Cuba in 1959 classified as "real" by broad consensus of Latin American observers. Social ("real") revolution and its relationship to civil-military relations will be discussed in a later section in conjunction with the fourth type (reform, development, and modernization). Although the two types differ in the basic political philosophies of their practitioners, they both arise in response to the contemporary "revolution of rising expectations" and thus are inseparable in their environmental base. The Wars for Independence need not be discussed further other than to note that they were not "real" social revolutions. Through them the Latin American colonies gained political independence from their imperial masters, but they did not significantly change the social structure. The traditional authoritarian societies remained with the small group of indigenous Spanish creole elites (*criollos*) replacing the foreign Spanish authorities (*peninsulares*) at the top of the political hierarchy. As Blanksten notes, "many may have argued that the revolution which did not come in the nineteenth century is now long overdue and may be expected in the twentieth." [11]

By far the most frequent form of revolution in Latin America has been the *coup d'etat* and its related forms. Even this "typical" form of Latin American violence is open to interpretation. The broadest definition of a *coup* is any unscheduled executive change in government that relies upon the threat or use of force for its success (i.e., an unconstitutional and violent executive change). A narrower definition restricts the label of *coup* to unconstitutional changes by an executive already in office of his own status, extending his own term of office. In Latin America this common type of *coup* is called *continuismo*, normally a bloodless method of relying upon military support and legitimized by constitutional amendment, plebiscite, or other technical legality.[12]

In the broader concept of *coup*, in which an executive may also be forced out of office, two additional basic forms are found in Latin America, both of which rely upon military force. The *golpe de estado*, also known as

---

Stokes, "Violence," in his *Latin American Politics* (New York: Thomas Y. Crowell, 1959); Kalman H. Silvert, *The Conflict Society: Reaction and Revolution in Latin America* (New Orleans: Hauser, 1961); Martin C. Needler, "The Army and Political Violence," in his *Latin American Politics in Perspective* (Princeton: Van Nostrand, 1963); and Needler, "Violence," in his *Political Development in Latin America* (New York: Random House).

[11] Blanksten, *ibid.*, p. 124.

[12] *Ibid.*, p. 122 and 122n.

the *golpe militar*, according to Stokes "is a direct personal assault on power through assassination or deposition of the president." [13] Another form of *coup* is the *cuartelazo*, also called the *golpe de cuartel*. Again relying on Stokes, the "classic pattern of the *cuartelazo* is the treason of a single barracks." In any event, whatever the particular form the *coup* may take, no fundamental social changes occur and the basic political order (and often even government policies) remains intact. The number of participants is highly limited, with government power merely shifting from one personality or group to another, not affecting the lives of most of the population in any substantial way.[14] Unlike Western Europe and the United States where such violence is considered aberrant behavior and elections the norm, *golpes* in Latin America occur with enough frequency to suggest that they are integral parts of several political systems, largely fulfilling the same "normal" functions for changing governments as elections in nonviolent systems.[15]

THE MILITARY ESTABLISHMENTS

Part of the explanation of political roles of the military depends upon an analysis of the institutional nature of the armed forces. What are their physical resources? What level of professionalism have they achieved? What are the social origins of military personnel? What is the extent of military factionalism and alliances with civilian political groups?

In terms of sheer numbers—military personnel levels and population-to-military ratios—Latin America generally is not a highly militarized area. The armed forces are small by the standards of the world's major nations. No Latin American state has achieved great power status (with the consequent international military commitments requiring large standing armed forces). As of 1970, no Latin American state, except Cuba, had a high ratio of population to military personnel (see Table 1).[16] The United States ratio in that year was 66 to 1 (based on a population of 204 million). Thus we may conclude at the outset that the frequency of military intervention does not necessarily depend on large military force levels.

[13] Stokes, "Violence as a Power Factor in Latin American Politics."

[14] See Kurt Conrad Arnade, "The Technique of the Coup d'Etat in Latin America," in Asher N. Christensen (ed.), *Evolution of Latin American Government* (New York: Holt, 1951); Peter Calvert, "The Typical Latin American Revolution," *International Affairs* [London], vol. 43 (January 1967), pp. 85–95; Egil Fossum, "Factors Influencing the Occurrence of Military Coups d'Etat in Latin America," *Journal of Peace Research*, IV (1967), pp. 228–251; F. Guillén, "Militarismo y golpes de estado en América Latina," *CAM,* XXIV (mayo/junio 1965), pp. 7–19.

[15] Merle Kling, "Towards a Theory of Power and Political Instability in Latin America," *Western Political Quarterly,* IX (March 1956).

[16] Source for Table 1: Institute for Strategic Studies, *The Military Balance,* 1970–1971 (London, 1970).

TABLE 1. THE MILITARY ESTABLISHMENTS

State	Population (thousands) and Rank	Size of Regular Armed Forces (numbers of personnel)				Para-military Forces	No. of Population per 1 Mil. and Rank	
		Total/Rank	*Army*	*Navy*	*Air Force*		*Regular Armed Forces*	*Reg. AF plus Paramilitary*
Argentina	24,350–3	137,000–2	85,000	35,000	17,000	25,000	178–4	140–4
Bolivia	4,925–11	21,800–9	20,000	—	1,800	5,000	226–7	184–7
Brazil	92,550–1	194,350–1	120,000	44,350	30,000	120,000	476–13	294–14
Chile	9,775–7	61,000–6	38,000	15,000	8,000	22,500	160–3	117–3
Colombia	21,025–4	64,000–5	50,000	8,000	6,000	35,000	329–11	212–10
Costa Rica	1,550–19	—19/20	—	—	—	1,200	—19/20	1292–20
Cuba	8,350–8	109,500–3	90,000	7,500	12,000	13,000	76–1	68–1
Dominican Rep.	4,310–13	19,300–12	12,000	3,800	3,500	10,000	223–6	148–5
Ecuador	6,090–9	20,000–11	12,800	3,700	3,500	5,800	305–10	236–11
Guatemala	5,170–10	9,000–14	7,800	200	1,000	3,000	574–15	431–17
Haiti	4,765–12	5,500–17	5,000	250	250	13,265	866–1	254–12
Honduras	2,575–16	4,725–18	3,500	25	1,200	2,500	545–14	356–15
Mexico	50,700–2	68,500–4	54,000	8,500	6,000	—	740–17	740–19
Nicaragua	1,985–18	7,100–15	5,400	200	1,500	4,000	280–9	179–6
Paraguay	2,378–17	20,200–10	17,500	1,900	800	8,500	118–2	83–2
Panama	1,350–20	—19/20	—	—	—	3,425	—19/20	394–16
Peru	13,585–5	54,650–7	35,500	10,150	9,000	18,000	249–8	187–8/9
El Salvador	3,515–14	5,630–16	4,500	130	1,000	2,500	624–16	432–18
Uruguay	2,886–15	15,400–13	12,000	1,800	1,600	—	187–5	187–8/9
Venezuela	10,490–6	30,500–8	15,000	6,500	9,000	10,000	344–12	259–13
Total	271,624	848,155	588,000	147,005	113,150	325,190	320	231

The largest individual establishments are those of Brazil (194,350) and Argentina (137,000), with other relatively large forces belonging to Cuba (109,500), Mexico (68,500), Colombia (64,000), Chile (61,000), and Peru (54,650). A large gap exists between this upper group of the 7 largest states and the remaining 13 states. Peru, the smallest state (in military terms) in the upper strata, has almost twice as many armed service personnel as Venezuela (30,500), the largest of the lower strata. The total armed forces in each of the 7 lowest-ranking states number less than a single infantry division of the U.S. Army. The only state comparable to the United States in its population-to-military ratio is Cuba (76:1). Ten states, of varying populations, have higher ratios than the Latin American average. Two states (Costa Rica and Panama) have no regular armed forces. The former disbanded its forces in 1948 and a small, politically impotent police force remains. In Panama the national guard plays military roles, including those involving intervention in domestic politics. The states with large military forces tend to be those with large territories, and they have sufficient strength to deploy troops fairly widely, unlike the small states where the military usually is concentrated heavily around the capital city.[17]

The military in Latin America is composed largely of the national armies. In all states (with the exception of Costa Rica and Panama) the army is the largest branch of service and, in almost all instances, the most politically active and significant. Most states have at least token navies (all but 3) and air forces (all but 2), and some are of significant strength (notably in Argentina and Brazil).

In several states paramilitary organizations are important. While the regular forces are generally the institutionalized reservoirs of specialization, organization, and planning for the professional application of forces by the state, a number of bodies presently exist or are adaptable to roles as paramilitary forces. They include such designations as gendarmerie (sometimes under army command), national maritime forces (sometimes subordinate to the navy), armed police, border and frontier guards, secret police, and civil guards. Paramilitary forces are important in a number of countries, not only because they significantly change the population-to-military ratio, but because of their political influence. Haiti is the leading example, where a militia of 8,000 men and secret police (*tontons macoutes*) numbering 5,000 were created as a counterpoise to the regular army's traditional role as political arbiter. [Since this chart was compiled, the *tontons macoutes* have been reduced considerably in numbers and importance.]

The role of the Cuban military is presently in flux and difficult to assess. The regular army was destroyed by Castro in 1959, and a revolutionary "party" army and militia were substituted; but, as Needler notes, it remains

[17] Gomez, "Revolution, Violence, Political Morality."

to be seen how long the new army "will remain without a separate corporate identity with divergent outlooks from the revolutionary government." [18] A similar situation obtained in Bolivia in 1952 when the regular military was virtually destroyed by revolutionary forces and a new army and rural militia were developed to support the revolutionary party and government. They were politically inactive for a time, but since 1964 the revamped regular forces have directly controlled government and politics.

The professional level achieved by Latin American military establishments has varied widely. All Latin American states have depended upon foreign powers for professional training and acquisition of arms and equipment.[19] Throughout the nineteenth century, and in some instances into the twentieth, Latin American armies were largely inadequately equipped, untrained militias led by officers lacking professional knowledge. Despite some tentative modernizing efforts in the nineteenth century, the armies tended to be undisciplined, ad hoc institutions. These bands of armed men were not loyal to the nation in the abstract or even to the national government, but retainers supporting charismatic regional strong men. Generally, the small navies were not much better off. At about the beginning of the twentieth century many Latin American governments consciously entered a period of "professionalization" of their armed forces involving, to a great extent, foreign military relations of various kinds.[20]

When discussing pre-World War II foreign military influences, a distinction must be made between the Caribbean area (including Central America) and the South American continent, where most of the major, more sophisticated states are located (with the exception of Mexico). The United States was dominant in the Caribbean region, while in South America several European states vied for influence and the United States was not a major competitor, except in naval affairs. In the Caribbean, the United States tended to be paternalistic and/or coercive, while South American international military relations were more cooperative in nature.

[18] Needler, *Latin American Politics in Perspective,* pp. 64–65.

[19] Irving Louis Horowitz, in an important sociological study, stresses the fact of international dependence as a major distinguishing feature setting Latin American military systems apart from those "in the highly developed portions of the world." He says that however firm their "ideological nationalism may be, the military is functionally dependent upon foreign support and foreign supplies for its place in the national power structures." Horowitz concludes: "Only by appreciating the contradictory roles and demands of the Latin American military, the strain between domestic legitimacy and international dependency, can the core problems of Latin American militarism be probed." "The Military Elites," in Seymour M. Lipset and Aldo Solari (eds.), *Elites in Latin America* (New York: Oxford University Press, 1967).

[20] See Robert J. Alexander, "The Military in Latin American Politics," in his *Latin-American Politics and Government* (New York: Harper & Row, 1965); and Lieuwen, *Arms and Politics in Latin America, passim.*

The United States intervened often in Caribbean affairs during the first third of the twentieth century, including the landing of troops. In the Dominican Republic, Haiti, and Nicaragua, once military occupation was begun, local military and police forces were trained in the hope that they would protect future constitutional governments when the United States withdrew its forces (a hope totally unrealized). The United States also pursued arms control in Cuba, Mexico, and Nicaragua, either through sales or embargos.[21] With the exception of Guatemala, where France had a military mission, the United States had almost exclusive military influence in the Caribbean.

In South America, foreign powers were called upon as sources of instruction and arms and equipment. Governments recognized the retarded state of their armed forces and that foreign military assistance was necessary if they were to be modernized. Many Latin American armies received foreign military instructors and training missions from Europe, especially Germany and France, to provide a variety of tasks. Britain and the United States were invited to train several navies. Latin American military personnel were sent overseas for professional training and education, regimental service, and observation at maneuvers (especially to Germany, France, and Italy). Armaments contracts were entered into with European munition firms and United States and European shipbuilders, committing most armies and navies almost completely to foreign manufacturers. The European efforts were part of the international political relations of the times and consonant with the European participants' world-wide military activities and competition.[22]

During the period surrounding the Second World War, the United States sought to displace European military influence in Latin America. Beginning in the late 1930s, the United States began to substitute its military missions and instructors for those from Europe and was especially successful with the air forces. Eventually the United States was the only external power maintaining missions in Latin America. After the fall of France in 1940, the United States negotiated with most Latin American states, attempting to develop closer military ties. In the interests of hemispheric defense a number of base agreements were completed and, later, Lend-Lease

21 See Marvin Goldwert, *The Constabulary in the Dominican Republic and Nicaragua* (Gainesville: University of Florida Press, 1962); Dana G. Munro, *Intervention and Dollar Diplomacy in the Caribbean* (Princeton: Princeton University Press, 1964) and J. Lloyd Mecham, *A Survey of United States-Latin American Relations* (Boston: Houghton Mifflin, 1965), Chps. 10–12.

22 The best general source is an unpublished manuscript by Fritz T. Epstein, *European Military Influences in Latin America.* This rough draft is on microfilm at the Library of Congress, file-card dated 1961, although the work appears to have been completed in about 1941.

agreements were signed, resulting in military cooperation and aid with almost all of Latin America (with the notable exceptions of Argentina and Chile) and the end of the European phase of military influence.

After World War II, to the present day, the United States has been Latin America's major source of military assistance, although arms purchases are made in several parts of the world, and Cuba in the Castro era has been militarily dependent on the Soviet Union. During the late 1960s and early 1970s, Peru and Chile have moved outside the U.S. orbit. In the first phase of the post-war period the United States rationalized military assistance in terms of the need for cooperative efforts toward common hemispheric defense, with standardized military equipment and training supplied under the aegis of the United States. With the Alliance for Progress and an emphasis on economic and social development in Latin America beginning in the early 1960s, the United States completed a policy shift from hemispheric defense to combatting internal subversion. Throughout the entire period, other United States military objectives have been to encourage domestic Latin American stability and exclude other foreign military influences. (Table 2 indicates the magnitude of United States public military assistance to Latin America since World War II.)

Latin American governments have been motivated to modernize their military establishments by a variety of considerations that, in modified form, continue to the present day as rationales for their maintenance. These goals have included the desire for international prestige (at least on the part of the larger states), the development of the army as a symbol and keeper of national identity, the practical concern of international security (involving boundary disputes and national rivalries), and domestic law and order. The effects of this long twentieth-century effort at military professionalization and modernization seem to be several. With foreign help, military academies, war colleges, and training schools were founded (by 1940 every nation had at least one such institution) and general staffs organized. A greater sense of discipline was imposed on the armed forces and the idea was instilled of the military as an institution serving the state instead of individuals (although not in all states). Technical military competence was increased and quality of equipment improved. The ultimate effects of foreign military influence ranged from copying models of military organization, training, doctrines, and tactics, to accepting foreign military philosophy and ideology. "Professionalism" has not necessarily been a cure for military intervention in politics. Rather than meaning an *apolitical* military establishment, "professionalism" seems to denote *nonpartisan political* involvement.

The Latin American armies long have been vehicles for social mobility, not to mention paths to political power. Historically, Latin American political activity has been monopolized by a restrictive elite, among whom military officers have been integral, often dominant, members. The general

TABLE 2. UNITED STATES MILITARY ASSISTANCE TO LATIN AMERICA (U.S. FISCAL YEARS, MILLIONS OF DOLLARS)†

	Marshall Plan Period	Mutual Security Act Period	Foreign Assistance Act Period										Total
	1949–52	1953–61	1962	1963	1964	1965	1966	1967	1968	1969	1970	1971	1949–71
Argentina	—	10.8	32.5	2.3	9.2	14.5	27.2	15.4	11.3	11.7	0.7	16.5	152.2
Bolivia	—	0.8	3.4	3.6	2.6	1.9	2.6	3.4	2.1	1.8	1.3	1.8	25.3
Brazil	—	148.0	49.6	17.5	41.2	11.2	28.9	32.1	36.6	0.8	0.9	12.2	379.1
Chile	—	41.8	17.8	30.6	9.0	9.9	10.1	4.1	7.8	11.8	0.8	5.8	149.5
Colombia	*	39.1	8.9	11.3	8.6	9.8	11.7	9.1	4.5	3.6	6.4	5.9	118.8
Costa Rica	—	0.1	0.2	0.7	0.3	0.2	0.2	*	—	—	—	0.1	1.9
Cuba	—	10.6	no activity subsequent to FY 1961										10.6
Dom. Rep.	—	6.1	1.5	3.1	2.0	1.7	2.9	2.7	2.5	2.6	2.0	1.4	28.3
Ecuador	0.1	25.6	5.2	5.4	3.8	4.0	3.3	6.4	2.3	2.3	1.9	0.4	60.6
El Salvador	—	0.1	1.0	1.4	0.9	0.5	0.7	0.3	0.4	0.4	0.6	0.4	6.9
Guatemala	—	1.5	1.9	3.5	1.8	1.3	1.3	2.1	1.0	2.3	1.2	6.6	24.4
Haiti	—	3.6	0.5	0.2	—	—	—	—	—	—	—	—	4.3
Honduras	—	1.1	1.8	0.3	0.1	0.9	1.0	0.8	0.8	0.8	0.4	0.6	8.6
Mexico	—	3.6	0.8	1.4	3.3	0.9	0.2	0.1	0.1	1.5	0.1	4.5	16.4
Nicaragua	—	1.9	1.2	1.9	1.3	1.1	1.3	1.1	1.1	0.8	0.9	0.9	13.6
Panama	—	0.1	0.3	0.7	0.2	0.2	0.6	0.5	0.2	0.3	0.8	0.5	4.5
Paraguay	—	0.4	0.7	1.8	1.2	2.9	1.5	1.0	1.0	1.2	1.0	1.0	13.7
Peru	0.1	66.3	21.6	15.1	8.7	11.5	9.8	5.0	1.4	0.6	0.6	0.6	141.3
Uruguay	—	22.0	4.4	3.2	2.2	2.8	5.0	1.4	1.7	1.4	1.4	5.2	50.8
Venezuela	—	31.2	18.1	15.4	15.4	11.7	11.9	0.9	1.0	0.8	0.8	8.4	115.6
Total	0.2	414.7	171.4	119.4	111.8	86.9	120.2	86.4	75.8	44.7	21.8	72.8	1,326.4

* Less than $50,000.

† Source: Agency for International Development, *U.S. Overseas Loans and Grants and Assistance from International Organizations, Obligations and Loan Authorizations, July 1–June 30, 1971* (May 24, 1972), pp. 34–60.

elitist pattern of the nineteenth century was a triad of the landed aristocracy, the church hierarchy, and senior military officers. The officers were newcomers to elite status—the authority of the other two groups had long been established during the colonial period—based on their personal prestige from the wars of independence and authority assumed during the chaotic national beginnings. Most military officers had arisen from non-elite ranks; in the highly stratified societies the army was almost the only way a person of such origins might successfully seek higher social status. A huge gap existed between the ruling elites and the lower-class masses. From the latter group were recruited the military rank and file—army service, miserable as it was, at least offered a subsistence existence and hope for survival. A tiny middle sector existed, which included junior and middle ranking officers. More often than not, they sought incorporation into elite elements.

Beginning in the late nineteenth century and gathering momentum in the twentieth, economic development in a number of states augmented and strengthened the middle sector and created new "proletarian" interests. This development coincided with military modernization and professionalization. These class and interest divisions have been reflected in the military structures. Fitzgibbon notes the social consequences of military professionalism, saying that a military career became more attractive for sons of socially elite families (most of them politically conservative), and at the same time the opportunities for status, advancement, and material perquisites also attracted middle-class candidates.[23] Silvert and Germani estimate "that throughout Latin America the sons of middle class families are more attracted to the military than are the sons of the upper groups." [24] One may generalize that today army officers and those of the air forces (separate since World War II) tend to come from the middle and upper classes and may favor the new quest for reform in Latin America, while naval officers continue to come from the "old families," tending to be politically and socially conservative.[25] The lower popular classes continue to fill the ranks.

It would seem that the imperatives of the military profession, its common training procedures and career patterns, would produce political and philosophical commonalities, especially among the officer corps. But military men identify with wider interests, ideologies, and pressures than their pro-

[23] Russell H. Fitzgibbon, "What Price Latin American Armies?" *Virginia Quarterly Review,* XXXVI (Autumn 1960).

[24] Gino Germani and Kalman Silvert, "Politics, Social Structure, and Military Intervention in Latin America," *European Journal of Sociology,* II (1961), p. 72.

[25] Karl M. Schmitt and David D. Burks, *Evolution or Chaos: Dynamics of Latin American Government and Politics* (New York: Praeger, 1963), p. 141. See also Thomas M. Millington, "The Latin American Military Elite," *Current History,* vol. 56 (June 1969), pp. 352–365.

fession alone would perhaps dictate. The result has been a lack of intellectual orthodoxy, factionalism, and alliances with civilian groups who urge the use of military force in their favor.[26] This fact of political fragmentation by the military is merely noted at this point, emphasizing that the military does not operate in a simplistic manner.

FUNCTIONS AND ROLES OF THE ARMED FORCES

In a purely military sense, the rationale for maintaining military establishments is to perform protective functions for the state, defending against both external and internal threats, or to act offensively against the state's foreign antagonists to compel them to accede to its demands. While defensive and aggressive use of domestic and international force at times have been important functions for the armed forces of Latin America, their domestic political roles and intervention into politics have been much more significant.

The national armies were born during the Wars for Independence in the early nineteenth century, and for the next three quarters of a century thereafter a number of them engaged in international (inter-American) wars and civil wars (actually involving, more accurately, regional rather than national armies). These wars have declined considerably in the twentieth century. While a number of states continue to keep a wary military eye on their neighbors (such as Argentina and Chile, Ecuador and Peru, and Cuban distrust of the United States), the only large-scale twentieth-century war was between Bolivia and Paraguay from 1932 to 1935 over the Chaco area. More recently, in 1967, El Salvador and Honduras fought a brief war, settled by the Organization of American States (OAS). No Latin American services participated in World War I, and in World War II only two states were militarily engaged—Brazil sent an expeditionary infantry division to Italy, and a Mexican air squadron was stationed in the Philippines. During the Korean war, Colombia contributed a unit to the United Nations forces. Several states contributed to the ad hoc Inter-American police force in the Dominican Republic in 1965. Hemisphere defense against Soviet attack has never been engaged beyond a "deterrent" role (of doubtful significance) and is today only a minor consideration. Defense against invasion has been centered in the Caribbean, especially in the 1950s against exile forces aligned with hostile neighbors.

[26] Germani and Silvert, "Politics, Social Structure, and Military Intervention in Latin America."

Military forces continue to be actively involved in internal military and police functions. They have long been involved in most countries in maintaining internal order, both alone and in conjunction with police forces, dealing with demonstrations, strikes, and the like. Antisubversion and counterinsurgency have significantly engaged their recent efforts, especially in the last decade, and been the primary rationale for United States military aid. Insurgent forces have generally been kept under control, as in Venezuela, Colombia, Argentina, and, most spectacularly, Bolivia, where the hero of the Cuban revolution, Ernesto "Che" Guevara, was killed in an encounter with the Bolivian army in 1967. Armies have not always been successful against revolutionary movements, however; they failed to defeat the Bolivian Revolutionary Movement in 1952 and the Cuban Revolution led by Fidel Castro beginning in 1956. The latter successful movement, and its subsequent "exportation of revolution," has made most military men sensitive to the problem of guerrilla warfare.

Another largely nonpolitical role has been the nonmilitary use of the military involving activities which have come to be known as "civic action." A number of enterprises fall under this rubric. By-products of military training may be transferable to civilian life, ranging from literacy training of recruits to teaching them technical skills which will provide them with civilian occupation opportunities. Other functions are directly aimed at assisting economic and social development, such as exploration of remote areas and opening new land, building schools and highways and communications installations, improving sanitation and health facilities, and other projects useful to civilians (especially those in rural areas). These functions are not new for many Latin American military establishments—a tradition of some sort of civic action (called something else in the past) exists in nearly every nation. The United States also has a tradition of similar projects in Latin America. The U.S. Army and Marine Corps carried out such activities between 1898 and 1932 during their occupations of Cuba, Panama, the Dominican Republic, Haiti, and Nicaragua. But in the early 1960s new emphasis was placed on civic action advocated by the United States as part of the Alliance for Progress. Thus, over the last decade, civic action has been established or reemphasized by Latin American governments and substantively supported by U.S. funds, equipment, and advisers.

As Barber and Ronning[27] note, a wide variety of objectives have been pursued (and variously stressed) as functions of civic action. One emphasis is economic and social development through nation-building and strengthening the economy by modernizing basic facilities and improving the infra-

[27] Willard F. Barber and Neale Ronning, *Internal Security and Military Power: Counterinsurgency and Civic Action in Latin America* (Columbus: Ohio State University Press, 1966).

structure. Related to this is the idea that the armed forces should justify their expensive public maintenance by helping to develop their nations through works of progress. It is also argued that this will help civil-military relations by keeping the military busy and perhaps out of politics. Another goal is improving the image of the military and the central government with a skeptical public. Special stress is placed on the relationship of civic action to counterinsurgency (the two doctrines were developed simultaneously in the 1960s). Here the goal is to rectify those conditions believed to inspire insurgency, such as poverty and unfulfilled expectations for a better life (that is, the *prevention* of insurgency). Barber and Ronning agree that the goals of civic action are desirable from a humanitarian and practical point of view, and they conclude that some limited objectives are being met in a few countries. However, they note some serious limitations and problems. In the first place, such activities meet Latin American opposition, from military officers who feel that they detract from the military's ability to defend their country by diverting military efforts into essentially civilian tasks and from civilian businessmen who feel their interests threatened by incursions of the military (road construction contractors, for example). Such activities also infringe upon the responsibilities of other government ministries (public works, development, and the like) and burden them when assigned follow-up maintenance of projects, as well as straining interdepartmental relationships. The improvement of public images is easier said than done—it is likely that most Latin Americans regard these activities as they have traditionally regarded all government: with suspicion and skepticism (e.g., rural villagers who assume that a road project is aimed at enhancing the property value for a local politician). Barber and Ronning wonder why the long tradition of civic action in some countries has not produced a more highly favorable public image. Finally, they feel it unlikely that civic action will play a crucial role in counterinsurgency: "It is as much a mistake to think that insurgency is merely a problem of poverty as to think that it is a problem posed by a few Communists."

The armed forces, especially the armies, have at some time in their nation's history exercised extensive political influence in every Latin American state, without exception. Today those military establishments perform different political roles in different ways, with varying degrees of scope and intensity. The only current example of nonmilitary involvement is Costa Rica. A typology of five basic roles may be posited, identifying the patterns of political behavior of the military over the years.[28] They are: (1) self-

[28] This scheme is adapted from the taxonomies of Kalman Silvert, "Political Change in Latin America," in Herbert Matthews (ed.), *The United States and Latin America* (New York: The American Assembly, 1959), p. 196; and Needler, *Latin American Politics in Perspective,* pp. 64ff.

interest pressure group; (2) constitutional guardian and protector of the "national identity"; (3) wielder of political veto power; (4) power support for personal dictatorship; and (5) the institution directly administering government (military rule). These categories, in turn, may be subdivided into more precise patterns of behavior. All of these forms have appeared at some time in the histories of all states, sometimes more than one existing simultaneously. In many states these patterns are unstable, and the situation may move up or down the scale of intensity.

Military establishments in Latin America, as almost everywhere else in the world, act at least minimally in politics as institutional pressure groups pursuing their own interests. In this sense the military is rarely apolitical, although it is under civilian control. It acts as a pressure group seeking the advancement of its professional self-interest—improving the image of the group, acquiring weapons, securing increased pay, promotion, and fringe benefits. Its level of influence varies from country to country. The military may have to compete with other groups for public resources and be accountable to the central government for what it gets, or it may have virtual *carte blanche* so far as its interests are concerned. In the latter case, the armed forces, besides deciding matters that relate to their own internal organization and functioning, may preempt for themselves such critical decisions as how large they should be and what weapons they should have, independent of higher authority. Presidents must also court the armed services with regard to budgets; they usually receive a disproportionate share of government allocations. Even reformist governments (such as the Betancourt administration in Venezuela) dare not cut military expenditures. The armed forces are generally the key interest group in all Latin American states, but in only one today is military involvement restricted to a pressure-group role. In Mexico the military has extensive power and interests, but it is unable to influence policy in areas in which it has no professional interest. The armed forces have been subjected to civilian control (and in the process their defense expenditures reduced). In the past, other armed forces have been under civilian control, such as in Argentina from the late 1800s until 1930, in Brazil from time to time until 1964, and in Uruguay and Chile until 1973, but today the military directly governs in the last three states and in Argentina relinquished power in 1973 after seven years of military rule.

Another stage of military behavior, going far beyond the role of pressure group, results from their self-identification as constitutional guardian and arbiter. The armed forces in this case act to protect constitutionalism even when it means overthrowing a government. In the event a tyranny is replaced, the military guardian establishes a provisional rule only and sponsors elections as soon as possible in order to return government to civilian authority. The military in Brazil traditionally played this role until 1964, when they opted for direct military rule. Ecuador also followed a guardian pattern in recent years until 1963, when they, too, ruled for a period of three years. The danger of guardianship is that a dictator may emerge in the guise of guardian, refusing to give up power, as did Rojas Pinilla of Colombia after replacing the dictator Gómez.[29]

The military may act as a policy-making elite, exercising a veto not only over their professional interests, but as orienters of national policies as well. In this role the military establishes the policy limits within which executives may act, with the threat of deposition imminent if the bounds are exceeded. Elected civilians rule, but only on the sufferance of the armed forces whom they must consult on major policy decisions and whom they must not antagonize. The military may decide which groups may participate in the political process and even who may (or more importantly, who may not) occupy the presidency. The Argentine armed forces played this role in limiting the actions of presidents between 1958 and 1966. Brazilian military men have also played this role often. Guatemala and the Dominican Republic are current examples of such a situation.[30]

The simplest military role is found in the traditional Latin American personalist dictatorship, known as *caudillismo*.[31] A *caudillo* is not by definition a military man, and a number of famous strongmen have been civilians, but most Latin American dictators have been military officers. As Needler observes, the *caudillo* does not rely on the armed forces as his exclusive base of power; in fact, his dictatorship is erected over the military in order to consolidate personal power; the *caudillo* attempts to keep the armed forces content through large military budgets, special privileges, and liberal perquisites; alienation of substantial groups within the armed forces may cause the downfall of the *caudillo*.[32]

Nineteenth-century political systems were typified by these unique

[29] Needler, *ibid.*, pp. 65–68.

[30] Silvert, in Matthews, p. 74.

[31] *Ibid.*

[32] Needler, pp. 70–72. A voluminous literature exists for this long-observed phenomenon, of which a few of the best known may be mentioned: J. Fred Rippy, "Dictatorships in Latin America," in Guy Stanton Ford (ed.), *Dictatorship in the Modern World* (Minneapolis: University of Minnesota Press, 1935 and 1939); Charles E. Chapman, "The Age of the Caudillos: A Chapter in Hispanic American History," *Hispanic American Historical Review,* XII (August 1932), pp. 281–300; R. H. Humphreys, "Democracy and Dictatorship," in Christensen, *Evolution of Latin American Government;* Cecil Jane, *Liberty and Despotism in Latin America* (London: Clarendon Press, 1929); Robert A. Humphreys, "Latin America: The Caudillo Tradition," in Michael Howard, *Soldiers and Governments* (Bloomington: Indiana University Press, 1959); Magnus Mörner, "Caudillos y Militares en la evolución Hispano-Americana," *Journal of Inter-American Studies,* II (July 1960), pp. 295–310. A good recent summary and interpretation is by William H. Beezley, "Caudillismo: An Interpretive Note," *Journal of Inter-American Studies,* XI (July 1969), pp. 345–352.

autocrats. Regional strongmen, usually dedicated to maintaining the status quo, would recruit personally loyal armies for power support. They were frequently accepted by large segments of the upper class as the defenders of order and property against liberal innovations. The *caudillo* has declined in the twentieth century, although several nineteenth-century-style dictators have appeared (e.g., Trujillo, Somoza, Batista). For two decades beginning in the mid-1930s a new form of dictatorship appeared, combining tyranny with social reform (Perón, Vargas), but none presently exist. Personal dictators today are found only in Paraguay and Honduras. Premier Castro of Cuba may also be described as a personalist dictator, but is unique in that he gained power not as a professional military man but via a guerrilla revolution.

Much more common than personal military dictators in the present stage of Latin American political development is military rule, also a tradition in the area. Military officers in this role occupy the most important governmental positions, including the presidency, remaining aloof from party politics. The general-president shares power with his officer colleagues as trustees for the military establishment.[33] This form of intervention has been popular in Latin America in the 1960s and early 1970s. At the present writing military rule is found in eight states, including three of the most important—Brazil, Chile, and Peru—as well as Bolivia, Ecuador, Panama, El Salvador and Uruguay. Here the danger is that an individual officer may use his position to build up personal power and transform himself from a military representative to a personal dictator. This seems a reasonable explanation for recent events in Argentina, where military rule was established from 1966 to 1973, but two military presidents were removed and replaced during this period with other military representatives of and by the armed forces.

The present state of civil-military relations in Latin America belies a view widely held in the late 1950s and early 1960s that the frequency of military rule was declining, the end of military intervention was predictable, and the armed forces were being progressively democratized. Based on a faith in the growth of "professionalism" in the armed forces and their inevitable "depoliticization," the view was supported by the overthrow of dictators in Argentina, Colombia, Venezuela, Cuba, and the Dominican Republic between 1955 and 1961.[34] This teleological view of Latin Amer-

[33] Needler, *ibid.*, pp. 69–70.

[34] Manfred Kossock, "Potentialities and Limitations of the Change of the Political and Social Functions of the Armed Forces in the Developing Countries: The Case of Latin America—Theses," paper presented to the Research Committee "Armed Forces and Society" of the 7th World Congress of Sociology, Varna (Bulgaria), September 14–19, 1970.

ican democratic development has been invalidated by the increase of militarism in the 1960s and 1970s. Today ten Latin American states, not including Cuba, encompassing about 55% of the total Latin American population,[35] are under military or dictatorial rule, and the political influence of the military is intense in several more.

SOCIAL REFORM AND THE "NEW MILITARY"

Most Latin American nations are experiencing rapid change, with outgroups demanding that it be accelerated. The Latin American military is caught up in this changing world and forced to respond to the dissatisfaction with the old political arrangements. As in most situations of change, three options present themselves: (1) to resort to repression and forcibly disallow change; (2) to reform within the existing order of things (at varying speeds); or (3) to engage in wholesale, probably violent, "real" revolution, overthrowing current institutions and establishing a new order. All three solutions have been attempted in Latin America, with the military, in some way, involved in each.

It was noted earlier in this chapter that two opposing schools view the role of the military in the process of social change in very different ways. Traditionalists view the military at best as a conservative, often as a reactionary, force; revisionists conceive of them as agents of reform. Revisionists claim that the "new military" is peculiarly suited to strike a balance between stability and change, as they embody a combination of authority and reform mindedness. In addition, ". . . a military government does not have to face obstruction from civilian politicians." [36] The reform-oriented military regimes themselves claim to have abandoned their role of defenders of the status quo and as allies of the upper class against civilian governments who sought reform.

Can the military play a radical revolutionary role? Can it be an effective force for reform, modernization, and development? Is it a vehicle for the maintenance of status quo stability? No simple answer is possible. Historically, military leaders by and large shared a desire with their ecclesiastical and landed aristocrat allies to maintain the status quo, and this desire remains evident among many military men today. But the military is not inevitably a traditional force nor inextricably committed to the status quo. The idea of a "new military" has a base in reality. Some examples exist even of radical social revolution on the part of professional military

[35] Based on the population figures in Table 1 (see page 236).

[36] Needler, "The Latin American Military: Predatory Reactionaries or Modernizing Patriots?" pp. 241–244.

men. In sum, military activities in Latin America with regard to change in the social order present a varied picture. (A major criticism of the Rockefeller Report is that it overstates its case, implying that all military establishments today are a modernizing force and that reform is their primary objective.)

The instances of professional military men joining radical revolutionary movements are dramatic but exceptional, and at present there is no discernible important trend in this direction. A major example from the past is Luiz Carlos Prestes, Brazilian Communist leader, who as an army lieutenant led a famous movement of junior officers (*tenentismo*) seeking popular revolution. Prestes' movement began in 1924, six years before he became a Communist in 1930. Another notable national revolutionary movement led by military men was the *febrerista* party of Paraguay, made up largely of discontented Chaco War veterans advocating a socialist program, led by Colonel Rafael Franco who gained power for a year after a revolt in 1936. "Military socialism" in Bolivia was led by Colonel David Toro, then Colonel Germán Busch, in power from 1936 to 1939, followed by Major Gualberto Villaroel, president for 2½ years after a military coup in 1943. In Guatemala, Lieutenant Colonel Jacobo Arbénz Guzmán came to power in 1951 in a rigged election. His radical administration was strongly influenced by Communism, culminating in the infamous events surrounding his deposition in 1954, including United States support of counter revolutionary forces.

"Real" revolution in Latin America today is associated by the Latin American military with *fidelismo* and, therefore, with Communism. Latin American Communists have always taken an ambivalent view of the military establishments, apparently taking their cue from Marx, who felt that regular armies could be agents of either revolution or reaction. As Poppino observes, Latin American Communists refer to the armed forces as both instruments of state repression and forces for "national liberation." [37] They "denounce traditional militarism," Poppino says, as well as praise "military sympathy for the aspirations of the people." Even Castro's defeat of the Cuban regular army "has not reduced Communist efforts to attract members from the armed forces in the rest of Latin America."

Since the Castro revolution there has been continuing ambiguity, but it appears revolutionaries are much more likely to view regular armed forces as integrally allied with United States and domestic Latin American "imperialism" than potentially with themselves. Fidel Castro, speaking in 1967 about guerrilla warfare as "the main form of struggle," recognized the possibility that "the uprising of military units may constitute a factor," but

[37] Rollie E. Poppino, *International Communism in Latin America: A History of the Movement, 1917–1963* (New York: Free Press of Glencoe, 1964).

no one "who considers himself a revolutionary will wait for a garrison to rebel in order to make a revolution." [38] Che Guevara in the same year wrote of "our great strategic objective, the total destruction of imperialism via armed struggle," and referred to "the armies of all American countries," allied with the United States, as "the enemy" who were "ready to intervene in order to smash their peoples." [39] This suspicion is generally reciprocated by professional military men. Not only do officers have an aversion to disorder and "radicalism" in the abstract; they also fear revolutionary communism because the Cuban example raises the spectre of the execution of senior officers and the destruction of the armed forces and their replacement by popular militias.

The Latin American military itself is ambivalent in its views toward change, torn between reform and the status quo. Military *coups* in the 1960s revealed a variety of mixed motives. In at least eight of these interventions (half of the total) constitutionally elected presidents were deposed (in Guatemala, Ecuador, the Dominican Republic, Honduras, Argentina, Peru, Bolivia, and Brazil) who, in each case, were at least hesitantly integrating the masses into national development. Also in each instance military intervention was made in the name of anti-communism and "national honor." [40] At the same time, reformist claims were made by most military governments appearing in the 1960s (in Ecuador, Brazil, Argentina, Panama, Peru, El Salvador, and Bolivia). The regimes differed greatly in their specific purposes, styles, sincerity as to reformist intentions, and, most importantly, their success in achieving change.

While this author cannot accept as generally applicable the proposition that Latin American nations "are gripped in military vises designed to hold back the pressures of social revolution," he does agree that military governments have "acquiesced" in reforms.[41] There is a relationship between anticommunism (identified with "real revolution") and "pro-reform." The "new military" regimes, ideologically anticommunist, make the realistic appraisal that if change continues to be resisted, communist chances for success will be enhanced, and conclude that their best option is to promote social and economic development. In this sense, their approach is counterrevolutionary, for reform is motivated primarily by a desire to undercut the appeal of violent change. However, the motives are inspired by more than a conspiracy to hold power for its own sake. One might argue that the

[38] Fidel Castro, "Waves of the Future," in Irving Louis Horowitz, Josué de Castro, and John Gerassi (eds.), *Latin American Radicalism* (New York: Random House, 1969), p. 554.

[39] Ché Guevara, "Message to the Tricontinental," in *ibid.*, pp. 611–612, 615–617, 619.

[40] Horowitz, "The Military Elites."

[41] Lieuwen, *Generals Vs. Presidents,* p. 130.

reasons for sponsoring reforms are not so important as the process of reforming. The reforms realized, however (at least on a region-wide level), have been meager.

Military reformist objectives complemented the goals of the Alliance for Progress promoted by the United States and specified in the Charter of Punta del Este, except for the idea that reform should be carried out within a democratic framework. The military approach was compatible with the concept that reform and development must take place in order to avoid violent revolution, which might be exploited by Communists. Even any reservation concerning democracy was arguable so far as the military governments were concerned. As soon as reforms were carried out, they said, the country would be returned to constitutional rule, which would find a more solid democratic base as a result of military-inspired reforms.

Military reformers have increasingly felt themselves not only qualified to deal with national economic and social development and the concomitant tensions and crises but also superior to civilian regimes in their ability to perform in these endeavors. This military confidence in their competence and superiority has been explained in terms of the "professionalization" of the armed forces. In order for the modern officer to keep up with the complexities of the modern world, he is assigned to study in advanced educational institutions, at home and abroad, not only technical military subjects, but the field of national security and defense policy as well. This in turn leads to interest in development theory and other "solutions" to national problems, perhaps in the context of counter insurgency. As this knowledge among military men increases and national problems become more intense, the notion is reinforced that the military is more competent than civilians to govern. That is, the "new military," feeling technocratically and bureaucratically more qualified, judges civilian performance by higher standards as a result of advanced training, finds it wanting, and decides to deal directly with social and economic problems. This was essentially the rationale of recent military rule in Brazil, Argentina, Peru, Ecuador, El Salvador, Bolivia, and Panama. Thus, in many instances, "professionalization" has not taken the military out of politics but, to the contrary, encouraged its intervention.[42]

It is difficult to separate the military superiority complex from fear and hatred of long-time political rival civilian groups. Military interventions and reforms have also been directed at undercutting the position of national reform (often personalist) parties such as the *peronistas* in Argentina, *getulistas* in Brazil, *apristas* in Peru, *velasquistas* in Ecuador, *panamenistas* in Panama, and so on. In any event, the military has developed its own views on the basic questions of economic and social change and increas-

[42] Alexander, *Latin-American Politics and Government,* pp. 90–91.

ingly has extended its functions far beyond simply preserving order. A major question is: can military reformism be more effective than civilian reformism? Military performance so far has generally been poor.

Despite the hopeful beginnings of military regimes genuinely interested in reform, their enlightened programs, support of the United States, and an authoritarian advantage, limited success has been achieved. Only in El Salvador and Peru has significant progress been made toward structural social change. Peru is an especially significant case. The current military regime is undertaking an ideologically coherent, systematic program of development, combined with nationalism, which may indeed be called radical, although it is non-Marxist and does not seek violently to eliminate the established order. A major unanswered question concerns the extent to which the Peruvian methods will or can serve as a model or inspiration for other military regimes, given the extensive communications among Latin American military men and their strong awareness of events in each others' policies. Qualified success may be credited to Brazil. While economic growth has been remarkable, the political and human cost of repression has been exorbitant. The outcome of the Ecuadorian and Argentine experiments must be judged failures.[43]

The obstacles to military modernization are several. Military rule is debilitated in part by the special circumstances and peculiar dynamics of their own political systems. Some problems seem to be applicable to most of them, however. In the first place, governing, for anyone, is a complex affair, vulnerable to internal and external pressures that may force compromise and modification of objectives or their outright abandonment. Powerful conservative interests, while detesting and fearing radical political movements, are unwilling to accept reforms that might undercut the appeal of those movements. Military relations with high school and university students are hopeless. Students are antimilitary as a reflex action. The military aggravate these poor relations when they clash with student demonstrators and invade normally inviolate and autonomous university campuses and close their doors. In other words, simply because the military is in power does not mean that they are free from obstruction from civilian politicians or political pressures. The Ecuadorian junta, for example, failed in its reform efforts and was eventually forced to resign because of opposition from powerful conservative business interests. In Argentina, leftist *peronistas* and the labor movement effectively disrupted the military government's "too moderate" attempts at economic development. Certain weaknesses seem to be inherent in the military approach to public adminis-

[43] For an analysis of the Ecuadorian experience, see G. P. Atkins, "La Junta Militar Ecuatoriana (1963–1966): Los Militares Latinoamericanos de Nuevo Tipo," *Aportes* [Paris], no. 24 (abril 1972), pp. 7–21.

tration, adversely affecting the viability of their modernization efforts. Janowitz has formulated a number of hypotheses concerning military intervention in the politics of the new nations of Asia and Africa that seem relevant in recent Latin American experience.[44] Among other things, Janowitz says that certain "common ideological themes are found which help to explain the professional officers' behavior," such as "a strong sense of nationalism, a puritanical outlook, acceptance of extensive government control of social and economic change, and deep distrust of organized civilian politics." This seems to describe the Latin American military governments of today.

The most pervasive theme in the military approach is what Janowitz calls an "anti-politics" outlook—the "politics of wanting to be above politics." The general public acceptance and initial political success of the various governments was partly because in the beginning of their rule they avoided this common attribute of military governments. However, they eventually revealed their puritan, self-righteous, nonpolitical approach to politics. They complained that legislatures, political parties and politicians made so many compromises that they were unable to arrive at concrete, forceful decisions. In their dealings with civilian opponents the military governors seem to take the attitude that "we are so obviously right, those who oppose us must be wrong." They appear to view public policy as a set of self-evident propositions that may be imposed rather than the result of a process of accommodating competing interests. To their credit (with the exception of Brazil), their rule lacks much of the harshness and repression often associated with Latin American military government, although this element is not entirely lacking.

Fulfillment of the military's promises depends not only on how long the public will support or accept military leadership, but also on how long the military establishment can act in unison with support from all the military services and of the various intraservice factions. Military regimes are especially susceptible to dissension in their own ranks and suspicion and discontent of different factions. Again referring to Ecuador and Argentina, a disunited military establishment, despite an initial facade of unity regarding goals and methods, complicated by personal ambition, strongly and adversely affected the level of performance in both cases.

It is doubtful that much progress has been made to promote democracy under the modernizing military governments. Little thought has been given by them to the problem of successorship once constitutionalism has been restored. If the military rulers really mean what they say about democratic goals, then they face a dilemma: they cannot "pacify" without

[44] Janowitz, *The Military in the Political Development of New Nations.*

suppressing political activity, but they cannot "prepare" without allowing political processes to function freely.

Within the larger context of the changing concepts of the role of the military in politics with which this essay was introduced, the significance of recent Latin American military regimes is that they defy being categorized in such a manner as to conform to either of the two points of view, traditionalist or revisionist. These cases support to some extent both positions, but do not conclusively demonstrate either. Empirically, conceptualization of civil-military relations in Latin America is still rudimentary.

12

The Politics of North African Armies

PHILIP A. MANGANO

This chapter is a survey of attitudes in Morocco, Algeria, Tunisia, Libya and the Sudan. The 3½ years since 1970 have witnessed major disturbances or upheavals involving national army leadership in two of the five countries of northern Africa stretching from the Atlantic to the western and southern borders of Egypt. The abortive mutiny in Morocco and the Communist-oriented *coup* followed by the counter-*coup* in the Sudan, all during the month of July, 1971, put a glaring spotlight on the internal strains and vulnerabilities of the political structures of these two states and on the inner tensions within their army officer class. An attempt was made in 1972 on the life of Moroccan monarch Hassan II, engineered by army and air force officers, including the King's most trusted former military adviser and Defense Minister. In two of the other three countries of the region, army leadership has either tightened its hold on governmental power and asserted increased nationalist militancy (the case of Libya) or has retained its position as a principal institutional mechanism from which the government derives authority and support (the case of Algeria). An exception to this developing pattern of dominance or special influence of the military is Tunisia. There, following the troubled National Congress of the Destour Socialist Party, the mood is changing, now that the question of the succession to political leadership has been formally posed though not, perhaps, clearly settled. Serious tests of the political and constitutional order appear to loom ahead during the inevitably waning phase of the heroic Bourguiba era.[1] Tunisian-Libyan talks on possible union add a note of uncertainty here.

Needless to say, the abrupt removal of Soviet military personnel from Egypt in July, 1972, and the dream that Libya and Egypt might bring off some kind of a limited merger of their two systems by the end of 1973 have induced other North African leaders to reassess their position

[1] For a perceptive look ahead on this subject, see Lorna Hahn, "Tunisia Prepares for Politics after Bourguiba," in *Africa Report,* June 1971.

vis-à-vis their fellow Arab rulers as well as the great powers. Moreover, the escalation of international terrorism by Palestinian extremists and the resort to extralegal retaliatory responses by Israel (not to mention the latest, fourth round of Arab-Israeli warfare) have kept the festering Arab-Israeli conflict unavoidably and harshly to the fore among their concerns. Finally, the growing concern in the world over an emerging "energy crisis" gives to Libya and Algeria, because of their oil resources and production, an economic and strategic role far beyond what would otherwise be the case.

To a considerable extent[2] the various North African systems, despite important differences of history, geography, and sociopolitical background, are coming to resemble one or another of the several patterns of political organization of the "Arab East" and of other developing countries. The orientation and political role of the military officer class in the countries here examined and their relations with civilian leadership groups deserve closer attention as they move into the seventies. A good deal of valuable research and perceptive writing has already been done on this dimension of nation-building or modernization in North Africa,[3] but more is deserved. Until recently, more attention has been given to both Sub-Saharan Africa and the "Arab East." This dimension of North African affairs merits renewed interest in view of the area's demonstrated strategic importance, its growing economic potential (especially in the world oil industry), and its valuable human resources. North African armies, even if we exclude Egypt, are, with only a few exceptions, considerably larger and better developed than the typical army of Sub-Saharan states.[4]

As noted for purposes of this essay, North Africa comprises an area of 2,830,000 square miles, about 25% of the total area of the African continent. It is nearly as large as the continental United States without Alaska. The countries have a total population of approximately 50,000,000. Their peoples are predominantly Arab or Arabized Berber in origin, language, and culture and Islamic in religion. Their combined coastlines constitute most of the southern shore of the Mediterranean west of the Suez Canal and Alexandria. While the Sudan may not fit completely into

[2] It would of course be misleading to stretch this analogy too far, but it can help for purposes of comparative analysis.

[3] Among recent works which make a major contribution to this field of study are: J. C. Hurewitz, *Middle East Politics: The Military Dimension* (Praeger, 1969), which has substantial sections on the North African countries; Claude E. Welch, Jr. (ed.), *Soldier and State in Africa* (Northwestern University Press, 1970); Clement H. Moore, *Politics in North Africa* (Little, Brown, 1970); and William B. Quandt, *Revolution and Political Leadership: Algeria, 1954–1968* (M.I.T. Press, 1969).

In addition there are numerous articles of value on this subject in such specialized journals or periodicals (for the past five years) as *Africa Report, The Middle East Journal, Jeune Afrique,* and *Africa.*

[4] Welch, *Soldier and State in Africa, loc. cit.*, pp. 40–41.

that cultural and geographic framework, its dominant, still substantially Arab-oriented Muslim leadership and its special relations with much of North Africa and the Middle East make its inclusion in this survey desirable. Egypt has not been included only because of the comparative wealth of published work on its political and military institutions and because that would have demanded a much greater concentration on the Arab-Israeli conflict than this study should attempt.

It is not suggested, simply because of the choice of the region surveyed, that the countries concerned have displayed in practice any marked sense of overall regional unity. Certainly they are not at the same level of social, economic, or political development. Even within the *Maghrib* or "Arab West" (Morocco, Tunisia, and Algeria), which shared a common experience of French colonial rule and whose national leaders periodically profess regional solidarity[5] and closer economic cooperation, the differences and contrasts are notable. Libya and the Sudan are closer physically and politically to the "Arab East" and in recent years have become considerably more involved in the politics and conflicts of that region. With them Egyptian example and influence have long been a key factor, though the Sudan now shows substantially equal interest in its African role and connections.

The "anti-colonial struggle," a theme constantly sounded by nationalist leaders in North Africa as elsewhere in the Third World, was immeasurably fiercest and most violent in Algeria, the only African country whose nationalist movement had to conduct a major, protracted, and bloody war against the European colonial power. Tunisia and Morocco won independence through a highly effective combination of nationalist agitation and organization, periods of negotiation, and intermittent resort to guerrilla or semi-guerrilla resistance. While neither Libya nor the Sudan needed any real "struggle" for independence, some Libyans (especially the Senussi of Cyrenaica) had strongly resisted the Italian Fascist regime. As for the Sudanese, under the *Mahdi* they had bitterly contested British-Egyptian occupation in the eighties and nineties of the last century. Twentieth-century Sudanese nationalism, however, was nurtured by the British, against Egypt's wishes. These differences of political landscaping along the respective paths to independence help to explain differences in the shaping and orientation of the respective national armies that have since emerged.

[5] The constitutional documents of all three, developed in the early post-independence period, declared that they formed a part of the *Maghrib*. Since 1964, a Permanent Consultative Committee of the *Maghrib* has engaged in planning and recommending measures for economic and financial cooperation among the countries of the region, but this program has so far been extremely limited in scope or in results. (Libya took part in this consultative relationship until the military *coup* of September 1969, but has looked eastward since then for its principal ties until recently when a revived interest in neighboring Tunisia has been shown.)

As North African countries move into a maturing phase of independent life,[6] political power has passed or is likely soon to pass from the hands of those who led or ruled at the outset of independence to a younger generation eager to try its hand at statecraft and to operate the levers of national authority. Domestic problems are complicated by pressures flowing from the continuing, if muted, U.S.-Soviet rivalry and the shifting strategic balance in the Mediterranean. There are residual difficulties, though in some cases opportunities to be seized, in their relations with former European colonial powers.[7] These countries are also exposed to the constant irritant of fiercely competing doctrines in the Arab world on such issues as inter-Arab relations, the monarchical principle versus socialistic republicanism, and appropriate Arab state behavior *vis-à-vis* the Arab-Israeli conflict and the Palestinian resistance.

Just how effective Egypt-Syria-Libya cooperation or the now fading Libyan-Egyptian union may be in dealing with the territorial dispute with Israel and the Palestinian cause remains to be seen. The Soviets may have lost some ground in Egypt, and Libya is vehemently anti-communist, but Russia's stock in Syria appears stronger than ever. Intertwined with these problems is the tangled web of relations between the West, particularly the United States, with the "moderates" and the "radicals" in the Arab world, especially with Egypt. Whatever the degree of interest or desire among Egypt's leaders to pursue a dialogue with the United States, and despite the improved atmosphere for progress along such lines that might have resulted from the Russian military withdrawal, the Syrian, Libyan, and Palestinian resistance pressures on Egypt ran counter to such trends. Some would argue, also, that American diplomacy was not sufficiently sensitive to the constructive opportunities inherent in such a situation, which might have been used to call for more flexibility or restraint in Israeli policy. The appearance is one of formally closer ties between Egypt and the other two partners, with the prospect of enhanced financial and military resources on which Cairo could draw. Yet these relationships can also be viewed, especially the Libyan dimension, as marking a relative decline in the dominance and dynamism of Egypt's leadership among its neighbors as compared with the Nasser era. The durability of such integrationist ties has yet to be tested, apart from war-time solidarity against Israel.

These are some of the main internal and external forces to which

[6] Clement H. Moore (*Politics in North Africa*, pp. 106–107). He develops the Bourguibist concept of a "second moment" or a "third moment" (stages) in the post-independence, nation-building process in these nations.

[7] Tunisia and Morocco have benefited, through economic ties with France, from advantageous arrangements with the European Common Market. Algeria, despite difficulties with France over the manner and extent of nationalization of the oil properties, has preserved fairly good economic and cultural relations with France. It too continues to develop special advantageous trade ties with the newly expanded EEC.

North African governments must respond in the period immediately ahead. Whether under civilian or military leadership, or a combination of the two, all aspire to more rapid economic development and the establishment of stable, popularly accepted political and governmental institutions. National armies, or their officer groups, are substantially involved in this process. Among scholars and publicists interested in such processes in Africa and the Middle East, there was at first an optimistic tendency (the whole field of study is relatively new) to emphasize the promising, potentially constructive aspects of military leadership in cementing national unity and in replacing outmoded practices in the governmental sphere with greater efficiency, integrity, and national fervor.

More recently, as military takeovers, *coups* and counter-*coups* have proliferated throughout Africa and the Middle East, including the North African area, a "revisionist" approach has been gaining adherents. It holds that, after an initial period of vigor, attempted reform, and patriotic zeal, military regimes almost inevitably become bogged down in the same unyielding economic and social problems with which their civilian predecessors or colleagues have wrestled and that despite their modern technical training, they are ordinarily less likely to have or to acquire the necessary skills or rapport with the people than regimes in which civilian political leadership is dominant.[8] In any case, where military regimes are in the saddle or share in the exercise of power in North Africa, they are faced with the problem of trying to shape more permanent governmental institutions and of creating popularly based political movements to replace or modernize the older political institutions. This may well mean creating conditions in which the military may ultimately find itself again with more limited functions and power, even if it does not unconditionally return to the barracks. Alternatively, such an evolution can be interrupted by additional military *coups* and postponement of the maturing process. In the country-by-country survey that follows, it is hoped to shed some light on the validity of these contending approaches as far as the role of the military in North Africa is concerned or on the merits of some middle ground for evaluation.

MOROCCO

Up to now the Moroccan army, developed after independence out of former French colonial forces and some infusions from the former "national liberation" movement, has been the main, dependable bulwark of the Moroccan monarchy and of the present ruler, Hassan II. The abortive

[8] Eric A. Nordlinger, "Soldiers in Mufti," *American Political Science Review*, December 1970, pp. 1131–1148; and Arnold Rivkin, *Nation-Building in Africa* (Rutgers University Press, 1969), pp. 74–76.

mutiny of July 12, 1971, and the further attempt on the King's life in August 1972 by Air Force pilots have ushered in a period in which the FAR (*Forces Armées Royales*) is itself becoming a special problem for the existing, more or less absolutist regime. One specialist commented on the national scene at the end of 1970:

> "Five years of absolutism has not only eliminated all representative institutions from Morocco, but has introduced a profound malaise which pervades all sectors, economic, agricultural, cultural, social, as well as political." [9]

It is obvious that this malaise has penetrated to some degree into the army officer corps. Even if it remains predominantly loyal in principle to the institution of monarchy and resistant to leftist revolutionary doctrines, it is an army whose younger, middle-level officers (and some at higher levels) are more politicized than at the dawn of independence. In any case, many share some of the impatience felt by other elites in Moroccan society over the stagnation in national life, the known corruption, and the lack of definite forward movement in the nation's economic and social development.[10] Hitherto "an arm of the Royal Household . . . rather than an instrument of the official government," [11] the army seems to be in the process of being propelled into a more active political role than before.

Since 1967 there has been no participation in the government by responsible members of any of the major political parties, which, though they survive, have been cowed or robbed of vitality. Since 1965, after the bloody suppression of the students and sympathetic workers' riots in Casablanca, the King has exercised full executive and legislative powers. The emergency condition, under which the constitution of 1962 was suspended, prevailed until 1970 under "state of exception" powers, when Hassan II promulgated a new, authoritarian constitution after mobilizing sufficient support to ensure its approval by national referendum.[12] Now, in the aftermath of the abortive *putsch* of 1971, and the almost miraculous escape of Hassan II from being shot down by officers of his own Air Force in the summer of 1972, there is a persistent air of suspense and uncertainty in the country over possible change that could bring reform and vitality to the nation. The monarch's several fruitless efforts to fashion constitutional changes that the political opposition would accept but that would not undermine the royal dominance in the whole system compound this uncertainty.

[9] William Spencer, "Morocco's Monarchial Balancing Act," *Africa Report*, December 1970, p. 21.

[10] Moore, *op. cit.*, pp. 212 and 292.

[11] *Ibid.*, p. 112.

[12] *Africa Report*, December 1970, p. 21. (There were reports of "rigging," but the overwhelming majority of Moroccans eligible to vote registered acceptance, despite opposition calls for a boycott.)

Morocco has an armed forces establishment of 50,000, with 45,000 in the army and the remainder divided between the Air Force (4,000) and the Navy (1,000). There are 20,000 to 30,000 more in para-military or auxiliary forces, including national police, mobile security battalions and several companies of royal guards. Approximately $80 million were spent for defense in 1969-70 out of an estimated GNP of $3.4 billion for that year.[13] Of the countries considered in this study, its army ranks second in size, after that of neighboring Algeria with which it tangled briefly but creditably in the border war of 1963. Most of its senior officers began careers in French or Spanish colonial forces, and a number were trained at French or Spanish military academies. The country has, however, its own national military academy at Casablanca and other training schools such as that for NCO's at Ahermoumou. It was the latter's cadet corps that were drawn, perhaps as unwitting pawns, into the insurgent forces that staged the attack on the King's summer palace at Skhirat (July 1971), where he was host at a celebration of his forty-second birthday.[14]

The army is a modernized, professional, and hitherto apolitical organization. Its arms, equipment, and training assistance have come mainly from western countries (chiefly France and the United States), with the United States the major source in recent years. Some arms and equipment have also been received from the USSR. Senior officers came mainly from the conservative and Berber tribal communities, which take pride in their military tradition and their Islamic orthodoxy. However, in the first five years of independence, when the army needed to build up its native officer corps, hundreds of young Moroccans were trained and commissioned. These came mainly from urban areas with the advantage of secondary school education, a requirement for admission to the officer candidate schools. They are the officers now at junior and middle levels. Many have been influenced by the years of revolution and by the reformist ideas of the nationalist parties, Istiqlal (moderate-conservative) and UNFP (*Union Nationale des Forces Populaires*, leftist), which played an important role in national life in the immediate post-independence years. Some of them have now had administrative experience in regional or local affairs, as the King has drawn upon army officers and militarily-trained civilians for such work under Interior Ministry supervision.[15] This has tended to produce a degree of fusion or interpenetration between the army and the bureaucracy in certain fields, particularly where problems of internal security are involved. With the political parties in a strait-jacket and the monarch insulated from the people except for his public image-building appearances, he

[13] Figures taken from Institute for Strategic Studies, London, *The Military Balance*, 1970–71, pp. 42–43, hereafter cited as I.S.S.

[14] *The New York Times*, July 19, 1971.

[15] Moore, *op. cit.*, pp. 291–292.

becomes increasingly dependent upon those who command the army. Therein lies his greatest vulnerability. The military is an institution in which traditionalism and particularistic interests are still strong, but it is also a modernizing, national power center, aware of its pivotal position and conscious of its political potential.

The bloody events of the military *putsch* at Skhirat and the attempted aerial assassination led, of course, to military trials and executions of those identified as ringleaders or important participants in the two plots.[16] General Oufkir, a former Interior and Defense Minister, ostensibly a strong right hand and strong-arm aide to the King, shot himself on learning that the King had discovered his complicity in the 1972 plot. Neither the Skhirat *putsch* nor the latest aerial attack on the King seem to have involved major elements of the armed forces. However, the purge and trials that followed have required drastic shakeups in the command structure, and the longer-range impact of these events on the officer class is not yet clear. The King seems anxious to gain limited participation by the parties in the government, but on his own terms, as a prelude to elections. On the other hand, he has hinted at possible contacts between certain UNFP leaders and General Oufkir, who directed the August 1972 plot. When UNFP leader Bouabid publicly denounced such allegations, and charges of suspected Libyan-UNFP contacts, the King switched tactics, saying that "the parties who desire freedom and democracy should help us in our work." Matters are still at an impasse. The UNFP wants creation of a "popular government" and a constituent assembly "to clarify relations between the hereditary institution of a monarchy and the people's legislative power."[17] Meanwhile, the nonpolitical technicians' cabinet continues, and the King's transparent fencing with the parties persists.

Suppression of the *coups* produced dramatic expressions of solidarity with the Moroccan monarchy from Jordan's King Hussein and of friendly sympathy from neighboring Algeria and Tunisia. In contrast, Libya's Col. Qaddafi, whose anti-Jordanian and pro-Palestinian fulminations have increased in intensity, applauded the rebel effort at Skhirat. He predicted the eventual success of efforts to overthrow the Moroccan monarchy and to bring about a revolutionary, Pan-Arabist reform of the entire Moroccan system, presumably along lines of the existing Libyan model. In this situation, Egypt's Sadat finds himself in an awkward position as would-be mediator; efforts to induce Qaddafi to come to Rabat, during the recent Organization of African Unity summit meeting to end the feud between him and Hassan II were unavailing. Another source of internal pressure on Hassan has been a reported demand by the Istiqlal Party for forceful action to

[16] *Africa,* No. 14, October, 1972, p. 31.
[17] *Ibid.*

help "liberate" the Rio de Oro territory (Spanish Sahara) to portions of which Morocco, Mauritania, and Algeria assert claims.[18] This "irredentist" cause probably appeals to strongly nationalist elements in the army, but Hassan cannot easily afford to risk breaking a common front with Mauritania and Algeria on this problem.

Morocco's ties with, and assistance from the West, especially with the United States and France, have helped to give the King time in considering how to modernize and reform his system. He has not yet done so in a manner responsive to mounting demands among the educated, politically conscious urban middle and labor classes, the youth and, to a growing extent, the military. The monarchy as an institution may still be widely regarded as the "principal cement for political life in contemporary Morocco." [19] But the shrinkage in the system's ability to get things done and to muster confidence makes it increasingly vulnerable to revolutionary change whether that be contrived by civilian political groups, by impatient elements of the military, or some combination of both.[20]

ALGERIA

The Algerian army grew out of the only major revolutionary war against the European colonial power in post-World War II Africa. It is an amalgam of elements from the so-called "external army" of that war (Algerian rebel units in training, based in the frontier areas of Tunisia and Morocco) and of the "internal army," i.e., the actual fighting forces organized in guerrilla units under the several regional (*Wilaya*) commands during the 7-year conflict with France. Together they formed the *Armée de Liberation Nationale* (ALN), the military arm of the nationalist-revolutionary movement known as the *Front de Liberation Nationale* (FLN). The present head of the Algerian government, Colonel Houari Boumedienne, became commander of the "external army" in 1960 and, at war's end, successfully pressed his claim to command of the entire ALN.[21] At that time Ahmed Ben Bella, rebel leader whose years in a French prison after his airplane kidnapping by French-Algerian security services in 1956

[18] *Africa,* No. 10, June, 1972, p. 52.

[19] *Current History*, March, 1973, p. 123 ("The Western Sahara-Suez Triangle," by William H. Lewis).

[20] See, in this connection, background statement by I. William Zartman, printed as Appendix D in: *The States of North Africa in the 1970's,* Joint Hearings of the Subcommittees on Africa and the Near East of House Committee on Foreign Affairs, GPO, 1972.

[21] Hurewitz, *op. cit.*, pp. 189–192. See also the penetrating chapter by I. William Zartman entitled "The Algerian Army in Politics," in Welch, *op. cit.*, pp. 225–249, for a full account of the rise to power of the Ben Bella-Boumedienne partnership.

enormously enhanced his standing among the Algerians, outmaneuvered the Provisional Government (GPRA) in the power struggle that followed the end of the war.

With the support of several key ALN commanders, including Boumedienne, he established a new FLN Political Bureau (the so-called Tlemcen Group) as a basis for his claim to government leadership and control. By late summer of 1962, after defeating or converting his principal opponents among the *Wilaya* commanders and among the politicians of the GPRA, this "Group" took over *de facto* authority at Algiers. It prepared the elections that made Ben Bella Prime Minister, and Boumedienne Minister of Defense in September of that year. From the beginning, the "primary authorship in shaping the Democratic and Popular Republic of Algeria could thus be ascribed to the civil-military alliance." [22]

The regime that emerged out of this immediate post-war confusion and rivalry, though it claimed political authority as the authentic leadership of the FLN, clearly depended on the support of the revolutionary army taking shape from the merger of "external" (regular) and "internal" (guerrilla) army units. The Ben Bella–Boumedienne combination continued formally until 1965, though Ben Bella had been seeking for some time to curb the power of his determined army chief. On June 19, 1965, Boumedienne and his military associates removed the excessively leftist-oriented Ben Bella from power by a *coup d'état*. Meanwhile Boumedienne, as Minister of Defense, had progressively eliminated many of the wartime guerrilla veterans from the army ranks and increased the proportion of regular, career personnel in the ANP (*Armée Nationale Populaire*) that he had been reorganizing. After 1967 the Revolutionary Council, a collegial executive body presided over by Boumedienne and dominated by army officers or politicized ex-ALN figures, ceased to meet, and Boumedienne assumed clear executive power. Thereafter the only serious challenge to his authority came at the end of 1967 from one of his former colleagues, ANP Chief of Staff Col. Zbiri, whose bid for power or changes in national policy sputtered out because Boumedienne had retained the real control and backing of the professional army.[23]

The ANP now has a total strength of about 60,000, of which between 3,500 and 4,000 are officers. If para-military forces are included, total armed forces strength comes to 70,000, with 2,000 each in the Air Force and Navy. This is the second largest national army among newly independent African states and the third largest in the Arab world. Since its relatively unsatisfactory showing in the 1963 border clashes with Moroccan forces, it has improved its proficiency, broadened the base for recruitment,

[22] Hurewitz, *op. cit.*, p. 193.
[23] Welch, *op. cit.*, p. 243.

and received substantial arms, equipment and training assistance from abroad, notably from France and the USSR.[24] For 1969–70, defense expenditures came to $174 million, or just under 6% of the nation's GNP.

The enlisted ranks are drawn from the semiliterate sons of the peasantry and city workers. The officer corps is a diverse group drawn from town and country, from the "external" ALN and the *Wilayas*, and even from student life. A totalitarian style of military training and psychological indoctrination is designed to neutralize regional ties and to inculcate loyalty to the professional military establishment as guardian of the national revolution. An overwhelming majority of the officers are in the junior ranks, a "higher proportion than in a classical army." [25] The regime seems to have had substantial success in subordinating social or regional attachments to professional military status and in stressing advancement through technical competence. In this sense, the officer class may be said to form part of that "new middle class" in North Africa and the Middle East that spells "personal modernization" for the individual and "rapid social advancement" for the group.[26]

Algeria, like Libya, possesses large petroleum resources. Developed mainly by French technology and capital investment from France and other western countries, this industry has now been brought substantially under nationalized control. Yet the returns from oil sales to France and other western countries have not yet produced any marked rise in the standard of living of the Algerian masses or greatly speeded overall economic development that the country sorely needs to relieve unemployment and improve educational opportunity. The present Algerian regime, then, is engaged in the battle of economic development with marked nationalist and socialist fervor but without the stabilizing support of a popularly-based, more solidly-structured system such as Tunisia, for example, has enjoyed.

In the political sphere, Ben Bella had tried to weld the FLN into a truly national political party and to make of the professional and political elite a cohesive force. But his methods and overly ideological approach

[24] Figures from I.S.S.: 1970–71, *op. cit.*, pp. 39, 110. The Soviets have had about 1500 military instructors or advisers in recent years in Algeria. The French military training mission has been less than one third that number.

[25] Welch, *op. cit.*, pp. 245–246. In his essay on Algeria, Zartman also points out that the "divorce between social origins and military status has been remarkably successful . . . ," and that in every case of army dissidence since independence, the "breakaway" officers could count on only a relatively small percentage of the junior officers and troops. Moore (*op. cit.*, p. 292) confirms the view that the Algerian officers have such privileges and benefits, as part of their separateness from other elements of society, that they could be said to be "coddled."

[26] Welch, *op. cit.*, p. 248. Manfred Halpern, in *The Politics of Social Change in the Middle East and North Africa* (Princeton, 1963) has particularly stressed this idea of army officer affiliation with the new, radicalized, educated, and change-oriented middle class in most Arab countries (see especially pp. 270–280).

aroused opposition from several directions, most importantly from the army. The FLN has not developed into a coherent political movement with any generally accepted ideology or political doctrine except nationalism. Boumedienne, on the other hand, less concerned with formal political structures, has managed to expand the role of the professional and intellectual elite, and of the administrative technocrats. Yet he has insisted upon maintaining good rapport with the military stability group with which his own fortunes have all along been associated. What has resulted is a coalition of technicians and professional military men with rather similar views on government and politics "because of their earlier socialization."[27] This posture of the Boumedienne regime has rallied little enthusiasm, and some tentative opposition, from such potentially important forces for the future as student and labor groups, the "secondary elite" as one specialist on contemporary Algeria calls them.[28] However, to judge from impressions of recent visitors and observers, there is an air of movement and progress in the Algerian centers and signs of a growing confidence in the nation's ability to cope with its problems in a practical and independent manner.[29]

In the field of foreign affairs and international security, the nation has had only one serious problem—the boundary dispute and clash with Morocco over Saharan territory, a dispute which now seems to have been resolved in an era of better Moroccan-Algerian relations. Though politically a vigorous supporter of the Palestinian "resistance," and strong in its public advocacy of no compromise with Israel, Algeria has not consistently participated in Arab state military planning sessions organized by the Egypt-Libya-Syria constellation. Boumedienne has appeared to harbor some reserve toward the flamboyant, warlike posture of Libya's Qaddafi. Indeed, he has gone out of his way to show stronger interest in allaying earlier anxieties over Algerian intentions in neighboring and moderate Tunisia and Morocco and to stress Algeria's need for peace. Ideologically committed to support for, and sympathy with, "anti-imperialist" or revolutionary movements in Africa, the Middle East (Palestinians), and elsewhere, Algeria has resisted the degree of cooperation which the United States, for example, would like in bilateral or multilateral (UN) measures to curb or punish acts of international terrorism, including hijacking. However, it has returned hijacked planes and money extorted by hijackers, though not the hijackers themselves, to countries whose airlines have been victimized by such acts.

The Algerian army continues to be a source of supply of arms and

[27] Moore, *op. cit.*, pp. 290–291.

[28] William B. Quandt, *Revolution and Political Leadership: Algeria 1954–1968* (Cambridge: M.I.T. Press, 1969), p. 253.

[29] *Jeune Afrique*'s keen-minded perceptive editor, Bechir Ben Yahmed (a Tunisian), has repeatedly made this point in editorials. The writer of this chapter saw confirmatory evidence during a visit to Algiers in the summer of 1972.

training for national liberationist guerrillas in the southern part of Africa, notably those of the Portuguese territories. Such action maintains or enhances Algerian prestige among the Sub-Saharan members of the African family and is, of course, consistent with Algeria's own strong anticolonial and revolutionary origins. Though Boumedienne has suppressed earlier Marxist influence in governing circles, official relations with both the USSR and mainland China are lively, as continued exchanges of official missions and other friendly contacts attest. On the other hand, despite absence of normal diplomatic relations with the U.S. since 1967, the state-owned oil company, Sonatrach, has not felt inhibited from entering into an agreement (completed early in 1973) with American business for a long-term supply of liquid natural gas for American markets.[30] The U.S. Export-Import Bank and others will finance construction of needed production and pipeline facilities in Algeria. Relations with France since the partial nationalization of French oil properties are improving and will remain important to Algeria, particularly in Algeria's developing trade relations with the European Common Market. One aspect of its nonalignment policy that has evoked some parallel response by neighboring Tunisia is a recurrent suggestion that the two superpowers would do well to withdraw their respective naval forces from the Mediterranean, leaving nations of the area not committed to any military or alliance grouping to join in fashioning a putatively more constructive security situation or zone of peace in that area. In that connection, despite criticisms of U.S. policy in the Far East and Middle East, Algeria has always refused any type of military facilities on its soil, or coastline, to the USSR.

At home, in contrast to the situation in Morocco, the army has been somewhat removed from day-to-day political processes and administration. Its active political role may even be declining as the independence war recedes into the background, as professionalization and technical training become key values, and as the proportion of revolutionary veterans grows smaller. It is worthy of note, too, that army personnel must resign their commissions before they can hold public office.

The nation still lacks a permanent constitution and popularly based institutions (the FLN has not become a valid party) that can give the regime in power a full measure of legitimacy. Its hold on national power, presently quite firm, depends on its ability to maintain a convincing momentum in economic development and social welfare, while retaining the con-

[30] The contract for large annual shipments of LNG over a 25-year period to El Paso Natural Gas Company as the U.S. distributor has met final approval at top U.S. Government levels. These arrangements have been worked out even in the absence of regular diplomatic relations between Washington and Algiers, broken off by the latter during the Six-Day War in the Middle East in 1967. The operation of a "U.S. Interests Section," operating under Swiss protection, has been a useful mechanism.

fidence of key military commanders. The latter, notwithstanding their apparent separation from active political affairs, possess ample means to seize power or to redistribute power, as in Turkey, should the technicians and politicians falter. For the present the civilian-technocrat-military partnership, buttressed by expanding revenues from oil and gas sales and by improving trade relations generally, is doing fairly well.

TUNISIA

Tunisia is unique among North African states in important respects. Smallest country of the area and most limited in natural resources, its population is relatively the most advanced, and its political and governmental institutions relatively the most stable. Its army officer class has no political role, has aspired to none (so far as can be observed), and is strictly confined to routine defense duties. Of the several states here considered, it has been outstanding for popular acceptance of government and political party leadership personified by President Habib Bourguiba and his chief associates of the Destour Socialist Party. The party still dominates the system and Bourguiba, though ailing physically and an unhappy witness to some loosening of his grip on the party hierarchy at the eighth Destourian National Congress at Monastir, in October 1971, still dominates the party. Critical to this grip was Bourguiba's success, apparently on threat of resignation if he were overridden, in shaping the new Political Bureau to his liking and confirming senior party stalwart Hedi Nouira as Prime Minister. This puts Nouira tentatively in line for succession to the presidency if Bourguiba were to step down or were to be incapacitated.

Missing from the new Political Bureau are long-time party leaders Bahi Ladgham (formerly number two in party and government hierarchy) and Ahmed Mestiri, erstwhile Minister of Interior. The latter's persistence in pressing for liberal constitutional reform and democratization of party and government practice brought his suspension from the party after the national congress. The downgrading of Ladgham, though less easy to explain, seems to reflect some jockeying for position in internal politics in which he lost ground to such figures as Nouira (Prime Minister) and Masmoudi (ex-Foreign Minister). Also, one may surmise that Ladgham, as head of the inter-Arab mediating commission supervising the truce between King Hussein and Palestinian guerrillas in Jordan in 1970, may have seemed to stray from the main line of Bourguiba's overall policy of moderation and conciliation on the Palestine problem. In any case, the Tunisian President obviously believes that his own primacy in national affairs is essential to the country's stability while his health permits him to go on and that the mantle of leadership must pass to men of sure commitment to continuance of Bourguibist policies when, in a few years, he leaves the scene.[31] Bordering on a larger, stronger, and postrevolutionary Algeria and on a militant, army-dominated Libya, Tunisia has gradually built up a somewhat larger military establishment than would have been the case if the country's experience had unfolded in a less turbulent atmosphere. With a population of 5,000,000, Tunisia now has a military establishment of 21,000. Of these, 20,000 are in the army and the remainder in the small, lightly equipped air force and navy. There are about 5,000 in the gendarmerie, and an equal number in the National Guard, auxiliary or paramilitary forces. For 1969-70, defense expenditures were $16,700,000, or 1.4% of the gross national product and 5% of the national budget, well below ratios in any other North African country.[32] Military supplies, equipment, and training assistance come mainly from the United States and France. The country now has its own officer-training facilities, but younger officers are also sent abroad, chiefly to western Europe.

The army, very small at the outset, grew out of the French colonial matrix. Initially its officers were Tunisians transferred from service with French forces. During the first years of independence, large numbers of Algerian rebel units were lodged in a training status in eastern Tunisia, while France retained air and land base rights at Bizerte and elsewhere in Tunisia. In this delicate situation, Bourguiba sought to build up a modest but credible national army to strengthen public confidence in his government's ability to keep its balance and to defend national interests in the face of these competing external pressures. During the period from 1956 to 1963 he pushed successfully for the progressive evacuation of the French bases, with the violent clash with the French at Bizerte in 1961 the main exception to that peaceful process. As the Algerian conflict neared its end, Tunisia was able to dispatch a contingent of 3,200 as a contribution to the UN forces in the Congo (1960–61). This enhanced the country's international prestige and gave seasoning and experience to the units involved. They were returned home in the summer of 1961, after the Tunisian-French clash at Bizerte in July of that year. That crisis subsided, and France withdrew its military presence completely by early 1963, after the Algerian war had ended and East-West tensions over Berlin had been eased.[33]

The only signs of political involvement or disaffection among some elements of the Tunisian army officer corps appeared late in 1962 when some officers, including one from the bodyguards, were implicated in a

[31] For a solid analysis of the internal political scene and of the "succession" problem, see Lorna Hahn, "Tunisian Political Reform," in *Africa Report*, Autumn, 1972.

[32] I.S.S. (1970–1971), *op. cit.*, p. 44.

[33] Hurewitz, *op. cit.*, pp. 412–413.

plot to assassinate the Tunisian President. While the political ideas of the conspirators are still obscure (a lingering "Youssefist" or revolutionary nationalist influence is suspected), the attempt caused interruption of Tunisian-Algerian relations when Ben Bella's Algeria gave asylum to several of the plotters.[34] Bourguiba severely admonished the military and the nation on the doctrine of civilian supremacy, and there has been no overt indication of *coup*-mindedness or hunger for a political role within the Tunisian army since that time.

Relations with Algeria have developed along generally favorable lines since the Tunisians dropped their claims to portions of Algerian territory in the Sahara, with its oil resources. Oil is now being discovered and exploited in modest amounts in Tunisia itself. Tunisian-Libyan relations since the advent to power of Col. Qaddafi are correct and relatively normal, at least on the surface. However, Libya spearheads and preaches the extremist, violent Arab position on Palestinian and related Middle East problems that Bourguiba has always rejected. Their relations could deteriorate if the Libyan chief is frustrated in his drive to mobilize the resources and cooperation of a wider grouping of Arab states in support of radical, militant policies or if, notwithstanding Bourguiba's hopes, an internal crisis over national leadership should develop in Tunisia when his rule is over. Such a situation, however unlikely it seems at present, could tempt the existing Libyan regime (which has hardly shrunk from various forms of intervention in areas more distant) to try to influence the Tunisian scene, directly or indirectly. Pressures from Algeria too, under such circumstances, might be expected, but hardly in support of Libyan objectives.

Those political figures who have been chastised or downgraded following the recent intraparty debate (Mestiri, for example) do not appear, on their records, to be the kind of men likely to be tempted, for personal or ideological reasons, to provoke internal turmoil or unrest of a nature to attract intervention by the army or to compromise the basic stability and cohesiveness of Tunisian society that they have helped to promote. Government and party have maintained a firm hand on national security forces, and no army officer has attained any national prominence or held any important post apart from strictly military affairs. There are, of course, evidences of discontent and restlessness among student, labor, and intellectual groups, and there has been slippage in the party's ability to attract the young into membership. Some observers see actual signs of boredom among Tunisia's trained professional and business elite. Also, it is obvious that, since Bourguiba's first illness in 1967 and following the "unpopular, costly and wasteful experiment in forced collectivization unrivaled outside

[34] *Ibid.;* and Moore, *op. cit.,* p. 293.

the Communist bloc" (the Ben Salah debacle for which Bourguiba himself took the blame), there has been some general erosion of public support for the party and loss of enthusiasm for the system.[35]

It may prove difficult, if not impossible, during the waning phase of the Bourguiba period to restore the "era of good feeling" that prevailed during the first decade of independence. Sooner or later, one might think, the unity and solidarity of the party are bound to be loosened as new conditions emerge and a younger generation begins to share in setting national policies. If not under Bourguiba, then afterward, it is possible to envisage some kind of limited opposition or independent movement or party—perhaps after the post-Ataturk Turkish model in Tunisia's moderate environment. Certainly there were hints at such an eventual evolution during the public discussions of constitutional and party reform that Bourguiba encouraged three years ago, a project that, save for minor changes, has faded from the fore more recently. Whether Tunisia itself is ready for such change and whether the international climate in North Africa and the Middle East makes such an evolution timely or safe in the near future appears to be the central issue. Bourguiba is convinced that it would be premature.

It would be strange if army commanders were not aware of, and touched by, these contending ideas in play on the Tunisian scene and in neighboring regions. But army commander Al Karawi maintains a very low profile, and the army has a high degree of loyalty to the national party and the nation's President. On balance, civilian primacy in Tunisia is well-grounded and it would seem to require domestic failures or breakdown of unusual proportions, coupled with substantial external interference, to change that balance. Recent evidence of Bourguiba's interest in a possible union with Libya, after Egypt cooled toward Qaddafi, seems out of character and also risky.

LIBYA

The political role of the military in the Libyan Arab Republic centers around the aggressive and spectacular personality of Colonel Mu'ammar al'Qaddafi who, with his principal associates on the Revolutionary Command Council (RCC), rules the country. Prior to the *coup* of September 1, 1969, which overthrew the floundering monarchy, Libyan policy, though generally neutralist in tendency, was mildly favorable toward the West and

[35] *Washington Post,* November 28, 1971. The recent escape of Ben Salah from prison and his flight to Europe created only a momentary stir. He has been quoted as disavowing political plans or ambitions.

cautiously responsive to cooperation with the Northwest African states of the *Maghrib*. Since the *coup*, it has turned strongly toward Egypt and other revolutionary and Arab-socialist countries of the Middle East, proclaiming its own strident version of anticolonialism and Pan-Arabism, and spearheading an impassioned campaign for larger Arab unity and Islamic solidarity. Fortified with large revenues from the oil resources developed during the sixties, this militant and somewhat puritanical young army officer has, in the view of many, taken on the mantle of Nasser as the paramount champion of militant Arab nationalism. Despite his youth and inexperience and the underdeveloped state of his country, he has asserted a forceful role in Arab state councils. His is the most warlike and uncompromising voice among them in espousing the cause of the Palestinians. He vehemently judges other nations—including the superpowers—by their policies and attitudes toward the Arab-Israeli conflict.

Qaddafi is a forceful advocate, probably the moving force, of the intended federation of Libya, Egypt, and Syria and of the abortive Libyan-Egyptian union. He pressed swiftly in the first months of his regime for evacuation by Britain and the United States of the air bases they had held by agreement with the monarchy of King Idris from the early period of independence in the 1950s. He has also been at the forefront of the successful campaign over the past year by the oil-producing countries for larger revenues from the international oil companies and for wider national control over their oil resources. He has sought to maintain a diffident, middle course in formal relations with the United States and the USSR. However, the Soviets' pro-Arab position on the Palestine problem and their heavy military assistance to Egypt and allied Arab countries, as contrasted with American military supply to Israel, have seriously undermined the American position in Libya. On the other hand, Qaddafi's uncompromising anti-Communist stance was shown in the summer of 1971 when he had two of the pro-Communist leaders of the abortive Sudanese military coup removed from a BOAC plane forced down while in Libyan air space. He turned them over promptly to the restored regime of General Nimeiri and bluntly warned the Soviet Union not to meddle in the internal affairs of the region.[36] Although Libya has since arranged for some arms purchases from the Russians, and there are indications of a Libyan-Soviet agreement to have Russian technicians assist in the operation of the nationalized, former British Petroleum properties in Libya, Qaddafi has made it absolutely clear that he wants no Communist activity in Libya.

The Libyan army has been surprisingly expanded during the past

[36] *The New York Times,* July 23, 1971. This extraordinary aerial intervention was strongly but ineffectually protested by Britain, as a matter of principle and of international law. It is also challenged in a strong editorial in *Africa,* No. 4.

several years, growing from a force of 6,000 to 7,000 to a level of approximately 20,000. A Libyan battalion has been stationed along the Suez Canal, a number of Libyans are being trained in Egypt, and some Egyptian forces appear to have been stationed in Libya.[37] Modern material and equipment, formerly supplied from British and American sources to the smaller army and air force during the sixties, are now provided mainly from Egypt and the USSR. In 1970 France agreed to sell Libya 100 Mirage jet-fighters over a period of several years after military supply arrangements with Britain were terminated.[38] French training, a supply of spare parts, and technical assistance in the use of these planes have been needed while the agreement is being carried forward. To date over half of the planes have been delivered.

Libya has its own officer-training school, where many of the younger army officers have been trained. Qaddafi himself, perhaps typical of younger officer experience, attended a rural secondary school and is a graduate of the Libyan military academy. He does not seem to have first-hand acquaintance with countries outside the Arab areas. Senior officers of the pre-*coup* period had been trained under the auspices of the British military mission or abroad. Some of these, if escaping punishment or disciplinary action, were used for a time as military attachés in a few Libyan embassies, but now seem to have been phased out of service.

Under King Idris development of a regular army had been slow, the monarch preferring to rely on regional security and police forces among which his own Cyrenaican Defense Force was strongly favored. In practice he chose to keep the tribal and regular forces separate, thus protecting his "elite eastern force against political contamination from steady exposure to the others." [39] Qaddafi's army regime has tightened centralization and administration, and the provincial forces have been largely absorbed into the regular army or relegated to more routine police functions. For 1971 defense expenditures were estimated at $84 million, only slightly under corresponding figures for much more populous Morocco and Algeria and four times the figure for Tunisia. Protracted tension between Libya and Chad, with reciprocal charges that the one was supporting subversive

[37] *I.S.S.*, 1971–72, *op. cit.*, p. 30, and *Jeune Afrique*, September 28, 1971, p. 23.

[38] The Libyan RCC chose France as a supplier of jet fighter-bombers, having removed both the U.S. and Britain from the air bases they had previously enjoyed. Soviet offers were rejected as bearing the risk of a tutelage more oppressive than that of the Egyptian dependence on Russian military aid. For France, apart from obvious business aspects, the deal offered prospects of improving her position in the Arab world, and helping to minimize French-Libyan differences over internal strife in Chad, and over political and security interests in the *Maghrib*. See *Africa Report*, June, 1970; "France Woos Libyans With Arms Aid," pp. 20–21.

[39] Hurewitz, pp. 236–237.

groups in the territory of the other, may have accounted for some of that increase, though the quarrel with Chad has recently been patched up. Most of it, however, must be attributed to Qaddafi's emerging strategy of maximizing Libya's role in a forceful Arab policy toward Israel[40] and perhaps to a desire to centralize control of Libyan internal administration far beyond past practice.

Potential opposition to Qaddafi within the ruling army officer group in the early period was quickly stifled in December 1969 when he forced from office (as Ministers of Defense and Interior) two senior officers most likely to contest his shift from low-key alignment with the *Maghrib* to one of intimacy with Egypt. Since then the path has led to the new three-way federation and the proposed closer union with Egypt. It has led to open friction with Morocco (Qaddafi openly applauded the attempted military *coup* against Hassan II in 1971) and to growing tension with the Sudan, which has backed away from joining the intended Egypt-Libya-Syria federation and has been shocked by the Palestinian terrorist murder of American diplomats in Khartoum. The Libyan chief has also aspired to offset or eliminate both western (NATO) or potential Soviet interests in Malta. There have apparently been substantial financial inducements offered to Malta's Dom Mintoff, so far without the success that Qaddafi seems to want. The Maltese leader, however, has kept alive the possibility of ending NATO rights, via British facilities, and the final outcome of this chess game is uncertain. All in all, the Libyan RCC seems to have embarked upon an extraordinarily ambitious and wide-ranging foreign policy, involving proffered support for revolutionary and antiwestern movements in areas well beyond the Middle East.[41] This policy, apart from adding to already troubled situations in such widely scattered places as Uganda, the Persian Gulf, Northern Ireland, and Panama, can drain the nation's resources and, more obviously, overreach the limits of its own national experience and stature. It is not unrealistic to imagine that Egypt's leadership may weary of having to calm or conciliate the Libyan leader, though Sadat has recurrent problems

[40] *Africa Report,* December, 1969, "Libyan Revolution Sorts Itself Out," by Charles E. Brown. See also William Lewis's article: "The Western Sahara-Suez Triangle," *Current History,* pp. 121–124, March, 1973.

[41] In his fiery speech of June 11, 1972, Qaddafi lashed out at what he called the "hated American imperialism," declared solidarity with the Black Muslim movement in the U.S., promised support for the Irish revolutionaries, denounced Britain and Iran for the latter's occupation of "Arab islands" in the Persian Gulf. Since then he has threatened to intervene in behalf of Uganda's General Amin against Tanzania-based Uganda exiles and has asserted a right to defend Muslim interests in the Philippines and to aid Panama in shaking off American control of the Canal Zone. (Text printed in Appendix J, pp. 223–235, in *The States of North Africa,* Joint Hearings before the Subcommittees on Africa and the Near East of the House of Representatives, 1972.)

with his own military and Libyan subsidies are important to Egypt's defense and development budgets. Egypt, however, now has financial aid from Saudi Arabia.

On the domestic front, where the Libyan system's longer-range future will probably be decided, pre-existing political parties are banned. Labor organizations, though tolerated, are expected to conform to the revolutionary spirit and Arab Socialist-Islamic programs of the regime. The RCC has created a national political movement intended to mobilize people from all classes, an Arab Socialist Union for Libya, modeled after that of Egypt. It is difficult to discern the generation of widespread popular support for or participation in this movement. There are also important and divisive regional differences in Libya. Efforts to unite with another Arab neighbor could aggravate such differences, though expanded economic opportunity, better housing, and improved social welfare measures help to encourage national solidarity. Libyans, perhaps as a result of their modern history, are known for their tendency toward xenophobic reactions, sometimes even where fellow Arabs are concerned.

There was a reorganization of the Libyan government in July, 1972, with the new cabinets, headed by Major Jalloud of the RCC, containing more civilians than previously. Had Quddafi's own position and policies been losing ground within the military's Revolutionary Command Council, and were these changes the symptoms of an emerging political crisis? Any such inference was quickly repudiated by Qaddafi, who pointed out that he would remain as head of the RCC and that he would, in due course, assume the title of President. Since then the militancy of Libyan foreign policy has been intensified, and additional stress has been laid on stricter Arabization (or further dewesternization) and on more rigid observance of traditionalistic Muslim orthodoxy in all aspects of national life.[42] This hardly suggests weakening of Qaddafi's policies within the military control group so far. The ministerial changes may even have been intended, in part, to prod the Libyan administration into more productive work on the problems of Libyan-Egyptian union, on which joint national commissions were supposed to have been at work. Now, Qaddafi seems to be interested in Tunisia.

Renewed Libyan militancy in the international arena has been exhibited in a number of developments. Its championship of the revolutionary Palestinian cause, extending to what much of the outside world can only regard as protection or encouragement of Palestinian terrorists, reflects that trend. In March 1973, one month after Israeli jet fighters shot down a Libyan commercial airliner apparently lost over Sinai, east of the Canal, Libyan Mirage fighters fired upon an American Air Force C-130 electronic intelligence plane in international air space 80 miles off the Libyan coast. Libya

[42] *Washington Post,* April 16, 1973.

seems to be claiming a 70-mile "security zone" beyond its shores, ostensibly on the basis of fears of possible Israeli raids into Libya. Their tendency to insist upon identifying American policy with Israeli actions or possible intentions is obvious, if misguided.

Disconcerting, of course, to the Israelis is the reported transfer of a number of Libya's French-built Mirage jet fighter-bombers to Egypt, or perhaps, rather, to Libyan air facilities at Egyptian bases, in April, 1973. France denies that such a shift in location under existing conditions amounts to a violation of the terms of the original sales agreement barring the handing over of such planes to any country directly involved in the Arab-Israeli conflict.[43] Libya did give air support only to Egypt during the recent October war.

Despite its large oil-industry revenues, the Libyan economy remains unbalanced, suffering from inadequate infrastructure and faulty contact between its various regions. Urban unemployment is still a significant problem, as migration from the depressed and unproductive interior to the cities continues. The military regime has expanded educational opportunities and launched new industrialization and development plans. There has been growth, as elsewhere in North Africa, of the civilian technician or managerial class needed to administer the country's development. But such a class is far from the position of partnership with the military attained by the technocrats and other office-holders in Algeria. The Libyan RCC has placed some civilians in ministerial posts, but there is little indication that they are afforded policy-making opportunities. Better defined and more permanent constitutional and institutional structures would engender a stronger claim to legitimacy for whatever system evolves out of the present military regime. All this, however, depends on what follows fading plans for Libyan-Egyptian union and on priorities such as between ambitious international ventures and the need for social and economic advancement at home. Apart from the military, no other cohesive or self-confident political force of national scope and purpose now exists, and none seems likely to be in a position to claim any share of power in the near future.

THE SUDAN

When the Sudan became independent in 1956 its army, trained and equipped by the British, was one of the best and most professional of all the armies in ex-colonial Africa. Enroute to independence, the army and the civil service were progressively Africanized. The new state began with more dependable performance from these two services than was the case

[43] *Ibid.*, April 11, 1973.

in most of the other African states. The army's rapid expansion, from 12,000 officers and men in 1958 to nearly 35,000 by 1970-71, was due largely to the rebellion in the non-Muslim, non-Arab South. Yearly defense expenditures more than doubled over that period.[44] Over half of the army was usually committed in the three rebellious southern provinces. With expansion and the influx of large numbers of junior officers, frustration grew over the interminable rebellion, and impatience mounted over internal army administration (pay and promotion policies, for example). At the same time political ideas, especially those emanating from Egypt, exercised considerable attraction. As the country seemed torn in purpose, younger army officers became exposed to competing ideologies or visions of the nation's destiny.

The Sudan had become less a bridge than an "area of confrontation for the increasingly self-conscious Arab world and the vehemently nationalistic African world." [45] The army became as much a product of that confrontation as a vehicle for its pursuit.

From the 1950s onward, though usually operating underground or camouflaged as adherents of popular or "progressive" movements, the Communists made significant headway, particularly in Khartoum. They began to make converts or attract sympathizers at junior and middle levels within the army officer corps. A sort of limited partnership then developed between younger, radical army officers and their counterparts in the "popular organizations." Then General Abboud's military regime was forced out in 1964, opening the way to 5 years of civilian government under a coalition of leaders from the revived, traditional parties, which rested on powerful religious sects. The affinity between certain Marxist-oriented younger officers and leftist labor leaders, students, and intellectuals continued.[46]

Nimeiri, who came to power by army *coup* in 1969, unseating the ineffective civilian regime, focused major attention on attempts to conciliate the South. No communist sympathizer, he banned the Party after an initial period of relative permissiveness. On the other hand, he accentuated an anti-western posture, embraced more fully the radical Arab position on all Middle East problems, leaned on the Russians for arms supply and economic aid, and implied readiness to join the Cairo-Tripoli-Damascus constellation when the time was ripe.

It was nevertheless the residual left-wing or pro-Marxist segment of the army officer corps that, impatient with Nimeiri and distrustful of his aims, engineered the ill-fated *coup* of July 19-22, 1971. This collided with

[44] Hurewitz, p. 175, and I.S.S., 1971–72, *op. cit.*, p. 31.

[45] *Rivkin*, p. 37.

[46] See Colin Legum, in "Sudan's Three-Day Revolution," *Africa Report*, October 1971, p. 13; and Ruth First, "Sudan: Behind the Coups," in *Africa*, No. 3, 1971, p. 61.

the brand of pro-Egyptian and Arab-Socialist-oriented nationalism dominant in the officer and noncommissioned officer corps and was doomed to failure. No sympathetic, popular insurrection in the capital city, as hoped for by the *coup*-makers, occurred. The grand strategy behind the *coup* was evidently masterminded by the Communist Party Central Committee and its Chief, Maghoub, who had returned clandestinely from banishment, as brought out at his trial. They guessed wrong in their estimate that the Sudan was "ripe" for this kind of revolution.[47] Maghoub and other convicted ringleaders, military and civilian, were executed. Hopes of slowing or blocking Sudan's absorption into the prospective Egyptian-Libyan-Syrian federation, unpalatable to the Soviet Union, may also have figured in the calculations of the *coup*-makers.

Thereafter Nimeiri determined to give absolute priority to ending the civil war. He also all but crushed the communist apparatus in Sudan, cooled toward the tripartite federation, and began to readjust his international position. For the first time in over a decade and a half the Sudan is at peace with itself. The nation has been able to move toward a more representative constitutional system with a broader national base.[48] A regionally autonomous government has been set up at the southern town of Juba, headed by Sudan's Vice President Abel Alier, a southerner. Some relaxation of the former drastic nationalization policy has been evident in order to reassure or attract foreign investment. Several hundred thousand refugees of the southern region have returned from neighboring countries or from the bush to their home districts. Such diverse sources as the UN High Commissioner for Refugees, Algeria, Morocco, the United States, Protestant and Catholic relief services and a Persian Gulf sheikhdom are contributing money, food, or services to aid in the huge rehabilitation process. Several thousand members of the former Anya Nya rebel forces have been absorbed into the national army or the regional police force, pursuant to the Addis Ababa agreement of 1972 that ended the conflict. Major General Joseph Lagu, ex-leader of the Southern Sudan Liberation Movement (SSLM), has been readmitted to the Sudanese army with special responsibility for supervision of this integration process. He appears optimistic, and claims that neither part of the country wishes to see the Sudan join an Arab federation and that opinion even in the North now looks as much toward Africa as to the Arab world.[49]

Parallel with the drive for internal reconstruction, Nimeiri has moved pragmatically toward a more balanced and businesslike international position in both Arab affairs and larger world matters. This stance has produced

[47] Legum, "Sudan's Three-Day Revolution," *loc. cit.*

[48] *Africa,* No. 17, January, 1973, p. 30, and *New York Times,* May 12, 1973.

[49] *Ibid.,* No. 20, April, 1973, pp. 40–41.

annoyance in Egypt and bitter resentment in Libya. Nimeiri contended that these two neighbors have created problems, Egypt by neglecting adequate consultation with Sudan over policy toward Israel and by failing to provide proper support to Sudanese troops stationed in Egypt, Libya by highhandedness generally and by reckless charges that the Sudan is a tool of those trying to block Arab unity.[50] The Sudanese obviously believe there is some connection between Libya and the Palestinian terrorists who murdered the American ambassador, his deputy, and a Belgian diplomat in the savage takeover of the Saudi Arabian embassy in Khartoum (March 1-4, 1973). Relations between the Sudan and Libya worsened for a time, and Nimeiri threatened to ban Al Fatah activity in the Sudan. He had announced that the assassins would be tried for murder under Sudanese law. More recently there have been indications that—under pressure from opinion widely shared by Arabs within the Sudan and in other Middle East countries —prosecution might be delayed or diluted. The subsequent Israeli commando-execution raid in Beirut, the fratricidal clashes between Lebanese army and Palestinians, and the latest round of Arab-Israeli war put a somewhat different light on the matter.[51] Such weakening in Nimeiri's original resolve, if borne out in practice, can only create new frictions in U.S.-Sudanese relations, which were restored only in July 1972. The trials, when they come, will have close international attention. The Sudanese attitude toward Russia has been cool since the communist-inspired *coup* of 1971, but Khartoum has cultivated expanding contacts with the Chinese People's Republic, West Germany and Britain. It has even opened diplomatic ties with the Vatican, perhaps in response to the Catholic Church's participation in relief efforts in southern Sudan where so much of the population is Christian. Warmer ties are also being revived with a number of neighboring Sub-Sahara African states, especially Ethiopia, and Nimeiri voices increased support for the Organization of African Unity.

In a recent revealing interview with a correspondent for the magazine *Africa,* President Nimeiri made the following observations on civil-military relations in Africa:

> . . . Armies are generally sensitive institutions in their countries. I can only speak for the Sudan in this regard and affirm that our army is there for the OAU to command when it needs it, for we consider it an integral part of a pan-African Army. This, in essence, stems from our belief that armies of independent African countries must owe justification for their existence to the protection and preservation of independence in all its forms and the liberation of still racist-dominated areas of the continent.
>
> If there is lack of cooperation on the continent, it is not due to military

[50] *Ibid.,* No. 10, June, 1972, pp. 44–45.
[51] *Ibid.,* No. 17, January, 1973, pp. 34–38.

> versus civilian. This is more fostered by negative visions of power on the one hand and positive ones on the other. A civilian government, or a military one, I believe, has no right to rule if its vision is not geared to the betterment politically and economically of its masses. . . .[52]

Apart from the reference to some future structure for a Pan-African army under the OAU (Nkrumah's dream), the statement might also serve as the Sudanese leader's rationale for civil-military relations in the Middle East. National leaders are judged by their deeds as well as their words, and Sudan's army and government head must be judged by both. There is doubtless a considerable mixture of idealism and expediency, or simply of practical nationalistic politics in the words and actions of Nimeiri. On overall performance, however, on the extraordinary problems he faces, his return to moderation and his commitment to national reconciliation are encouraging signs in an area caught up in tensions.

CONCLUSION

The approach of this chapter was to examine and describe the nature of the respective national and military leaderships in the countries considered, with emphasis on how they have achieved prominence or dominance, to what ideological and political ends they shape their armies, and how they have sought to mold their military's sense of national mission and destiny. As the focus has been on performance or participation in the political and nation-building process, this chapter is more a study of domestic and international politics, without an atempt to amass detailed, comparative data on the social, economic, educational, or regional background of segments of these military systems. The analysis is set against the background of the broader international scene and *detentist* trends and what Professor Zartman calls the problem of "Unity of Ranks" vs. "Unity of Purpose" among Arab states where Israel and related problems are concerned.[53]

It is difficult and risky to generalize about the politics of so volatile an area as North Africa or to draw conclusions on the role of the military or other political phenomena that have provable validity for the region

[52] *Africa,* No. 21, May, 1973, pp. 26–27.

[53] J. C. Hurewitz (ed.), *Soviet-American Rivalry in the Middle East,* Academy of Political Science, New York, 1969 (pp. 75–76).

Since preparation of this chapter, Professor Zartman has brought out, as editor and major contributor, a unique, comprehensive book entitled: *Man, State and Society in the Contemporary Maghrib.* This new collection of essays on that area should prove indispensable to scholars, politico-military specialists and diplomatic practitioners concerned with North Africa.

as a whole. Even if our focus were exclusively on the *Maghrib,* as noted at the outset, the differences in post-World War II experience and in the types of national leadership which that experience has brought forth in Tunisia, Morocco, and Algeria are unmistakably reflected in the markedly different roles of the military in each of these nations. As between Libya and the Sudan, where army leadership is in charge and where, in each case, efforts are being made to create a single, national political movement (as Nasser did in Egypt during the sixties) internal conditions are vastly different, and the style and goals of their respective chiefs are in contrast.

In summing up the indications at hand, in awareness that the situation is fluid and that the time span over which interested observers can assess army-influenced systems in the area is relatively short, a few evaluative comments seem in order:

1. National and military leadership in most of the countries concerned (Libya is a partial exception) appear to recognize that they had better devote major attention and resources to internal development, social progress, stabilization of their regional and international positions, and, if possible, avoidance of conflict.

2. Over the short term, at least, prospects for orderly progress and pragmatic adjustment to emerging needs seem relatively good in such otherwise contrasting systems as those of Algeria, Tunisia, and the Sudan.

3. Militant Libya, with huge oil revenues to draw upon for an adventurous foreign policy and caught up in a relentless drive to forge a larger, more formidable Arab power system, with partnership with neighbors as a foundation, has become a major storm-center in the area; it may well find itself in trouble at home, with the possibility of a counter-*coup* from within the military itself, should present stringent domestic policies backfire or if determined opposition is encountered from a number of its Arab and African neighbors.

4. The Moroccan army, long the bulwark of the monarchy, and now aware that it holds the balance of power between King and opposition, is no longer screened away from the political scene. As its potential for reformist intervention has increased, its function as a stabilizing force in the region may have been impaired.

5. A conclusion somewhat intuitively reached (with the current Sudanese example in mind) is that military leadership—like that of civilians—is capable of learning from its experience and mistakes and sometimes shows equal capacity for setting realistic goals and pursuing them by pragmatic methods.

6. Algeria seems to possess both the means and the determination eventually to become the leading and strongest power in North Africa, at least west of Egypt; it appears bent on avoiding excesses or diversions that might compromise that prospect.

Since this chapter was prepared still another, and hopefully the last, round of Arab-Israeli warfare has erupted in the Middle East. Relations between the superpowers, concern of the industrialized and oil consuming states over the mounting energy crisis, questions of solidarity among Arab nations, speculation on possible modification of Israel's previously rather rigid position on territorial and related issues, UN involvement in renewed peacekeeping operations—all of these currents and factors have come into play. It is too early to attempt a measured assessment of the longer range political and military impact of the latest "round" on Middle East and North African politics and leadership. It is, in any case, beyond the scope of the present chapter. The crisis has, it might be noted, tended to increase public awareness of the growing importance of the North African countries and their region not only in the calculations of the major and the superpowers, but in those of their fellow Arab nations and of the Third World generally.

13

Civil-Military Relations in the People's Republic of China and Indonesia

LT. CHARLES R. D'AMATO, USNR

The purpose of this chapter is to make a comparative analysis of civil-military relations in China and Indonesia. In Indonesia, as in so many other parts of the underdeveloped world, the inability of modern civilian regimes to cope with or channel the various pressures toward "modernization," to develop their economies or to integrate disparate "primordial" [1] groups has enhanced the role of the military organization. In China, the inability of the civilian party to fulfill Mao Tse-tung's expectations for his society led him to give increasing responsibilities to the military. On first impression one might surmise that the hierarchical characteristics of the typical military organization, together with such typically military traits as discipline, dispatch, loyalty, and accountability, would prove beneficial to a developing country. One might conclude that such traits equip an army with inherent advantages over civilian bureaucracies, parties, or charismatic leaders.

During the last several decades in both nations, the military—particularly the army—has played an even more important political role, and at present these armies sit at the hearts of their respective polities. The People's Liberation Army of China has played a dramatic and central role in keeping the "revolution" in China alive, has taken an increasingly more powerful political role in the 1960s, and has been set up as an ideological model for the rest of Chinese society. The Indonesian army came to power under highly unusual circumstances and is presently committed to a program of rapid economic change. Civilian-military relations in both countries are complicated and in a state of becoming.

Perhaps the central question these case studies revolve around is this:

[1] A term used by Clifford Geertz in his article, widely quoted, "The integrative revolution," in Geertz (ed.), *Old Societies and New States* (N.Y.: Free Press, 1963), pp. 105–158.

in the underdeveloped world, can military organizations be more successful in bringing "modernity" to these countries than various forms of civilian regimes? How successful has the military been in the third world in bringing economic development, political maturity, and a sense of "nation" over more basic diversity or givens within the society? Two related questions are: How successful can armies be in cajoling civilian organizations to work with them and yet not share in the heights of political power? How willing and able are armies to share political power (or, as in China, be a willing instrument of political power) so that genuinely stable relationships with skilled civilian groups can be formed?

One must be careful in generalizing about military organizations. Indeed, as these cases develop, we will find many significant differences among the complexions, goals, and attitudes of the armies in question. Clearly, attempts at sweeping theories concerning the viability of military regimes, like other experiences in theorizing about the underdeveloped world, are probably doomed to failure at this stage of our knowledge and research. Two decades after independence, it is now clear that the development process is much tougher than was originally thought and that military organizations do not possess any formulae that easily bypass the stupendous problems that proved insoluble for civilian regimes. Gunnar Myrdal, the author of undoubtedly the most exhaustive study of development in Asia, has found the state of theory on development in this area in a state of shambles. "Never," he writes, "have I felt so far from being able to present something resembling the final truths about a matter." Many of the theories he examined were founded on a slim basis of facts, most of which were crude guesses and often wrong. "Worse," he continues,

> . . . as I worked on I became increasingly aware that many of the concepts and theories commonly used in analyzing the problems of the underdeveloped countries of South Asia broke down when criticized from the point of view of their logical consistency and their realism, that is, their adequacy to reality.
>
> . . . I sincerely believe that at the present stage an important contribution to the advance of knowledge about these countries is the negative act of destroying constructs that we have rapidly put together and exposing to criticism masses of more or less worthless statistics collected within the framework of these constructs, which we are using all too confidently. I believe this because these constructs and statistics now stand in the way of scientific progress.[2]

Where specific ethnic groups in Asian countries are concerned, even their central governments have a very imperfect understanding of the characteristics of these people that could effectively be utilized to help integrate

[2] Gunnar Myrdal, *Asian Drama,* Vol. I (N.Y.: Pantheon, 1968), pp. xi–xii.

them into a more national culture. Westerners engaged in research may understand even less.[3]

Perhaps even more importantly for this analysis, there is a great lack of detailed studies on the internal dynamics of the military organizations in question, their activities, and their relations with specific civilian institutions and groups in both countries.

With these provisos, let us proceed to a discussion of Asian armies in politics and draw up some modest generalizations concerning the role of armies in development and civil-military relations in Indonesia and China.

CHINA

Civil-military relations in mainland China today can be understood only in the context of the way in which the communists came to power and in light of the fact that those who led the struggle against the Nationalist Chinese still occupy the seats of power.[4]

In analyzing civil-military relations in China, it is difficult to make any fundamental distinction between what is "military" and what is "civil." The dividing line is not usually clear, and the overlap in function has been without parallel in any other communist system. As Edgar Snow has remarked, "All China is a great school of Mao Tse-tung Thought and the Army is its headmaster. 'We are all connected with the Army,' said Premier Chou En-lai, and he might have added, 'the Army connects all of us.' "[5] Chou, generally considered at the time of this writing (1973) to have solidified his control over China's political system after an unsuccessful attempt at *coup d'etat* by Defense Minister Lin Piao, was himself at one time a general in the Army. The army has just experienced a purge of major proportions in its upper echelon, yet its prestige remains high and unimpaired. In its modernization process, Chinese society has been penetrated from above as never before and "militarized" in an organizational sense. Its language has been

[3] Lee Huff, who has worked extensively with the Thai in the northeast area of Thailand, for instance, remarks that "very little is known about the basic characteristics of target audiences exposed to government development programs. In particular, there is inadequate recognition that many of the populations involved have been undergoing considerable change and that perhaps older 'basic characteristics' have indeed been replaced by new ones." See Lee W. Huff, "Thai Mobile Development Unit Program," in Kunstadter (ed.), *Southeast Asian Tribes, Minorities and Nations* (Princeton, N.J.: Princeton Univ. Press, 1967), p. 472.

[4] The average age of 118 of the 170 full members of the 9th Central Committee is 61.4 years, with only 3.4% below the age of 50. *Current Scene,* Vol. IX, No. 2, Feb. 7, 1971, p. 6.

[5] Edgar Snow, "The Army and the Party," *New Republic,* May 22, 1972 (U.S. and world copyright), p. 9.

one of discipline to doctrine and externalization of personal motivation, but it is not militaristic in the Prussian sense. An old China hand like John Service has remarked that the PLA is an "oddly unmilitary army. One never sees units of marching men, or hears a military band." Everyone wears the "same shapeless, unstarched and unpressed cotton uniform." [6] There is, then, no hint of spit and polish, of swagger and strut. As Snow points out:

> From Kindergarten up, China's schools are organized in squads, companies and brigades. So are factories and communes. And all able-bodied adults see service in the militia, run by the Army. But it is the first duty of the PLA to propagate Mao's Thought, which is not *Mein Kampf*. It contains no doctrines of racism, foreign conquest or the export of revolution. At home it teaches liberation through class revolution as well as service to the people and preparedness against war.[7]

The range of roles and duties played by the PLA in Chinese society today is staggering. As far as performing functional work and getting along with society, the PLA has no rival in the world. The range of its tasks and its intimacy with the peasant society is constantly stressed by the leadership, is firmly entrenched in the doctrine, and constantly remarked upon by visitors. Service calls the PLA the "paragon of civic virtue and the model of political reliability." He claims joining the PLA is the top career goal among high school seniors.[8] "Any visitor to China," says Snow, "can quickly see that the armed forces are popular. The Soldier's public behavior is exemplary and among the people he seldom carries arms." [9] According to Tilman Durdin, the 2.8 million members of 1972's armed forces do a multitude of "civilian" jobs:

> They grow vegetables, raise pigs, operate small factories and state farms, reclaim waste land, spread Mao Thought, act as adjudicators of political orthodoxy in universities, and do manual labor with workers and peasants on dam projects, on farms and in steel mills.[10]

Does this mean that the army is more civic organization than anything else, that it does not contain a body of officers with definite points of view counterposed to other organizations? It would be deceiving to maintain the civic-action model. The PLA has a pride of its own, though it is not clear how unified it has been over time, how definite the allegiances of personalities to the top national leaders has been, or what relationship has developed over time between regional powers and national leadership.

[6] John Service, editorial, *New York Times,* Jan. 27, 1972.

[7] Snow, *op. cit.,* p. 10.

[8] *New York Times,* Jan. 26, 1972.

[9] Snow, *op. cit.*

[10] Tilman Durdin, "China's politicized armed forces are performing a host of civilian tasks in farms, schools and factories," *New York Times,* Feb. 17, 1972.

Controversies within China over undue bureaucratization of the military have focused on the question of "professionalism" in the Chinese officer corps and the relationships over the years between party leaders and professional military officers and within the career officer corps over the propriety of professionalism itself.[11] It seems to make analytical sense to view the army as one of several layers Mao has used to develop his dream of a highly conscious, dynamic (i.e., "revolutionary") society basically motored by spontaneous initiative or mass action from the local levels. A power struggle between the civil and military organizations is not the central issue; the issue is which organizations and groups can be relied upon to fulfill Mao's goals. Over time, several organizations failed, or succeeded and then failed; the spotlight shifted. This in itself is not inconsistent with Mao's goals. He has feared the Djilas-described development[12] of centralized bureaucracies that accumulate more and more power in society and in which powerful elites grow, vie for power, and rob initiative from the mass level. Mao believes this phenomenon has occurred in the Soviet Union, and most analysts would quickly agree. He has thus fought the tendency of the major institutions in China—the party, the army, and the state bureaucracy—to mature into settled, plodding organizations and has displayed his willingness to throw them into chaos to achieve his goal.

Generally speaking, "professionalism" connotes an officer corps with a high degree of training in a wide range of military specialities, associated with military technologies and weapons systems. The complexity of these technologies and systems usually means years of training, study, and experience. It is considered important in the American military, for instance, to be considered a "real professional," to be an expert on and proficient manager of one or another of America's sophisticated weapons systems and platforms, to be part of a community of officers associated with that technology, and to become deeply involved in the further development of those systems. The process of military modernization China embarked upon in 1949 would appear logically to cause the growth of communities of such officers in the Chinese military.

There were two difficulties for the officers involved in this growth. First, the political demands made by Maoism—the "struggle sessions" through which one was supposed to raise one's understanding of what needs doing and to raise one's "revolutionary consciousness"—interfered with the task of military modernization in the narrow sense. Second, Joffe argues that

[11] An excellent study on this topic is by Ellis Joffe, *Party and Army: Professionalism and Political Control in the Chinese Officer Corps, 1949–64* (Boston: East Asia Research Center, Harvard Univ., 1965).

[12] See the classic indictment of the Communist system by Milovan Djilas in *The New Class* (New York: Praeger, 1962).

> professionally oriented officers have developed views and values which in some basic respects differ drastically from those of the politically oriented party leaders and the officers who support the leadership's point of view. This divergence of views has brought part of the army into conflict with the party on a number of issues.[13]

This conflict, Joffe maintains, is between generations, that is, between the veteran leaders of the "guerrilla generation" and a younger group of officers who tend to be more "professional." Though both generations are members of the party and all agree on the necessity for military modernization, there is a crucial difference of emphasis. Those who emphasize politics are termed more "red," the others more "expert." An additional problem in the course of modernization has been the privileges granted by the regime to the developing professional army, creating (as the 1950s wore on) a visible class of officers differentiated from the population at large and from the enlisted ranks. Their privileged status tended to make some of the officers "caste-conscious." [13A]

During the revolutionary war the Army was anything but professional in the way we have used the term. The nature of the conflict with the more mechanized Nationalists and Japanese necessitated an irregular army that was very democratic in character, that is, the relationship between officers and men was close. The men were treated very "fairly and respectfully," and criticism and self-criticism of leaders in open meetings was common. This was in accord with Maoist doctrine of the "mass line," in which leading cadres (activists) were enjoined to go to the masses to receive knowledge, act on that knowledge, and return to the masses to implement party decisions in an intimate and educative fashion.

There were no outward formal distinctions between enlisted men and officers, such as the wearing of ranks and insignia. There was no difference in wages. Men were encouraged to voice suggestions on the conduct of military affairs before the battles and review the results afterwards.[14] The war also necessitated extremely close liaison between the guerrilla forces and the population. In Mao's famous phrase the army was the "fish" that to survive had to be at home in the "sea" of China's masses. It meant close attention to public relations and to development of popular militia forces that supported the guerrillas. It meant popular mobilization on a mass scale. The *political* allegiance of the masses was inseparable from *military* success. It meant, ultimately, then, very tight political control over the armed forces. In addition, because of the decentralization of organization during the revolution, the army often had to support itself by engaging in agricultural

[13] Joffe, *op. cit.*, p. x.
[13A] *Ibid.*
[14] *Ibid.*, 1, pp. 31–32.

and production work. Tight central control of the armed forces was impossible.

This revolutionary model of intimate relations with the masses, the pre-eminence of politics, self-sufficiency, decentralization of control, and democratic behavior within the armed forces was of absolute necessity prior to 1949.

Further and very important, the political control system developed during the revolutionary era served as a workable tool of the party leadership down until Mao lost faith in the party in the middle and late 1960s. The system consisted of political commissars attached to military units, theoretically down to the platoon level, who had authority over the military leaders and responsibility for conducting education and propaganda, enforced "democracy" in the company and good relations with the local population. Party branches were organized down to the company level as early as 1928.[15]

If one were to pin down the basic relationship between civil and military organizations, one would have to start from Mao's premise that "political power grows out of the barrel of a gun. Our principle is that the party commands the gun and the gun shall never be allowed to command the party." [16] The doctrine is elaborated as follows:

> The Chinese People's Liberation Army is an armed organization built by the Chinese Communist Party to win victory in the revolution and realize socialism and Communism in China. Only under the leadership of the Party can our army grow into a powerful people's army, win victory in revolutionary wars, and fulfill the glorious task of defending the motherland. Whenever our army separates itself from the Party leadership, the revolutionary cause will suffer a loss. For this reason, we must resolutely fight against all tendencies towards separation from Party leadership. We must enforce a system of Party leadership.[17]

The classic statement on party control of the army was made by Mao at a conference of the Fourth Red Army at Kutien in Fukien Province in 1929. It disparaged the "purely military viewpoint which saw political and military affairs in opposition to each other," and emphasized political control from top to bottom. Political work was "regarded as a totality which embraces all aspects of the army's everday life, of its cultural, educational and sparetime activities." [18] Central Party leaders were to maintain control over the military leadership, ensuring that party policies were carried out.

[15] John Gittings, *The Role of the Chinese Army* (London: Oxford University Press, 1967), pp. 102–103.

[16] *Selected Writings of Mao Tse-tung* (Peking, 1963), p. 272.

[17] *Chieh-fang-chün Pao* (Liberation Army Newspaper), editorial, July 1, 1958 (XCMP 1881), as quoted in Gittings, *op. cit.*, p. 99.

[18] *Ibid.*, p. 105.

Two hierarchies were developed, separate from each other, to fulfill these functions. First, a system of party committees was developed extending down in parallel to the military organization, and reporting up a separate chain of command ending in the Military Affairs Committee of the Party Central Committee. Second, a hierarchy termed the "Political Department" was made part of the Army hierarchy and reported from the Political Office of the regiment up to the General Political Department of the PLA. It implemented the decisions of the party committee and "is responsible for the detailed implementation of measures intended to educate the rank and file of the army." [19]

Additionally, of course those officers who wished to succeed became party members, adding another safeguard to the political control system. This system worked as designed during the revolution, especially in light of the fact that there was great overlap between military commanders and political commissars.

The First Post-Revolutionary Decade

Between 1949 and 1959, this revolutionary model atrophied in favor of a more narrow-minded officer corps, preoccupied with professionalism. In particular, very heavy losses of men during the Korean war drove home the necessity for mechanization to the leadership.[20] In place of revolutionary focus on the human or political factors in conflict came an emphasis on weapons, technologies, and professionalism. At the same time came massive aid from the Soviet Union and, as in other fields (especially in the first part of the decade), close copying of the Soviet model of a more hierarchical military. Military modernization thus proceeded apace up until 1960. The military drifted from its intimacy with society, and its previous self-sufficiency declined. In place of the irregular, democratic revolutionary era came regularization, more rigid hierarchies, obvious ranks and insignia, and specialties. Conscription was introduced, as was the "distinction between the amateur citizen-soldier and the professional officer." [21] There developed a resistance to agricultural and production work, i.e., "nonprofessional" tasks. Thus developed a contradiction between the needs of modern defense and the doctrinal desire to preserve a revolutionary army under tight political control.[22] Centralization of the armed forces was brought about by the creation of a very powerful Military Affairs Committee under the Party Central Committee.

During the revolutionary era political control of the army was epit-

[19] *Ibid.*, p. 110.

[20] Gittings suggests a casualty figure of, very roughly, 600,000. *Ibid.*, p. 76.

[21] Joffe, p. 39.

[22] See Gittings for an excellent discussion of this conflict.

omized by the fact that there was "little to distinguish the political from the military leaders. The top military commanders were in almost every case important leaders of the party, while even party leaders who held no direct command played key roles in the direction of military affairs." Modernization meant a division of function in the leadership, as is the case in all societies where the military does not control the polity (Indonesia being an example of the opposite). The division was between, on the one hand, the professional leaders who implement decisions and those veterans who have become professionals in the course of modernization, and, on the other hand, the top policy-makers who are the veteran guerrilla leaders whose views coincide with the revolutionary model.[23]

By the mid-1950s the army had moved well in the direction of the professional model and had lost much of its intimacy with the party and the masses. As the strong relationship between officers and men had weakened, "democracy" was no longer prevalent. The party viewed these developments with concern and as a result during this period introduced various campaigns to counter them. The campaigns grew in intensity from 1956 to 1959, and the extent of professional opposition was revealed dramatically when changes occurred in the military leadership in 1959, including the purging of Marshal P'eng Teh-huai, Minister of Defense and head of the Military Affairs Committee. He was relieved by Marshal Lin Piao. The specific issue underlying the dispute was one's attitude toward the relative importance of men and weapons in a modern military establishment. The professionals argued that technological factors predominate over humans, in contrast to the revolutionary period, which in their view was a situation no longer applicable to the present world situation. Lin charged that these officers felt that men and political considerations were no longer critical factors. The party leaders and their supporters in the military argued the revolutionary model still stood, that as men will always be superior to machines, the political factor—mobilizing and educating the men—is decisive.[24] These men do not disparage technology—witness the continuing expenditures to catch up to the major powers in the fields of nuclear weapons and delivery systems. Yet the revolutionary experience instructs them that the human factor will win even against significant technological odds. Given the difference in emphasis it seems that the hierarchy of political controls in the army irritated the professionals over time and led to disputes.

The party also became concerned with the behavior of some caste-conscious officers toward the people, charging that the officers treated the people arrogantly. Further, it became clear that many officers resented the party's use of the army for nonmilitary production tasks. The party, how-

[23] Joffe, pp. 44–45.
[24] *Ibid.*, p. 49.

ever, remained committed to this usage because it was considered vital to the economic development, necessary for the proper political conditioning of the army, and kept the troops close to the masses.[25]

The campaign against professionalism reached new intensity in conjunction with the Sino-Soviet dispute and the Great Leap Forward in the later 1950s. Now that it was clear that the Soviet Union was not going to provide nuclear weapons and technology, the revolutionary model of people's war was reemphasized. The militia was expanded. P'eng Te-huai was accused of "modern revisionism," which meant that his erroneous line of thinking called for ideological concessions to the Soviets in order to obtain further Soviet aid. He apparently was also guilty of opposing the economic policies of the Great Leap and right political control over the military.[26] It is certain that the political control system had deteriorated very significantly. Decision-making by many party branches was turned over to the military commanders, and party branches met irregularly.

In reaffirming the revolutionary model the party leaders in the late 1950s strengthened its indoctrination of the professional officers and attempted to beef up its political control system. This was done by requiring that numerous courses on doctrine be taken by officers and by attempting to strengthen the party branches associated with the army. Campaigns against bureaucratism (isolation from the masses) and autocratic behavior by officers were developed by the General Political Department. Measures were taken to reduce the obvious difference in living standards between the officers and the population at large. Dependents, for example, were moved on a massive scale off military bases and told to go back to their home villages. In 1957 the "officers to the ranks" movement was inaugurated, in which officers were required to spend a month each year working at the basic military levels as common soldiers. Such a campaign would be considered highly inefficient in modern armies and signifies the seriousness with which the leadership believed in its revolutionary model. Lin Piao's leadership was dedicated to political renewal, and it took him several years before Mao was satisfied that he had decisively reversed the tide of affairs and, in fact, had reinvigorated the primacy of politics and attention to ideology so well that

[25] *Ibid.*, p. 87.

[26] *Ibid.*, p. 108. Joffe's source for this is the *Kung-tso t'ung-hsun* (bulletin of activities), high-level internal Chinese documents obtained by the West through intelligence sources. Partly because of these documents analysts in the West have been able to determine that these debates did go on and that public statements of doctrine by the Chinese on the question of the primacy of men and politics genuinely reflect the real thinking of the Chinese leadership, i.e., they are not propaganda smokescreens covering other considerations. For an analysis of these documents see Ralph Powell, *Politico-Military Relationships in Communist China* (U.S. Department of State, Washington, D.C.: Policy Research Study, External Research Staff Bureau of Intelligence and Research, Oct., 1963).

the nation as a whole was exhorted in 1964 to "learn from the PLA." There was nothing new, ideologically speaking, in these campaigns; it was an intense reaffirmation of Mao's Kutien philosophy. Its extent was symbolized in 1965 by the abolition of ranks and insignia and the awards that had been established in the 1950s.[27]

The PLA was used from this time forward, especially during the Cultural Revolution, as the model for the civilian organizations and even the population at large to follow to enable them to root out elements of "revisionism." The PLA's Political Department structure was introduced in industrial enterprises and government bureaucracies in the hope that the revolutionary spirit would permeate the civilian sector as well.

The Cultural Revolution and Its Aftermath

If the political sins of the army in the 1950s were rectified by Lin in the early 1960s, Mao's general concern that revolutionary fervor and local dynamism were disintegrating in China grew. His attention turned from the military to the civilian sector, and the techniques used to rectify the situation became more severe. In his view, the party was becoming corrupted: it was now becoming a status-oriented organization with privileged elites and caste-consciousness. It had become institutionalized and bogged down in bureaucratic procedures. It was, therefore, "bourgeois" and "revisionist." The ideology, it can be assumed, was being treated in a more perfunctory way. In fact, in the Party, a crisis of confidence in Mao's policies had grown from the failure of the Great Leap. As is well known, chaos had been the result of the Great Leap in the economy: what with the attempt at "backyard furnaces," the disparagement of statistics, and the lack of careful central economic planning, the process of growth that had reached a reasonably impressive stage by 1957 slowed to the point of near stagnation in the early 1960s. Clearly the focus on the revolutionary model had been at the expense of modernization in the conventional sense. It was again necessary to arouse mass support for Mao's programs, and if the Party dragged its heels in implementing his policies, then the party must be cleansed. As Mao later

[27] Again, it should be noted that both conventional and nuclear technologies developed apace, though it is not clear to what extent, if any, they have been held up by the political campaigns. Suffice it to say that by 1972 the West "conservatively estimated that China has at least 50 to 100 tactical nuclear weapons in her arsenal. Other estimates range two to three times that high, based on the fact that China now has three plants turning out uranium and plutonium of a grade suitable for producing weapons." Additionally, her delivery systems have proceeded seemingly untroubled by political events: she has already deployed operational medium-range (600 mile) and intermediate-range (1500 mile) missiles. William Beecher in *New York Times*, July 25, 1972.

stated, he had delegated substantial political power to the party leaders and stepped back from direct control of events. That is, he stepped back into the "second line" while Liu Shao-chi and Secretary-General of the Party Teng Hsiao-ping moved into the "first line." In 1962 Mao abolished the second line, reverting to the tactic of using the mass movement from below to support his actions.[28]

Interestingly enough, though the army was now adjudged politically loyal and a willing tool, Mao returned to his basic faith in mass action first. The intent was to free society from the stifling overlay of a bureaucratic party and somehow allow a dynamism to develop, particularly among the younger generation, that would bring out worthy revolutionary successors, tempered in an environment (however artificial) of struggle. The ultimate object of the struggle became the revisionist civilian organizations. The basic idea was to create a "new Communist man, imbued with proletarian consciousness and able to act in all social roles. . . . persons in all walks of life—soldiers, laborers, peasants, intellectuals, party cadres, and others—should be trained in politics, culture, and military affairs so as to become useful in industry, agriculture, and warfare, or whatever else was needed." [29]

At first the Party was in charge of this revolution, but Mao perceived that the party's inherent conservatism was stifling the campaign within bounds or order, to stem the developing chaos in which persons in positions of authority in all walks of life were "struggled against," sometimes verbally, sometimes violently. Mao's reaction then was to confer authority directly on the masses, sanctioning attacks by "revolutionary students" on the party itself.

By the end of 1966, the mantle was removed from the Red Guards and placed on "Revolutionary Rebels" (adult workers). Workers were urged to remove "capitalistic" influences in industry by setting up revolutionary councils. The Red Guards were warned by Chou En-lai not to interfere with the economy. The relaxation of party control opened the society to the development of numerous conflicting organizations and groups, all acting ostensibly in the name of Mao. The original organization directing the Cultural Revolution consisted of (1) Cultural Revolution committees selected by the "revolutionary masses" in schools, factories, villages, and other organizations to provide general guidance to the Red Guard units; (2) a top-level Cultural Revolution Group of the Central Committee led by Mao and his new associates, which was to provide general guidance; and (3) inter-

[28] See W.A.C. Adie, "China's Second Liberation in Perspective," in *China After the Cultural Revolution* (a selection from the Bulletin of Atomic Scientists, New York: Vintage Press, 1970), pp. 27–57.

[29] Unpublished directive by Mao of 7 May 1966 as discussed by William F. Dorrill, in "Power, Policy and Ideology," in Thomas W. Robinson (ed.), *The Cultural Revolution in China* (Berkeley: University of California Press, 1971), p. 93.

mediate-level ad hoc Cultural Revolution committees composed of party members loyal to Mao whose function was unclear. In practice, the differentiation between who was and was not loyal to Mao was difficult to make. For several months there was a great deal of violence. Resistance to the Red Guard units was greater than Mao expected and his tactics shifted in the direction of discipline and the protection of production. We see again, as in the Great Leap, the dictates of Mao's revolutionary model at conflict with the process of economic development.

The resistance put up initially by the Party organization indicated it had wide support in the society. The Revolutionary Rebel campaign was as indecisive as the Red Guard campaign, and confusion grew: for example, in Shanghai alone there were 31 Revolutionary Rebel and Red Guard organizations. There were reports of Rebels striking for higher wages and better economic conditions, rather than concerning themselves with politics at all. By the beginning of 1967 the Army had intervened and initiated a more orderly policy. Former provincial and municipal administrations were replaced by Revolutionary Committees based on a "triple alliance" of Revolutionary Rebels, Army men, and "cadres" (reliable party members). The upshot of these developments was army control of the situation. Within the next two years, as new organs of administration were developed, the PLA might have disengaged itself from politics. Instead, it played an increasingly greater role in a wide range of tasks and institutions in the civilian sector.

Some sense of the events of the late 1960s was provided by Lin Piao in his report to the 9th Party Congress in April of 1969. It is evident that it was not formal organized opposition to Mao that forced him into these drastic measures but his perception of what was needed to maintain life in his ideological beliefs. The Cultural Revolution cannot be explained as a classic power struggle. As Lin described it, the problem was how to arouse the creativity of the masses to progress along the road to socialism and increase their revolutionary consciousness. One social group after another was allowed to have its head to achieve these goals; all fell short. Finally, Lin concludes, the revolution was saved by the PLA and by a revolutionary upsurge among the workers.[30]

A preliminary result was enhanced army visibility, as reflected in the statistical breakdown of the composition of the 9th Central Committee: Representation for civilian organizations dropped from nearly 75% of the full members in the 8th Central Committee to just under 50% of the 9th, while representatives from military organizations rose from 25% to 47%. Furthermore, there is a sharing of political power between center and region;

[30] See John Gittings, "Lin Piao's Gospel," *Far Eastern Economic Review,* May 8, 1969.

representation of national-level organizations dropped from almost 70% in the 8th Central Committee to about 40% in the 9th, while 45% of the members "hold positions on regional Revolutionary Committees, suggesting the rising prestige of regional leadership. Further representation of regional military organization rose from a mere two percent in the 8th Central Committee to 25% in the 9th." [31]

Also revealing in the statistics of the 9th Central Committee is the percentage of "revolutionary successors" in the body. Despite the hoopla over renewing revolutionary dynamism we find that in comparing this Committee to that of the 7th in *1945* that "Mao's much-heralded inner core remains largely intact. There is no significant cluster of men of relative youth who hold significant posts." [32]

By 1969 the army had widened its arm of activity in the civilian sector very significantly. It was heavily represented in the Party Central Committee, was the dominant partner in the Revolutionary Committees at the provincial level and below, and "has apparently played a commanding role in the rebuilding of the civilian Party apparatus at the grass roots." [33] Though the rebuilding of the party went rather slowly, it seems that the new party committees will be heavily influenced by the people in uniform (though not necessarily the military as an organized and unified interest group). This massive entry of the army into the party constituted, certainly, a fundamental reversal of the relationship between party and army that had been dogma since the Kutien speech. The army "intimately mingled with the life of the nation and the party," according to *Le Monde*. For instance the army took direct control of the armament industry. And, in the autumn of 1971, of the 29 party first secretaries in the provinces and municipalities, 20 were career soldiers.

> The interpenetration of the state, the army, and the party was such that one wondered whether the country was not governed by a college where melted together the civil, military, and party influences. Lin Piao himself incarnated the new conglomerate since he was at once, Vice President of the Party, Deputy Prime Minister, and Minister of Defense. . . .[34]

Despite this upsurge in military influence, however, it became clear that, from a policy point of view, there were strong elements of moderation in the army as well as in the party. By 1969 the political environment was

[31] Jurgen Domes, "The Ninth CCP Central Committee in Statistical Perspective," in *Current Scene,* vol. IX, no. 2, Feb. 7, 1971, pp. 11–12.

[32] Donald W. Klein and Lois B. Hager, "The Ninth Central Committee," *China Quarterly,* no. 45, Jan.–March 1971, pp. 39, 42.

[33] "Mainland China 1970: Old Problems and New Solutions," by the editors of *Current Scene,* Vol. IX, no. 2, Feb. 7, 1971, p. 2.

[34] Alain Bouc in *Le Monde,* July 29, 1972.

extremely confused. Military district commanders were warned to refrain from "declaring mass organizations 'counter-revolutionary' without prior approval from Central authorities," and from discriminating against civilians. The army, it can be concluded from various directives from the Party Central Committee and the Central Military Affairs Commission, had "failed to properly execute its Maoist mandate to aid the revolutionary leftists in many—if not most—instances of local factional conflict." In fact the army was playing factional politics, and in many instances there had been military support for "conservative forces." It has been argued that by the end of 1968 the revolutionary left had declined as the "major force in local politics in China." [35]

The 9th Congress indicated compromise and an attempt at national unity. In such an inconclusive situation, the power broker, who was Chou En-lai, apparently had the most decisive influence on policy. Chou wore several hats on center stage during the Cultural Revolution:

> Chou was at the center of almost every important Cultural Revolution decision . . . for several months he was the organizer of and chief consultant to the Red Guards. Occasionally he played a role in the military. He centered in himself China's foreign policy. At times he evidently ran several ministries when their heads were under criticism or purged. Chou thus stood between the government bureaucracy, the Party ideologue, the youthful revolutionary, and the military activist turned governor.[36]

We shall see later that Chou was able to capitalize on the fact that the military was not unified in purpose or organization, that significant elements of moderation were to be found in both civilian and military institutions, and that there seemed to be a general willingness to compromise to bring a measure of needed stability to China's policy.

Modernization and the Economy

There can be little question that the effects of the revolutionary model have been extremely deleterious for "modernization" in the narrow sense of economic development. The economy suffered a major setback as a result of the Great Leap. After an extraordinarily good beginning during the early years, all indices indicate a dramatic reversal with the Leap, followed by a period of recovery necessary for several years thereafter. The best economic analysis available indicated that during the period of 1952 to 1957 there was steady growth of both total and per capita product. In fact, the

[35] See Richard Baum, "Cultural Revolution in the Countryside" in Robinson, *op. cit.*, p. 437.

[36] Thomas W. Robinson, "Chou En-lai and the Cultural Revolution," in Robinson, *op. cit.*, p. 167.

rate of growth of the "domestic product was higher in China (9%) than in practically all of the more than 40 other nations analyzed" in a major study.[37]

> The performance of the Communist economy during 1952–55 . . . must be considered a most outstanding success, exceeding . . . West Germany and Japan. It approaches a miracle if one considers the very limited technical knowledge and personnel the Communist regime had to start with.

Yet this was all thrown away during the period from 1958 to 61 when the economy took a "serious leap backwards," and a total of seven years (1958–65) was lost "without any growth." [38] The total production of agriculture, which is the crucial sector of the economy for a number of reasons, was probably slightly higher in 1966 than it had been in 1957, but meanwhile the population had increased by 100 million people.[39]

We have little information about what happened to the economy as a result of the Cultural Revolution. Initially, the party tried to insulate it from the effects of the Red Guards. In the communiqué issued by the Central Committee of the Party in August 1966, scientists and technologists were to be excluded from the campaign. But the communiqué was not honored and the campaign affected even those at the heart of China's national defense effort.[40] It is certain that serious, though temporary, disruptions occurred in the transportation network; and as the centers of the Cultural Revolution—Shanghai, Wuhan and cities in Manchuria—are also industrial centers, it is clear that production was hampered, but the extent of the damage is unknown.

Generally speaking, China's problems remain. "No major breakthrough in sustained economic growth" occurred, although there have been great improvements in the methods of distribution and China has not suffered a major famine since the Communists took power.[41]

Does this mixed economic record mean that modernization has failed? There are other elements to modernization besides economic development. If we also consider national unity and responsiveness to national direction, then the role of the military in the revolutionary model at the local level appears to make it a modernizing agency par excellence. Clearly the center has, through the mass line, been able to penetrate the village as never before

[37] Ta-Chung Liu, "Economic Development of the Chinese Mainland, 1949–65," pp. 643–5, in Ping-ti Ho and Tang Tsou, *China's Heritage and the Communist Political System,* vol. 1 (China in Crisis), Book Two (Chicago: University of Chicago Press, 1968).

[38] *Ibid.,* p. 648.

[39] Robert F. Dernberger, "Economic Realities and China's Political Economics," in *China after the Cultural Revolution* (New York: Vintage, 1969), p. 96.

[40] See Michael B. Yahuda, "China's Nuclear Option," in *China in Crisis, op. cit.*

[41] Dernberger, *op. cit.,* p. 113.

in Chinese history and has shortened the traditional distance between Peking and the village. The extremely important role of the military certainly has not been duplicated in Indonesia or in any other Southeast Asian country, save North Vietnam.

In addition it is not certain that the final gains from the Cultural Revolution might not offset the economic losses. If Mao was trying to secure a commitment to the nation, to the "building of a more just society, a commitment that arises from participation in the revolutionary act of defying authority" [42] on the part of the younger generation, the results are not yet in. Mao would rather, apparently, sacrifice industrialization than put that industrialization in the hands of elites. Thus, one must agree with Oksenberg that to "the extent that Mao's desire is to insure that industrialization serves the interests of his society, he is dealing with the central intellectual problem of our age." [43] Although beyond the scope of this analysis, it is certainly true that concepts of modernization in the Western sense, as a desirable thing, are open to attack. If urbanization is an index, then the current Chinese policy *not* to consciously urbanize would not be "modern." But the problems of many Western cities—particularly from the point of view of the individual —throw doubt upon their value to society. If exposure to mass media, literacy, participation of the masses in their fate, and "orientation to change and innovation" [44] are used as indices, then in most of these respects the Chinese, and even, to some extent, the Indonesian polities have been committed to "modernization."

The Lin Piao Affair

It should be noted that throughout the period of rule of the Chinese Communists until 1971 there is no evidence of any fundamental disloyalty on the part of the military to civilian leadership. Up until Mao decided the party was betraying the revolution, the party and government did have primacy. The Peng Te-huai incident dealt with policy and not power. The question was not civilian control of the military, but the narrower issues of modernization in the armed forces, economic policy, and the proper functions of the armed forces in the larger society.

It is only in the hindsight of an attempted *coup* by Lin Piao that we can speculate about the political situation of the 1969 to 1971 period. Obviously the coalition of people at the national center who were associated with Chou favored moderate domestic and foreign policies. Certainly this policy heavily compromised any further attempts at intense cultivation of the revolutionary

[42] Michael Oksenberg, "Comments," in Tsou, *op. cit.*, p. 493.

[43] *Ibid.*

[44] For an interesting discussion on this point concerning China, see S. N. Eisenstadt, "Tradition, Change and Modernity: Reflections on the Chinese Experience," in Tsou, *op. cit.*

model as in the days of the Great Leap and the early Cultural Revolution. And quite obviously these were major disputes over the direction of these new policies. Lin Piao did not command loyalty throughout the army to the point where he could motor a takeover. It seems that the army was divided "along regional, generational, doctrinal, and service lines," [45] although it was for a time the primary source of stability in the nation.

Information on the attempted *coup* by Lin in September, 1971 has been made available in two documents provided by the Nationalist Chinese, the authenticity of which is not absolutely proven but whose existence was previously referred to by the Chinese Communists and whose content coincides with other facts revealed by Mao to various visitors. The first document entitled "Struggle to eliminate the counter-revolutionary plot of the Lin-Chen clique" [46] indicates that Mao "reorganized the military region of Peking in January of 1971, which removed all possibility of success of their plans which they had been developing in the capital and northern China." According to Agence France Press, Lin attempted to "manipulate" the Central Committee during the course of a secret meeting of part of that committee in December of 1970. This led Mao to throw his weight behind Chou.[47] After this, the document charges that Lin, his wife, and his son travelled to various Chinese cities to coordinate a *coup* (termed "project 571") attempt. The second document, incorporated into the first, purports to have been written by the plotters and explains the reasoning behind it: (1) Mao's new policies of gradualism have "abused the confidence of the Chinese people," (2) the "clique in power is extremely unstable at its core and is subjected to constant struggles for power," (3) the "armed forces are subject to all forms of persecutions and the intermediate and superior cadres of the armed forces who hold actual power in the army are discontent," (4) the Red Guards were "duped and manipulated, were used as fodder for the cannon during the first phase of the Cultural Revolution and as scapegoats during the second phase," (4) generally, the "clique in power takes measures which defy good sense, persecute the masses; the economy stagnates . . . and discontent becomes more and more obvious." The army is praised for its "remarkable results, militarily, organizationally, and ideologically." The second document also describes the army as riven

[45] "Mainland China," in *Current Scene, op. cit.*

[46] See *Le Monde,* September 2, 1972. The Chen referred to is Chen Po-ta, formerly a member of the Central Revolutionary group. All quotations (unless otherwise noted) referring to these events are translations by the author and come from this issue of *Le Monde*. This version of events had been publicly supported by Mao in discussions with French Minister of Foreign Affairs M. Schumann and the Ceylonese Prime Minister, Mme. Bandaranike. See *Le Monde,* weekly edition July 27–Aug. 2, 1972, p. 1.

[47] Patrice de Beer, "The successor had forgotten that the party commands the gun," *Le Monde,* July 23, 1972, p. 1.

with conflict within itself, "making difficult the constitution of a united front under our control." More Maoist than Mao, unable to ride with the change in atmosphere, Lin and his group, it is claimed, contacted the Soviets. Very possibly the cause, as has been suggested, was the policy shift in favor of détente with the United States.[48] Apparently the airliner shot down with Lin aboard the night of September 12, 1971, was bound for Irkutsk, Soviet Union.

In the aftermath of Lin's demise has come the most far-reaching shake-up of the central leadership of the CCP since 1967. As of January, 1972 only 9 members of the 21-man Politburo were still active.[49] Mao told Snow in the fall of 1970 that it was *not* the army that was exercising power and that this would become clear in the months to follow.[50] The best terms for the political situation are: fragmentation, broker politics, and moderation. Power has been shared between the provinces and the center. In the provinces, the local and regional military leaders are ascendant, dominating the party committees[51]; in the center, a coalition of state bureaucrats, perhaps some radicals, and central military welded in some fashion around Chou. There is factionalism within the military, certainly, but it seems that at the province level the traditional civilian party control of the military has been seriously eroded, while the central authorities are unable to eradicate, at present, a large measure of local autonomy. Those in ascendancy in the center are not "revolutionary successors" but, by and large, the older generation now forging policies more appropriate to a maturing nation. In fact several men who opposed Red Guard activity with armed force in the city of Wuhan during 1967 have been visibly rehabilitated. And other personalities —both military and civilian[52]—rehabilitated during the summer of 1972 give ample evidence of the politics of moderation, pragmatism, and renewed emphasis on professionalism. Chou is apparently reconstructing the administration with "experienced senior management men." [53] At the center, then, the demise of Lin and those central military authorities who supported him means for the short run that "politics commands the gun." It is, however, a more moderate politics, which has largely abandoned the shrillness of the revolutionary model.

[48] Stanley Karnow, in the *Washington Post,* Jan. 11, 1972.

[49] Tilman Durdin in *New York Times,* December 29, 1972.

[50] *Le Monde,* July 23, 1972.

[51] See Harry Harding, "China: The Fragmentation of Power," *Asian Survey,* vol. XII, no. 1, Jan. 1972, for a good summation of the political situation at the end of 1971. According to Harding, "Of the 158 secretaries of the 29 provincial Party Committee, 94 (59%) are military, 55 (35%) are civilian cadres. Of the 29 first secretaries, 11 are military commanders, 9 are professional military commissars, 9 are civilian cadres." Pp. 2–3.

[52] "China: the Old Order Returns," in *Newsweek,* Aug. 14, 1972, p. 27.

[53] Robert Guillain in *Le Monde,* Aug. 2, 1972.

Summary Remarks on China

In traditional China, there was a saying that "good iron is not wrought into nails, good men do not become soldiers." This attitude toward military life was, as we have seen, reversed by the Communists during the revolutionary war. What role has the army played in China's modernization? In emphasizing the human factor, the regime has used the army to reinvigorate ideology in the belief that, properly motivated, people can do anything, thereby shortening the time span in the development process. The economic failure of the Great Leap proved to be wrong, but the primacy of politics continued into the Cultural Revolution. The professionals were, in both the army and the party, modernizers in the Western sense; but the campaigns against them proved that modernization at the expense of revolutionary fervor was not acceptable to Mao and his supporters. In the process, the pace of modernization has been start and stop, political power fragmented and now more moderate policies finally come to the fore. At the present a balance has been struck between the needs of modernization and the primacy of politics. A coalition, its looseness or stability uncertain at this time, has been built between numerous groups including, undoubtedly, both ideologues and modernizers. It is clear that the army will be a vital factor in China's future modernization as a partner with civilian organizations. It has been proven in the past that modernization breeds bureaucracy in China, that the two appear to go together there as elsewhere. The reality of this seems to have been forced on the leadership.

Chinese politics do not appear to be as susceptible to analysis along civil-military lines as might first appear to be the case, given the role of the PLA in the Cultural Revolution. Though we have pointed out problems between officer and party communities (particularly in the 1950s) and, of course, between Lin and his supporters in the central military leadership with Chou and his associates in the 1970s, the real division in politics depends more on one's policy orientation than on one's uniform.

At present it appears that there has been a deep restructuring of Chinese policies. Softened foreign policies, epitomized by the Nixon visit, are clear for all to see. Internally, there is a refocusing on serious modernization at the expense of concessions from the ideology (i.e., a shifting of emphasis from "red" to "expert"). Techniques from abroad are being welcomed. Trade is sought, highlighted by a wheat deal with the United States in the fall of 1972.

After the bewildering kaleidoscopic sequence of events in China over the past decade, it is hazardous to be conclusive about anything in the Chinese polity today. There has clearly been a settling-out since the dramatic events of September 1971. Competent observers comment upon the seeming stability reigning in China today. The population has come through the events of the Cultural Revolution and its aftermath, according to Durdin, "cheerful and relatively at ease with their government."[54] The shifting of administrative organs in the last 6 years sometimes has taken on the air of fantasy. Despite the seemingly tumultous changes, one finds familiar faces: the "controlling revolutionary committees usually are made up of people who held leading positions in the same or similar organizations before the Cultural Revolution."[55] Yet, in fact, it appears that Chou's coalition has given the army a good report card: in general, it performed its political duties well, is loyal, and enjoys the trust of the nation.[56] Further, it appears that in practice at the local level the revolutionary model is at least partly operative. As discussed at the beginning of this Chapter, the army is anything but estranged from the masses. Ranks, insignia, and privilege are still forbidden. The army attempts to be as self-sufficient as possible. Officers to the ranks remain operational. Performing a host of civilian duties is considered "natural and commonplace."[57] The purges of the plotters in the central military have not seriously affected the prestige of the military, although propaganda using the military as models in society is over. It is uncertain whether the national leadership under Chou has allowed the continued influence of military men throughout the structures of power in provincial China because the army, despite Lin, has been adjudged fundamentally loyal to the regime or because it is too powerful to be tampered with now, given the over-all priority of order, moderation, and modernization. Nevertheless, a campaign is underway today to reiterate the traditional relationship of party and army. A combined party-government statement in January 1972 enjoined Revolutionary Committees at all levels and leading bodies of the army to implement the primacy of politics: "The people are the source of the strength of the people's army. . . . The PLA should modestly learn from the people throughout the country."[58]

Thus the part of the revolutionary model regarding the primacy of politics is reemphasized from the center (though in some provinces the responsiveness of powerful local leaders is certainly questionable), but the other part of the model emphasizing ideological purity at the expense of professional modernization is currently muted.

INDONESIA

Indonesia has had a military regime since the army assumed power in 1965 as a result of a confusing series of events involving divisions within

[54] Tilman Durdin, "Report on a Visit to China: Stability seems to Reign," *New York Times,* May 10, 1972, p. 1.

[55] *Ibid.*

[56] Guillain, *Le Monde,* Aug. 2, 1972.

[57] Durdin, *New York Times,* Feb. 17, 1972.

[58] *Washington Post,* Jan. 5, see also *New York Times,* Feb. 7, 1972.

the military, tensions among the military and the PKI (Communist party) and the personality of President Sukarno. This assumption[59] of power eventually spelled the end of the political career of Sukarno and for the PKI in the foreseeable future. It did not kill Western-style democracy, as that experiment had been deceased for several years, and it did not halt economic development, for the roof had already fallen in. The military had arrived to save the nation from economic chaos, mismanagement, foolhardy foreign adventures, galloping communism, and polemics.

What tendencies can be seen in the colonial, revolutionary and immediate post-revolutionary era tending to unite or fragment Indonesia as a "nation?" The nation Sukarno and his fellow revolutionaries fought to liberate had not been created, willy nilly, out of whole cloth to the convenience of the imperial powers. The Dutch had ruled over a territory roughly the same as that of the two great Indonesian empires of the ninth and fourteenth centuries, Shrivijaya and Majapahit. This is in contrast to the drawing of borders on the peninsula of Southeast Asia which often cut through ethnic configurations and was stimulated not by the attitudes of indigenous groups so much as the convenience of the metropolitan powers.

The guts of the Indonesian military effort against the Dutch was the PETA, a militia created by the Japanese and originally intended for use against the allies, but which eventually fought both the Japanese and the Dutch. The heaviest and most successful effort by the Indonesians occurred on the central islands of Java and Sumatra, where the revolutionists set up a Republican government, solidly supported by the indigenous populations. However, the Dutch retained most of their power on the other islands (Borneo, Celebes, Lesser Sunda, Moluccas). Although the physical linkages of the Dutch-controlled islands to the Republic-controlled islands were cut, the psychological tie was strong; the outer islands definitely considered themselves part of any Indonesian nation and during the occupation "looked wistfully to those areas of Java and Sumatra still able to hold out against the Dutch, regarding them as champions of their own cause." [60] A nationalist outlook on the part of the younger generation was particularly promising because the old societal order, which had been propped up by a Dutch administration unwilling to engage the Indonesians in their own fate, crumbled with World War II. New social groups arose quickly under the Japanese and the occupiers encouraged the development of mass organizations to support the Japanese war effort. In the process, the society was shaken fundamentally. These new groups shed much of their former ethnic

[59] I use the term "assumption" advisedly because, as will be explained in more detail, the army literally had to be threatened with its very existence before it was willing to take the reins of power. This is in contrast to other countries in Southeast Asia, e.g., Thailand and Burma, where the word "takeover" is applicable.

[60] George McT. Kahin, "Indonesia," in Kahin (ed.), *Major Governments of Asia* (Ithaca, N.Y.: Cornell University Press, 1963).

loyalties and value systems and took on wider perspectives. When the Dutch returned to take power again after the defeat of the Japanese, the new perspectives gained maturity in conflict. This nationalism, despite internal bickering, disappointments, and great violence, remains as a seemingly permanent feature of society. The revolutionary experience, even though basically more against something than for something, definitely heightened an archipelago-wide sense of national identity.

It is nevertheless true that the history of the nationalist movement in Indonesia was marked by internal divisions and fits and starts and was checked at intervals by Dutch and Japanese repression. The Indonesian experience in nationalism, then, was in marked contrast to that of the Chinese. No single nationwide, mass-based, reasonably unified movement developed in Indonesia as it did in China. The techniques of mobilization and the development of ideological underpinnings that sustained the Chinese Communists both before and after victory did not have parallels in Indonesia. The Indonesian Communists eventually came closest to building such a mass base, but this base was not as deeply developed as was needed to sustain assaults from rival groups in the society and was decimated in the middle 1960s. There were several main currents to the nationalist movement, including religious political groups centering around Islam, a Communist party dating back to 1920, and intellectuals educated in the West (Sukarno falls into this category). Primarily these political divisions reflect the fact that Indonesia has always been a fragmented society, in part because of a geographical diversity that spans some three thousand islands, in part because of the existence of several hundred ethnic groups, about a dozen of which claim over a million members each, and in part because of a number of social and religious attitudes and influences over time, including Hinduism, Islam, and Dutch Christianity. The product has been a rich and complicated structure of socio-cultural groupings, or "alirans." The aliran pattern, as described by Hindley, can be analyzed "through an examination of two fundamental cleavages that cut across society: one religious, the other between holders of traditional and modernist world views."[61] Although Indonesia is about 90% Moslem, only about half of these are devout in the political sense of supporting specifically Moslem organizations. This devout group has a high degree of cohesion and by virtue of dress and customs, visible group identification, and are termed "santris." Non-santri (or "abangan") Moslems both oppose and fear political domination by santri organizations.

To complicate matters, the santri Moslems are divided along modernist and traditional lines, with widely differing attitudes concerning authority and

[61] Donald Hindley, "Alirans and the Fall of the Old Order," in *Indonesia* (Cornell Modern Indonesia Project), no. 9, April 1970, pp. 23–66, quote from p. 23. The discussion concerning alirans is drawn primarily from this source.

modernization. Political parties in the modern era developed around rival traditional and modernizing santris, the Nahdatul Ulama representing the former and the Masjumi party representing the latter. They are centered in differing parts of Indonesia, Masjumi in the urban areas of West Java, and particularly in Sumatra, Nahdatul Ulama in villages in East Java.

The other half of the population who are not political santri are also divided along a traditional-modernist axis and have also been represented by political parties. First, the non-santri traditionalist by the Partai Nasional Indonesia (PNI) are centered in the "aristocratic-bureaucratic stratum of Central and East Javanese society." [62] Second is the non-santri modernizers, who can be broken down into two further groupings or alirans: the highly educated elite of the major cities (represented for a time by the Partai Sosialis Indonesia, PSI, banned by Sukarno in 1960) and, second, a larger group of non-santri modernizers, not highly educated but not bound by traditional outlooks, who grouped around the PKI. There have been, in addition, Christian modernist alirans.

The aliran pattern has provided promises and dangers for Indonesian society. The aliran, as a group of organizations clustered around a party, provided a place in modern society for many, as the parties could control patronage, licenses, civil service positions, and the like. At the same time, its close association with an ethnic or socio-religious community posed a danger for national integration.[63] When the parties later lost their effectiveness in the political order, it seemed evident that the potential for particularistic loyalties and rivalries could easily overwhelm the benefits of marginal participation in the national polity. As will be discussed, much of the terrible violence of the 1965 events bears out the reality of this danger.

Some analysts have found the basic cleavage to be between Javanese aristocrats and outer-island entrepreneurs, the clearest tensions between Sumatran Masjumi elements and the Javanese parties and groups, exacerbated by Javanese control of the Civil Service on both islands.

Another approach to understanding recent Indonesian politics, somewhat different from the aliran analysis, focuses on the relationship between Jakarta and Javanese groups not part of the capital city's cultural milieu. This approach is used in a highly interesting analysis at Cornell that provides a different version of the power struggle in 1965 than that generally accepted.

Java itself has its own distinct cultural milieu, which distinguishes it from the other islands, particularly the wealthier island of Sumatra. Containing two thirds of the population, Javanese have dominated the military,

[62] *Ibid.*, p. 25.

[63] See also Herbert Feith, "Indonesia," in Kahin (ed.), *Governments and Politics of Southeast Asia* (Ithaca, N.Y.: Cornell Univ. Press, 1964), for a good discussion of the aliran pattern.

civil service, and other important nonmilitary sectors of society. The Javanese belief system is steeped in the occult and is a conglomeration of animism and various religions, with a very humanistic and harmonious way of looking at man and nature. Its basic idea is one of broad consensus among many unequals in a social hierarchy that is not rigid, but whose existence depends on the mutually harmonious relations of all its parts. This is not a caste system but a rich integrated cosmos complete with wondrous mythological beings, gurus, soothsayers, and wise men who interpret natural forces. It is a moral order, as everything depends on the existence of everything else. The magical orientation of these beliefs tend to inhibit practical problem-solving, as Western rationalism does not play a part. This belief system is important to Indonesian politics because it is generally taken seriously even among many of the highly educated—Sukarno and Suharto included—and often practical politics makes little sense without reference to it.

Jakarta has developed its own distinct personality, which is perhaps as Javanese as San Francisco is American—a cosmopolitan city which, as is usually the case, modernized more quickly than the rest of Indonesia and perhaps loosened its roots to Javanese society. It is possible for regional Indonesian elements to look upon Jakarta disparagingly as immoral and untrustworthy.

The Sukarno Years

The men who emerged from the Japanese occupation to challenge the return of the Dutch in a revolution which spanned 5 years (1944 to 1949) were without pre-war administrative experience. The Dutch (as in contrast to the British) did not permit the development of Indonesian administrative skills, nor any experience in self-government. "Thus during the colonial period, Indonesians were denied access to constructive political roles." [64]

The long struggle for liberation, coupled with this lack of prior political experience, meant that the political education of the emerging leaders was one of violence, rebellion, and conspiracy. In contrast to this the leaders of the revolution tried to install a government along the lines of Western-style parliamentary democracy when they finally secured independence in 1949. The experiment in the Western model was short-lived. The parties feuded and the system shifted from coalition to coalition, none of which succeeded in modernizing society or bringing sustained economic development, as was the case in the early years of the Chinese Communist regime. Mutually

[64] For a broad and balanced introduction to Indonesian politics in the revolutionary era see Kahin in Kahin, *op. cit.*, pp. 535–688. Quotation is from page 537. For the classic statement on the Indonesian revolution, see his *Nationalism and Revolution in Indonesia* (Ithaca, N.Y.: Cornell Univ. Press, 1952).

strong suspicions and lack of cooperation among the parties made the political system during this period of "liberal democracy" unworkable along the lines of its western model.

By 1956–57, the system was floundering, and there was increasing discontent that the "country's condition was rotten." [65] Regionalism and fratricidal politics began destroying the ability of the central government to extend its control beyond Java. The seven military regions of Indonesia of that time were being run by their commanders as autonomous kingdoms, with troops generally loyal first to region, then to Jakarta. Bloodless *coups* against Jakarta-appointed civilian officials occurred across the critically important (economically) island of Sumatra, power being taken by army-led regional councils headed up by indigenous military commanders and supported primarily by the modernist Masjumis.[66] The given reason for the action was corruption and red tape in the central government and the inability of this government to bring financial satisfaction to Sumatra. Shortly thereafter another *coup* occurred in East Indonesia (Celebes, Moluccas, and Lesser Sunda Islands), power being assumed by an army-led council. With the developing chaos, ethnic divisions were inflamed, particularly between ethnic Javanese (about 59% of the population) and various ethnic groups of the outer islands. Yet there was enough of a sense of nationalism overlaying these problems that a serious solution was sought. It is here that we can see plainly the value of a truly charismatic figure in the creation of a sense of unity in a fragmented nation. Yet his charisma was not quite enough. In order to restore central control it was necessary for Sukarno to rely on the army to use force to end the threat of national dissolution posed by the regional councils. Martial law was declared and within a short time, involving very little resistance by the rebels, national integrity was restored.

But the experiment in liberal democracy was over, and in its place several developments occurred: First came a period of "guided democracy," which centered primarily around the magic of Sukarno's personality and second, enhanced army powers. The Indonesian military has always sought to play an active role in politics, but it never attempted to seize power until virtually forced to in 1965. It played a major role in quelling disturbances on behalf of the civilian government several times, but it offered no specific political program of its own and took no concrete ideological position except anti-communism. Yet it shared a general discontent over the lack of progress in the early post-revolutionary years and felt a need to provide skills and energy in those areas where the civilians had failed. The

[65] Feith, in Kahin, *Governments and Politics,* op. cit., p. 208.

[66] For a good account of these events, see Herbert Feith and Daniel S. Lev, "The end of the Indonesian Rebellion," *Pacific Affairs* XXXVI (Spring 1963), pp. 33–46.

rebellion of the late 1950s and the accompanying period of martial law gave the army commanders of "every district immense authority, subordinating civilian administration to military orders and making it possible everywhere except Jakarta for officers to exercise paramount influence in government." [67] At the same time the army began organizational efforts to draw support of various groups in the society away from the political parties, which the army considered inept; needless to say this alarmed the parties and Sukarno and the effort was not particularly successful. The army, then, under General Nasutian, during the turmoil stepped into a range of heretofore unfamiliar civilian administrative and political positions (in particular in formerly Dutch enterprises that Sukarno had nationalized). In addition, in restoring national unity, the prestige of the army rose greatly.

The third development after the end of liberal democracy was that, with the important exception of the Communist Party, the political parties lost much of their credibility, and, in turn, the alirans lost their channel for national participation. Being blocked by normal political routes (Sukarno dissolved Parliament in 1960), Party leaders looked now to the army to support their cause.

The Sukarno period of guided democracy no longer attempted to weld a viable order on the basis of pluralistic politics of compromise but established a more authoritarian pattern that he attempted to legitimize through charisma and a sort of pop-ideology focused on the ideal of national consensus. Sukarno often resorted to the "outside enemy" to help build unity and personal support. Thus, for example, he successfully challenged the Dutch on the question of sovereignty over Western New Guinea, played a major international role in the 1950s and early 1960s when "nonalignment" was in vogue, beat the drum in a highly artificial "crush Malaysia" campaign, and finally turned against the West and moved dramatically closer to mainland China. It must be credited to Sukarno that in much of this he succeeded. Though he took few tangible measures (including an attempt to extend a national language, bahasa Indonesia, across the country, with mixed results) to put unity in Indonesia on sound footing, one must agree with Robert Shaplen that:

> For twenty years, with a combination of glamour and gall, he sustained the Indonesian revolution in his own image; whenever it flagged or threatened to disintegrate, he managed by sheer bravado or improvisation to piece it together again. The non-stop revolutionary momentum he provided, often in the manner of an interlocutor of an old-time minstrel show, was his unique contribution. . . .[68]

[67] Daniel S. Lev, "The Political Role of the Army in Indonesia," Pacific Affairs, XXXVI (Winter 1963–4), p. 350.

[68] Robert Shaplen, *The Lost Revolution* (Harper and Row: N.Y., 1969), p. 17.

In general, the central government became more pervasive throughout society but over time administered its program poorly and failed to bring general economic benefits to the society. It would be misleading to term the Sukarno period "totalitarian" even though he extended controls into all areas—economic, intellectual, and social organization—the controls were often superficial, poorly implemented, and unworkable. When he finally was driven from power, the economy was in nearly hopeless shape. The basic causes appeared to be inflation (the rate reaching 1200% annually in 1965), capital losses with the departure of foreign business, corruption, and an inability on the part of the Sukarno regime to create any effective plan for development. The present regime is attempting to correct these deficiencies.

The Sukarno era shows to what extent it is possible to govern an underdeveloped nation of 100 million people through the use of symbols more than a workable problem-solving government and also that in the long run if the government is not workable then forces are set off which that government cannot control and will probably bring it down.

It would seem that charisma, which in itself brings expectations of progress in the society, must be accompanied by some tangible achievement in the long run or it will eventually wear itself out.

Sukarno came to rely increasingly on the support of the army, but there were limits beyond which he could not exert control over it. Sukarno–army relations were basically a bargaining situation. Regardless of division within the officer corps there is the feeling that, having been primarily responsible for winning independence it has a continuing major role in the affairs of state. As described by Feith, Sukarno and the army informally recognized different areas of government as predominantly their respective fiefdoms. The army's areas of influence were "regional government, state enterprises, mostly ex-Dutch, and matters directly connected with civil security," while Sukarno's power was "great in matters of ideology and the formal organization of government and in the area of foreign policy." [69] Thus, the two were uneasy partners in the exercise of power, and in fact there were several attempts by different sections of the army to unseat him. Thus the President could not easily play the game of divide and rule, and as a consequence he found it necessary to use the Communist Party to counterbalance army influence.

As of 1964, the party was growing in numbers (approximately 2 million members), had successfully established a number of mass organizations on the typical communist model, and was generally considered to be popular among significant segments of the population. The political bias of the army is heavily anti-communist, and Sukarno's favoritism toward the

[69] Feith in Kahin, *op. cit.*, p. 243.

party had inherently explosive implications. The army favored groups who agreed with this political bias, and in its political bailiwicks protected them against the Communists. Sukarno gained leverage for himself through their rivalry, but at the same time played a dangerous balancing act, for both sides waited for the opportunity to do the other in. Without Sukarno the prospects for violent conflict were grave.

Sukarno–army competition, in fact, took on a roughly regional coloration, with the Army representing the interests of the Outer Islanders and West Java (areas of Masjumi strength) and Sukarno representing, very roughly, interests in East and Central Java (areas of PNI and PKI strength and ethnically Javanese).[70] The army, then, served as a conduit for pressures from civilian groups in these areas, serving as their proxy, enhanced by the fact that commanders in these areas were often indigenous to their area of responsibility. The army then played, in a very real political way, the role of a political party in the modern sense. By the same token, both the army and Sukarno sought support from these various groups to enhance their powers. During this period of guided democracy the army played such a strong political role that there was little need for a *coup*; indeed, a *coup* would pose more problems than it was worth. Nasutian saw the army's role as neither the banana republic model nor the passive model of Western Europe.[71] It would play a very active role, including at the highest levels much in the way of a political party.

The *Coup* of 1965 and Its Aftermath

The high army officer corps, although representing ethnic and religious diversity, generally is non-santri modernist. The army, although individually perhaps sympathetic to aliran background, has not sympathized with the political groupings representing those alirans and has, in fact an elan of its own which has over time led it to deprecate the squabblings of the political parties. This does not mean, however, that the military is a tightly woven body, politically unified. Many of the more senior officers shared in the revolutionary experience, which, as in China, was characterized by decentralized guerrilla action. Yet there are, naturally, many younger officers who did not serve in the revolution who are not close to the older group. We have already commented upon the strong regional caste of much of the military, and the restlessness exhibited by various sections of the military over time. This all adds up to potential divisions within the military. As in China, when independence came and the army transformed itself from the popular

[70] *Ibid.*, pp. 246–247.

[71] See Lev, "Political Role," *op. cit.*, for an account of the army's political maneuverings during this period. See also footnote 86 for the army's self-description.

force of revolution to a more modernized and centralized organization, problems arose. In China it brought campaigns against professionalism; in Indonesia it brought, apparently, schisms between the Central military elite and the regional forces.

It has been generally assumed that in October 1965 the PKI initiated violence against the military (assassinating six top generals) to swing the political balance decisively in its favor once and for all, especially in light of rumors of Sunkarno's ill health. The evidence has been confusing, most particularly because the reaction from the military group around General Suharto brought almost no resistance from the Communists, who were subsequently slaughtered by the hundreds of thousands. By far the most careful study yet available indicates, surprisingly enough, that this was not the case at all, and that the scenario began with an attack on the central leadership by a group of middle-level army officers (the key figure of which was a Lieutenant colonel Untung) from the Diponegoro Division of Central Java.[72]

The Diponegoro Division is "the most Javanese of the major constituent units of the Indonesian Army and displays much of the typical character of rural and small-town Central Java, both psychologically and sociologically." In this close reflection of the society from which it comes, it is similar to other Divisions in East and West Java. Thus it is suspicious of outsiders, is alienated from what it considers the "metropolitan decadence" of Jakarta, "nostalgic for the days of the national revolution when Army and people were nearly as united as they ever could be." True to Javanese tradition, it was alarmed at the "spiritual decline evinced by widespread corruption, 'materialism,' and Westernized life styles." It was frustrated by the importance of the central government, although, true to the army style, very anti-Communist. The target of the enterprise was apparently the "political generals of the General Staff" who had become corrupted by the good life of Jakarta and who were opposed to the Sukarno policies; internally, they saw the generals resisting the "revolutionary spirit of 1945." As such they were romantics attuned to Sukarno's charisma. An additional factor of some importance was the suspicion that the generals may have been involved in a plot against Sukarno, supposedly supported by the CIA. These rumors were apparently fanned by the PKI, and as a result, the General Staff's patriotism was questioned. It appears that they expected that elimination of the "political generals" in Jakarta would remove a major

[72] This analysis is taken entirely from Benedict R. Anderson and Ruth T. McVey, "A preliminary analysis of the Oct. 1, 1965, coup in Indonesia," (Cornell Modern Indonesia Project, Southeast Asia Program, Cornell Univ., Ithaca, N.Y., 1971). There has been no comparable study on these events. However, it was completed in 1965 and not updated to include fresh and important information on the communist role revealed during political trials conducted by Suharto.

obstacle in Sukarno's path, that he would then assume full political power, and have "an army in which they themselves or men they trusted would hold the key positions." [73]

Service politics also played its part. The army conspirators received substantial active support from air force elements, the air force having had a history of rivalry with the army.

The Cornell analysis finds that the PKI was left in the dark through most of the scenario, though some lower level groups were used by the conspirators without the knowledge of PKI leaders. Aidit, the PKI leader, was kept under lock and key by the plotters, and the PKI was not encouraged to make any moves. The analysis finds the plot a spectacular gamble: convince Sukarno a generals' *coup* was underway against him, that the PKI had committed itself to the Untung group in defense of the President, and that if he wished to sustain his leftist politics he had no choice but to support the Untung group.[74] Without reciting the details of the failure, the summary results were: (1) the group miscalculated that General Suharto would remain neutral or favorable; (2) Sukarno dragged his feet, played for time "until it became clear that any such proclamation would unleash civil war rather than crown a successful internal Army *coup*";[75] Sukarno played for time too long, which severely compromised his position in Suharto's view; (3) Aidit successfully restrained the PKI from taking advantage of the situation in the hope that the Communists would be exonerated from any culpability in the affair, knowing that militarily the PKI was no match for the army; (4) the use of lower-level PKI groups by the plotters, plus a rash editorial in *People's Daily* (the communist newspaper), gave Suharto's group an excuse to crush the PKI; (5) since the affair, the army has placed the blame "squarely on the PKI (and, *sub rosa,* Sukarno) both because of actual PKI involvement, however confused, and because all groups now in power wish to believe it, since for years they lived in growing fear of a possible PKI takeover." [76]

Testimony subsequent to the completion of the Cornell analysis, during political trials in the late 1960s, surely shows major communist complicity and, probably, overall direction of the plot (unless the testimony was doctored) and that Untung was more of a tool than a mover. This version sees the "progressive" military group under Untung speedily replaced by a "Revolutionary Council" dominated by the Communists. Sukarno comes out from the testimony deeply implicated in the leftist conspiracy.[77] An ex-

[73] *Ibid.,* pp. 1–2 of synopsis.

[74] *Ibid.,* p. 7 of text.

[75] *Ibid.,* p. 3.

[76] *Ibid.,* p. 4 of introduction.

[77] Shaplen, *op. cit.,* pp. 91–114, for a readable analysis based on this testimony; see also Justus M. Van Der Kroef, "Gestapo in Indonesia," *ORBIS X* (Summer, 1966), pp. 458–487, for a brief, but balanced, discussion.

planation offered for the poor timing of the *coup* is that Sukarno forced the PKI to move faster than it wanted and, further, that there may have been additional pressure from China during the period of intense American build-up in Vietnam. It should be noted that the PKI had given the army pause to consider a potential PKI *putsch*, since the PKI (with Sukarno's active support) had negotiated a deal with China for 100,000 small arms to be delivered through channels bypassing the army, apparently to be used by the PKI to establish a so-called "fifth force" composed of an armed peasantry.[78]

Be these various versions as they may, for purposes of this analysis, the role, background, and characteristics of the military plotters is instructive for an understanding of the divisions within the Indonesian military. The Diponegoro Division was not rent by generational cleavages but was a close-knit group, with the senior officers passing the mystique of the revolutionary days on to the more junior members. A particularly strong characteristic of the group was the ideal of the courageous leader exhibiting high moral qualities. The home area of the Division is one of the poorest in Java, where communist sympathies are especially strong. The hostility of the officers from this background for the "intellectual" [79] Jakarta General Staff can be readily appreciated, and there have been instances in the past, particularly in 1952, when there were major clashes between officers of these two syndromes. As rivalry between Sukarno and the General Staff developed, the revolutionary syndrome, let us say, of the deeply Javanese officers of Central and East Java saw the Staff as betraying the revolution.

Suharto is a Diponegoro officer but represents the man-in-the-middle, neither succumbing to the good life of Jakarta nor remaining confined to the geographical area of Central Java (he was head of the Strategic Army Command when the *coup* occurred). His personal life is more akin to the "revolutionary" style, and he remains "psychologically close to the 'Diponegoro world,' largely speaking and thinking in Javanese." It was for these reasons he was spared in the *coup*.[80] Also for these reasons it can be seen that he blends several characteristics necessary for leadership in Indonesia today: true to Javanese heritage, yet a modernizer in the Western sense.

Events immediately after the abortive *coup* revealed the pent-up frustrations of Indonesian society after years of stagnation. The army decided to take action against the PKI, closed down its press, and opened up its own press campaign against the PKI. It is stressed by the Cornell analysis that the abortive army *coup* and the anticommunist campaign that began in earnest 3 weeks later on October 21 were entirely different and unrelated

[78] John Hughes, *The End of Sukarno* (London: Angus and Robertson, 1968), pp. 11–12.

[79] Anderson, *op. cit.*, p. 4 text.

[80] *Ibid.*, p. 6.

affairs.[81] Particularly important were the long-standing resentments between the Communists and the rightist Masjumi and military, leading to the killing of upwards of a half-million people. It was clear that the communist support among the masses was not nearly as great as had previously been supposed. The events were incomprehensible in terms of the Javanese cosmos of consensus previously described, although they must have been at least partly due to long-standing agitation brought about by the Communist party among the peasants for radical reforms. The army did not help to dampen the violence.

Suharto, sensitive to the great residual influence of Sukarno's magical personality in society, was careful not to assume power too quickly and in fact exasperated his supporters both in and out of the military for going too slowly. Indeed, had Sukarno not given all indications that he was bent on restoring the pre-*coup* political situation of extreme pro-PKI sympathies, Suharto might have faltered. Involved, too, was the use of the occult, careful and thorough exposure through the *coup* trials of Sukarno's complicity, and continuous discussion among military and civilians until a general consensus had been achieved, or, one might say, it was clear to everyone that the Sukarno magic was done. His political fate was finally sealed about 18 months after the *coup*.

This process was extremely important in order not to cause perhaps irreparable divisions within the military. The process of dismantling Sukarno was implemented by five groups of the "least provincial, most Western-educated, Westernized, cosmopolitan segment of the officer corps." [82] We have seen that a dichotomy between this orientation and the more traditional orientation played a heavy role in the 1965 events. Thus it was essential to discredit Sukarno thoroughly, implicate him completely, and permit civilian groups, particularly the children (in the form of "action fronts," most importantly of high school students and university graduates), to expose his bankruptcy and pinch his charisma. Suharto's traditionalist background undoubtedly aided in easing this process.

Suharto was reluctantly named Army Chief of Staff by Sukarno in mid-October. From that time forward he was concerned with four things: (1) to consolidate centralized control over the armed forces; (2) to put the economy out of its morass; (3) to rebalance Indonesia's relations with the international community, with the particular goal of enticing foreign capital back into the country; (4) put off a new experiment in parliamentary democracy—except one with the dice heavily loaded in Suharto's favor—in fear of a return to the old politics of squabble, although to gain mass support for his regime from the younger generation he would tolerate some party politics. It would appear that Suharto is less interested in complete military

[81] *Ibid.*, p. 63.
[82] Hindley, "Alirans," *op. cit.*, p. 46.

power for its own sake than he is trusting in the ability of the military, with substantial aid of economic experts, to get the nation moving. Nevertheless there is restiveness among large segments of the civilian community, including the students, over the prospects of indefinite military rule; and pressure continued for more formal civilian political participation until elections were held in 1971, which significantly legitimized Suharto's mandate. The viability of the Suharto government will clearly be dependent on its ability to bring home the bacon.

Suharto set out to reorganize the military in the direction of enhanced centralized control. Those officers in power in the central command who had remained committed to Sukarno were removed and replaced by Suharto loyalists. Finally, a major reorganization occurred in 1969–70. As might be expected because of the deep air force involvement in the *coup,* particularly the direct role of the pro-Communist head of the air force, the power of the service chiefs was eliminated and the power of the air force, navy, and police was reduced in favor of deeper army control. A complicated "system of regional commands has been created to ensure . . . greater subordination to the center," and the new structure has involved "a massive transfer of personnel" at all levels.[83] It is too early to determine whether this structural reorganization will bring lasting military control by the center, but it seems probable that the outcome will depend in large measure on the ability of the Suharto regime to bring significant economic progress throughout the archipelago.

Under Suharto the military has assumed greater involvement in civilian affairs than ever before. This has made militarism a major political issue, and Suharto has made a continuing attempt to put civil-military relations on a firm functional foundation. Indeed, intimate cooperation between civilian managers, technical experts, and the military is an essential for progress. A new development Cabinet was created, composed primarily of civilians, including eight members of political parties and seven university professors. Yet the cooperation with civilians was basically an administrative cooperation; Suharto remained suspicious of the value of political parties, a suspicion strongly shared throughout the military.

The economic measures taken by Suharto have been effective enough to give him a legitimacy to rule for some time to come. Foreign investment has been enticed back to Indonesia.[84] The rate of inflation has been reduced to manageable proportions. Most important of all the regime has demonstrated a willingness to plan rationally on the basis of the best economic advice available. Economic progress was given a fresh beginning; and com-

[83] "Current Data on the Indonesian Military Elite after the Reorganization of 1969–70," by the editors of *Indonesia,* no. 10, Oct. 1970, p. 195.

[84] See Sumner Scott, "The Challenge to American Corporate Investment in Indonesia," *Asian Survey,* May 1972, Vol. XII, No. 5, for a round-up.

pared to the situation the regime began with, Suharto's efforts have given him a latitude in politics that he began to take advantage of in 1971.

Parliamentary elections were held in 1971. The regime has responded to pressures for a better break for the political parties by permitting nine parties to function legally. The PKI, of course, will not share in this development, and steps have been taken to ensure the PKI is not a major problem for some time to come. However, the army has created a new political form, an organization called Sekber Golkar (Joint Secretariat of Functional Groups), which is designed to compete with the parties. The parliament was to have 460 seats, and the combination of 100 seats automatically allocated to Presidential selection (75 of which would be members of the armed forces) and the seats won by Golkar were thought to ensure Suharto's mandate. Other safeguards taken by the regime included the right of the Suharto government to screen the lists of candidates, divisive politicking against the regime was forbidden, and the government counted the ballots. Even taking these factors into consideration Golkar did extremely well, taking nearly two thirds of the entire vote and a majority in all electoral districts save three. Only the Nahdatul Ulama withstood the sweep;[85] thus Golkar controls 336 out of the 460 seats, and, of course, it is tightly controlled by Suharto's army and technocrat supporters.

Democracy as an operationally effective system, with real protection of minority rights, adequate expression of majority sentiment, protection of civil liberties and close adherence to parliamentary procedure, has not yet appeared in any Southeast Asian country. Legitimacy through progress and a measure of participation for the major groups in society would appear to be the prerequisite for effective government, and the military in Indonesia is at present as promising in this attempt as anyone else in the area.

In both the administration and the parliament, civil-military relations have been placed on a footing designed to give the regime legitimacy, to prick any massive discontent by out-groups, and give Suharto room to bring rational economic reform. Suharto has been careful not to appear to be too radical and, although the predominant power is military, has played a broker role among civilian radicals, army radicals, and party leaders much the same way as Chou En-lai in the post-Cultural Revolution period.

CONCLUSION

In both China and Indonesia, the army has, from the late 1960s to the present, assumed a range of civilian functions that might lead one to question the future of the civilian sphere in those polities. Yet in both nations

[85] Donald Hindley, "Indonesia 1971: Pantjasila Democracy and the Second Parliamentary Elections," *Asian Survey,* January 1972, Vol. XII, no. 1, gives a summary of the election results.

forms of coalitions have developed in which nonmilitary elements are playing crucial roles. In China the military is powerful in the center and even more powerful in the regions. But it is both unwilling because of the tradition of the primacy of politics (and unable because it lacks cohesion, amply demonstrated by Lin Piao's aborted plot) to take central control of the polity. It has grown in influence because of the chaos of the early Cultural Revolution, but this growth was, in the first place, due to its supposed loyalty to the ideology and rule of the civilian leadership. In Indonesia the army was at one time also unwilling to usurp the reigns of government but was finally forced into power—the result, in the long view, of the politics of bankruptcy of Sukarno and an army philosophy that it has a duty and a right to participate in the affairs of state and bring progress to Indonesia.[86] The army thus has become, it would seem, a more centralized and cohesive organization than we find in China, and its share of power in Indonesia at the center is greater than that of the army in China. Yet the Indonesian army accepts the need for participation of all groups in the system who are oriented toward modernity; it does not really welcome the political parties but is willing to tolerate party activity within certain limits (i.e., the participation must be positive and not divisive).

The army professionals are predominant in Indonesia, and it would seem that a general new Chinese emphasis on moderation would include more toleration of professionalism in the armed forces there.

Recent turmoil and violence in both nations would seem to bear out Huntington's thesis that "civil violence is . . . more likely when aspirations and capabilities are changing and when the gap between them is increasing." [87] We see this both in the demands made by Revolutionary Rebels for better working conditions and in the frenzy of violence that succeeded the *coup* in Indonesia. But the effects of civil violence as he sees them (further "praetorian violence, political repression and communal conflict")[88] are not clear in either case. In Indonesia violence came because of the frustrations of Huntington's gap but was also encouraged by the army in order to eliminate its competitor. In China it came because organizational develop-

[86] This was reiterated by the army in an all-Indonesian political seminar held in August 1966. A document issued by the seminar stated the position: "The Indonesian army is above all the fighter for independence, the defender of justice and truth, and the People's Shield against . . . exploitation and tyranny. . . . It cannot be neutral about the direction of the State, about whether the Government is bad or good, about the welfare of society. . . . [It] is a fact that the people entrust their fate to the Indonesian Armed Forces." Sumbanagan Fikiran TNI/AD Kepada Kabinet Ampera (Jakarta, 1966), pp. 19, 37; quoted by Hindley, "Aliran," *op. cit.*, pp. 56–57.

[87] Samuel Huntington, "Civil Violence and the Process of Development," in *Civil Violence and the International System, Part II: Violence and International Security,* Adelphi Paper no. 83, Institute for Strategic Studies, London, December 1971, p. 1.

[88] *Ibid.*, p. 15.

ments were not to Mao's liking, though economic progress was coming rather satisfactorily. When chaos arrived in both countries it was only the discipline of a military organization that could bring peace, although in both nations strong Communist parties existed that could also have brought a semblance of stability.

In both nations the armed forces are committed to change, and the civilianization of the armies (i.e., the new economic roles taken over by the army in China, the creation of an army political party, Golkar, in Indonesia) is allowing them to become more versatile in their abilities to bring change.[89] Conversely there has been little militarization of civilian groups, with the exception of the now-decimated PKI.

It is interesting to note that attempted *coups* by both Lin Piao and Colonel Untung represented the voice of tradition; for Lin the issue was the abandonment of the pure ideology (in addition, of course, to the question of personal power); for Untung, the issue was the betrayal of Javanese morality (along with the lack of economic progress). We should not be surprised to see future frictions along this axis.

One's conclusions concerning civil-military relations in both nations in many respects depends on one's understanding of the complexities of each of the army organizations in question. In this regard we know much too little to construct really meaningful models.[90] Has Suharto been able to centralize the military and at the same time require regional and local leaders to have intimate ties with indigenous populations in order to ensure the army does not become alienated from the society? Given the dominance of non-santri modernizers, generally Westernized, at the center, is there enough social cohesion in the Indonesian army for the center to get the response it needs to accomplish its goals? Can, indeed, there be central control at the same time that local army "representation" is a reality? How responsive are China's regional leaders to the center? We do not have enough data to be meaningful about this, although we know regional leaders are involved in coalition politics in Peking and that centralization under Lin was clearly less potent than previously believed. Civil-military relations have to be understood both at the center and at the regions, and there may be a significantly different mix of emphasis from one to the other. Tentatively we might suggest more military influence at the local-regional levels in China than at the center, but then how is the building of a renewed

[89] This would bear out Janowitz's proposition that for a military organization to succeed at politics, it "must develop a political apparatus outside of the military establishment but under its direct domination." Morris Janowitz, *The Military in the Political Development of New Nations: An Essay in Comparative Analysis* (Chicago, Ill.: Univ. of Chicago Press, 1964), p. 29.

[90] *Ibid.*, for a broad discussion of models, and see also Jacques Van Doorn (ed.), *Armed Forces and Society* (The Hague: Mouton, 1968).

party effecting this emphasis? What changes in civil-military politics will it bring? Some of the alternatives would be: reversion to the traditional pure ideological model, control by the military, or varying coalitions from area to area. Will the experiments in civil-military partnership in Jakarta be reflected in the rest of Indonesia? The information is not readily available, though the technocrats will most likely be concentrated at the center.

In both systems there appears to be a genuine partnership between civilian and military elements, though in China the former hold the ultimate keys to power while in Indonesia the latter sit in the dominating position. These situations are in large part in accord with the view of politics that developed in the revolutionary period in both countries, the Chinese military conforming to Mao's political primacy, the Indonesian military feeling justified in playing a major role in getting things done in Indonesia. In the long view, the role of the military has been in large part a function of the performance of the civilian sector in both nations.

14

Civil-Military Relations in the USSR

HARRY J. GILMORE
FSO-4

The aim of this chapter is to present an interpretive survey of civil-military relations in the USSR from three vantage points: first, the present institutional relationships between the Communist Party of the Soviet Union (CPSU) and the Soviet military establishment[1] in the making of national security policy; second, the ideological and practical rationale for the Party's[2] supremacy over the Soviet military establishment, the methods of control the Party has devised to ensure its supremacy, and the reaction of the military to these controls; and finally, the dynamics of civil-military relations in the USSR at the present time, insofar as they are evident to foreign observers examining the public record, and the prospects for the immediate future.

In the course of this chapter the reader will encounter in both the text and footnotes references to monographs and articles in English pertaining to Soviet civil-military relations. It should be understood that these studies, while illustrative of the English-language literature on the Soviet military, represent only a modest cross-section of the substantial body of this literature. Readers who desire to delve into the subject should consult the bibliographies contained in the referenced studies as well as the indexes to such periodicals as *Problems of Communism, World Politics,* and *International Affairs*. Rand Corporation studies constitute another important source of current scholarship on Soviet military affairs.

In reading this essay it is important to keep the following considerations firmly in mind. Security considerations and censorship practices in the USSR

[1] The terms "the military" and "the military establishment" will be used in this essay to denote both the corps of professional officers—as distinct from political officers responsible for ensuring the political reliability, from the point of view of the CPSU, of all military units—as a collective entity or institution and the Ministry of Defense of the USSR in its role as spokesman for the institutional interests and views of the professional officer corps.

[2] Unless otherwise specified, the word "Party" will refer to the Communist Party of the Soviet Union or its predecessor (before October 1952), the "All-Union Communist Party (of Bolsheviks)."

combine to inhibit, when they do not flatly prohibit, any public discussion in the Soviet media and in Soviet scholarship of policy differences among Soviet political and military leaders. Statements based upon a few hard facts and a certain amount of educated conjecture are, therefore, unavoidable in studies such as this.

Civil-military relations in the USSR are acted out in an environment that differs radically from any that now prevails—or has ever existed—in the West. In fact, until the end of World War II, the pattern of civil-military relations that evolved in the USSR following the Bolshevik Revolution of November 7, 1917, was unique in the world.[3] With the establishment, by means of Moscow-engineered revolutions, of peoples' republics in Bulgaria, Czechoslovakia, Hungary, Poland, Romania, and North Korea and the successful seizure of power by indigenous communist movements in Albania, Yugoslavia, and China in the 5-year period from 1944 to 49, however, the uniqueness of the Soviet system came to an end. Soviet practice in the area of civil-military relations, like Soviet practice in virtually every area of government and politics, became the model for all the regimes belonging to what Moscow soon came to call the "Socialist Camp."

In the more than 20 years since their establishment—years that witnessed the death of Stalin, the autocrat, the growth of polycentrism,[4] and the ever-widening rift between the Soviet Union and the People's Republic of China—these peoples' republics have developed practices in civil-military affairs varying from those of the USSR. Still, the study of Soviet practice remains the central point of departure for any comparative study of civil-military relations in the communist world.

The study of civil-military relations in the USSR eventually may also come to occupy an important place in the study of comparative civil-military relations in one-party revolutionary regimes. When considered in this context, the Soviet model may be examined as one configuration, albeit an extreme and perhaps atypical one, that civil-military relations may assume under regimes that Robert Tucker has grouped under the category "revolutionary mass-movement regimes under single party auspices." [5]

An important practical consideration in the study of civil-military relations in the USSR is the fact that the Soviet Union shares with the United

[3] The Mongolian People's Republic, founded in November 1924 and closely linked with the USSR ever since, did, of course, pattern its political, military, and governmental systems on the Soviet model.

[4] "Polycentrism" is a term coined in 1956 by Palmiro Togliatti, then the Secretary General of the Italian Communist Party, to describe the growth of doctrinal independence from Moscow of the ruling and nonruling parties of the Socialist Camp and the emergence of Peking as well as Belgrade as rival centers of communist doctrine and influence.

[5] Robert C. Tucker, *The Soviet Political Mind,* rev. ed. (New York: W. W. Norton and Company, Inc., 1971), p. 7.

States the double distinction of being one of the world's two superpowers as well as the central political force and chief source of military and industrial power of a major military bloc. Consequently, the Soviet Union—and, at present, only the Soviet Union—is capable of threatening the United States with unacceptable levels of destruction in the event of thermonuclear war. At the same time, it is the Warsaw Pact alliance, led by the Soviet Union, that is the potential antagonist of the U.S.-led NATO alliance should armed conflict break out in Europe. Finally, the Soviet Union is the only state other than the United States that possesses or is likely soon to possess the ability and will to pursue a truly global foreign policy. The global interest and policies of the U.S. and the USSR can, potentially, lead to conflicts ranging in magnitude from backing rival candidates for the right to govern a given territory to proxy wars by client states threatening to lead to military confrontations by the superpowers themselves. This fact is borne out by even a cursory review of international events on almost any given day.

In short, in examining civil-military relations in the USSR we are examining both the prototype of a system of civil-military relations that exists in variant forms in every communist regime around the world and a system whose inner dynamics directly influence the political and military stability of the world.

THE CPSU, THE MILITARY ESTABLISHMENT AND THE MAKING OF NATIONAL SECURITY POLICY

When we speak of civil-military relations in the USSR we must understand from the outset that we are speaking primarily about relations between the leaders of the CPSU, on the one hand, and the Soviet military establishment, on the other. This is not readily apparent to the foreign observer. In fact, it is not apparent at all to an outsider looking only at the formal governmental structure of the USSR as delineated in the Soviet Constitution.

Article 30 of the Soviet Constitution states that the Supreme Soviet (Council) of the USSR, a bicameral, quasilegislative body normally convoked only twice annually for sessions of 3 to 7 days, is the "highest organ of state authority" and, as such, is charged with responsibility for deciding "questions of war and peace." The Presidium of the Supreme Soviet of the USSR, the executive body charged with exercising the Supreme Soviet's authority between convocations, is empowered under Articles 48 and 49 of the Constitution to appoint and remove the supreme command of the Soviet armed forces, proclaim a state of war during periods when the Supreme Soviet itself is in recess, declare general or partial mobilizations, and proclaim martial law.

Meanwhile, Article 64 designates the Council of Ministers of the USSR, a 120- to 130-man body headed by a chairman and several deputies and composed of the heads of all central ministries, state committees, and other important central administrative agencies, as "the highest executive and administrative organ of state authority." This same provision of the Soviet Constitution grants the Council of Ministers supervisory authority over the Ministry of Defense as well as the various central ministries engaged in producing weapons and war materiel. Other provisions of the Constitution grant the Council of Ministers such specific powers in the military sphere such as the right to "fix the annual contingent of citizens to be called up for military service," the right to "direct the general organization of the armed forces of the country," and the right to "set up, wherever necessary, special committees and chief (central) administrations . . . for defense." [6]

In reality, however, the ultimate decision-making authority in the USSR in military as well as political matters has always been exercised by the leadership of the CPSU. In the 55 years of communist power in the USSR, decision-making authority has been vested either in the Politburo (Presidium) of the Central Committee of the CPSU,[7] or in the person of the General Secretary of the Central Committee (First Secretary from 1952 to 1966) of the CPSU. The General Secretary is an ex-officio member of the Politburo and presides over its meetings. The prime example of the latter type of leadership is that portion of the period of Stalin's ascendancy dating from the conclusion of the Great Purges at the end of 1938 to Stalin's death in March 1953, during which time Stalin ruled both the CPSU and the country as a virtually unchallengeable autocrat.

[6] The several citations from the Soviet Constitution quoted in this paragraph are taken from Harold Berman and Miroslav Kerner's *Soviet Military Law and Administration* (Cambridge: Harvard University Press, 1955), pp. 5–7. The present author's discussion of the distinctions between formal and actual decision-making authority in military matters is based on the discussion of the constitutional framework of civil-military relations in the USSR found on pages 5 through 9 of that study.

[7] The Politburo of the Central Committee of the CPSU was recast as the Presidium in 1952. In 1966, however, it reverted back to its original name. Theoretically, the Politburo is elected by the Central Committee of the CPSU, which is, in turn, elected by the All-Union Party Congress, the assembly proclaimed by the CPSU statutes to be the "supreme organ" of Party authority. In fact, however, the Politburo determines its own membership by the twin processes of cooptation and ouster except when the General Secretary has consolidated his authority in or over the Party to the extent that he is able to name the membership. At the present time the Politburo has 16 full (voting) members and seven candidate (nonvoting) members.

At the time of the Revolution (November 7, 1917) and for approximately two years thereafter, it was the Central Committee itself, which then numbered about 25 persons, that served as the chief decision-making body in the Soviet Republic. From March 1918 to March 1919 there was no Politburo at all, according to Leonard Schapiro. For a fuller discussion of this question see Schapiro's *The Communist Party of the Soviet Union* (New York: Random House, 1959), pp. 239–241.

In sum, despite the implications of the cited provisions of the Soviet Constitution, the Supreme Soviet and its Presidium and the Council of Ministers and its Presidium[8] have possessed and continue to possess only ministerial and executive powers to announce and implement policy decisions taken by the CPSU leadership. And, whether the important policy decision on national security matters have been taken collectively, by vote in the Politburo (Presidium), or a smaller executive body thereof, or by the General Secretary himself, it has always been the leadership of the highly-centralized Party that has exercised final policy-making authority in the military and civilian spheres.

Although supreme policy-making power has always been wielded by the leader or leaders of the CPSU, the chain of command through which the Party's decisions have been transmitted to the military and the military establishment's views and recommendations presented to the Party leadership has often been a mystery to outsiders. This mystery has been the product of two interrelated factors: the extreme secrecy that has always prevailed at the highest levels of the Soviet government and the fact that authority at the apex of the Soviet power pyramid has traditionally flowed through personal rather than well-defined institutional channels. The personalized nature of political power at the top of the Party-government complex can, in turn, be explained largely in terms of the well-established practice of the concurrent holding by Politburo members of other high party and state positions or, what is merely another way of stating the same thing, the cooptation of officials selected to head important state and governmental bodies into the Politburo. For example, Leonid I. Brezhnev, the present General Secretary of the CPSU, is both the ex-officio head of the Secretariat of the Central Committee of the CPSU[9] and a member of the Presidium of the Supreme Soviet. Certain other present members and candidate members of the Politburo concurrently hold the post of Secretary of the Central Committee (see footnote 8). Moreover, Politburo members Aleksey N. Kosygin and Nikolay

[8] The Presidium of the Council of Ministers is composed of the Chairman, First Deputy Chairmen, and Deputy Chairmen of the Council of Ministers. The Presidium actually directs the work of its parent body and frequently acts in its name.

[9] The Secretariat of the Central Committee of the CPSU, the executive arm and staff agency of the central Party apparatus, is headed by the General Secretary of the CPSU and administered by the several Secretaries of the Central Committee (the number has varied from three to more than ten) who are often called "Party Secretaries." Although the Party Secretaries are ostensibly elected by the Central Committee, they are actually chosen by the General Secretary or, at times of collective leadership, by the collective leadership. The Secretariat is organized into various "otdely" (departments) such as the Party Organs Otdel and the Administrative Organs Otdel, each supervised by a Party Secretary or department chief. Each *otdel* is responsible for supervising some segment of the Party or government apparatus. For a more detailed discussion of the functions of the Secretariat see John S. Reshetar, Jr., *The Soviet Polity: Government and Politics in the USSR* (New York: Dodd, Mead & Co., 1971), pp. 144–146.

V. Podgorny serve as Chairman of the Presidium of the Council of Ministers and Chairman of the Presidium of the Supreme Soviet, respectively. Also, the head of the security (secret) police has often been either a member or a candidate member of the Politburo. (The present head of the Committee of State Security, known usually by its Russian initials "KGB," Yuriy Andropov, is a full member of the Politburo.) Politburo members have also served frequently as members of the Presidium of the Supreme Soviet. On two occasions, one of which shall be discussed in more detail later, career officers of the uniformed military have attained full membership in the Politburo (Presidium). The first career military officer to attain membership in the Politburo, then known as the Presidium, was Marshal Georgy K. Zhukov, who as Minister of Defense attained candidate membership in 1956 and full membership for a brief period in 1957. The only other career military officer to rise to membership in the Politburo is the present Minister of Defense, Marshal Andrey A. Grechko, who was named a full member by a plenary session of the Central Committee held on April 26-27, 1973.

As a result of this fusion of state and governmental functions in the persons of the members of the Politburo, decisions made by this body are often conveyed personally to the appropriate action organ of the bureaucracy by one of the decision-makers himself. A second result of this fusion of functions is that the decision-makers frequently tend to represent or at least articulate the interests of important institutions or interest groupings. This was true, as we shall see, in the case of Minister of Defense Zhukov during the brief period of his membership in the Presidium (Politburo).

Because of the personalized nature of political power in the USSR and the secrecy in which policy decisions are made and transmitted to the appropriate action organs, the formal chain of command through which important decisions of the Party leadership are communicated to the Ministry of Defense and policy inputs from the Ministry of Defense reach the Politburo is largely a matter of conjecture. On the basis of the very limited information available, however, it is possible to make certain educated guesses about these processes.

The Ministry of Defense, it should be noted, is headed by Marshal Andrey A. Grechko, a professional military officer. In the years since Stalin's death in 1953 it has become established practice for a professional military officer to hold this post. As a result, the Soviet military is, in the words of Raymond L. Garthoff, "more the master of its own house than it would be if it had a civilian defense minister." [10] Although there are Party and security police control systems operating in the Ministry of Defense itself and in all military units down to and including the regimental level—and perhaps

[10] Raymond L. Garthoff, *Soviet Military Policy: A Historical Analysis* (New York: Frederick A. Praeger, 1966), p. 61. Hereafter cited as Garthoff, *Soviet Military Policy*.

even battalion and company levels—the Ministry, which is highly centralized, often seems able to present and defend the majority views of the military establishment on specific policy issues in dialogues with the Party leadership.

Until the changes in the membership of the Politburo promulgated by the April 26-27 plenum of the Central Committee of the CPSU, the chief forum for the discussion of national-security policy by representatives of the Party leadership and the military establishment seems to have been the Defense Committee.[11] The Committee's exact membership is unknown, but it is probably chaired by the General Secretary of the CPSU, Brezhnev, and numbers among its members other key members of the Politburo such as Chairman of the Presidium of the Council of Ministers Kosygin, Chairman of the Presidium of the Supreme Soviet Podgorny, and Secretary of the Central Committee and candidate member of the Politburo Dimitriy F. Ustinov, a Party apparatchik who has spent virtually his whole career as a specialist on defense industry matters. Military members would include Defense Minister and full member of the Politburo Grechko, Commander-in-Chief of the Warsaw Pact Forces Marshal Ivan I. Yakubovsky, and the commanders of the Ground Forces, Strategic Missile Forces, Air Force, Navy, and Air Defense Forces.

While it seems likely that real differences of view are aired at Defense Committee sessions, it is highly improbable that anything resembling voting on policy questions takes place at this level. What is more likely is that final decisions on important policy questions are made—after careful consideration of both military and nonmilitary inputs—either by the entire Politburo or a smaller grouping thereof. Many of the decisions taken by the Politburo may be communicated formally to the military at sessions of the Defense Committee. Other Politburo directives on national-security matters may be transmitted to the Ministry of Defense either via the Presidium of the Council of Ministers or, in cases involving changes in the high command, the mobilization of troops, or other matters relating to the constitutional prerogatives of the Supreme Soviet, via the Presidium of the Supreme Soviet. Because he

[11] David Mark of the Bureau of Intelligence and Research of the U.S. Department of State confirmed the existence of the Defense Committee in testimony concerning the ABM question before the Subcommittee on Economy in Government of the Joint Economic Committee of the U.S. Congress in June, 1969. Mr. Mark's testimony may be found in "The Military Budget and National Economic Priorities" (Part III), 91st Congress, First Session, June, 1969, U.S. Government Printing Office, Washington, 1969, p. 956.

During World War II and again during the period of Krushchev's ascendancy, bodies similar in function to the present Defense Committee are known to have existed. The World War II body was known as the State Defense Committee, while the one that functioned during at least part of the Khrushchev period seems to have been called the Supreme Military Council.

has a seat on the Politburo, Minister of Defense Grechko is, of course, in a position informally to alert appropriate elements of the military establishment of impending Politburo directives before these directives can be disseminated in written form.

The Defense Committee seems to be concerned only with problems of over-all military and national-security policy. It does not seem to get involved in more routine military matters. Although the chain of command from the Politburo to the Ministry of Defense for more routine matters is a closely held secret, the following hypothesis seems plausible. Politburo directives affecting military matters are transmitted formally to the Presidium of the Council of Ministers, often, perhaps, through the office of the Chairman of the Presidium of the Council of Ministers, who is a Politburo member. The Presidium of the Council of Ministers, in turn, transmits them to the Ministry of Defense. Memoranda from the Ministry of Defense containing recommendations for action or describing options for decisions to be made by the Party leadership would seem to be sent first to the Presidium of the Council of Ministers and then to the Secretariat of the Central Committee. The Party Secretary (or Secretaries) responsible for handling defense matters in the Secretariat, who may himself be a member or candidate member of the Politburo, and his staff presumably screen such memoranda and decide whether they raise questions to be decided only by the Politburo or whether they can be decided in the Secretariat on the basis of previously-established policy.

It is possible—although not, in the present writer's view, probable—that the recent elevation of Minister of Defense Grechko to the Politburo will lead to a situation in which the Politburo itself will gradually eclipse the Defense Committee as the locus of discussion and resolution of all important national security questions. It is evident that Grechko's elevation to the Politburo will enable him to act as a spokesman for the military establishment on questions of national security policy—insofar as there may be a concensus among the Ground Forces, Navy, Strategic Missile Forces, Air Defense Forces, and other components of the military establishment. It seems reasonable, nevertheless, to assume that the top Party leadership will desire to hear the views of the heads of the individual services and other high-ranking officers as well as those of the Minister of Defense himself before making decisions on such important matters as force structures and posture and the amount of resources to be allocated to various defense-related industries. If this assumption is correct, we can postulate the continuing existence of the Defense Committee or the creation of a similar body.

Although it is based partly on conjecture and should not, therefore, be accepted as established fact, the foregoing account of the institutional relationships between the Party leadership and the military establishment in the making of national-security policy does give us some insight into the ways in which the Party has dominated this process. As we shall see, however, domination of the military establishment by the CPSU leadership, a leadership which presently includes the Minister of Defense himself, has not been restricted to the Party's control of policy-making. Ideological and practical considerations have combined to lead the CPSU throughout Soviet history to seek and, in significant measure, achieve complete supremacy over the military establishment and all other potentially autonomous institutions in the USSR.

THE RATIONALE FOR PARTY HEGEMONY, THE METHODS OF PARTY CONTROL, AND THE REACTION OF THE MILITARY

The uniqueness of the environment in which civil-military affairs are conducted in the USSR cannot be explained solely in terms of the peculiarity of Soviet institutions, the largely personalized nature of political power, and the dominance by the leadership of the CPSU of the national-security policy-making process. These are, to be sure, important aspects of the unique Soviet environment. The *roots* of the uniqueness of the Soviet environment, however, are to be found in Marxist ideology as interpreted and transformed by Lenin, the Bolshevik concept of the nature and role of the revolutionary party, and the circumstances prevailing in Russia at the time of the Bolshevik Revolution.

The ideological convictions of Lenin and his fellow Bolsheviks and their successors have influenced the nature of civil-military relations in the USSR in several important respects. Of fundamental importance was Lenin's conviction that the revolutionary party was to be "the vanguard of the proletariat," the class destined in the Marxist-Leninist view to revolt against the existing capitalist order. Once in power the vanguard party would, in Lenin's view, establish a revolutionary dictatorship that would crush the remnants of the capitalist economic order, demolish the existing social and governmental systems, and lead society first in the construction of socialism, the lower stage of communism, and ultimately in the construction of communism itself. In the view of Lenin and his followers, they and their party alone among the political factions contending for power in the weakened, war-weary Russia of 1917 possessed an infallible doctrine based on the "scientific" laws of history discovered by Marx and Engels. Consequently, it was they and their Party, a small, highly centralized group of Marxian socialists who were willing to regard the making of revolution as their vocation, who were destined to be the instrument of historical change in Russia and, indeed, the harbingers of change in the world.

In the view of the Bolsheviks, the Party's decisions were historically correct, because they were based on a correct understanding of the dialectical laws of historical development. They believed it was only those who had mastered the teachings of Marx and Engels and who had become members of the Party, and not the working masses themselves, who could become truly conscious of the historical role of the proletariat and thus deduce the appropriate strategy for attaining its revolutionary goals. Therefore, they believed it was the Party which was destined to lead the working masses of Russia in the building of the classless society of the future.

A logical corollary of this belief was the Party's claim to hegemony—once it came to power—over the entire polity and every institution within it. The continuing effort on the part of the CPSU throughout the half-century of Soviet power to maintain hegemony over the military establishment and all other institutions in the USSR is thus a natural outgrowth of the view of the Bolsheviks and their successors of the historical role of the Party.

The 22nd Congress of the CPSU proclaimed in 1961 that the Party had become "the vanguard of the whole people" during the period of transition from socialism—which the CPSU leaders claim had already been achieved—to communism. This change in the description of the Party's role reflected the CPSU leaders' contention that by 1961 antagonistic classes no longer existed in the USSR. Not surprisingly, the change had no discernible practical effect on the Party's role within the Soviet policy. Indeed, the CPSU continues today to press its claim to hegemony over all elements of Soviet society.

When the Bolsheviks seized power by *coup* on November 7, 1917, they and their followers and allies represented only a minority of the population.[12] Once in power they faced the problem of developing a reliable military arm as soon as possible. Russia was still technically at war with the Central Powers, and although the Bolsheviks decried the war as an "imperialist" conflict and sued for peace, they were not at first willing to accept the terms of the Central Powers. Consequently, the new Soviet Government needed an organized military force to stem the renewed advance of the armies of the Central Powers. Meanwhile, the new regime was soon faced with an even greater requirement for armed force as the result of the outbreak of civil war followed by limited armed intervention by Great Britain, France, Japan and the United States.

The forces immediately available to the Bolsheviks in 1917-18 were, in the words of the prominent American sovietologist Merle Fainsod "a motley lot" consisting of armed workmen recruited in the Petrograd and

[12] In the November 25, 1917, election to the Constituent Assembly (although the election was held more than two weeks after the Bolshevik seizure of power, it had been scheduled by the Provisional Government), the Bolsheviks received only 25% of the votes. On January 19, 1918, the Bolsheviks dissolved the Constituent Assembly by force.

Moscow factories and organized into Red Guards, sailors from the Baltic fleet and a few units of the Petrograd garrison.[13] Ensuring the loyalty of these forces as well as the peasants who were to become the chief source of manpower for the newly created Workers' and Peasants' Red Army, and the NCO's and commissioned officers from the old Imperial Army who were, together with a few Bolsheviks, to become its officer corps became a primary task of the new regime. The Soviet Government decided to combat this problem by appropriating and adapting to its own requirements a scheme devised by the Provisional Government earlier in 1917: the appointment of commissars (commissioners), political representatives of the Soviet Government, to all large units of the armed forces.[14]

The network of political officers or commissars that grew up during the earliest months of Soviet power was conceived originally as a temporary expedient destined to last only until the Party could train a new officer corps composed of reliable communists. In fact, however, the institution of the political officer (commissar) gradually evolved into a permanent system of Party surveillance and control over the military, parallelling the military chain of command and extending from the highest levels of the Ministry of Defense down to regimental and batallion level and, occasionally, even company level. A control system descended from this original institution is functioning today.

In the course of the 50-odd years of its existence, the Party's control and surveillance system in the military has undergone substantial modification from time to time.[15] The most significant aspects of these modifications have involved the role of the political officer in professional military matters. The specific issue has been whether he should exercise the right of veto over all orders issued by the commanding officer of the unit to which he is assigned or whether his role should be restricted to the education and political indoctrination of the troops, the overseeing of the work of Party organizations in the armed forces, and serving as adviser to the commanding officer. During periods when his functions have been limited, at least formally, to education, indoctrination, and advising the commanding officer, the political officer at regimental and battalion level has held the title "Zampolit" (Deputy

[13] Merle Fainsod, *How Russia Is Ruled,* rev. ed. (Cambridge: Harvard University Press, 1963), p. 463.

[14] For a discussion of the role of the commissar under the Provisional Government and in the early years of the Soviet regime see Dmitrii Fedotoff White, *The Growth of the Red Army* (Princeton: Princeton University Press, 1944), pp. 74–75, and John Erickson, *The Soviet High Command: A Military Political History* (London: Macmillan and Co., Ltd., 1962), pp. 41–42.

[15] For a more detailed account of the historical background and institutional development of the Party's control system see Roman Kolkowicz, *The Soviet Military and the Communist Party* (Princeton: Princeton University Press, 1967), Chapter IV and V, pp. 80–173. Hereafter cited as *Kolkowicz.*

Commander for Political Affairs). At times when he has possessed the authority to veto the orders of the commanding officer, he has held the title of Military Commissar. The role and title of the political officer have oscillated since the early forties between the two poles of "Zampolit" and Military Commissar depending on the degree of control over the military the Party deems necessary at any given period of time.

Since May 1919 the Party's control system in the military has been administered by the Main Political Administration (MPA) of the Soviet Army and Navy (formerly the Main Political Administration of the Red Army). Although it operates formally as a component of the Ministry of Defense and, as such, is formally subordinate to the Minister of Defense, it also constitutes a section of the Central Committee of the CPSU and is directly responsible to the Secretariat and, through the Secretariat, to the Politburo itself.[16] Representatives of the MPA are assigned to all important levels in the military chain of command from the headquarters of the individual force commands (Ground Forces, Strategic Missile Forces, and the like) down to regimental and battalion and sometimes also company level.

At the present time the political officers of the MPA at regimental and battalion level carry the title "Zampolit" and do not have the formal authority to veto the orders of the regimental and battalion commanders. Still, the influence of the "Zampolit" on all the officers of the units to which he is assigned is substantial. He is first of all in charge of the political education and indoctrination of all the personnel in the unit. His authority is not limited to indoctrination and education, however. He has a voice in deciding which officers will be recommended for promotion. And finally, because he exercises control over both the Party and Komsomol (Communist League of Youth) organizations serving the personnel of his unit, the "Zampolit" is able to arrange for officers whose conduct is, in his judgment, contrary to the interests of the Party to be subjected to a ritual known as "kritika-samokritika" (criticism–self-criticism) at Party and Komsomol meetings.[17] If we add to these powers of the "Zampolit" the more generalized power he exercises as the representative as well as the eyes and ears of the Party in the unit to which he is assigned, we can see that his authority is formidable.

16 For a more detailed description of the organization and functions of the MPA see Kolkowicz, pp. 84–87 and p. 376.

17 "Kritika-samokritika" is an institutionalized ritual that occurs in all Party organizations throughout the USSR. It involves criticism by the "collective," i.e., by the members of the Party organization, of the alleged failure of one of the members to maintain proper Party discipline or to carry out his responsibilities as a member of the Party. The recalcitrant member is then expected to criticize himself by acknowledging the correctness of the criticism of the collective and promising to mend his ways. Military officers are reported to dislike this practice intensely because they regard criticism by those under their command as tending to erode their authority as commanding officers.

Although the role of its representative as the eyes, ears, and conscience of the Party in the military makes the MPA a powerful instrument of control indeed, the MPA is not the Party leadership's only control system in the military. A separate, parallel system of external control over the military in the form of a network of Special Sections presently known as Counterintelligence Sections has also existed from the earliest months of Soviet rule. This system is operated by the security (secret) police.

The All Russian Extraordinary Commission for Combating Counterrevolution, Sabotage and Speculation, usually referred to by its Russian acronym "Cheka," organized the first Special Sections in the Red Army in 1918. Their task was to maintain security and guard against counterrevolution. Except for a brief hiatus in 1919, the security police, in their various institutional guises—OGPU, NKVD, or MVD—have always maintained networks of Counterintelligence Sections in the military similar to the one which exists today.[18]

At present it is the Main Directorate of Counterintelligence, known by its Russian acronym GUK (or GUKR), that controls the network of Counterintelligence Sections in the military. (The GUK should not be confused with the Main [Military] Intelligence Administration, whose acronym is GRU, whose duties are focused largely on the gathering of intelligence on the military capabilities of foreign countries.) The GUK presently functions as a department of the Committee of State Security (KGB), the security police, and is therefore, actually subordinate to the head of the KGB rather than to the Minister of Defense. (The present head of the KGB, as we noted in Section II of this essay, is a member of the Politburo.) The formal role of the GUK is, in the words of ex-Red Army Colonel I. Dmitriev, "to combat foreign espionage and hostile penetration into the Soviet armed forces."[19] In fact, however, the GUK and its network are designed primarily to report on the morale of all military units, check on the loyalty of every officer and enlisted man, and to detain deserters and other military personnel whose activities are considered subversive.

Officers of the GUK, like those of the MPA, are assigned to units at various levels of the military chain of command down to regimental and perhaps even battalion level. All Counterintelligence officers are given assimilated military rank and wear the uniform and insignia of the units to which they are assigned.[20] Thus their identity is usually known only to the "Zam-

[18] Although it is somewhat dated, the single best English-language source on the operation of the Counterintelligence Sections in the military is Zbigniew Brzezinski, ed., *Political Controls in the Soviet Army,* Research Program on the USSR (Ann Arbor, Mich.: Edwards Brothers, 1954), pp. 54–83. The present discussion of the organization and activities of the Main Directorate of Counterintelligence is based in large measure on that study.

[19] Brzezinski, p. 54.

[20] Brzezinski, p. 56, footnote no. 2.

polit" and perhaps a handful of regular officers of the unit. The Counterintelligence officers' primary source of information about the personnel of the units to which they are assigned is a network of secret informers they recruit by various means, including blackmail and threats. Counterintelligence officers are also given copies of all orders issued by the commanding officer of the respective units. They are, therefore, in a position to know virtually everything that is happening in the unit to which they are attached.

In peacetime and under normal circumstances the authority of the Counterintelligence officers rests in large measure on their participation in the officer promotion process.[21] No officer can be recommended for promotion without the approval of both the "Zampolit" and the Counterintelligence Section of his division. Therefore, any professional military officer who has run afoul of the GUK apparatus may find himself unable to be promoted.

The reaction of the military establishment to the Party controls just outlined has not always been easy to gauge. A close reading of military journals and the military daily *Red Star* occasionally reveals hints of disgruntlement with these controls on the part of the military establishment. There has only been one period in recent Soviet history, however, when the military made any overt attempt to modify and weaken the system of controls thrust upon it. This was the period of the rise of Marshal Georgy K. Zhukov to the posts of Minister of Defense and candidate member and later full member in the Presidium (Politburo) of the Central Committee of the CPSU.

The circumstances of Marshall Zhukov's rise from the post of Deputy Minister of Defense to that of Minister of Defense and, more importantly, his rise to membership in the Presidium (Politburo) have been analyzed admirably by a number of scholars.[22] In broad outline, Zhukov's rise and the consequent ability of the military establishment to play, through him, an important role in the making of military and even national policy for the first time in Soviet history should, in this writer's view, be seen against the background of developments stemming from the death of Stalin, the autocrat, in March, 1953. As Stalin's successors maneuvered to gain all or even a

[21] During World War II the Counterintelligence Sections became known collectively and individually as "SMERSH," an acronym stemming from the Russian phrase "Smert' Shpionam," "death to spies," and possessed broad authority to mete out summary punishment, including execution, to suspected traitors, deserters, and shirkers. See Brzezinski, p. 54 and pp. 71–73 for a fuller account of the role of "SMERSH" during World War II.

[22] Among the best analyses of this subject are Zbigniew Brzezinski and Samuel P. Huntington, *Political Power: USA/USSR* (New York: The Viking Press, 1963), Chapter 8; Raymond L. Garthoff, *Soviet Strategy in the Nuclear Age* (New York: Frederick A. Praeger, Inc., 1962), Chapter 2; Raymond L. Garthoff, *Soviet Military Policy* (see footnote 10), Chapter 3; and Roman Kolkowicz, see page 16 of present essay, footnote 16, Chapters V-VII.

portion of the power he wielded, they looked to the military establishment as a source of countervailing armed force against Lavrenty Beria, the head of the security police, who had amassed great personal power including control over a number of military units belonging to the police apparatus. After Beria's ouster in June, 1953, several Party leaders continued to look to the military, in the person of Zhukov, as a potential ally or at least a benevolent neutral in the struggle for power in the Party. By siding with or at least backing Khrushchev and Bulganin, and later with Khrushchev alone against other leaders and factions in the Party, Zhukov gave Khrushchev important and perhaps indispensable help in consolidating his authority within the Party. In return, Zhukov was elevated to the post of Minister of Defense in February 1955 and then became the first professional military officer to be elected candidate member (February 1956) and then full member (July 1957) of the Presidium (Politburo). Zhukov's tenure as a member of the Presidium proved to be relatively brief, however, as he was ousted from both the Presidium and the Ministry of Defense in October, 1957.

Students of Soviet civil-military affairs are deeply interested in the whole range of Zhukov's attempted reforms as Minister of Defense. Within the framework of this essay, however, we are interested chiefly in his attempts to diminish certain of the MPA controls in the military. Interestingly enough, Zhukov's reforms, so far as we know, did not affect the operation of the Counterintelligence Sections in the military.

As Minister of Defense, Zhukov succeeded in abolishing the position of "Zampolit" at company level and moving the battalion-level "Zampolit" up to regimental level.[23] More significantly, he increased the authority of military commanders in relation to the "Zampolits" by restricting the role of the latter to the areas of education and morale and relegating these activities to times when they would not detract from the performance of military duties.[24] Finally, he instituted a number of reforms designed to appeal especially to officers. These included placing the study by officers and enlisted men of Party history and ideology on a voluntary basis, granting officers the option to substitute combat training for political education, and perhaps most important of all from the officers' point of view, attempting to restrict the scope of "kritika-samokritika" by exempting purely military aspects of the commanders' activities from Party and Komsomol criticism.[25]

Several days before Zhukov's demise the Presidium (Politburo) adopted a resolution designed to increase the scope of the functions of the political organs in the military. In the period between Zhukov's ouster and the April 26-27, 1973, plenum of the Central Committee of the CPSU when

[23] Kolkowicz, p. 129.
[24] Kolkowicz, p. 127.
[25] Kolkowicz, p. 129.

the present Minister of Defense, Marshal Grechko, was named a full member of the Politburo, the military establishment had no voice in the highest policy-making body in the Party and, consequently, no real opportunity to attempt to limit the scope of Party controls over the military. Available indicators, such as military newspapers and journals, suggest, however, that at least some elements in the military establishment remain unconvinced of the utility of Party controls, at least in their present degree. In the coming weeks and months students of Soviet political-military affairs will be watching for signs that Marshal Grechko may attempt to use his influence as a member of the Politburo to reduce the scope or even modify the structure of Party controls over the military establishment.

The present writer considers it unlikely that Grechko will attempt to effect any dramatic changes in Party controls over the military. Grechko must be well aware of the connections between Zhukov's unceremonious ouster from his posts as full member of the Presidium (Politburo) and Minister of Defense and his efforts to limit the influence within the military establishment of the MPA and its personnel. Presumably Grechko is also conscious that he lacks the power base in the Party and particularly its Central Committee to mount a successful challenge to the authority of the MPA, an institution that in all likelihood enjoys the protection of General Secretary Brezhnev who briefly held the position of First Deputy Chief of the MPA in the period following the death of Stalin.

THE DYNAMICS OF CIVIL-MILITARY RELATIONS IN THE USSR AT THE PRESENT TIME AND PROSPECTS FOR THE IMMEDIATE FUTURE

The CPSU is still firmly committed to its leading role in Soviet society. In practice, as we have seen, this role has been characterized by a compulsion to dominate—or at least strive to dominate—the entire Soviet polity and the economy and, consequently, to manipulate and control all institutions in the society. The Party seems more concerned about maintaining its dominance over the military establishment than over any other institution, except, perhaps, the security police. This is in part because the Party leadership is keenly aware that the leaders of the military establishment control the largest single concentration of the means of physical coercion in Soviet society.[26] It is also a consequence of the Party's traditional fears of Bonapartism and elitist separatism on the part of military leaders.

[26] The Soviet Armed Forces do not, however, have a monopoly on the means of coercion. Both the Committee of State Security (KGB) and the Ministry of Internal Affairs (MVD) have armed military and paramilitary forces at their disposal. The KGB forces include Border Guards, Government Signal Troops, and perhaps guard

The Party leadership continues to deem it necessary to maintain special controls over the military establishment, despite the fact that important military leaders are themselves not only Party members but often also members of the Party's Central Committee and the Minister of Defense is a member of the Politburo itself. The system of "Zampolits" under the MPA and the system of Counterintelligence officers employed by the KGB are still in place and functioning. And there is no evidence that the ritual of "kritika-samokritika," [27] which is apparently disliked by many military officers, has been abolished or fallen into disuse. It seems reasonable, therefore, to postulate some continuing tension between the military and the CPSU leadership over the two control and surveillance networks. It also seems safe to assume that barring some severe, unforeseen shock to the Soviet system such as the strains that would result from a protracted land war with the People's Republic of China, as envisaged by the dissident Soviet journalist and historian Andrey Amalryk in his book *Will the Soviet Union Survive Until 1984?* [28] Party rule in something like its present form and both the political and police control systems in the military and the tensions they engender will persist.

In the period from the ouster of Marshal Zhukov from his positions of full member of the Presidium (Politburo) and Minister of Defense in October 1957 until the plenary session of the Central Committee of the CPSU of April 26-27, 1973, the pattern of civil-military relations in the USSR was clearly one of subordination of the military establishment to the CPSU leadership in the making of national-security policy. It is possible that the designation at this plenum of the Central Committee of the incumbent Minister of Defense Grechko as a full member of the Politburo may alter this pattern of military subordination to the Party. As of this writing, however, there is no evidence in the public domain that Grechko's accession to the Politburo has been accompanied by a turn toward a more belligerent or nationalistic line in Soviet foreign policy. In fact, General Secretary Brezhnev, in his policy address at the same plenary session of the Central Com-

---

troops as well. The MVD forces include Internal Troops, the Militia (uniformed police), and Fire Guard. For a cogent discussion of the role and organization of KGB and MVD forces as well as an estimate of their size, see J. T. Reitz, "Soviet Defense-Associated Activities Outside the Ministry of Defense," in "Economic Performance and the Military Burden in the Soviet Union: A Compendium of Papers Submitted to the Subcommittee on Foreign Economic Policy of the Joint Economic Committee of the Congress of the United States," U.S. Government Printing Office, Washington, D.C., 1970, pp. 135–165.

[27] See footnote 17.

[28] Andrey Amalryk, *Will the Soviet Union Survive Until 1984?* (New York: Harper and Row, 1970).

mittee, reportedly stated that the present atmosphere was propitious for the further improvement of relations between the U.S. and the USSR as well as between the "socialist" countries, i.e., the USSR and the Communist Countries of Eastern Europe and the Federal Republic of Germany. He also said that "favorable conditions" had been established "for the development of peaceful collaboration among the countries of Europe.[29] This address hardly signaled a tougher line in Soviet foreign policy. There is also no evidence at this early date that Grechko has made any moves toward curbing the role and influence of the MPA and GUK in the Soviet military.

The present writer considers it likely, but by no means certain, that the well-established pattern of subordination of the military establishment to the CPSU will persist, notwithstanding Marshal Grechko's accession to the Politburo. So long as the professional Party bureaucrats in the Politburo are able to reach a consensus on major policy decisions on such national-security questions as the relative levels of investment in the capital goods sector of the economy, on one hand, and the consumer-related industries sector on the other, the balance between nuclear and non-nuclear weapons and delivery systems, the size of the defense budget, force levels, and the specific types of weapons systems to be built, the role of the military establishment is likely to continue to be that of (a) adviser—and advocate of the military consensus—on matters such as military strategy and weapons systems, (b) planner, and (c) executor and administrator of the policy directives of the Politburo.

As the Zhukov case illustrates, however, at times of acute intra-Party tension, such as periods when as the result of the death or ouster of a powerful Party leader there is an open struggle for supremacy within the Politburo and Secretariat, or when the Party leadership is faced with unreconcilable policy differences—which in the context of the modus operandi of the Politburo can be resolved ultimately only by the ouster of one leader or faction or the other—the military establishment may find itself able to advance its institutional interests and play a greater role in the formulation of national-security policy by means of a tacit alliance with one of the Party leaders or factions contending for power. Such an alliance, while it may prove quite beneficial to the military for the period of its duration, is likely to last only until a single Party leader—or coalition of leaders—consolidates his authority within the Politburo and Secretariat and, consequently, within the entire Party apparatus. Once this occurs, the Party leadership, given its operational code calling for Party dominance and manipulation of all the

[29] See the April 30, 1973, edition of the *New York Times* for an unofficial translation of excerpts from Brezhnev's address as carried by the April 29 edition of *Pravda,* the daily newspaper of the Central Committee of the CPSU.

other elements of the polity,[30] will maneuver to relegate the military establishment once again to a position of subordination in the national-security policy-making process.

Once united, the Party leadership possesses a whole panoply of techniques to eliminate what it considers to be dangerous elements in the military. These techniques include: (a) encouraging the development of factionalism in the military by the promotion to high rank and important commands of officers well-disposed toward the Party leadership;[31] (b) engineering the election to the Central Committee of the CPSU of those military officers willing to accede to Party domination and dropping those who do not; (c) assigning potentially dangerous military leaders to relatively unimportant commands; and (d) the use of Party discipline—every officer holding a top command is a member of the CPSU—including in extreme circumstances public censure in the media against those who persist in their opposition to Party domination.

Because they are well aware that the military establishment has vast powers of coercion at its disposal, the Party leaders are likely to move both circumspectly and gradually to undermine what they judge to be dangerous elements in the military leadership. Over the long pull the Party is virtually certain, in the author's view, to reassert successfully its domination over military leaders who threaten its position.

Some sovietologists have seen the Soviet military establishment as acquiring increasing institutional autonomy in the post-Stalin era. One of the most prestigious of these is the American specialist on Soviet military affairs Roman Kolkowicz. In his book *The Soviet Military and the Communist Party*,[32] published in 1967, Kolkowicz argues that the Soviet military has been moving gradually toward the attainment of greater institutional autonomy despite the setback suffered when Marshal Zhukov was removed

[30] Nathan Leites' books, *The Operational Code of the Politburo* (New York: McGraw-Hill, 1951), and *A Study of Bolshevism* (Glencoe, Ill.: The Free Press, 1953), are classic studies in the psychological aspects of the behavior of the leaders of the CPSU. For a more recent study of the structure of beliefs and assumptions about the nature of politics of the Bolsheviks and their successors see Alexander L. George, "The 'Operational Code': A Neglected Approach to the Study of Political Leaders and Decision-Making," the RAND Corporation, RM-5427-PR, September, 1967. For a discussion of the operational code of the CPSU in relation to Marxian ideology see Chapter 4, "The Operational Code," of Alfred G. Meyer's *Leninism*, (New York, Washington: Praeger, 1956).

[31] The Presidium of the Supreme Soviet of the USSR is empowered by the Constitution to confer the title "Marshal of the Soviet Union" and to appoint and dismiss top commanders in the armed forces. In reality, however, it is the section of the Secretariat responsible for military affairs or the Politburo itself which decides who the top commanders will be.

[32] See footnote 15.

from his posts as member of the Presidium (Politburo) and Minister of Defense in 1957. Kolkowicz also contends that although Stalin's terror and Khrushchev's promotion of military officers closely associated with him during his days as a Military Commissar on the Stalingrad Front in World War II have hampered the ability of the military establishment to play "its great potential role in Soviet politics," the military is likely to play a more active role as "the last of the Bolsheviks in the Party are on their way out, and their followers in the military are ready to retire." [33]

Kolkowicz believes that the Party has become deeply concerned with what he alleges to be the growing desire of the Soviet officer corps to indulge itself in the kinds of elitist behavior observable in the military establishments of noncommunist societies. The Party, he feels, has moved to counter this growing elitism. In his view, however, the Party's program not only has been unsuccessful but has actually added to the friction between the officer corps and the Party and, consequently, underscored the necessity of a more radical solution to the problem. The solution, Kolkowicz suggests, is likely to be an enhanced role for the military in Soviet politics. He identifies four interrelated developments with the Soviet polity as working to produce an atmosphere conducive to the growth of the military as a powerful, self-conscious institution. They are:

> (1) the progressive ideological disillusionment of Soviet society, (2) the stress on functional and professional excellence, (3) the emergence of a mild form of pluralism, and (4) the absence of the terror machine. . . .[34]

Kolkowicz does not spell out what specific phenomena he has in mind when he speaks of "progressive ideological disillusionment" in the USSR. It seems fair to assume, however, that he is referring, at least in part, to the increasingly vocal protests against various aspects of the Soviet system by dissentient intellectuals like physicist Andrey Sakharov, biochemist Zhores Medvedyev and his brother, historian Roy Medvedyev, journalist-historian Andrey Amalryk, and poet Vladimir Bukovsky. Telling and courageous as their criticisms and the criticisms of other dissenters may be to certain of their fellow Soviet intellectuals, as well as to the general newspaper reader in Western Europe and the United States, their protests have, as yet, evoked no visible response whatsoever from the overwhelming mass of Soviet citizens. It should be emphasized, too, that judging from the available evidence, the number of these dissenters is exceedingly small. What is more, the few scattered triumphs they have achieved as a result of their many confrontations with the security police have resulted in large measure from their success, through contacts with resident foreign journalists and foreign

[33] Kolkowicz, p. 346.
[34] Kolkowicz, p. 347.

tourists visiting the USSR, in having their grievances publicized abroad. Thus it has been the potential embarrassment to the Soviet Government and damage to its foreign policy interests rather than support from groups or institutions in the USSR that have gained a measure of autonomy that explain nearly all the successes of the dissenters.[35] More important, however, is the fact that in most instances the dissenters have not achieved success. The convictions and incarceration of Larissa Daniel and Pavel Litvinov as a result of their protest against the Soviet-led invasion of Czechoslovakia in August 1968 and the conviction and incarceration of historian Andrey Amalryk and poet Andrey Bykovsky in recent months are illustrative of both the Soviet Government's tough line on dissent and the dissenters' lack of public support.

Presumably the factors on which Kolkowicz's assertion that a "mild form of pluralism" has emerged in Soviet society rest are an allegedly observable increase in the autonomy of specialized elites such as the scientific and managerial elites and, perhaps more significantly, the emergence of the military itself as a conscious and increasingly assertive institution. Aside from the Medvedyev case, the present writer is unaware of any instance where a significant number of Soviet scientists, acting collectively, have successfully confronted the Party leadership on an issue involving their interests as a group. Similarly, there seems to be no evidence to indicate that industrial managers have been able to assert their interests as a collective entity. Finally, it is moot whether even the Soviet officer corps—which tends, as Kolkowicz notes, to be a closed, elitist group with common values stemming from the peculiarities of the educational process at military academies, shared experiences both in the field and in the military bureaucracy, use of common jargon, and the habit of commanding others and being part of a chain of command[36]—has attained the degree of autonomy he imputes to it.

The question of whether the military establishment is gaining increased institutional autonomy turns on the more fundamental question of whether a type of pluralism is developing within the Soviet polity. As we have seen, Kolkowicz flatly asserts that a "mild form of pluralism" has in fact emerged in Soviet society. He does not, however, indicate how he defines the concept of pluralism within the context of the Soviet polity.

[35] The one important exception to this generalization is the case of biochemist Zhores A. Medvedyev, who was seized by the secret police and placed in a mental institution because of his exposé of the effects of Stalinism on freedom of scientific inquiry in the USSR. This exposé took the form of a book entitled *The Rise and Fall of T. D. Lysenko* (New York, 1969), which was smuggled to the West to be published. Protests by Medvedyev's fellow scientists as well as unfavorable publicity in the foreign press of his detention led to his release and return to laboratory work.

[36] Kolkowicz, p. 21.

Since the mid-sixties a number of scholars in the West have addressed the question of the existence of a form of pluralism in the USSR. At the root of their effort has been the conviction that by viewing Soviet society in terms of the concept of a monolithic totalitarianism, Western scholarship has created a self-imposed limitation on its ability to detect and evaluate change in the Soviet system. The scholarly debate over both the utility of the concept of pluralism as a tool in the analysis of the Soviet polity and the question of the existence of pluralism in any form continues. The number of proponents of the utility of some concept of pluralism as an analytic tool seems to be growing.

This writer agrees with those who believe that the development of a concept and model of pluralism applicable to the Soviet polity will be useful as a device for measuring change in the political system. At the same time he takes the view that pluralism in the Western—and especially the American—understanding of the concept does not now exist and is unlikely to evolve in the USSR. Autonomous institutions able to organize freely and represent openly the interests of their members in the political decision-making process do not exist in the USSR. As the Canadian scholar Bohdan Harasymiw has observed in a recent paper, the only groups able to represent their interests in the political decision-making process in the USSR are those which the CPSU leadership regards as legitimate.[37] This means, as Harasymiw notes, that there are no groups in Soviet society that are autonomous in the sense that they exercise control over their internal affairs and over the lives of their members.

A number of the other aspects of the Soviet system also work to prevent the rise of pluralism in the sense that the term is understood in the West. The communications media are tightly controlled by the bureaucracy on behalf of the Party; as a result there is no freedom of the press, and would-be interest groups are unable to articulate their objectives publicly. Nor is there freedom of association. Soviet citizens are not free to form or join associations other than those approved by the Party. Most important of all, the Party itself is hostile to the very idea of institutional or sub-group autonomy. In its view, Soviet society is and should remain "monolithic."

It seems clear, then, that pluralism in the Western sense does not exist in the USSR and that there are no autonomous institutions—when measured in terms of the criteria for institutional autonomy commonly used in the West—in the Soviet polity.

Military, managerial-technocratic, scientific, and cultural elites do exist in the USSR, however. And, as Harasymiw indicates, recent studies have

[37] Bohdan Harasymiw, "Application of the Concept of Pluralism to the Soviet Political System," *Newsletter on Comparative Studies of Communism,* vol. v., no. 1, November, 1971, pp. 40–54.

shown that more members of at least one of these elites, the managerial-technocratic, have found their way to positions of political leadership in the post-Stalin period than in the Stalin era.[38] Although professional (career) Party apparatchiks still have the inside track in gaining access to political offices—this is chiefly the result of the Party's control of all appointments to important Party and governmental positions—leadership selection has, in Harasymiw's words, "moved toward the pluralistic type." [39]

We must not overestimate the significance of this phenomenon, however. The overwhelming majority of the top political and governmental apparatus leaders in the USSR continue to be Party careerists. The members of the military establishment and technocratic elite who have gained greater access to positions of political leadership in the post-Stalin period have been able to do so because at some point in their careers they became Party careerists as well. What we have witnessed in the post-Stalin period is a gradual broadening of the sources from which the Party draws its leaders to include promising technocrats. With the exception of Marshal Zhukov's rise to membership in the Presidium (Politburo) during 1955–57, however, the present Minister of Defense Marshal Grechko has been the only career military officer to rise to the summit of political leadership in recent years.

Insofar as the members of the military establishment and other elites develop and retain attitudes that challenge Party dominance of the decision-making process and are able and willing to articulate these views in high Party and government councils, it may be argued that a type of pluralism—albeit one far different from those which exist in Western societies—is developing in the USSR. One of the few scholars who has studied the development of elite attitudes that question Party dominance of the decision-making process is Milton Lodge. In a book entitled *Soviet Elite Attitudes Since Stalin*,[40] Lodge maintains that specialist elites are indeed developing attitudes that stress their right to participate in the decision-making process and, therefore, constitute a challenge to Party supremacy. If Lodge's conclusions are supported by further studies, we may conclude that a type of extremely limited pluralism may slowly be evolving in the USSR. This incipient Soviet-style pluralism, to the degree that it exists at all, would seem to differ so radically from the pluralism found in a number of Western countries as to deserve a special name.

The Soviet military establishment may be viewed conceptually as an elite group of experts in military art and science bound together by certain military traditions and the shared experience that results from military life.

[38] Harasymiw, p. 52.

[39] Harasymiw, p. 52.

[40] Milton Lodge, *Soviet Elite Attitudes Since Stalin* (Columbus, Ohio: Charles E. Merrill, 1969).

As such its input into the decision-making process in national-security affairs may be likened to that of a quasi-interest group. It possesses a clearly-defined, homogeneous institutional base, the Ministry of Defense. It is headed by a professional military officer and need not filter its views on security policy matters through any civilian chief. Consequently, it is able to aggregate the views of the military elite and, insofar as either a consensus or a set of clearly-defined options can be agreed upon, its head, the Minister of Defense, is able to articulate them at sessions of the Politburo meetings of the Defense Committee and in other official encounters with the Party and government leadership. The military establishment's near-monopoly, in an age of increasingly sophisticated technology, on expertise concerning the capabilities of weapons systems including those of the putative enemy, the logistic requirements of modern forces, and related matters strengthens significantly its ability to speak with a distinct and often very persuasive institutional voice in its dealings with the Party leadership.

Weighty though the voice of the military establishment in the making of decisions on national-security matters seems to be, the limits on its autonomy as an institution should not be underestimated. These limitations include the MPA and GUK control systems, the Party leadership's control over promotions and assignments of top military leaders, and the susceptibility of high military leaders—as members of the CPSU—to "kritika-samokritika" and other forms of Party discipline. Finally, we must continually bear in mind the fact that it is the Party itself, and especially the Politburo, that constitutes the arena in which major policy decisions are made. Although, as we have seen, the military establishment has recently acquired representation in the Politburo after a hiatus of more than fifteen years, it is impossible as of this writing to assess the impact of this change. Newspaper columns and editorials that interpret the elevation of Marshal Grechko and Chairman of the Committee of State Security (KGB) Andropov, to full membership in the Politburo as an indication of a power shift in the Kremlin in favor of more militant elements seem to be based solely on conjecture.[41]

Abrupt changes in the dynamics of Soviet civil-military relations over the next few years are not likely, despite Marshal Grechko's accession to the Politburo. It seems possible, nevertheless, that we may now be witnessing the onset of a new phase in civil-military relations, a phase characterized by the emergence of a new generation of military leaders who, in the words of Raymond Garthoff, would be "more professional and less bound to the

[41] I refer specifically to an unsigned editorial in the May 2, 1973, edition of the *New York Times* entitled "Moscow Power Shift" as well as to an article by Joseph Alsop entitled "A New Power in the Politburo," which was printed in the May 4, 1973, edition of the *Washington Post.*

political (Party) leaders either by ideology or by the personal bonds of wartime service." [42] As Garthoff indicates, however, the rise of a new generation of increasingly professional military leaders does not necessarily imply direct conflict between the military establishment and the Party leadership.[43] In fact, it is Garthoff's view—and the present writer agrees with him—that the military establishment is "not likely to try to assume a leading role in the political realm unless there is a collapse in the Party's rule." [44] It seems possible, then, that instead of leading to a larger voice for the military in the making of political decisions, the impact of the ascendance of a new generation of officers to high positions in the military establishment may be restricted, initially at least, to formalizing and professionalizing the dialogue between the Party leadership and the military on national-security questions.

Surveying the Soviet civil-military relations horizon in mid-1969, Thomas W. Wolfe advanced the view that the Soviet military establishment as an interest group operating within the ruling elite had acquired greater prestige and influence during the Brezhnev-Kosygin tenure than it enjoyed under Khrushchev.[45] Marshal Grechko's accession to the Politburo certainly symbolized the greater prestige and influence the military establishment has acquired since the deposition of Khrushchev. At the same time, Wolfe voiced the opinion that behind the facade of tranquility and harmony between the Party leadership and the military were "intractable issues which generate continuing internal controversy and tension." [46] The present writer shares this view and believes it applies equally to the atmosphere of civil-military relations that prevails in the USSR at the present time. Tensions over Party and KGB controls over the military, the percentage of resources to be allocated to defense-related industry and new weapons systems, nuclear strategy and the question of negotiated limitations on strategic weapons, and no doubt other issues of which we are not aware are almost certainly present. What is more, there is nothing to indicate that they will not persist in the foreseeable future.

We must, of course, keep our sense of perspective in assessing the

[42] Garthoff, *Soviet Military Policy* (see footnote 10), p. 61.

[43] An article by Drew Middleton in the April 22, 1973, edition of the *New York Times* reports that over the past 18 months a number of younger Soviet officers with technical backgrounds have been transferred to commands that had been the preserve of Ground Forces officers of World War II vintage. The implications of these changes in terms of Soviet military strategy are not yet clear.

[44] Garthoff, *Soviet Military Policy*, p. 61.

[45] Thomas W. Wolfe, "Are the Generals Taking Over?" in *Problems of Communism*, July-October, 1969 (Vol. XVIII), pp. 106–110.

[46] Wolfe, p. 110.

significance of these tensions. Party and police controls over the military have existed, as we have seen, since the earliest days of the Soviet regime. Although they have generated tension on a continuing basis, this tension has not ever, so far as the available evidence indicates, erupted into collective resistance by the military or any individual units thereof. This would indicate that, irksome and harmful from the point of view of military efficiency as individual officers may find them, these controls do not produce violent or extreme behavior on the part of the officer corps. Likewise, there have been no indications on the public record that tensions in the military establishment resulting from the continued domination by the Party leadership of the making of national-security policy have led to any confrontations that would threaten the stability of the Soviet system.

In this writer's view, institutional tension between the Soviet military establishment and the Party leadership is endemic in the Soviet system as presently constituted. The present leaders of the Party have been conditioned by the Leninist doctrine of the guiding and manipulative role of the Party as well as years of experience in intra-Party struggles to strive for total domination by the Party of all aspects of organized endeavor. Despite the fact that approximately 80% of the armed forces and an even higher percentage of the officer corps may be comprised of members of the CPSU and the Komsomol [47] and despite the absence of even a single attempt at a *coup* by the Soviet armed forces in the 55 years of Soviet power, the present Party leaders, like their predecessors, consider the military establishment a potential threat to Party rule and maintain the traditional controls over it.

Although it is impossible to foresee what changes, if any, in the institutional relationships between the Party and military a new generation of Party and military leaders is likely to bring about, two things seem clear. First, there is no evidence pointing to any significant early change in the unique socialization process through which all leaders of the CPSU pass; therefore, it seems reasonable to expect that, at least initially, the new leaders of the CPSU will have much the same compulsion to dominate and control the whole of Soviet society, the military establishment included, as the present leaders. Second, there is little evidence of the development of more than a nascent form of meaningful pluralism in the Soviet Union. Speculation in the press in the U.S. and Western Europe notwithstanding, there is simply no hard evidence to indicate that any group in Soviet society such as the scientific community, the managerial elite, or even the military establishment itself, has yet attained or is even close to attaining real institutional autonomy in relation to the Party. As we have noted, however, the military establishment does seem to be able to function as a quasi-interest

[47] Kolkowicz, p. 12.

group that is often able to articulate the military consensus both at meetings of the Defense Committee and in other high-level Party and government councils including the Politburo.

Unless the Soviet Union is undergoing political and social changes not apparent to outsiders, it seems safe to state that the CPSU leadership, providing it remains united, will complete the sixth decade of its rule over the Soviet Union with its final authority at the pinnacle of the pyramid of political and economic power unimpaired. At the same time, the institutional tensions between the CPSU and the military establishment that have existed in varying degree for most of the Soviet era seem destined to live on.

Index